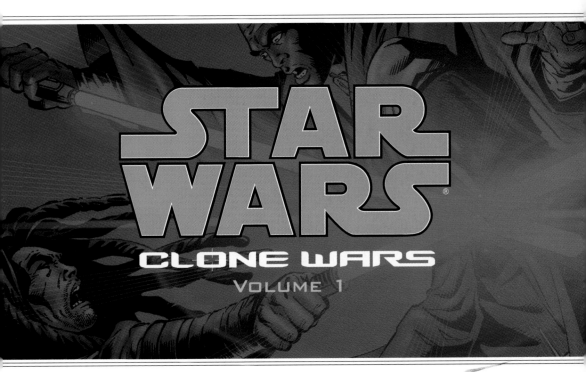

STAR WARS®

CLONE WARS

VOLUME 1

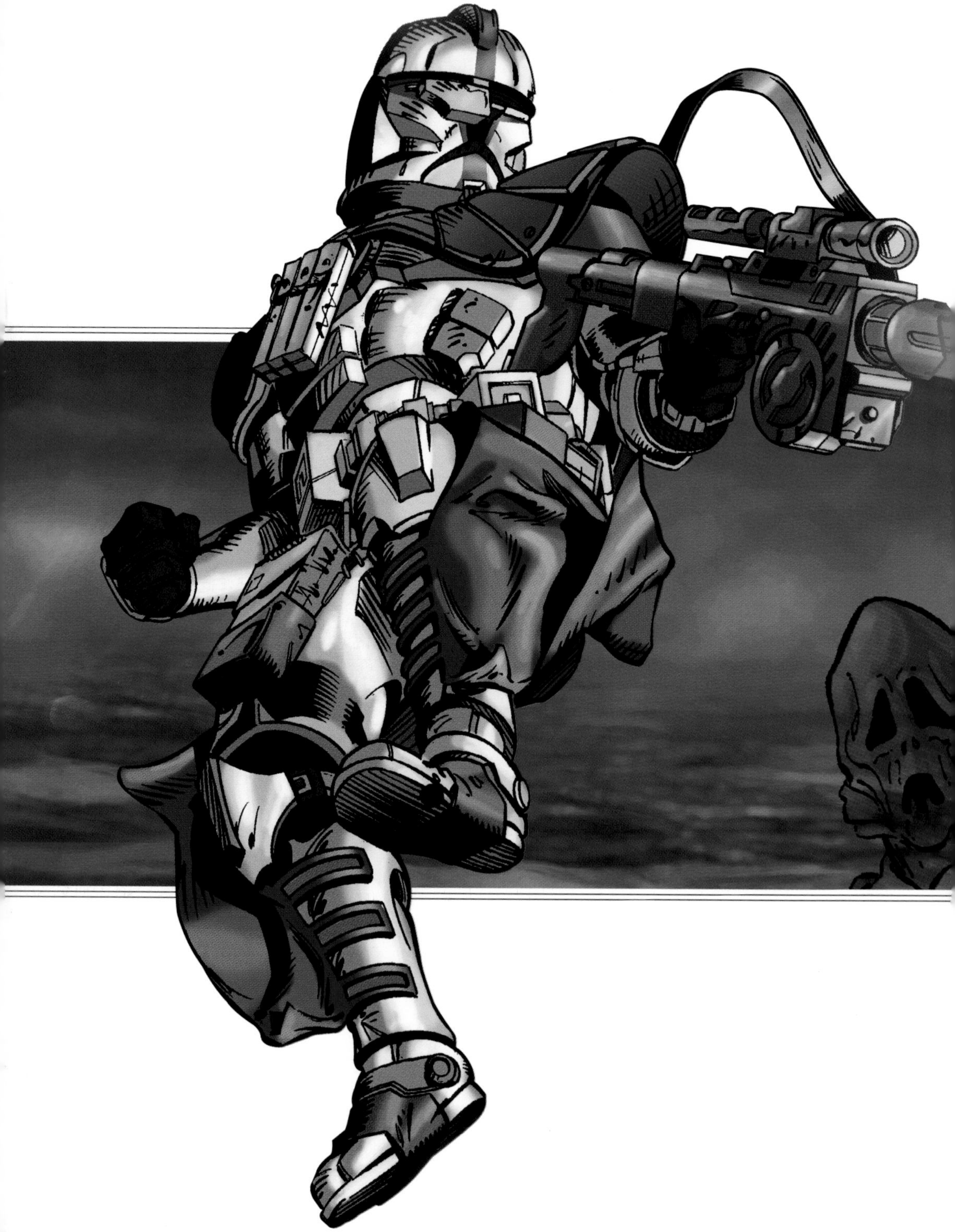

The events in this story take place between two and three months after the battle of Geonosis (as seen in *Star Wars: Attack of the Clones*)

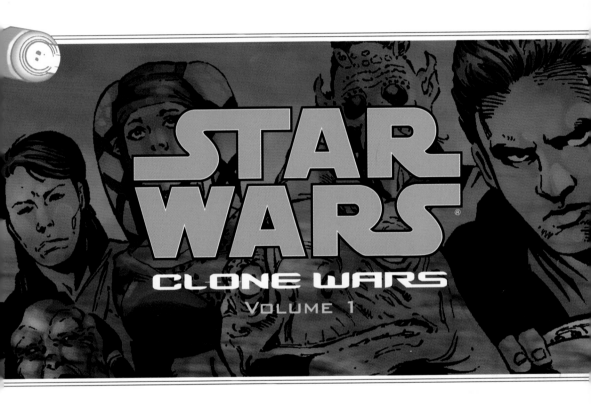

STAR WARS

CLONE WARS

VOLUME 1

The Defense of Kamino
and other tales

Dark Horse Comics®

colors by **Joe Wayne**

lettering by **Digital Chameleon**

cover illustration by **Carlo Arellano**

publisher **Mike Richardson**

collection designer **Darin Fabrick**

art director **Mark Cox**

assistant editor **Jeremy Barlow**

editor **Randy Stradley**

special thanks to **Chris Cerasi** and
Lucy Autrey Wilson at Lucas Licensing

STAR WARS®:CLONE WARS VOLUME 1

THIS VOLUME COLLECTS *STAR WARS: REPUBLIC* **#49-50 AND** *JEDI: MACE WINDU*

PUBLISHED BY DARK HORSE COMICS, INC.
10956 SE MAIN STREET · MILWAUKIE, OR 97222

WWW.DARKHORSE.COM
To find a comics shop in your area, call the Comic Shop Locator Service
toll-free at 1-888-266-4226

FIRST EDITION: ISBN: 1-56971-962-4
3 5 7 9 10 8 6 4
PRINTED IN CHINA

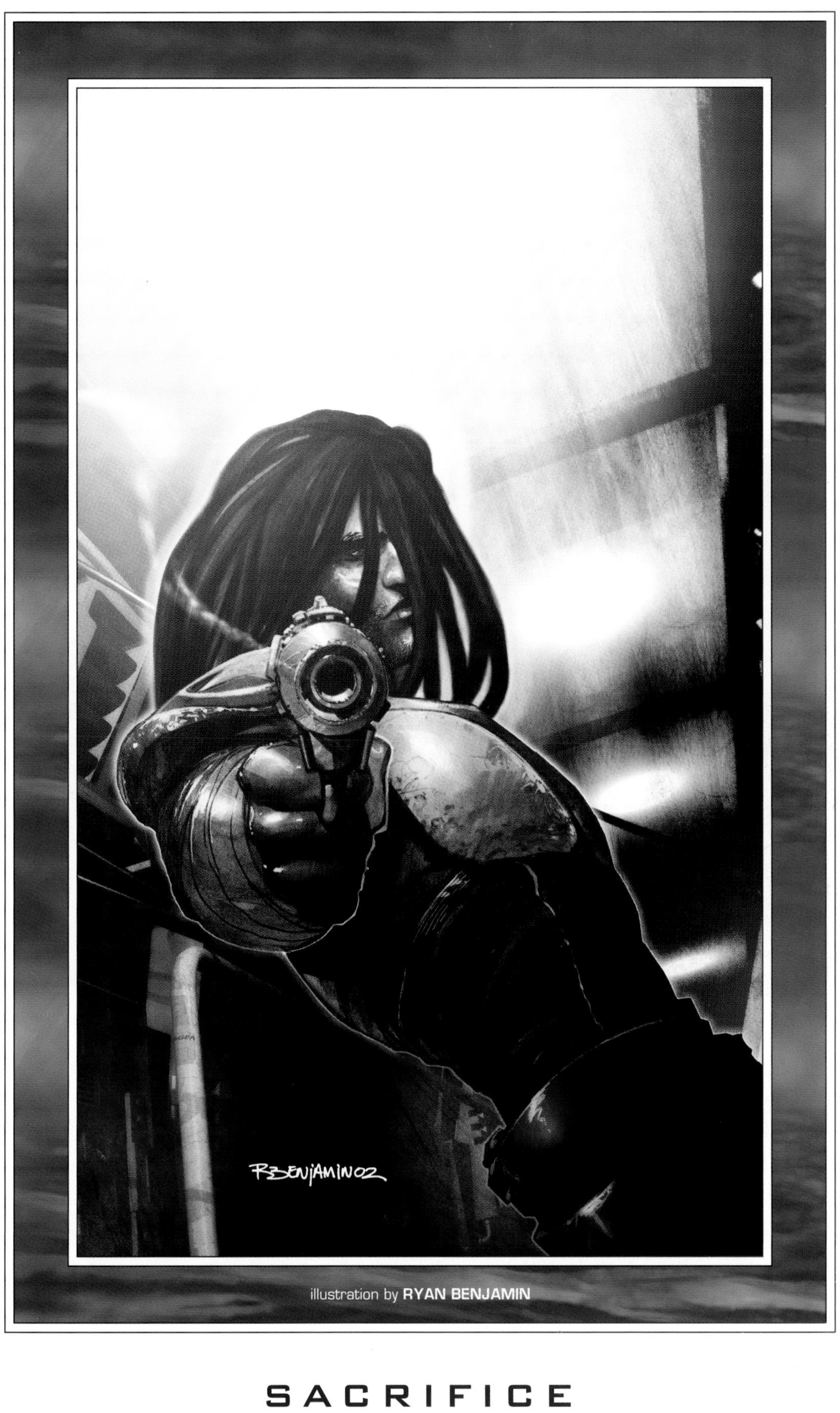
RBENJAMIN02

illustration by **RYAN BENJAMIN**

SACRIFICE

Approximately one month after the Battle of Geonosis...

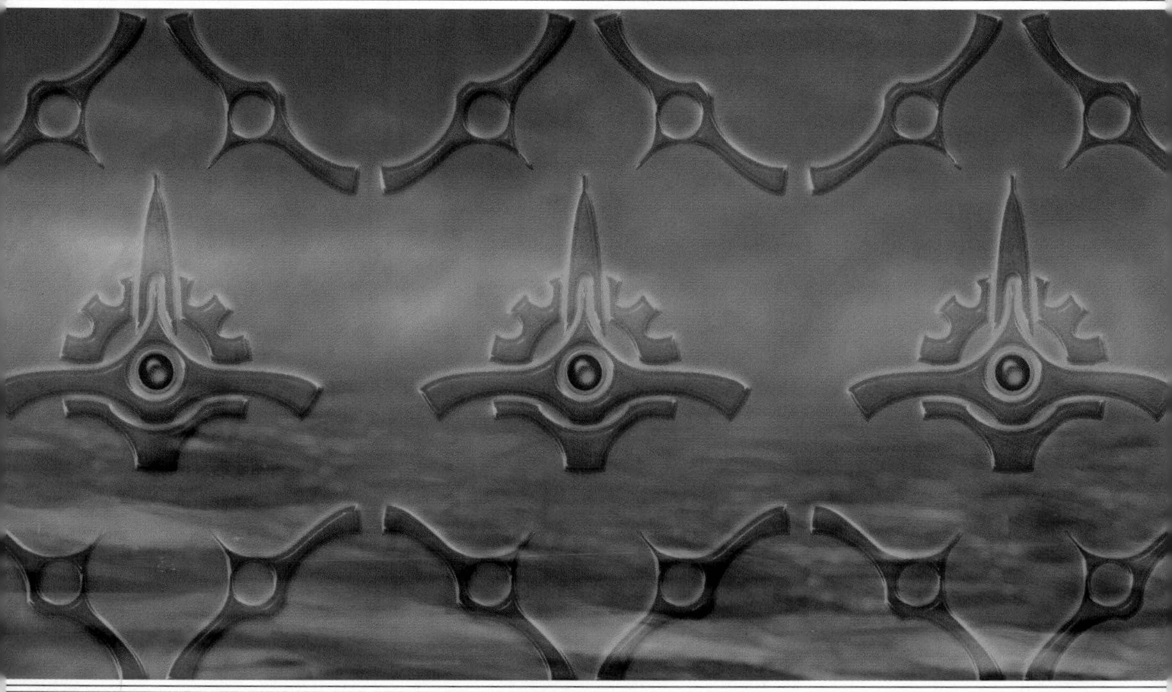

"Sacrifice"
written by **John Ostrander**
pencilled by **Jan Duursema**

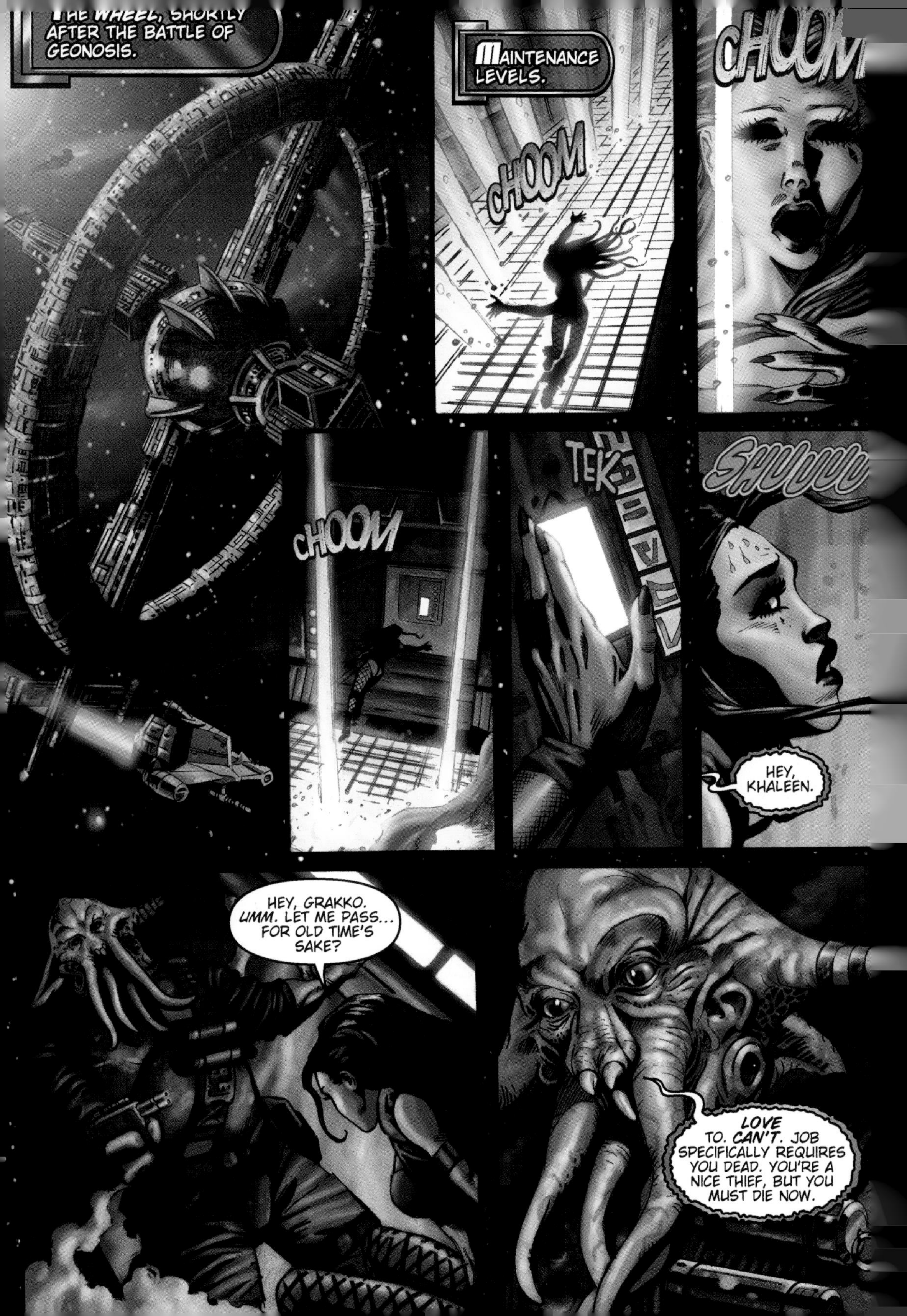
THE WHEEL, SHORTLY AFTER THE BATTLE OF GEONOSIS.
MAINTENANCE LEVELS.
CHOOM
CHOOM
CHOOM
TEK
SHUUUU
HEY, KHALEEN.
HEY, GRAKKO. UMM. LET ME PASS... FOR OLD TIME'S SAKE?
LOVE TO. CAN'T. JOB SPECIFICALLY REQUIRES YOU DEAD. YOU'RE A NICE THIEF, BUT YOU MUST DIE NOW.

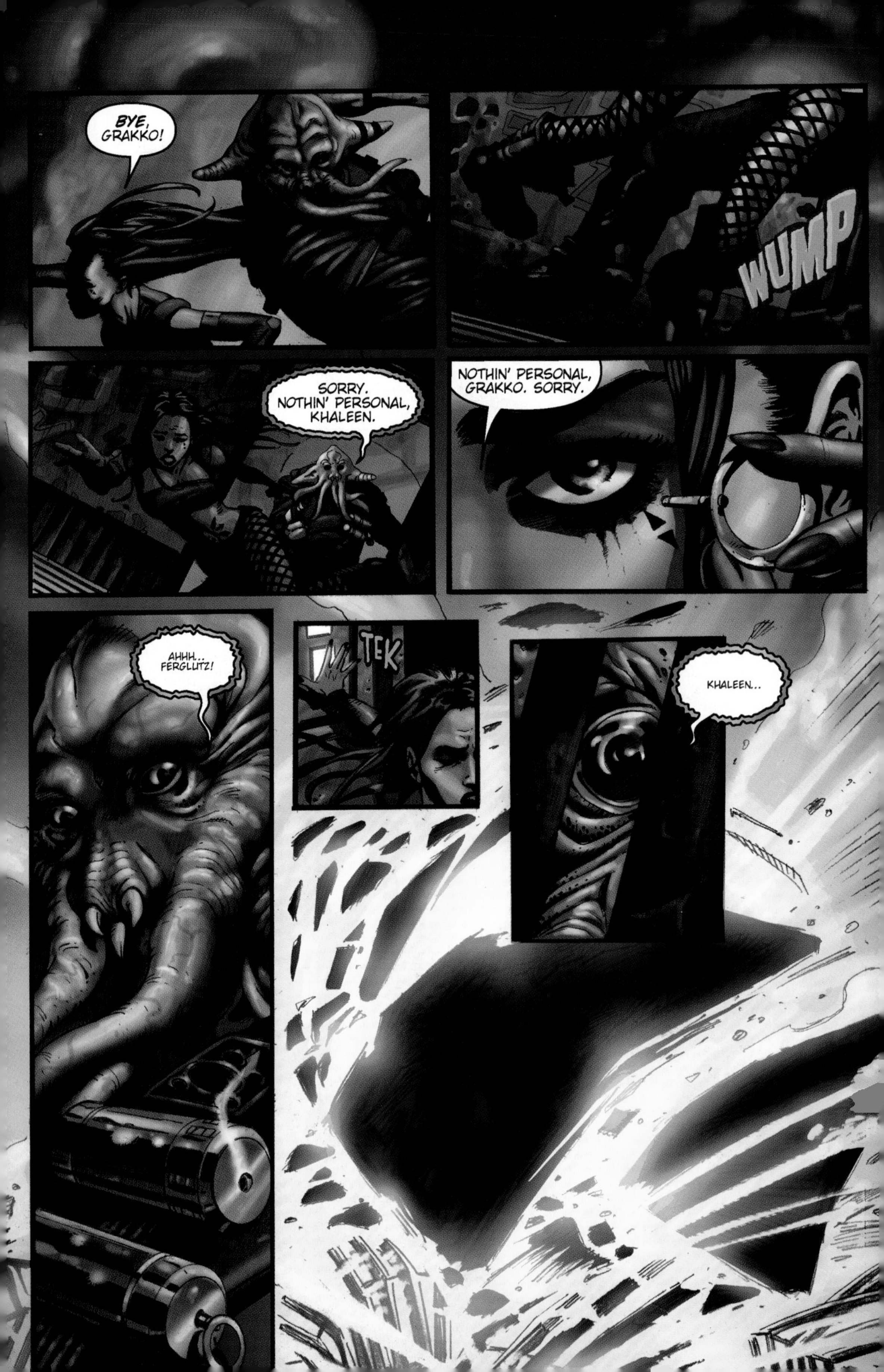
BYE, GRAKKO!
WUMP
SORRY. NOTHIN' PERSONAL, KHALEEN.
NOTHIN' PERSONAL, GRAKKO. SORRY.
AHHH... FERGLUTZ!
TEK
KHALEEN...

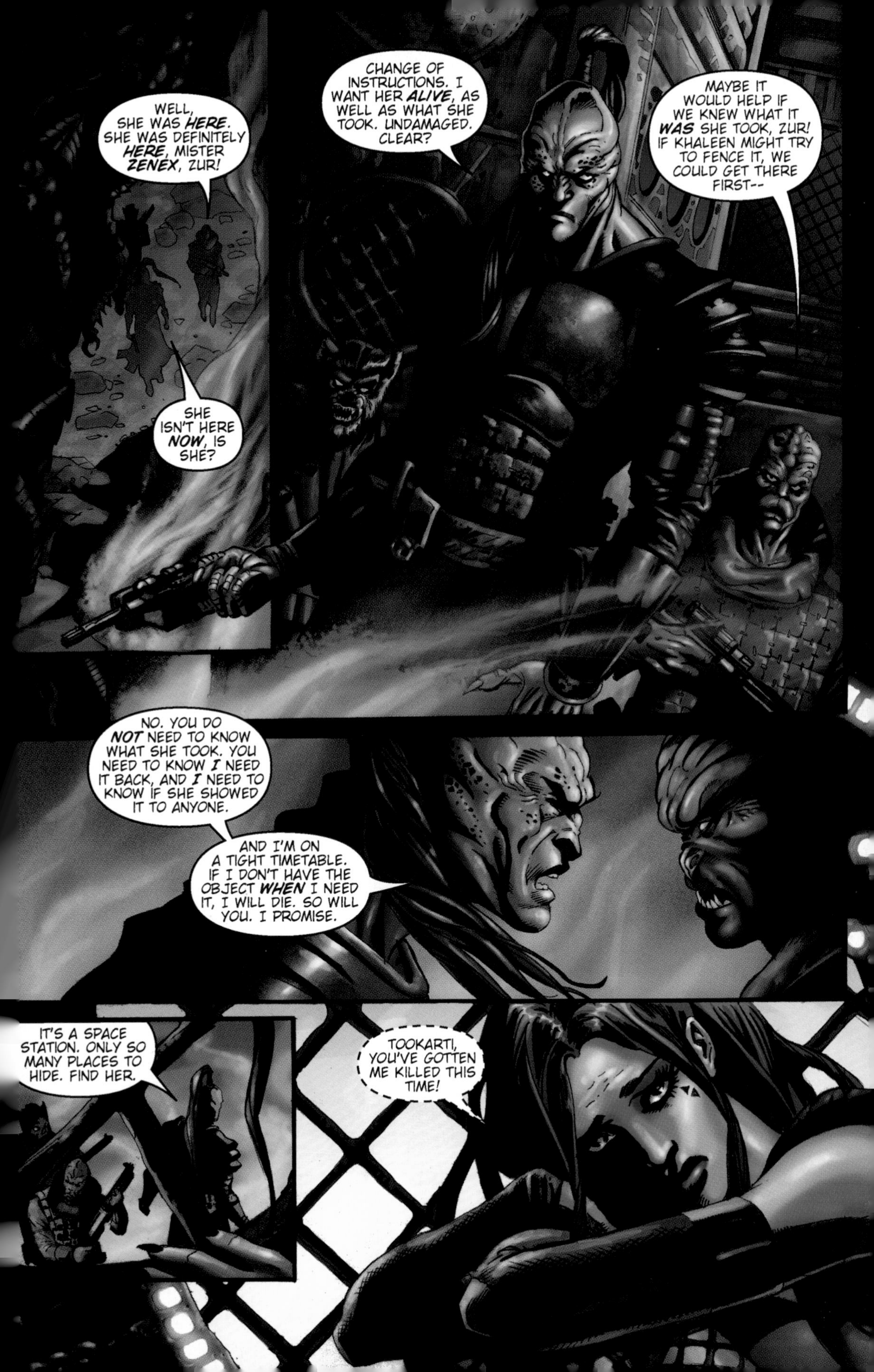
WELL, SHE WAS HERE. SHE WAS DEFINITELY HERE, MISTER ZENEX, ZUR!
SHE ISN'T HERE NOW, IS SHE?
CHANGE OF INSTRUCTIONS. I WANT HER ALIVE, AS WELL AS WHAT SHE TOOK. UNDAMAGED. CLEAR?
MAYBE IT WOULD HELP IF WE KNEW WHAT IT WAS SHE TOOK, ZUR! IF KHALEEN MIGHT TRY TO FENCE IT, WE COULD GET THERE FIRST--
NO. YOU DO NOT NEED TO KNOW WHAT SHE TOOK. YOU NEED TO KNOW I NEED IT BACK, AND I NEED TO KNOW IF SHE SHOWED IT TO ANYONE.
AND I'M ON A TIGHT TIMETABLE. IF I DON'T HAVE THE OBJECT WHEN I NEED IT, I WILL DIE. SO WILL YOU. I PROMISE.
IT'S A SPACE STATION. ONLY SO MANY PLACES TO HIDE. FIND HER.
TOOKARTI, YOU'VE GOTTEN ME KILLED THIS TIME!

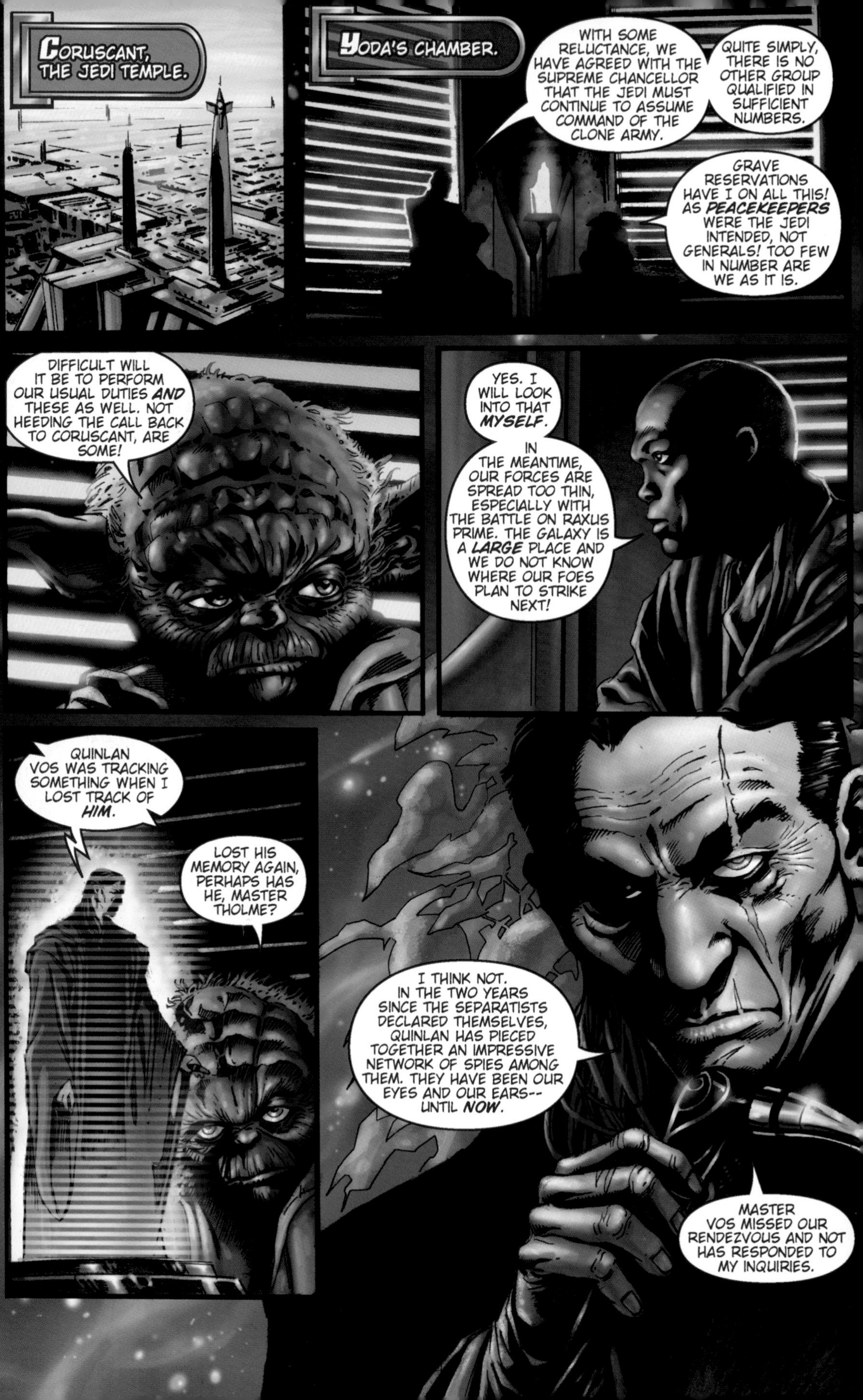
CORUSCANT, THE JEDI TEMPLE.
YODA'S CHAMBER.
WITH SOME RELUCTANCE, WE HAVE AGREED WITH THE SUPREME CHANCELLOR THAT THE JEDI MUST CONTINUE TO ASSUME COMMAND OF THE CLONE ARMY.
QUITE SIMPLY, THERE IS NO OTHER GROUP QUALIFIED IN SUFFICIENT NUMBERS.
GRAVE RESERVATIONS HAVE I ON ALL THIS! AS *PEACEKEEPERS* WERE THE JEDI INTENDED, NOT GENERALS! TOO FEW IN NUMBER ARE WE AS IT IS.
DIFFICULT WILL IT BE TO PERFORM OUR USUAL DUTIES *AND* THESE AS WELL. NOT HEEDING THE CALL BACK TO CORUSCANT, ARE SOME!
YES. I WILL LOOK INTO THAT *MYSELF*.
IN THE MEANTIME, OUR FORCES ARE SPREAD TOO THIN, ESPECIALLY WITH THE BATTLE ON RAXUS PRIME. THE GALAXY IS A *LARGE* PLACE AND WE DO NOT KNOW WHERE OUR FOES PLAN TO STRIKE NEXT!
QUINLAN VOS WAS TRACKING SOMETHING WHEN I LOST TRACK OF *HIM*.
LOST HIS MEMORY AGAIN, PERHAPS HAS HE, MASTER THOLME?
I THINK NOT. IN THE TWO YEARS SINCE THE SEPARATISTS DECLARED THEMSELVES, QUINLAN HAS PIECED TOGETHER AN IMPRESSIVE NETWORK OF SPIES AMONG THEM. THEY HAVE BEEN OUR EYES AND OUR EARS-- UNTIL *NOW*.
MASTER VOS MISSED OUR RENDEZVOUS AND NOT HAS RESPONDED TO MY INQUIRIES.

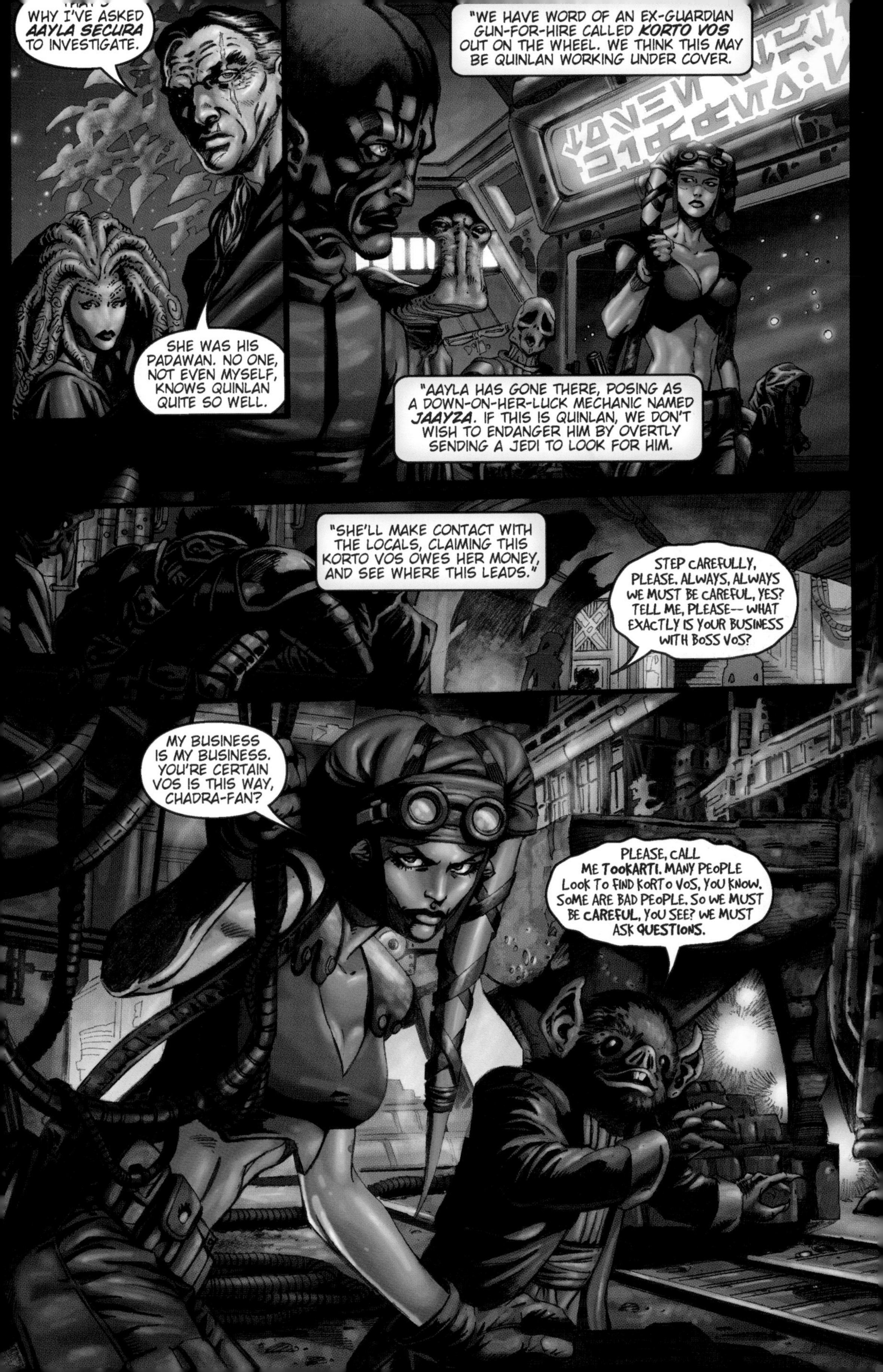
WHY I'VE ASKED AAYLA SECURA TO INVESTIGATE.
SHE WAS HIS PADAWAN. NO ONE, NOT EVEN MYSELF, KNOWS QUINLAN QUITE SO WELL.
"WE HAVE WORD OF AN EX-GUARDIAN GUN-FOR-HIRE CALLED KORTO VOS OUT ON THE WHEEL. WE THINK THIS MAY BE QUINLAN WORKING UNDER COVER.
"AAYLA HAS GONE THERE, POSING AS A DOWN-ON-HER-LUCK MECHANIC NAMED JAAYZA. IF THIS IS QUINLAN, WE DON'T WISH TO ENDANGER HIM BY OVERTLY SENDING A JEDI TO LOOK FOR HIM.
"SHE'LL MAKE CONTACT WITH THE LOCALS, CLAIMING THIS KORTO VOS OWES HER MONEY, AND SEE WHERE THIS LEADS."
STEP CAREFULLY, PLEASE. ALWAYS, ALWAYS WE MUST BE CAREFUL, YES? TELL ME, PLEASE-- WHAT EXACTLY IS YOUR BUSINESS WITH BOSS VOS?
MY BUSINESS IS MY BUSINESS. YOU'RE CERTAIN VOS IS THIS WAY, CHADRA-FAN?
PLEASE, CALL ME TOOKARTI. MANY PEOPLE LOOK TO FIND KORTO VOS, YOU KNOW. SOME ARE BAD PEOPLE. SO WE MUST BE CAREFUL, YOU SEE? WE MUST ASK QUESTIONS.

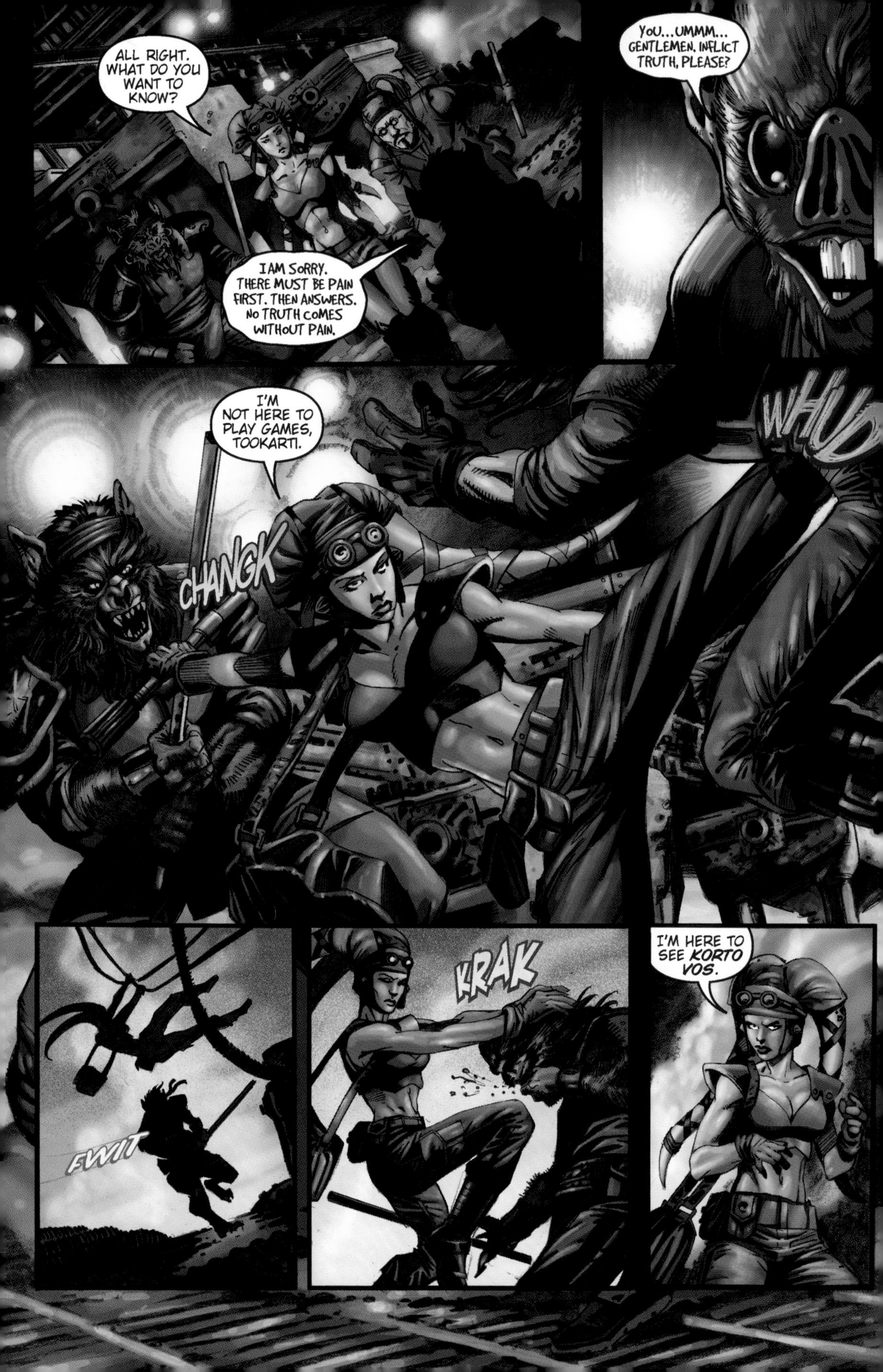
ALL RIGHT. WHAT DO YOU WANT TO KNOW?
I AM SORRY. THERE MUST BE PAIN FIRST. THEN ANSWERS. NO TRUTH COMES WITHOUT PAIN.
YOU...UMMM... GENTLEMEN, INFLICT TRUTH, PLEASE?
I'M NOT HERE TO PLAY GAMES, TOOKARTI.
WHUD
CHANGK
FWIT
KRAK
I'M HERE TO SEE KORTO VOS.

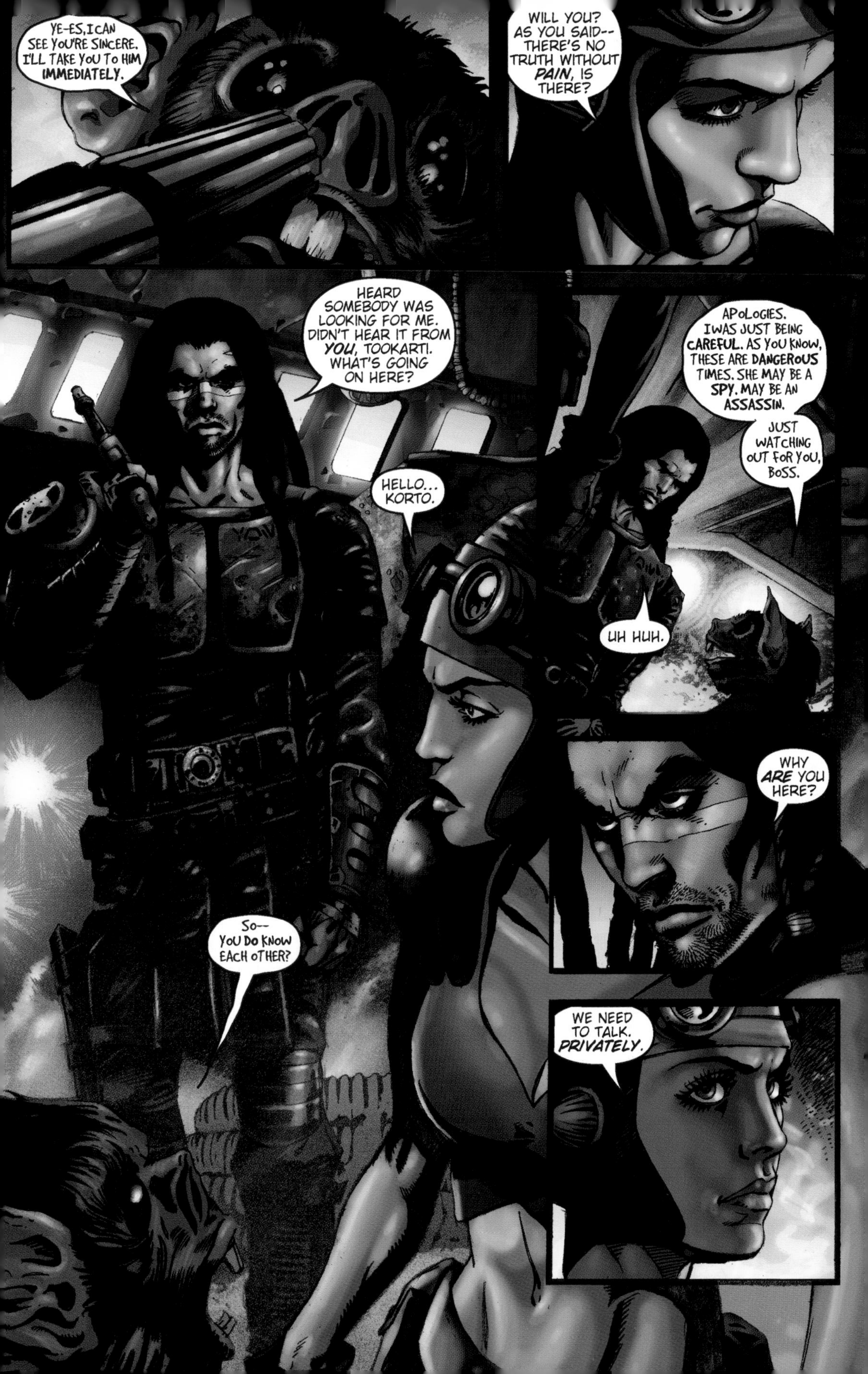

YE-ES, I CAN SEE YOU'RE SINCERE. I'LL TAKE YOU TO HIM IMMEDIATELY.
WILL YOU? AS YOU SAID-- THERE'S NO TRUTH WITHOUT PAIN, IS THERE?
HEARD SOMEBODY WAS LOOKING FOR ME. DIDN'T HEAR IT FROM YOU, TOOKARTI. WHAT'S GOING ON HERE?
HELLO... KORTO.
SO-- YOU DO KNOW EACH OTHER?
APOLOGIES. I WAS JUST BEING CAREFUL. AS YOU KNOW, THESE ARE DANGEROUS TIMES. SHE MAY BE A SPY. MAY BE AN ASSASSIN.
JUST WATCHING OUT FOR YOU, BOSS.
UH HUH.
WHY ARE YOU HERE?
WE NEED TO TALK. PRIVATELY.

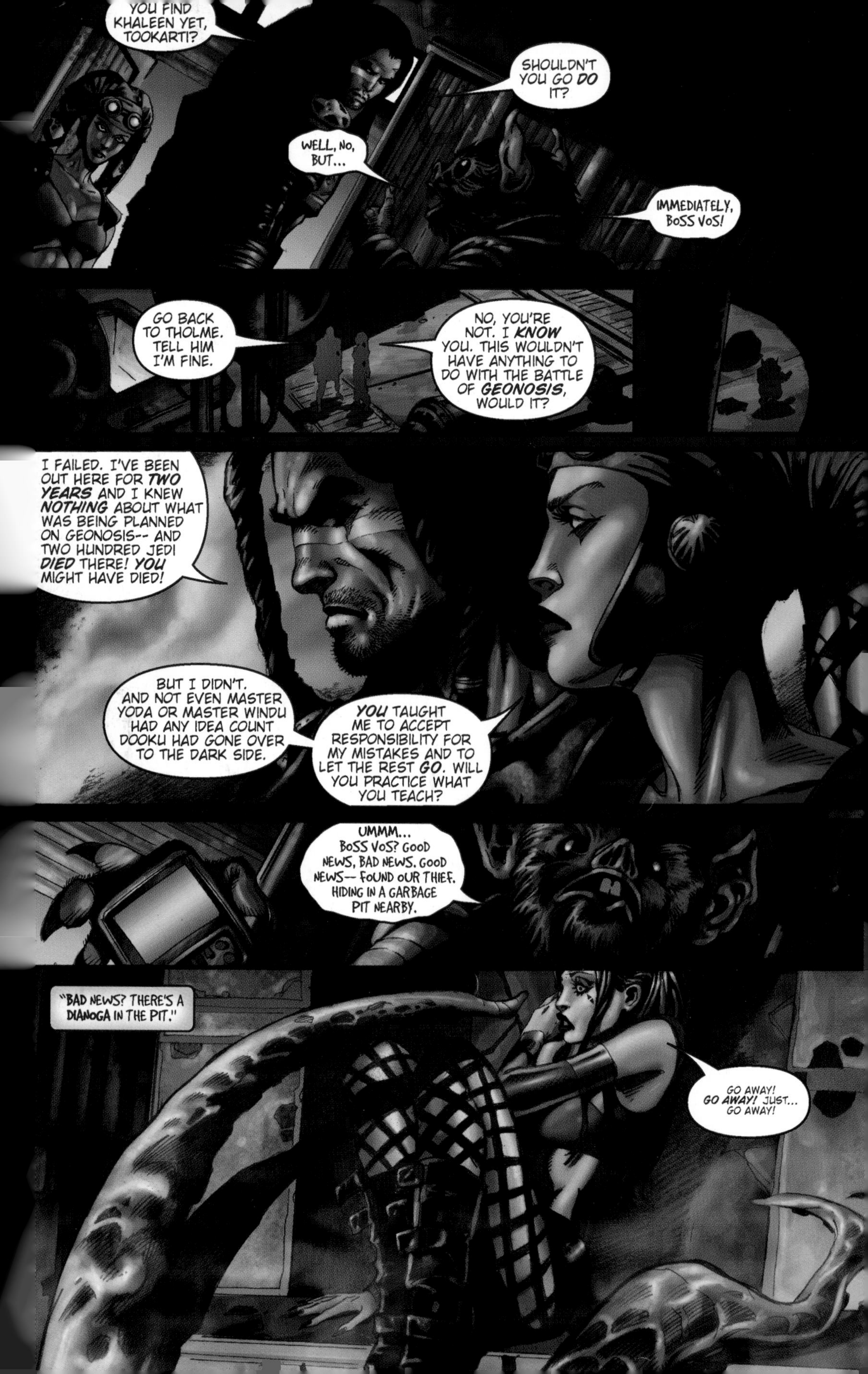
YOU FIND KHALEEN YET, TOOKARTI?
SHOULDN'T YOU GO DO IT?
WELL, NO, BUT...
IMMEDIATELY, BOSS VOS!
GO BACK TO THOLME. TELL HIM I'M FINE.
NO, YOU'RE NOT. I KNOW YOU. THIS WOULDN'T HAVE ANYTHING TO DO WITH THE BATTLE OF GEONOSIS, WOULD IT?
I FAILED. I'VE BEEN OUT HERE FOR TWO YEARS AND I KNEW NOTHING ABOUT WHAT WAS BEING PLANNED ON GEONOSIS-- AND TWO HUNDRED JEDI DIED THERE! YOU MIGHT HAVE DIED!
BUT I DIDN'T. AND NOT EVEN MASTER YODA OR MASTER WINDU HAD ANY IDEA COUNT DOOKU HAD GONE OVER TO THE DARK SIDE.
YOU TAUGHT ME TO ACCEPT RESPONSIBILITY FOR MY MISTAKES AND TO LET THE REST GO. WILL YOU PRACTICE WHAT YOU TEACH?
UMMM... BOSS VOS? GOOD NEWS, BAD NEWS. GOOD NEWS-- FOUND OUR THIEF. HIDING IN A GARBAGE PIT NEARBY.
"BAD NEWS? THERE'S A DIANOGA IN THE PIT."
GO AWAY! GO AWAY! JUST... GO AWAY!

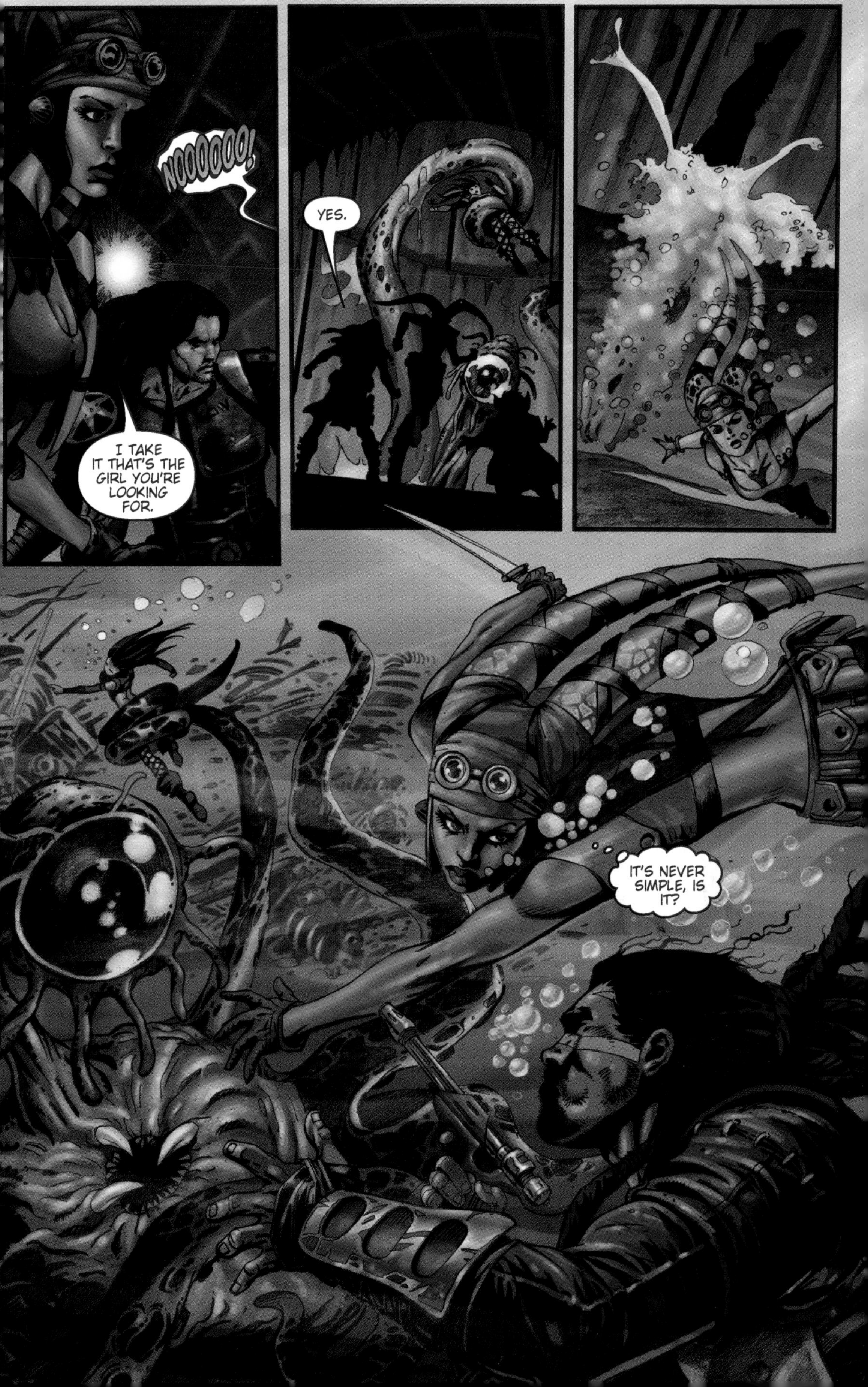
NOOOOOO!
I TAKE IT THAT'S THE GIRL YOU'RE LOOKING FOR.
YES.
IT'S NEVER SIMPLE, IS IT?

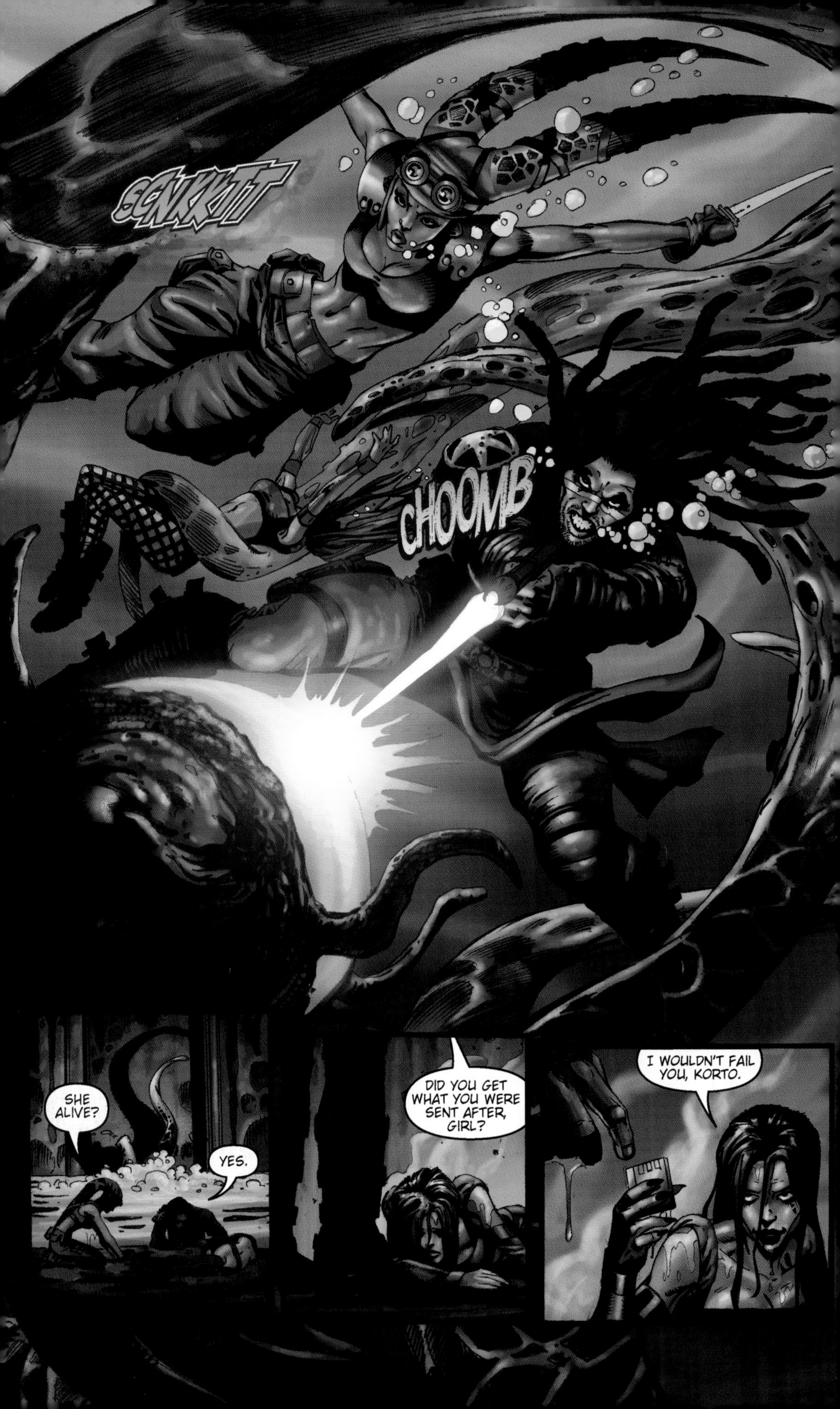
SCNKKTT
CHOOMB
SHE ALIVE?
YES.
DID YOU GET WHAT YOU WERE SENT AFTER, GIRL?
I WOULDN'T FAIL YOU, KORTO.

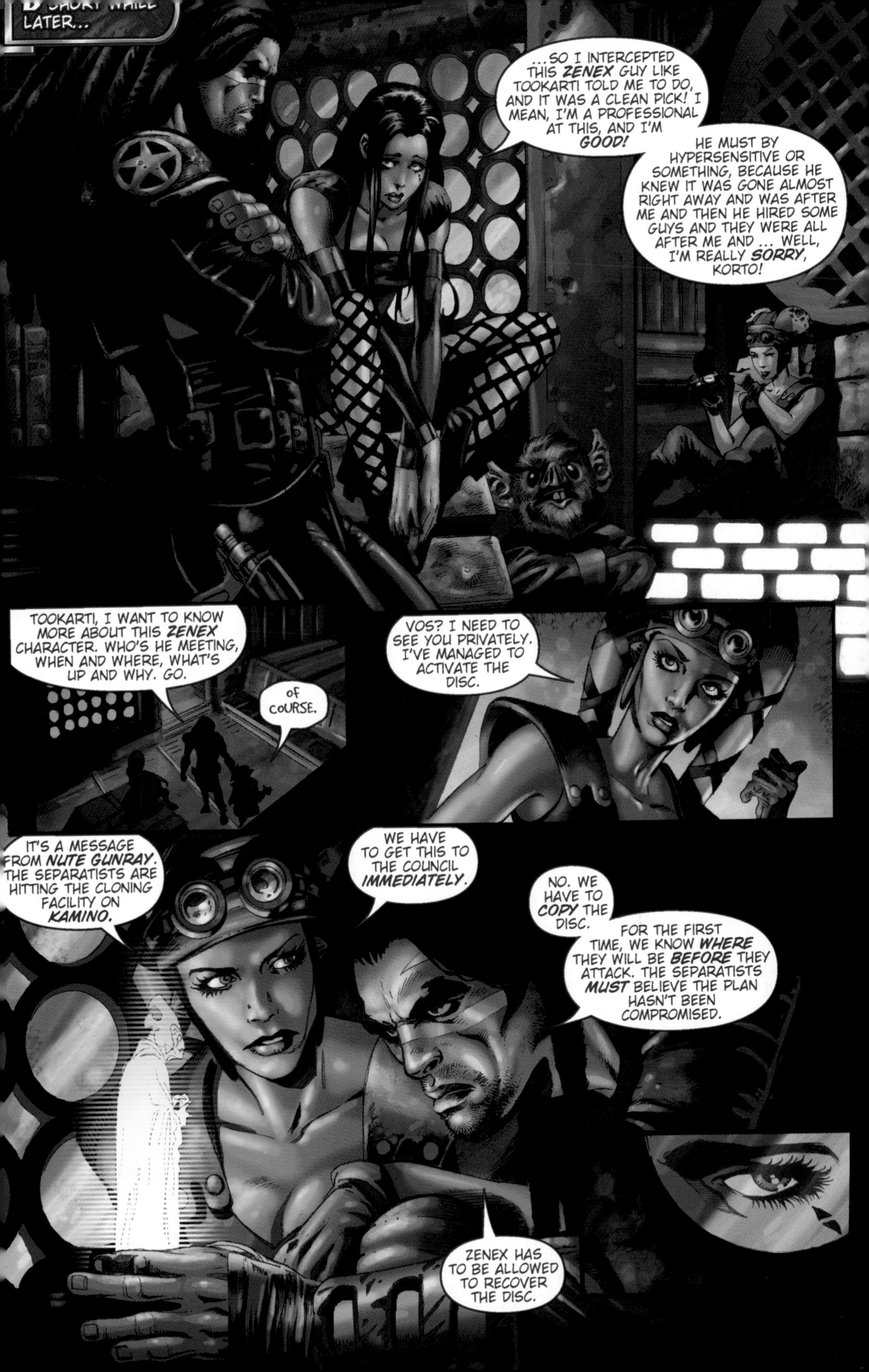

LATER...
...SO I INTERCEPTED THIS ZENEX GUY LIKE TOOKARTI TOLD ME TO DO, AND IT WAS A CLEAN PICK! I MEAN, I'M A PROFESSIONAL AT THIS, AND I'M GOOD!
HE MUST BY HYPERSENSITIVE OR SOMETHING, BECAUSE HE KNEW IT WAS GONE ALMOST RIGHT AWAY AND WAS AFTER ME AND THEN HE HIRED SOME GUYS AND THEY WERE ALL AFTER ME AND ... WELL, I'M REALLY SORRY, KORTO!
TOOKARTI, I WANT TO KNOW MORE ABOUT THIS ZENEX CHARACTER. WHO'S HE MEETING, WHEN AND WHERE, WHAT'S UP AND WHY. GO.
OF COURSE.
VOS? I NEED TO SEE YOU PRIVATELY. I'VE MANAGED TO ACTIVATE THE DISC.
IT'S A MESSAGE FROM NUTE GUNRAY. THE SEPARATISTS ARE HITTING THE CLONING FACILITY ON KAMINO.
WE HAVE TO GET THIS TO THE COUNCIL IMMEDIATELY.
NO. WE HAVE TO COPY THE DISC.
FOR THE FIRST TIME, WE KNOW WHERE THEY WILL BE BEFORE THEY ATTACK. THE SEPARATISTS MUST BELIEVE THE PLAN HASN'T BEEN COMPROMISED.
ZENEX HAS TO BE ALLOWED TO RECOVER THE DISC.

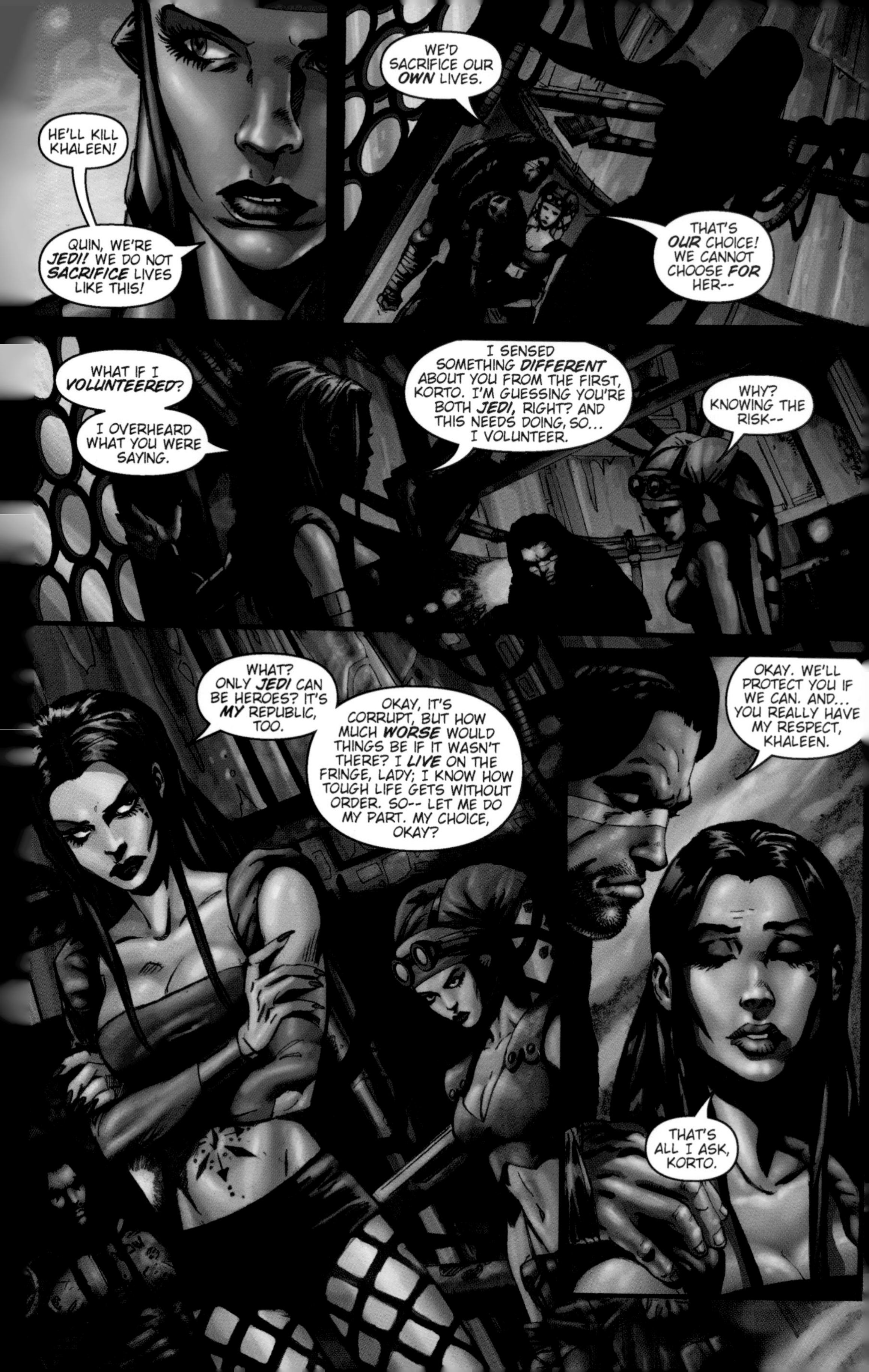
HE'LL KILL KHALEEN!
QUIN, WE'RE JEDI! WE DO NOT SACRIFICE LIVES LIKE THIS!
WE'D SACRIFICE OUR OWN LIVES.
THAT'S OUR CHOICE! WE CANNOT CHOOSE FOR HER--
WHAT IF I VOLUNTEERED?
I OVERHEARD WHAT YOU WERE SAYING.
I SENSED SOMETHING DIFFERENT ABOUT YOU FROM THE FIRST, KORTO. I'M GUESSING YOU'RE BOTH JEDI, RIGHT? AND THIS NEEDS DOING, SO... I VOLUNTEER.
WHY? KNOWING THE RISK--
WHAT? ONLY JEDI CAN BE HEROES? IT'S MY REPUBLIC, TOO.
OKAY, IT'S CORRUPT, BUT HOW MUCH WORSE WOULD THINGS BE IF IT WASN'T THERE? I LIVE ON THE FRINGE, LADY; I KNOW HOW TOUGH LIFE GETS WITHOUT ORDER. SO-- LET ME DO MY PART. MY CHOICE, OKAY?
OKAY. WE'LL PROTECT YOU IF WE CAN. AND... YOU REALLY HAVE MY RESPECT, KHALEEN.
THAT'S ALL I ASK, KORTO.

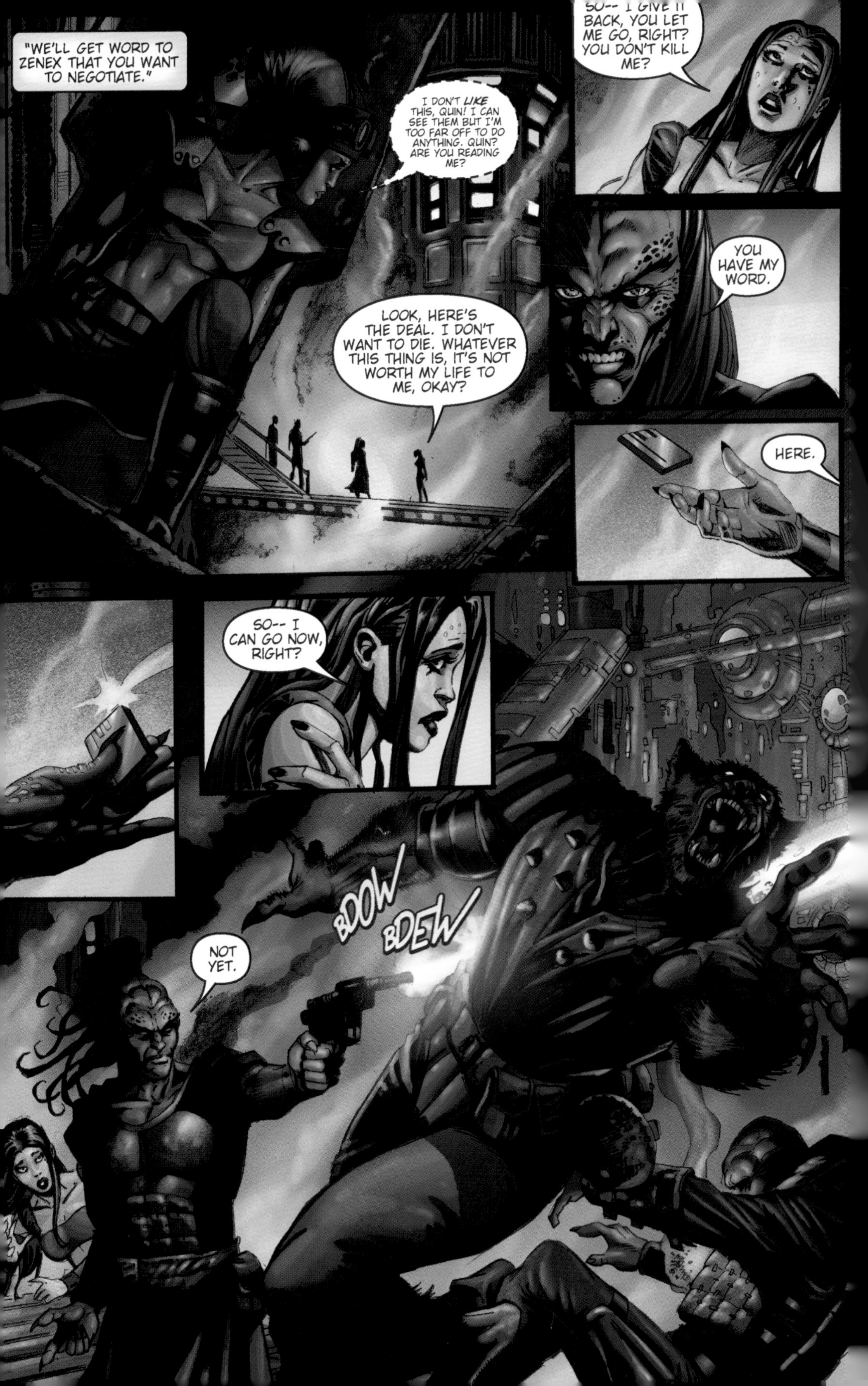
"WE'LL GET WORD TO ZENEX THAT YOU WANT TO NEGOTIATE."
I DON'T LIKE THIS, QUIN! I CAN SEE THEM BUT I'M TOO FAR OFF TO DO ANYTHING. QUIN? ARE YOU READING ME?
LOOK, HERE'S THE DEAL. I DON'T WANT TO DIE. WHATEVER THIS THING IS, IT'S NOT WORTH MY LIFE TO ME, OKAY?
SO-- I GIVE IT BACK, YOU LET ME GO, RIGHT? YOU DON'T KILL ME?
YOU HAVE MY WORD.
HERE.
SO-- I CAN GO NOW, RIGHT?
NOT YET.
BDOW
BDEW

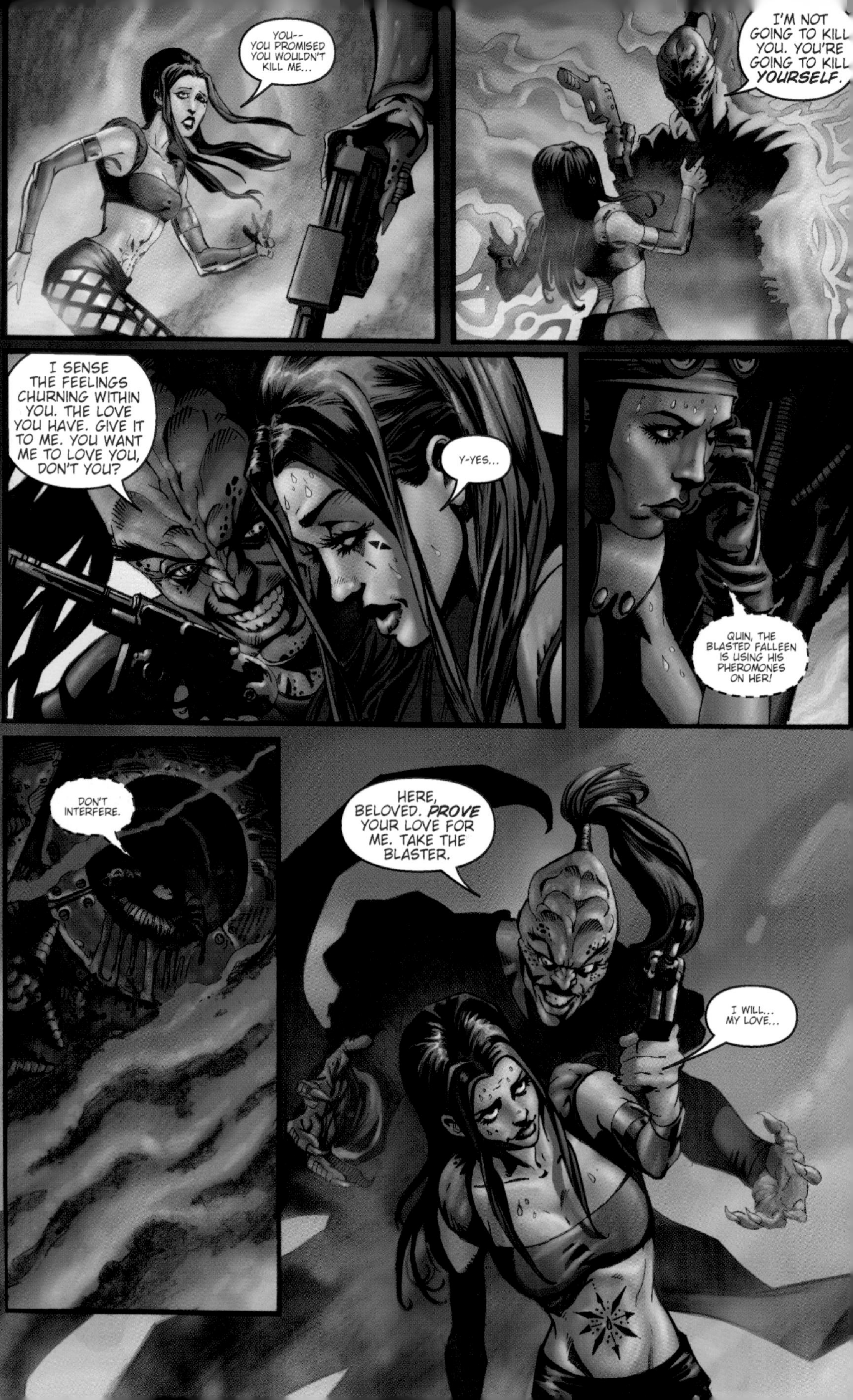

YOU-- YOU PROMISED YOU WOULDN'T KILL ME...
I'M NOT GOING TO KILL YOU. YOU'RE GOING TO KILL ***YOURSELF***.
I SENSE THE FEELINGS CHURNING WITHIN YOU. THE LOVE YOU HAVE. GIVE IT TO ME. YOU WANT ME TO LOVE YOU, DON'T YOU?
Y-YES...
QUIN, THE BLASTED FALLEEN IS USING HIS PHEROMONES ON HER!
DON'T INTERFERE.
HERE, BELOVED. ***PROVE*** YOUR LOVE FOR ME. TAKE THE BLASTER.
I WILL... MY LOVE...

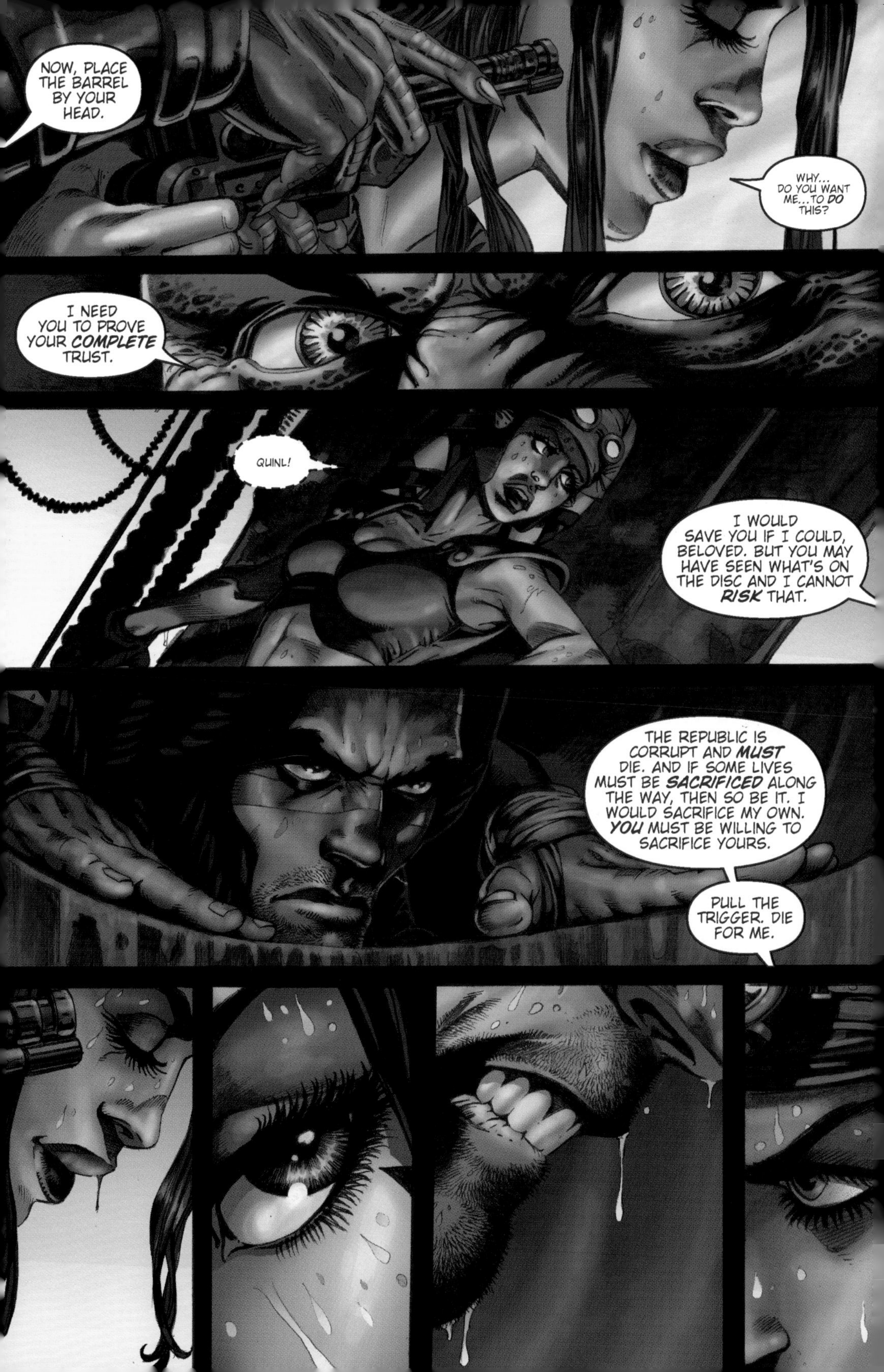
NOW, PLACE THE BARREL BY YOUR HEAD.
WHY... DO YOU WANT ME... TO DO THIS?
I NEED YOU TO PROVE YOUR COMPLETE TRUST.
QUINL!
I WOULD SAVE YOU IF I COULD, BELOVED. BUT YOU MAY HAVE SEEN WHAT'S ON THE DISC AND I CANNOT RISK THAT.
THE REPUBLIC IS CORRUPT AND MUST DIE. AND IF SOME LIVES MUST BE SACRIFICED ALONG THE WAY, THEN SO BE IT. I WOULD SACRIFICE MY OWN. YOU MUST BE WILLING TO SACRIFICE YOURS.
PULL THE TRIGGER. DIE FOR ME.

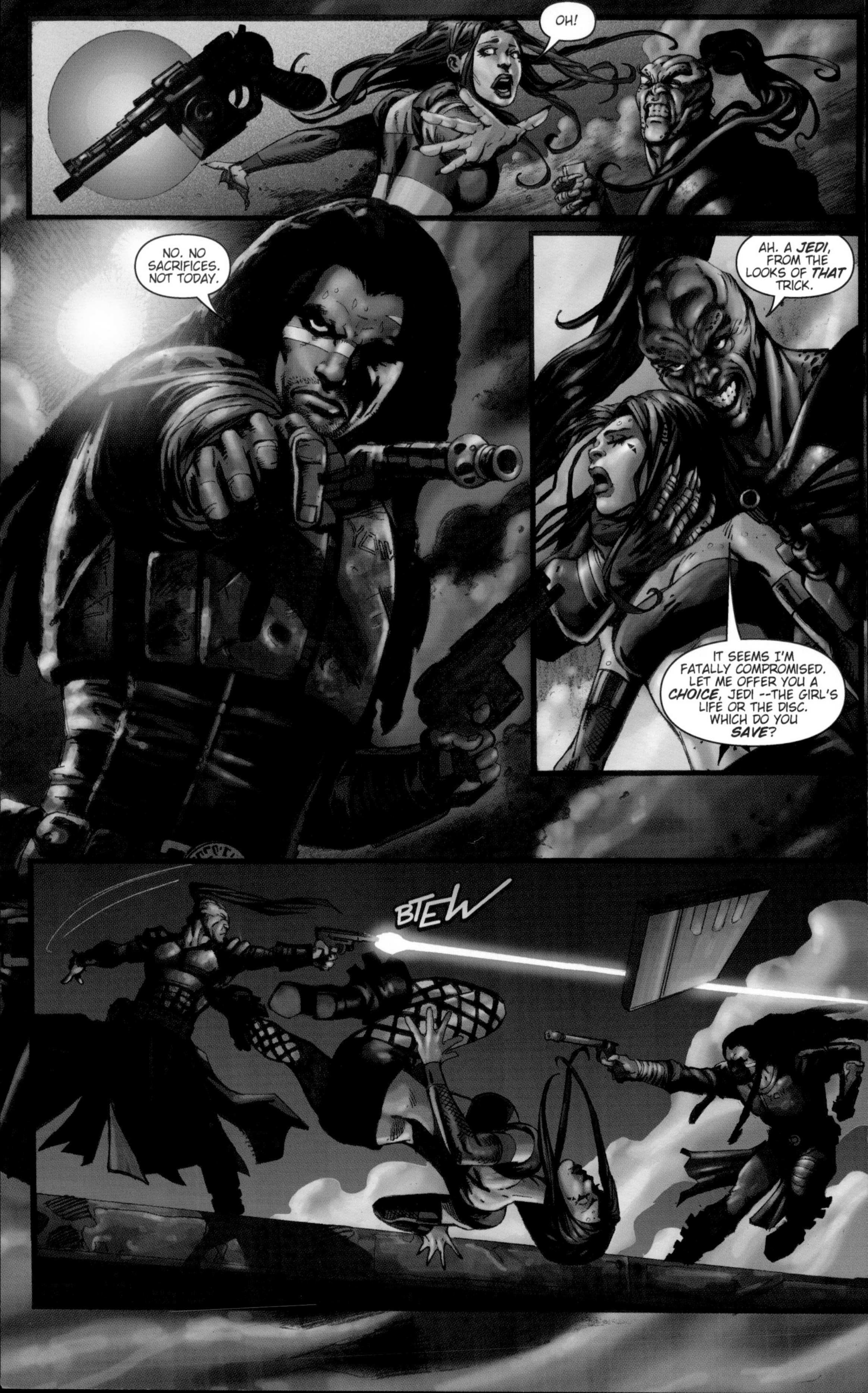
OH!
NO. NO SACRIFICES. NOT TODAY.
AH. A JEDI, FROM THE LOOKS OF THAT TRICK.
IT SEEMS I'M FATALLY COMPROMISED. LET ME OFFER YOU A CHOICE, JEDI --THE GIRL'S LIFE OR THE DISC. WHICH DO YOU SAVE?
BTEW

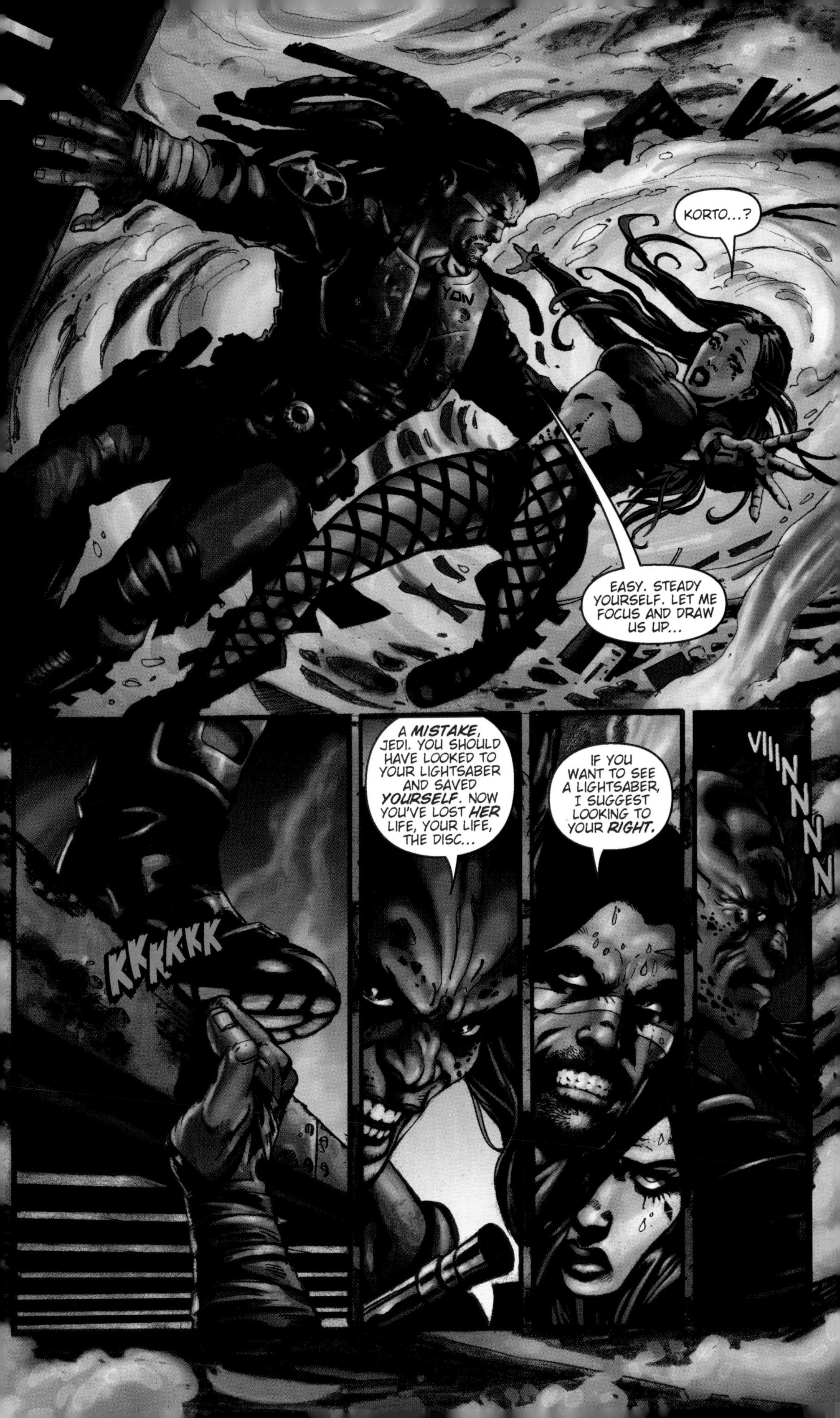
KORTO...?
EASY. STEADY YOURSELF. LET ME FOCUS AND DRAW US UP...
KKKKKK
A **MISTAKE**, JEDI. YOU SHOULD HAVE LOOKED TO YOUR LIGHTSABER AND SAVED **YOURSELF**. NOW YOU'VE LOST **HER** LIFE, YOUR LIFE, THE DISC...
IF YOU WANT TO SEE A LIGHTSABER, I SUGGEST LOOKING TO YOUR **RIGHT**.
VIIINNNNN

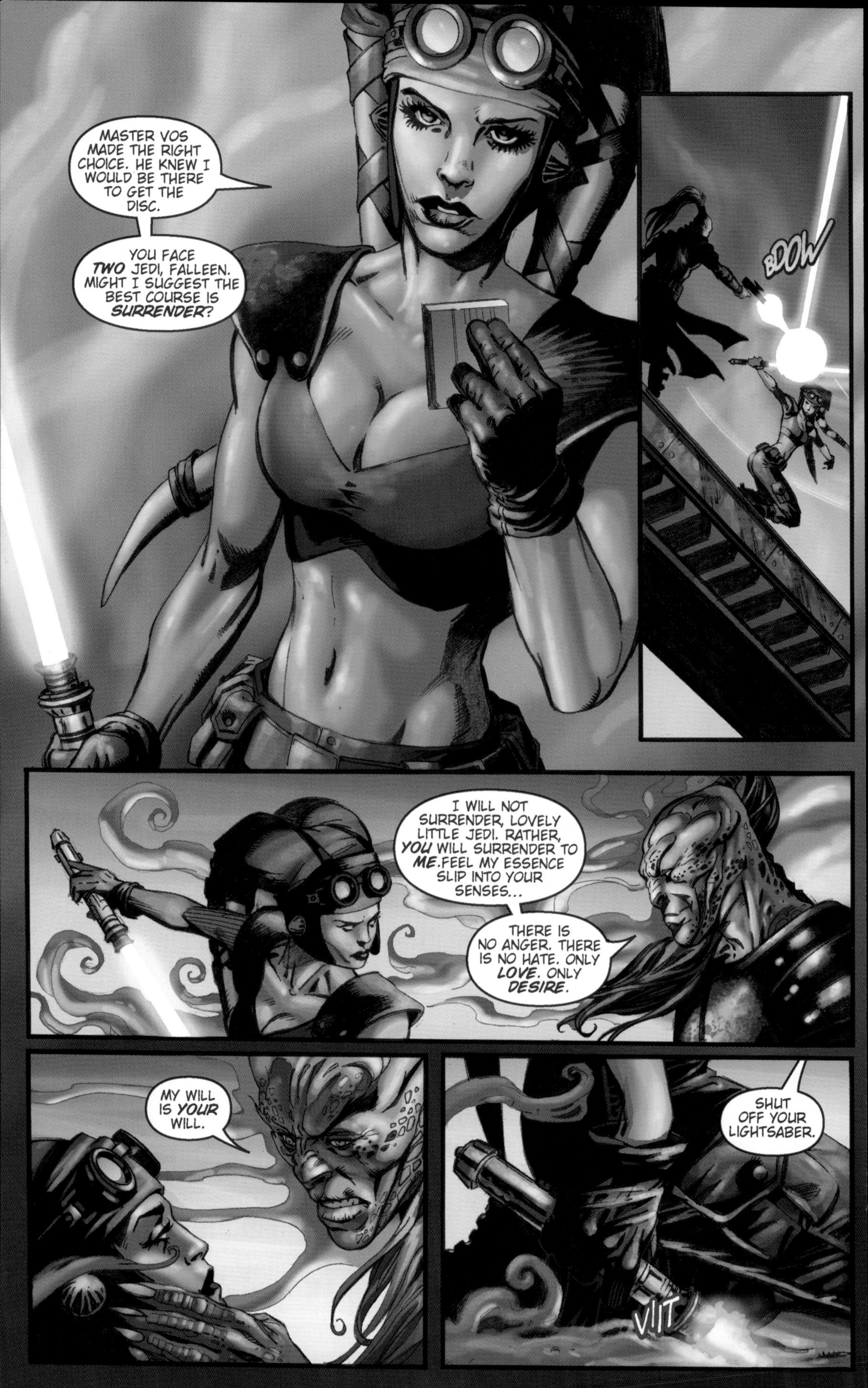
MASTER VOS MADE THE RIGHT CHOICE. HE KNEW I WOULD BE THERE TO GET THE DISC.
YOU FACE **TWO** JEDI, FALLEEN. MIGHT I SUGGEST THE BEST COURSE IS **SURRENDER**?
BDOW
I WILL NOT SURRENDER, LOVELY LITTLE JEDI. RATHER, **YOU** WILL SURRENDER TO **ME**.FEEL MY ESSENCE SLIP INTO YOUR SENSES...
THERE IS NO ANGER. THERE IS NO HATE. ONLY **LOVE**. ONLY **DESIRE**.
MY WILL IS **YOUR** WILL.
SHUT OFF YOUR LIGHTSABER.
VIIT

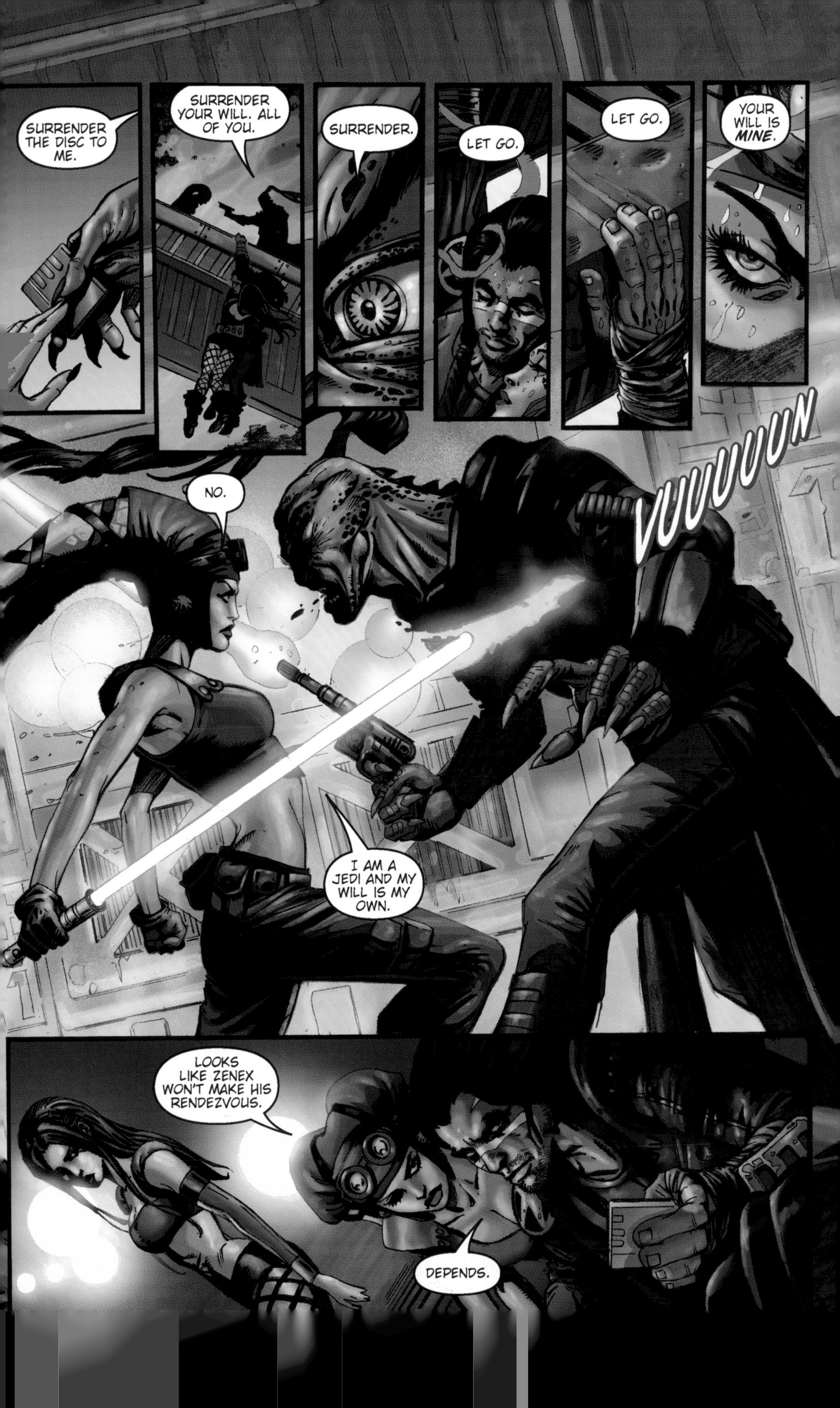
SURRENDER THE DISC TO ME.
SURRENDER YOUR WILL. ALL OF YOU.
SURRENDER.
LET GO.
LET GO.
YOUR WILL IS *MINE*.
NO.
VUUUUUN
I AM A JEDI AND MY WILL IS MY OWN.
LOOKS LIKE ZENEX WON'T MAKE HIS RENDEZVOUS.
DEPENDS.

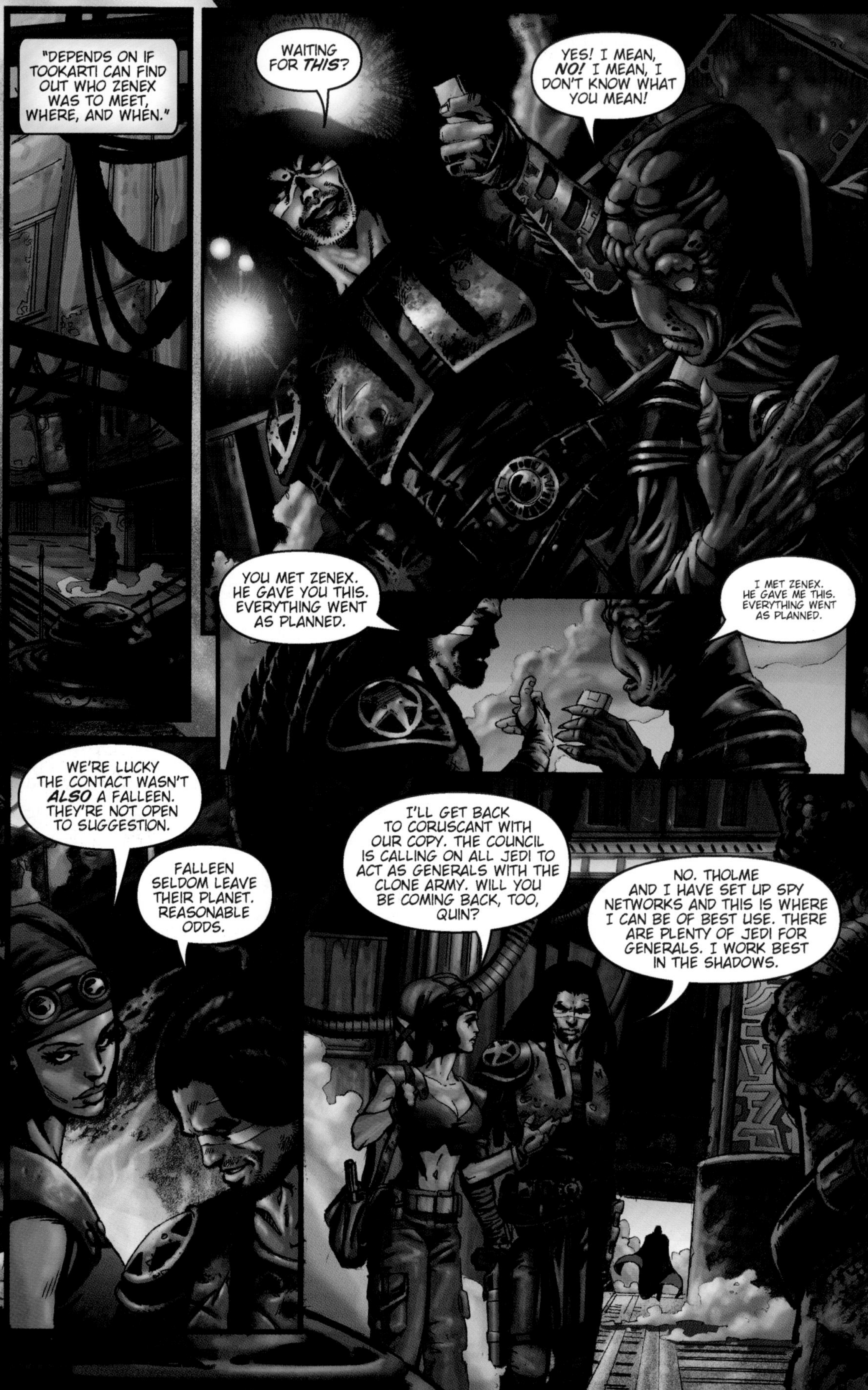
"DEPENDS ON IF TOOKARTI CAN FIND OUT WHO ZENEX WAS TO MEET, WHERE, AND WHEN."
WAITING FOR *THIS*?
YES! I MEAN, *NO!* I MEAN, I DON'T KNOW WHAT YOU MEAN!
YOU MET ZENEX. HE GAVE YOU THIS. EVERYTHING WENT AS PLANNED.
I MET ZENEX. HE GAVE ME THIS. EVERYTHING WENT AS PLANNED.
WE'RE LUCKY THE CONTACT WASN'T *ALSO* A FALLEEN. THEY'RE NOT OPEN TO SUGGESTION.
FALLEEN SELDOM LEAVE THEIR PLANET. REASONABLE ODDS.
I'LL GET BACK TO CORUSCANT WITH OUR COPY. THE COUNCIL IS CALLING ON ALL JEDI TO ACT AS GENERALS WITH THE CLONE ARMY. WILL YOU BE COMING BACK, TOO, QUIN?
NO. THOLME AND I HAVE SET UP SPY NETWORKS AND THIS IS WHERE I CAN BE OF BEST USE. THERE ARE PLENTY OF JEDI FOR GENERALS. I WORK BEST IN THE SHADOWS.

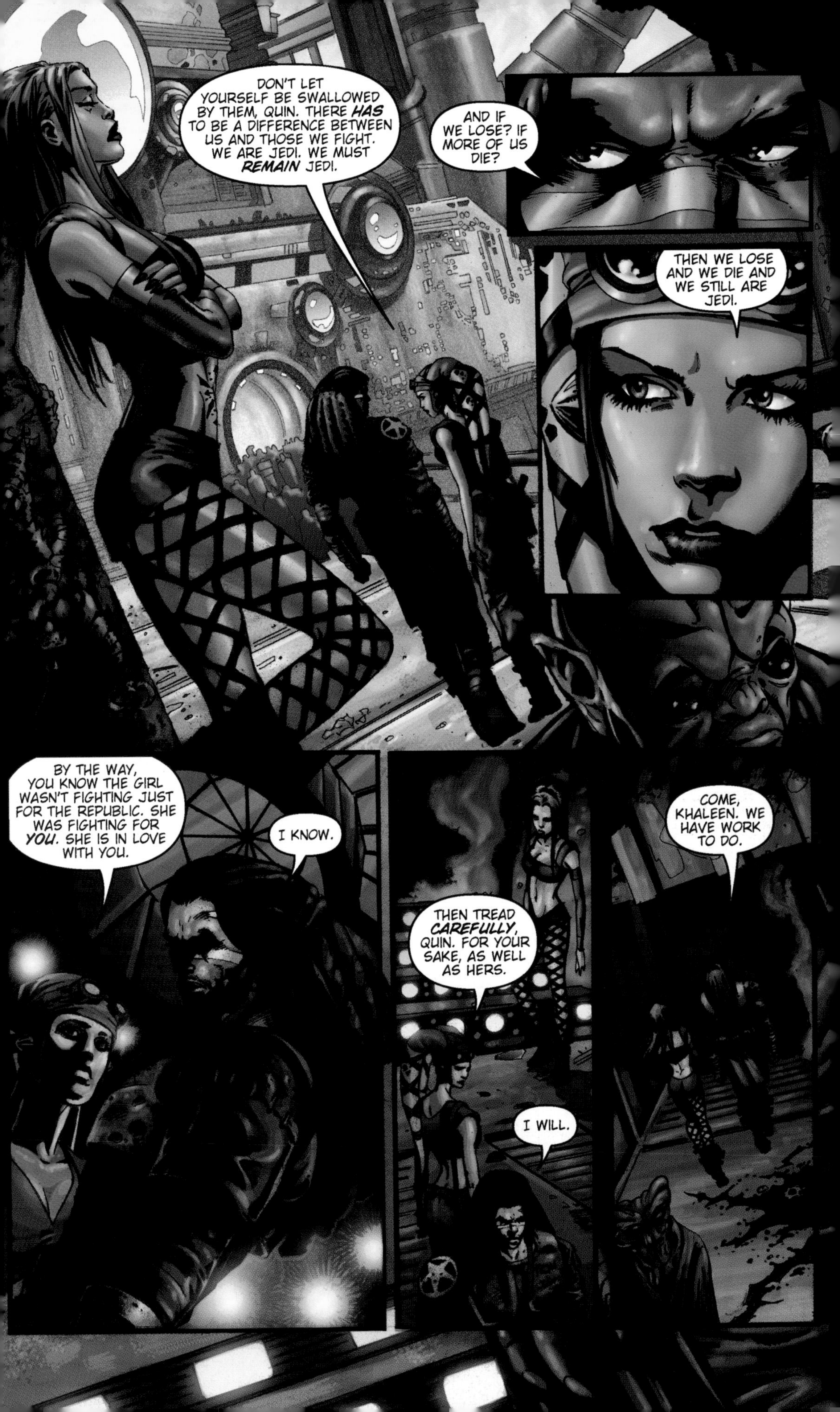
DON'T LET YOURSELF BE SWALLOWED BY THEM, QUIN. THERE HAS TO BE A DIFFERENCE BETWEEN US AND THOSE WE FIGHT. WE ARE JEDI. WE MUST REMAIN JEDI.
AND IF WE LOSE? IF MORE OF US DIE?
THEN WE LOSE AND WE DIE AND WE STILL ARE JEDI.
BY THE WAY, YOU KNOW THE GIRL WASN'T FIGHTING JUST FOR THE REPUBLIC. SHE WAS FIGHTING FOR YOU. SHE IS IN LOVE WITH YOU.
I KNOW.
THEN TREAD CAREFULLY, QUIN. FOR YOUR SAKE, AS WELL AS HERS.
I WILL.
COME, KHALEEN. WE HAVE WORK TO DO.

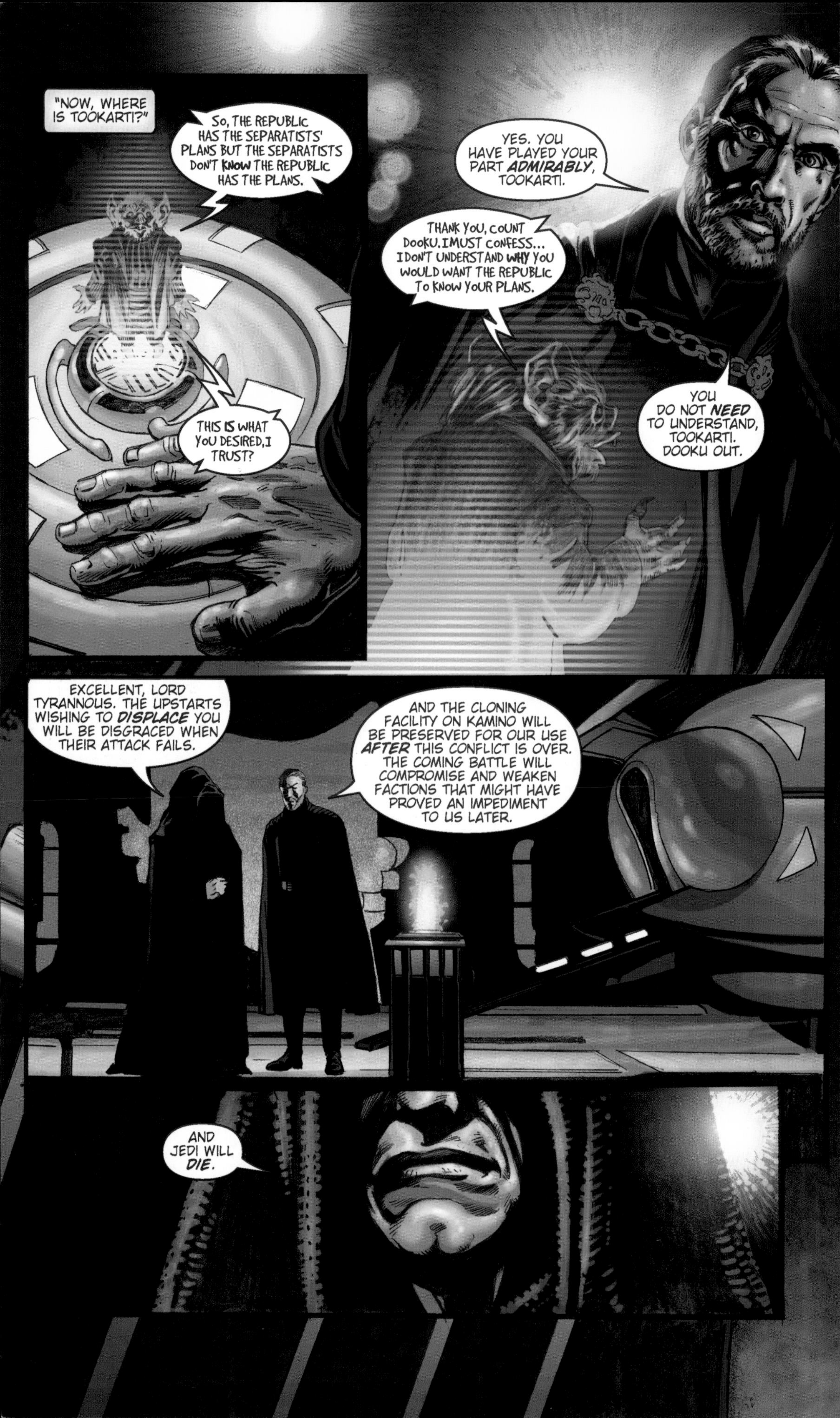
"NOW, WHERE IS TOOKARTI?"
SO, THE REPUBLIC HAS THE SEPARATISTS' PLANS BUT THE SEPARATISTS DON'T KNOW THE REPUBLIC HAS THE PLANS.
THIS IS WHAT YOU DESIRED, I TRUST?
YES. YOU HAVE PLAYED YOUR PART ADMIRABLY, TOOKARTI.
THANK YOU, COUNT DOOKU. I MUST CONFESS... I DON'T UNDERSTAND WHY YOU WOULD WANT THE REPUBLIC TO KNOW YOUR PLANS.
YOU DO NOT NEED TO UNDERSTAND, TOOKARTI. DOOKU OUT.
EXCELLENT, LORD TYRANNOUS. THE UPSTARTS WISHING TO DISPLACE YOU WILL BE DISGRACED WHEN THEIR ATTACK FAILS.
AND THE CLONING FACILITY ON KAMINO WILL BE PRESERVED FOR OUR USE AFTER THIS CONFLICT IS OVER. THE COMING BATTLE WILL COMPROMISE AND WEAKEN FACTIONS THAT MIGHT HAVE PROVED AN IMPEDIMENT TO US LATER.
AND JEDI WILL DIE.

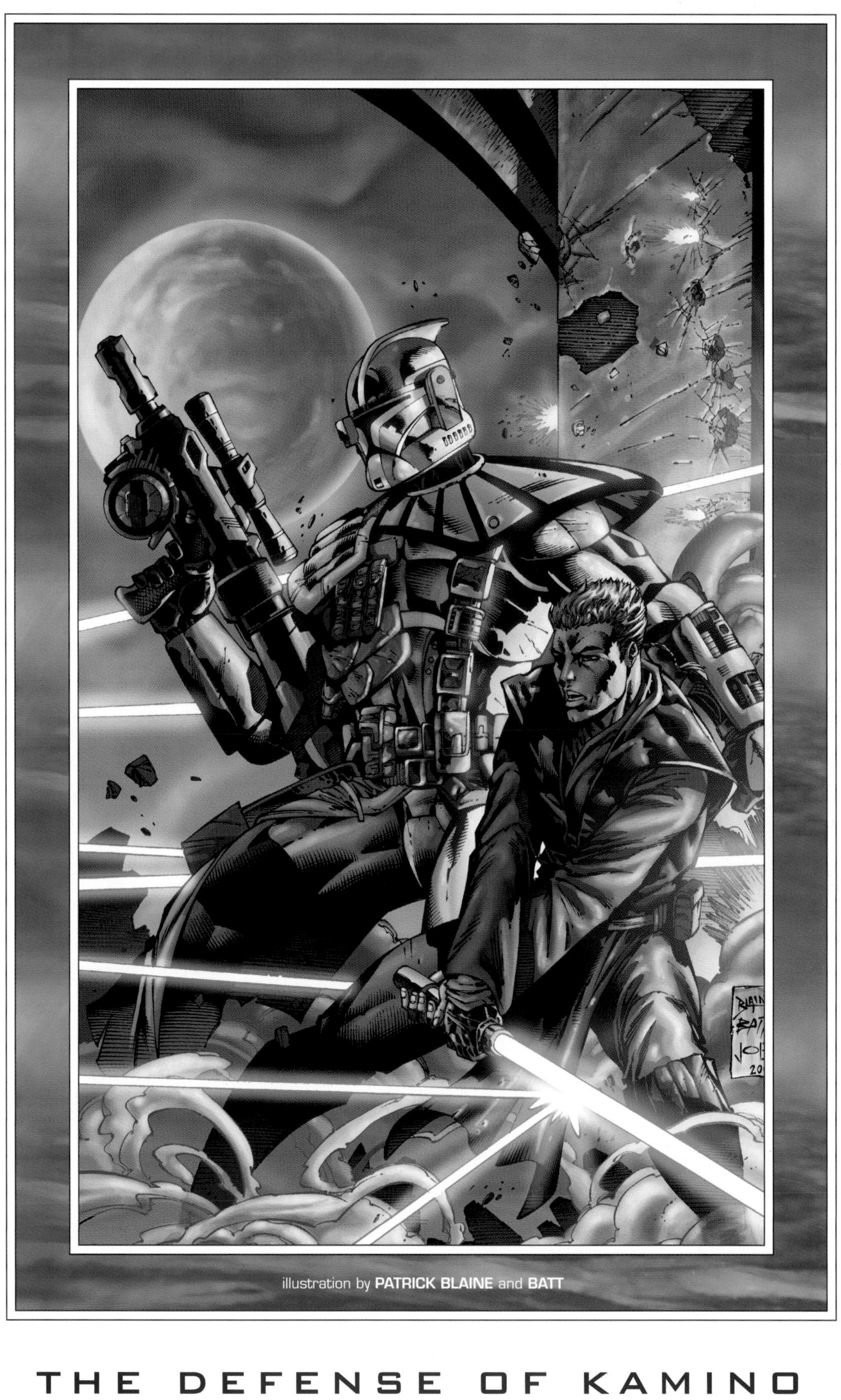

illustration by **PATRICK BLAINE** and **BATT**

THE DEFENSE OF KAMINO

"Brothers in Arms"
written by
John Ostrander
pencilled by
Jan Duursema
inked by
Dan Parsons

"Jango's Legacy"
written by
Haden Blackman
pencilled by
Stephen Thompson
inked by
Ray Kryssing

"No End in Sight"
written by
Scott Allie
pencilled by
Tomás Giorello
inked by
Ray Kryssing

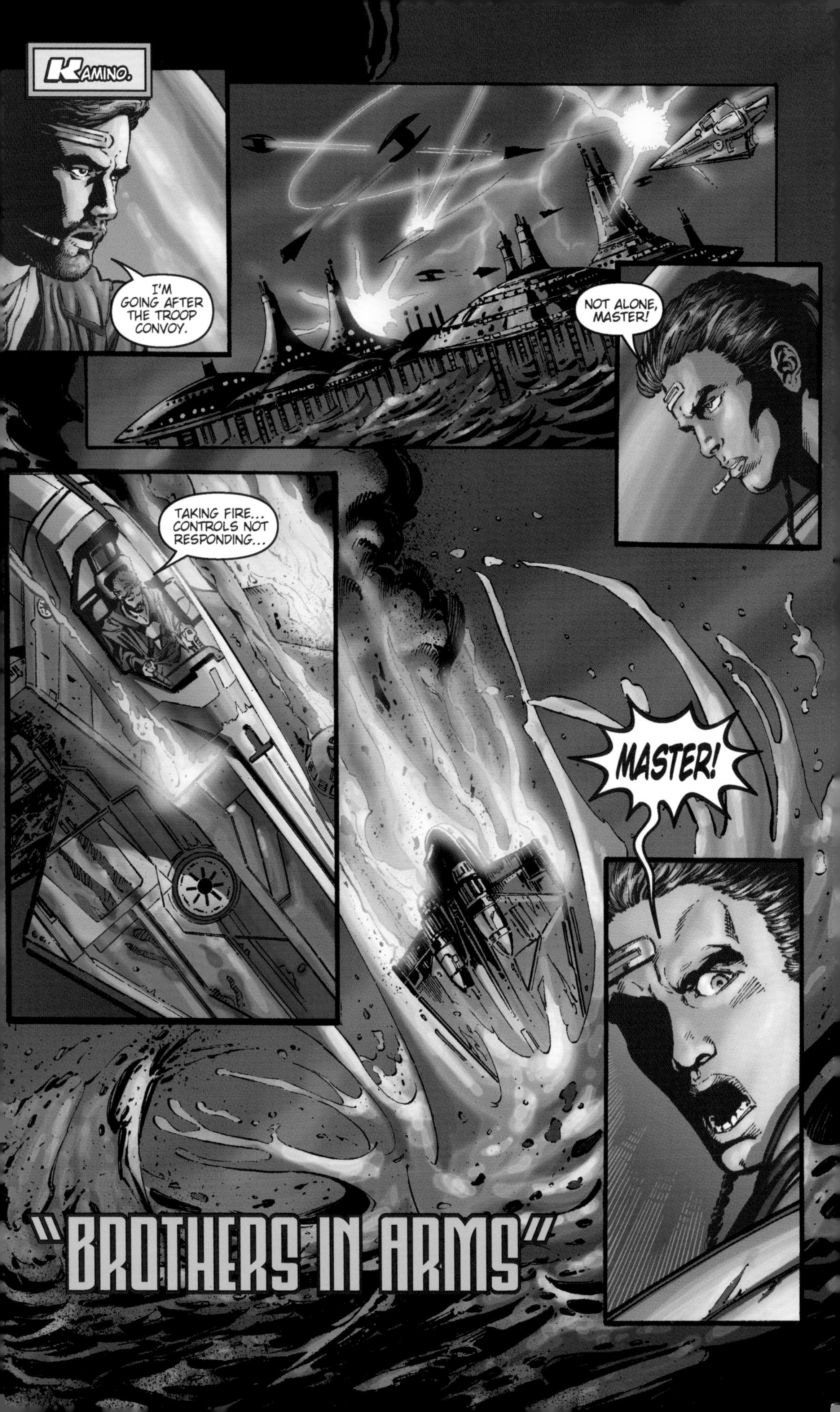
KAMINO.
I'M GOING AFTER THE TROOP CONVOY.
NOT ALONE, MASTER!
TAKING FIRE... CONTROLS NOT RESPONDING...
MASTER!
"BROTHERS IN ARMS"

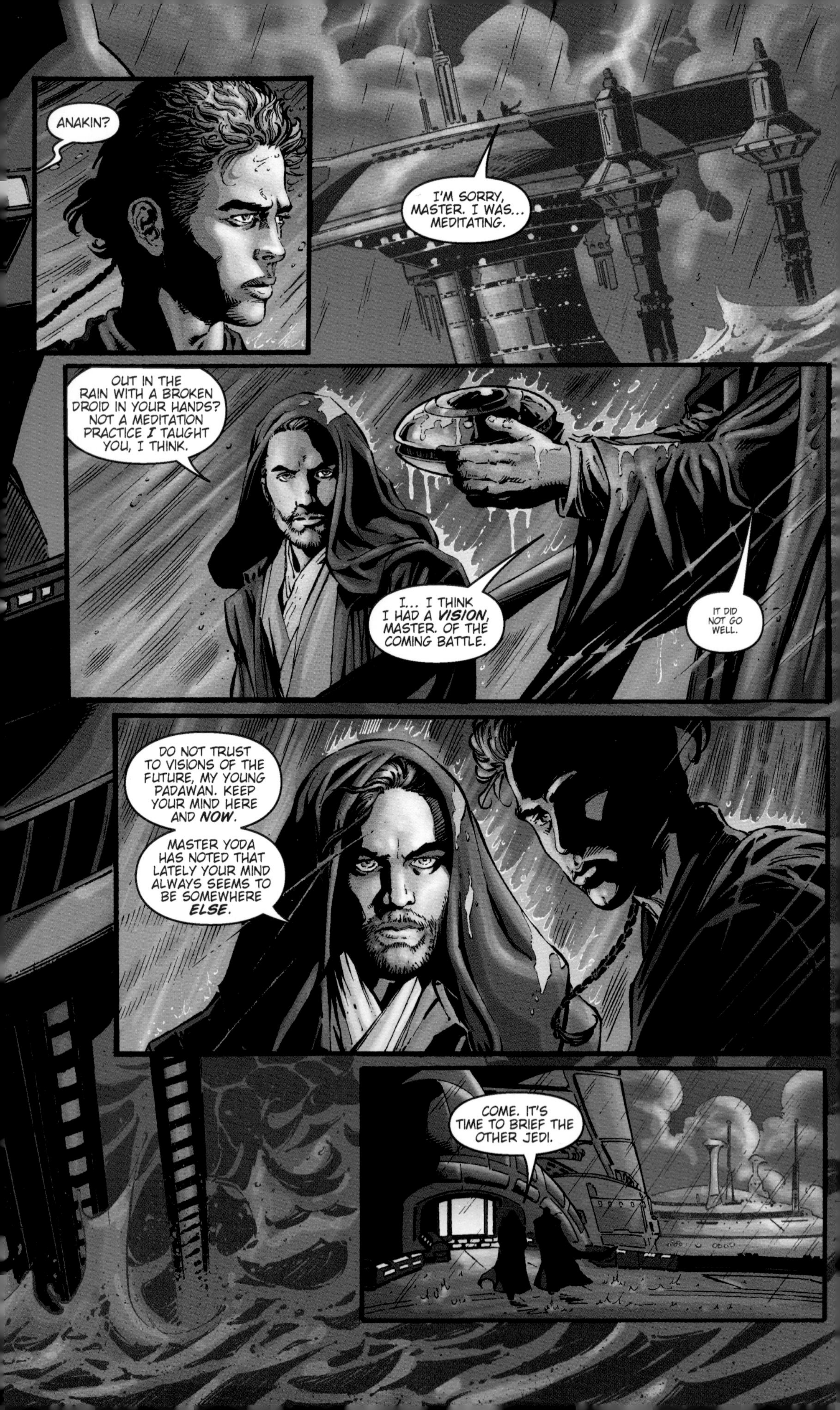
ANAKIN?
I'M SORRY, MASTER. I WAS... MEDITATING.
OUT IN THE RAIN WITH A BROKEN DROID IN YOUR HANDS? NOT A MEDITATION PRACTICE *I* TAUGHT YOU, I THINK.
I... I THINK I HAD A *VISION*, MASTER. OF THE COMING BATTLE.
IT DID NOT GO WELL.
DO NOT TRUST TO VISIONS OF THE FUTURE, MY YOUNG PADAWAN. KEEP YOUR MIND HERE AND *NOW*.
MASTER YODA HAS NOTED THAT LATELY YOUR MIND ALWAYS SEEMS TO BE SOMEWHERE *ELSE*.
COME. IT'S TIME TO BRIEF THE OTHER JEDI.

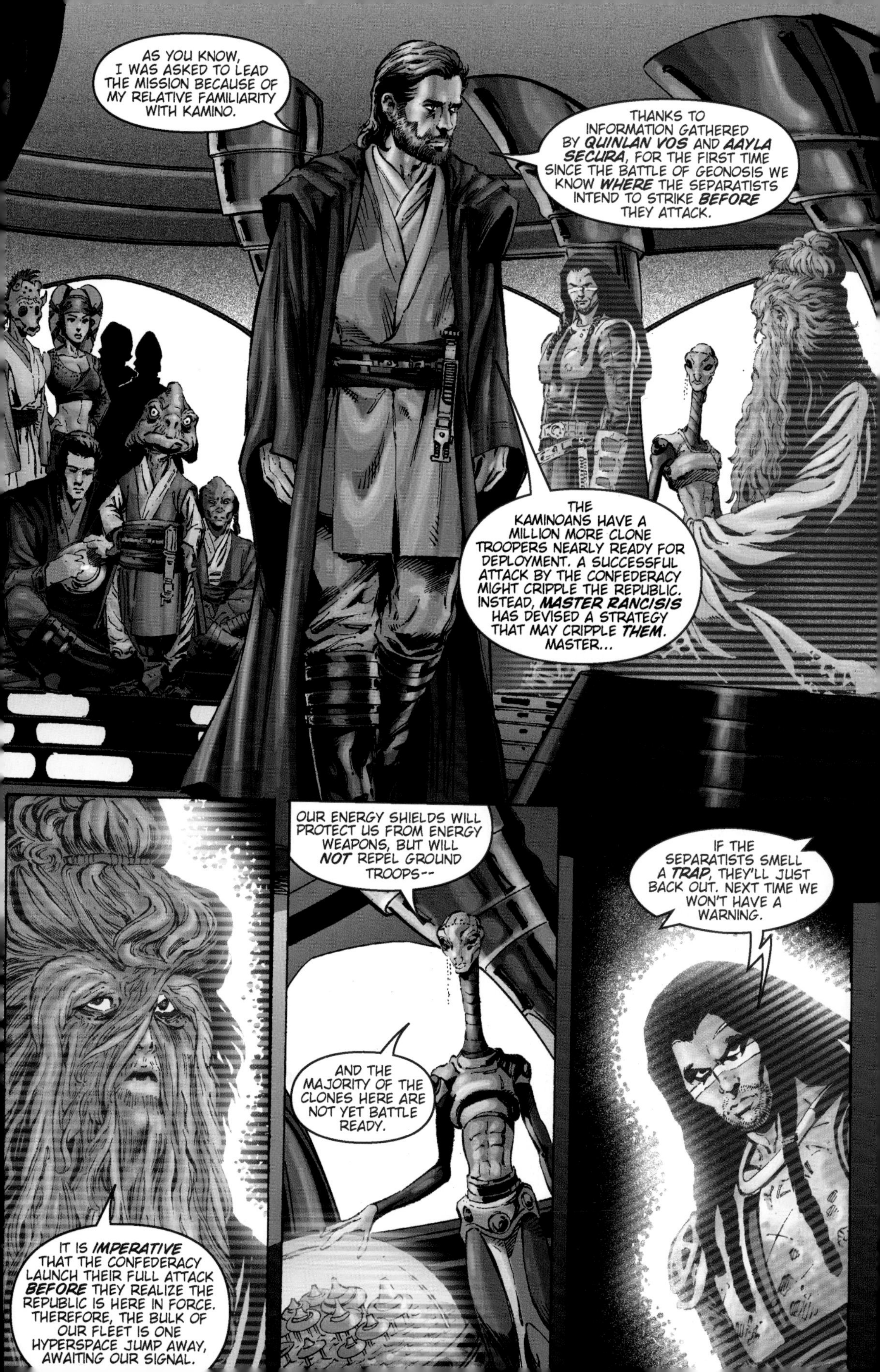
AS YOU KNOW, I WAS ASKED TO LEAD THE MISSION BECAUSE OF MY RELATIVE FAMILIARITY WITH KAMINO.
THANKS TO INFORMATION GATHERED BY QUINLAN VOS AND AAYLA SECURA, FOR THE FIRST TIME SINCE THE BATTLE OF GEONOSIS WE KNOW WHERE THE SEPARATISTS INTEND TO STRIKE BEFORE THEY ATTACK.
THE KAMINOANS HAVE A MILLION MORE CLONE TROOPERS NEARLY READY FOR DEPLOYMENT. A SUCCESSFUL ATTACK BY THE CONFEDERACY MIGHT CRIPPLE THE REPUBLIC. INSTEAD, MASTER RANCISIS HAS DEVISED A STRATEGY THAT MAY CRIPPLE THEM. MASTER...
IT IS IMPERATIVE THAT THE CONFEDERACY LAUNCH THEIR FULL ATTACK BEFORE THEY REALIZE THE REPUBLIC IS HERE IN FORCE. THEREFORE, THE BULK OF OUR FLEET IS ONE HYPERSPACE JUMP AWAY, AWAITING OUR SIGNAL.
OUR ENERGY SHIELDS WILL PROTECT US FROM ENERGY WEAPONS, BUT WILL NOT REPEL GROUND TROOPS--
AND THE MAJORITY OF THE CLONES HERE ARE NOT YET BATTLE READY.
IF THE SEPARATISTS SMELL A TRAP, THEY'LL JUST BACK OUT. NEXT TIME WE WON'T HAVE A WARNING.

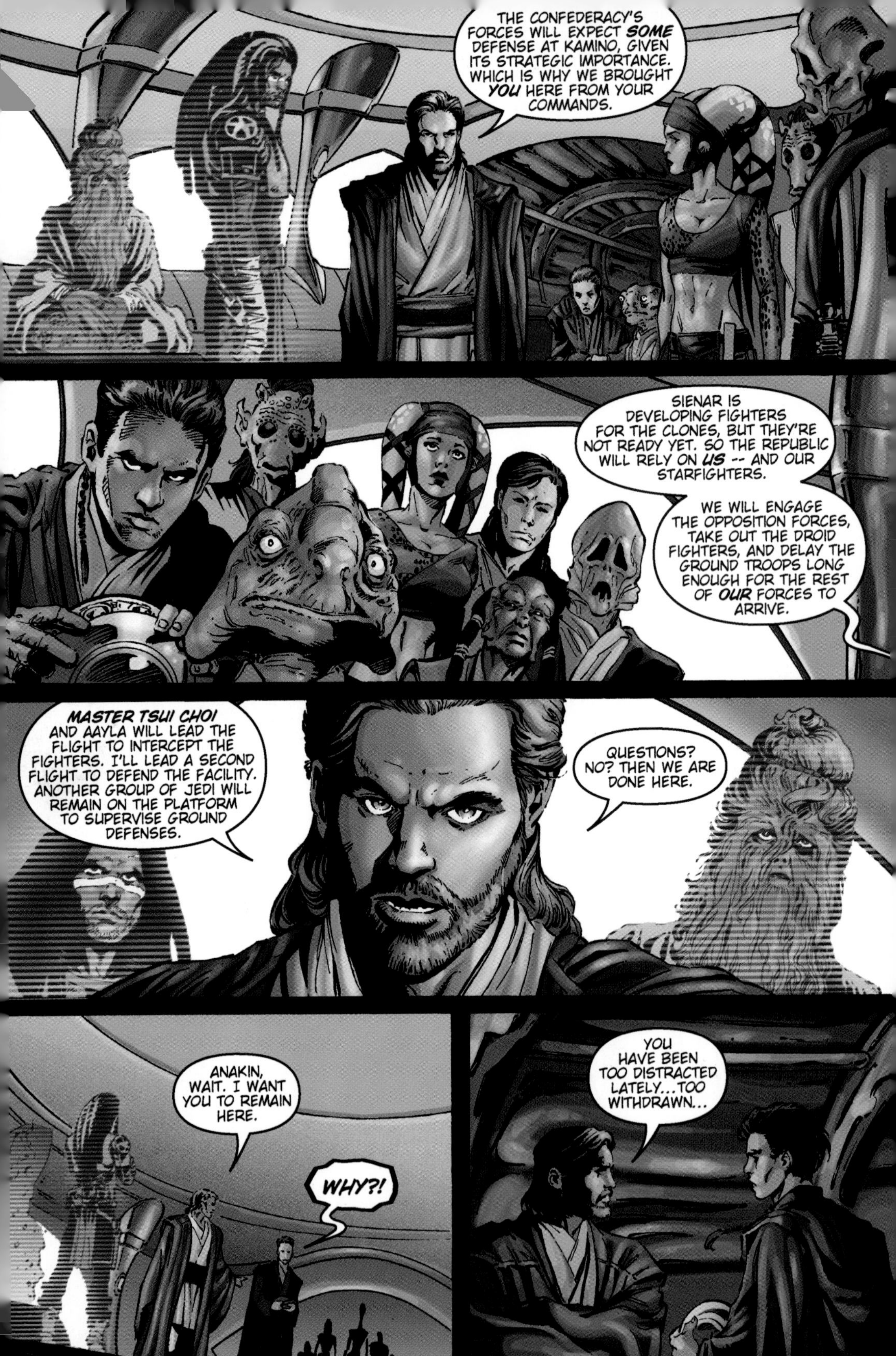
THE CONFEDERACY'S FORCES WILL EXPECT SOME DEFENSE AT KAMINO, GIVEN ITS STRATEGIC IMPORTANCE. WHICH IS WHY WE BROUGHT YOU HERE FROM YOUR COMMANDS.
SIENAR IS DEVELOPING FIGHTERS FOR THE CLONES, BUT THEY'RE NOT READY YET. SO THE REPUBLIC WILL RELY ON US -- AND OUR STARFIGHTERS.
WE WILL ENGAGE THE OPPOSITION FORCES, TAKE OUT THE DROID FIGHTERS, AND DELAY THE GROUND TROOPS LONG ENOUGH FOR THE REST OF OUR FORCES TO ARRIVE.
MASTER TSUI CHOI AND AAYLA WILL LEAD THE FLIGHT TO INTERCEPT THE FIGHTERS. I'LL LEAD A SECOND FLIGHT TO DEFEND THE FACILITY. ANOTHER GROUP OF JEDI WILL REMAIN ON THE PLATFORM TO SUPERVISE GROUND DEFENSES.
QUESTIONS? NO? THEN WE ARE DONE HERE.
ANAKIN, WAIT. I WANT YOU TO REMAIN HERE.
WHY?!
YOU HAVE BEEN TOO DISTRACTED LATELY...TOO WITHDRAWN...

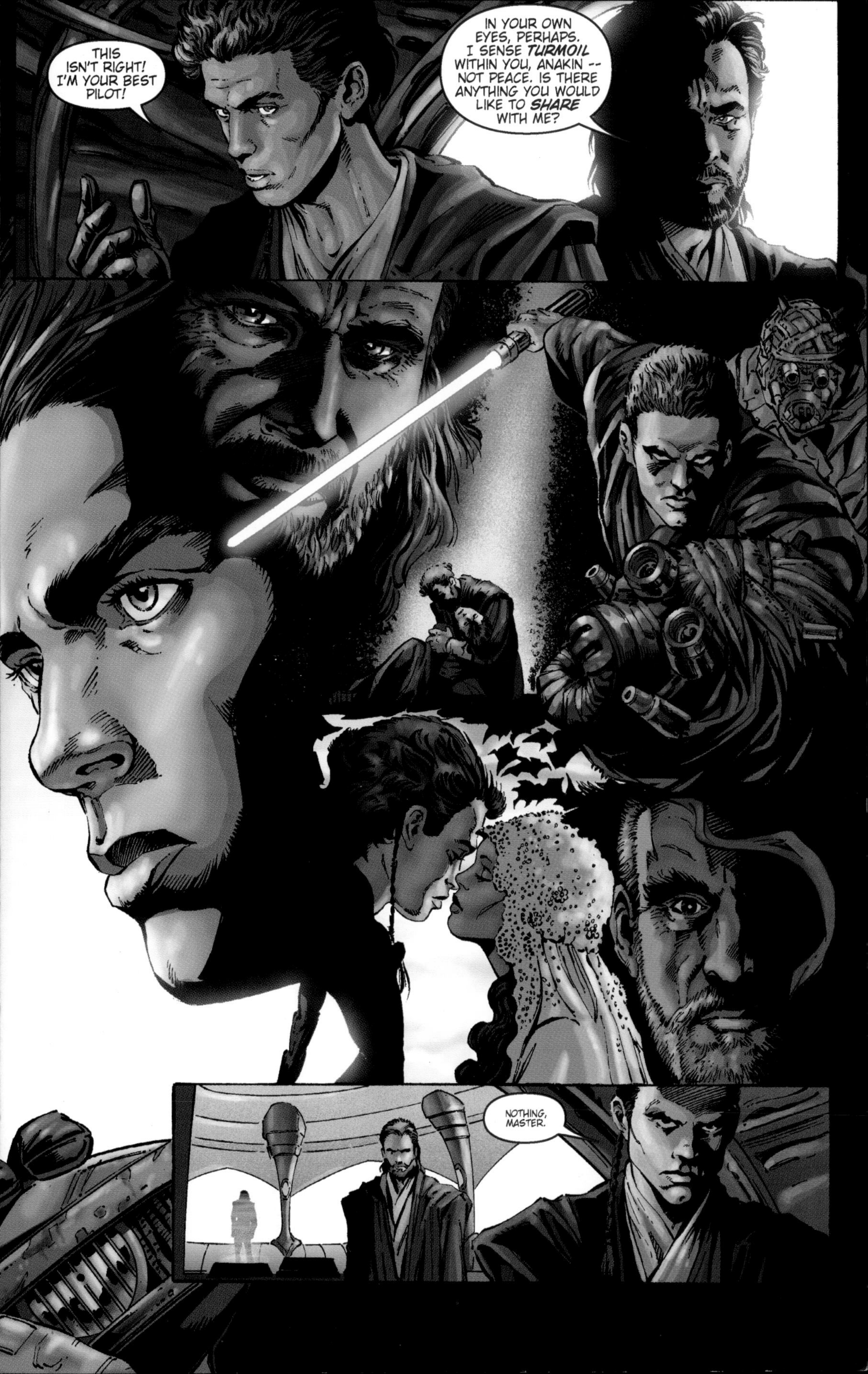
THIS ISN'T RIGHT! I'M YOUR BEST PILOT!
IN YOUR OWN EYES, PERHAPS. I SENSE TURMOIL WITHIN YOU, ANAKIN -- NOT PEACE. IS THERE ANYTHING YOU WOULD LIKE TO SHARE WITH ME?
NOTHING, MASTER.

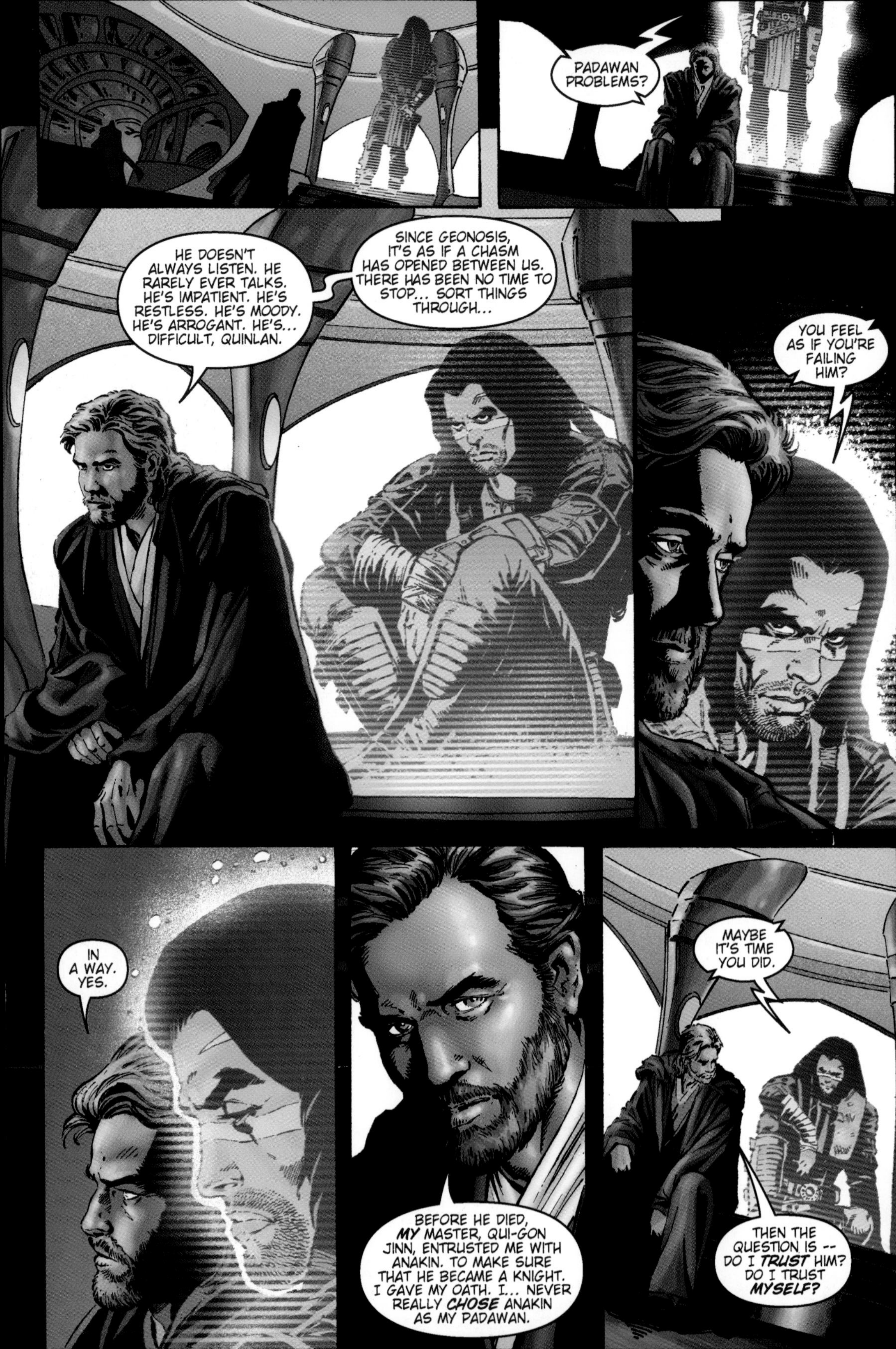
PADAWAN PROBLEMS?
HE DOESN'T ALWAYS LISTEN. HE RARELY EVER TALKS. HE'S IMPATIENT. HE'S RESTLESS. HE'S MOODY. HE'S ARROGANT. HE'S... DIFFICULT, QUINLAN.
SINCE GEONOSIS, IT'S AS IF A CHASM HAS OPENED BETWEEN US. THERE HAS BEEN NO TIME TO STOP... SORT THINGS THROUGH...
YOU FEEL AS IF YOU'RE FAILING HIM?
IN A WAY. YES.
BEFORE HE DIED, MY MASTER, QUI-GON JINN, ENTRUSTED ME WITH ANAKIN. TO MAKE SURE THAT HE BECAME A KNIGHT. I GAVE MY OATH. I... NEVER REALLY CHOSE ANAKIN AS MY PADAWAN.
MAYBE IT'S TIME YOU DID.
THEN THE QUESTION IS -- DO I TRUST HIM? DO I TRUST MYSELF?

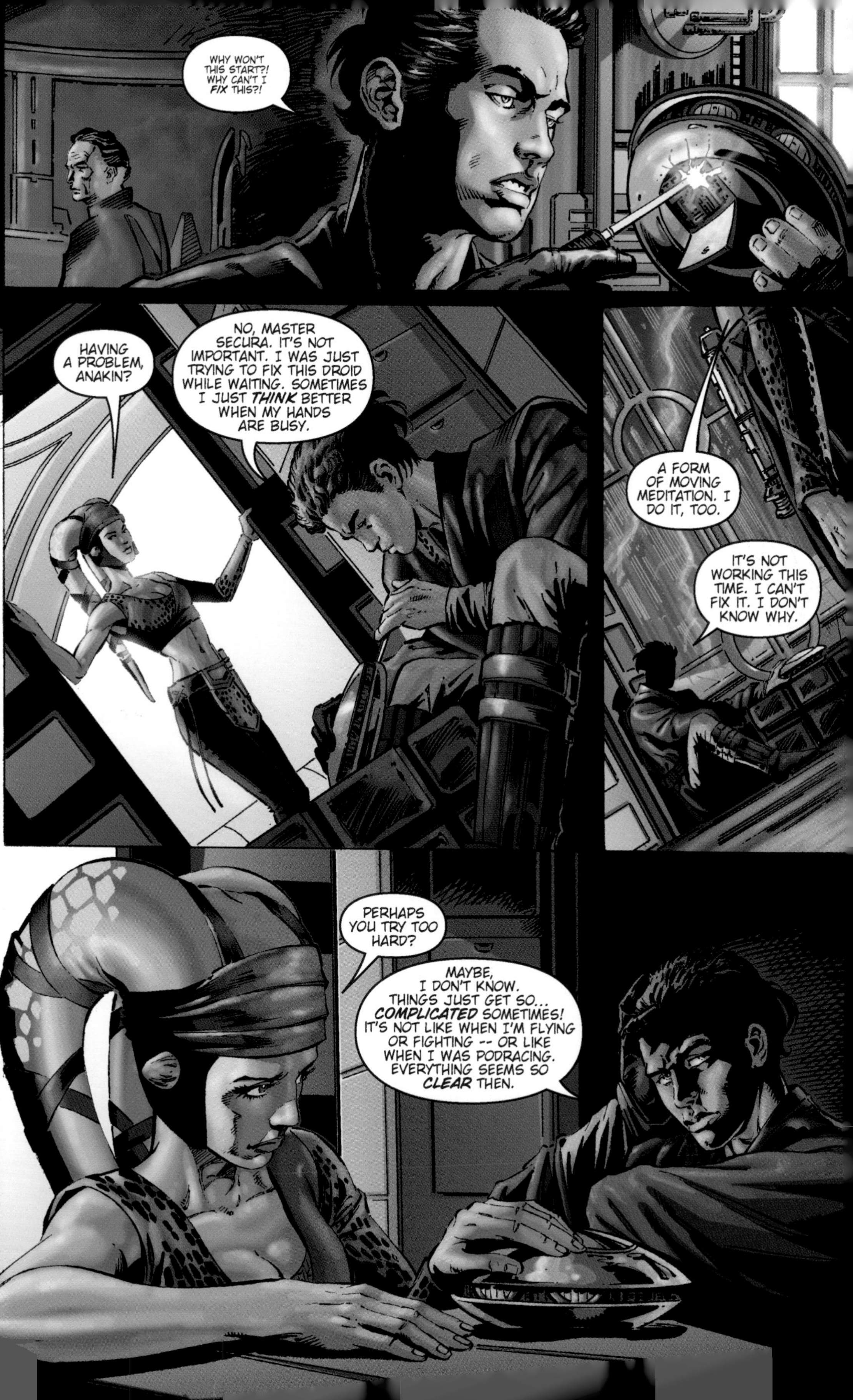
WHY WON'T THIS START?! WHY CAN'T I *FIX* THIS?!
HAVING A PROBLEM, ANAKIN?
NO, MASTER SECURA. IT'S NOT IMPORTANT. I WAS JUST TRYING TO FIX THIS DROID WHILE WAITING. SOMETIMES I JUST *THINK* BETTER WHEN MY HANDS ARE BUSY.
A FORM OF MOVING MEDITATION. I DO IT, TOO.
IT'S NOT WORKING THIS TIME. I CAN'T FIX IT. I DON'T KNOW WHY.
PERHAPS YOU TRY TOO HARD?
MAYBE, I DON'T KNOW. THINGS JUST GET SO... *COMPLICATED* SOMETIMES! IT'S NOT LIKE WHEN I'M FLYING OR FIGHTING -- OR LIKE WHEN I WAS PODRACING. EVERYTHING SEEMS SO *CLEAR* THEN.

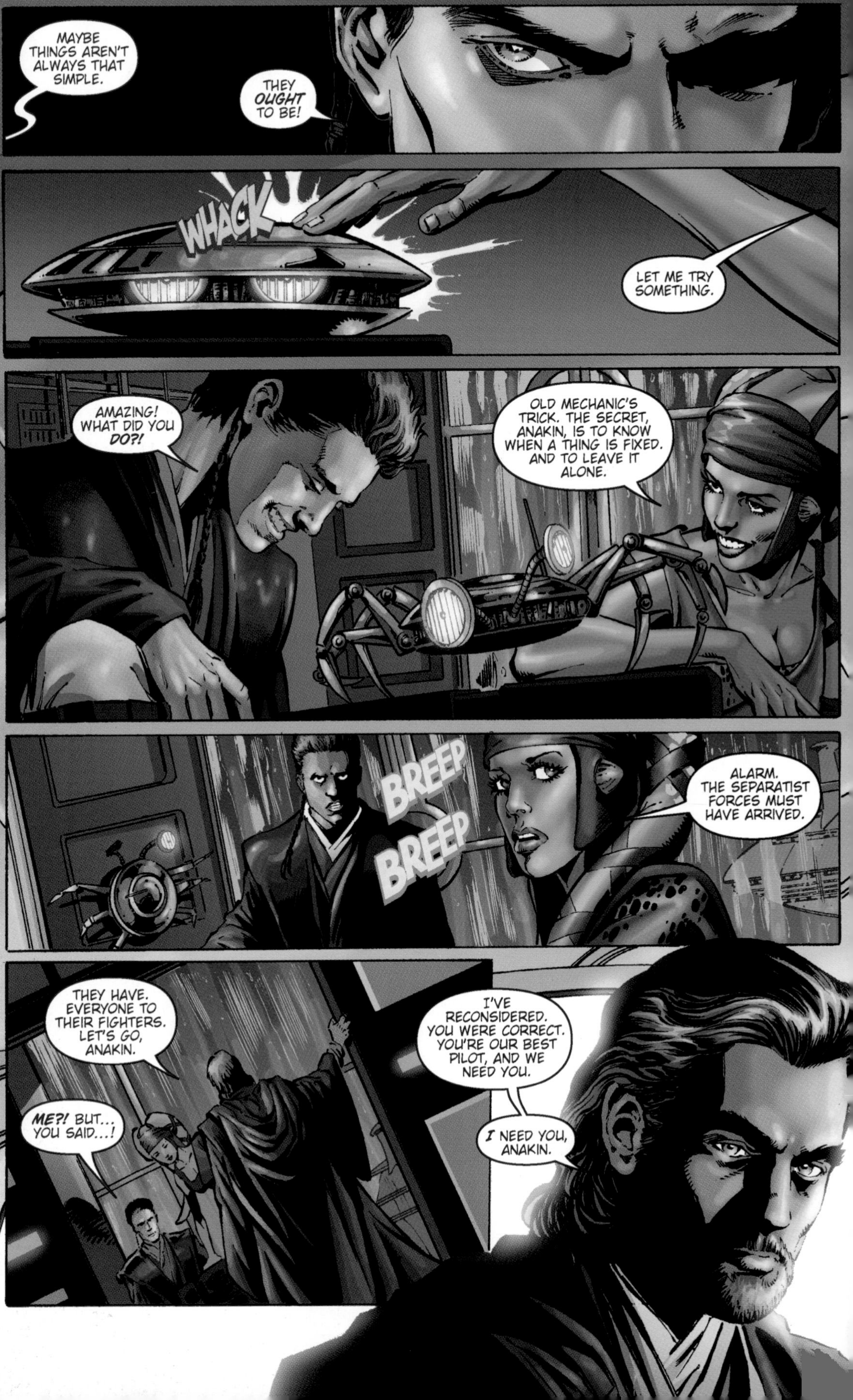
MAYBE THINGS AREN'T ALWAYS THAT SIMPLE.
THEY OUGHT TO BE!
WHACK
LET ME TRY SOMETHING.
AMAZING! WHAT DID YOU DO?!
OLD MECHANIC'S TRICK. THE SECRET, ANAKIN, IS TO KNOW WHEN A THING IS FIXED. AND TO LEAVE IT ALONE.
BREEP
BREEP
ALARM. THE SEPARATIST FORCES MUST HAVE ARRIVED.
THEY HAVE. EVERYONE TO THEIR FIGHTERS. LET'S GO, ANAKIN.
ME?! BUT... YOU SAID...!
I'VE RECONSIDERED. YOU WERE CORRECT. YOU'RE OUR BEST PILOT, AND WE NEED YOU.
I NEED YOU, ANAKIN.

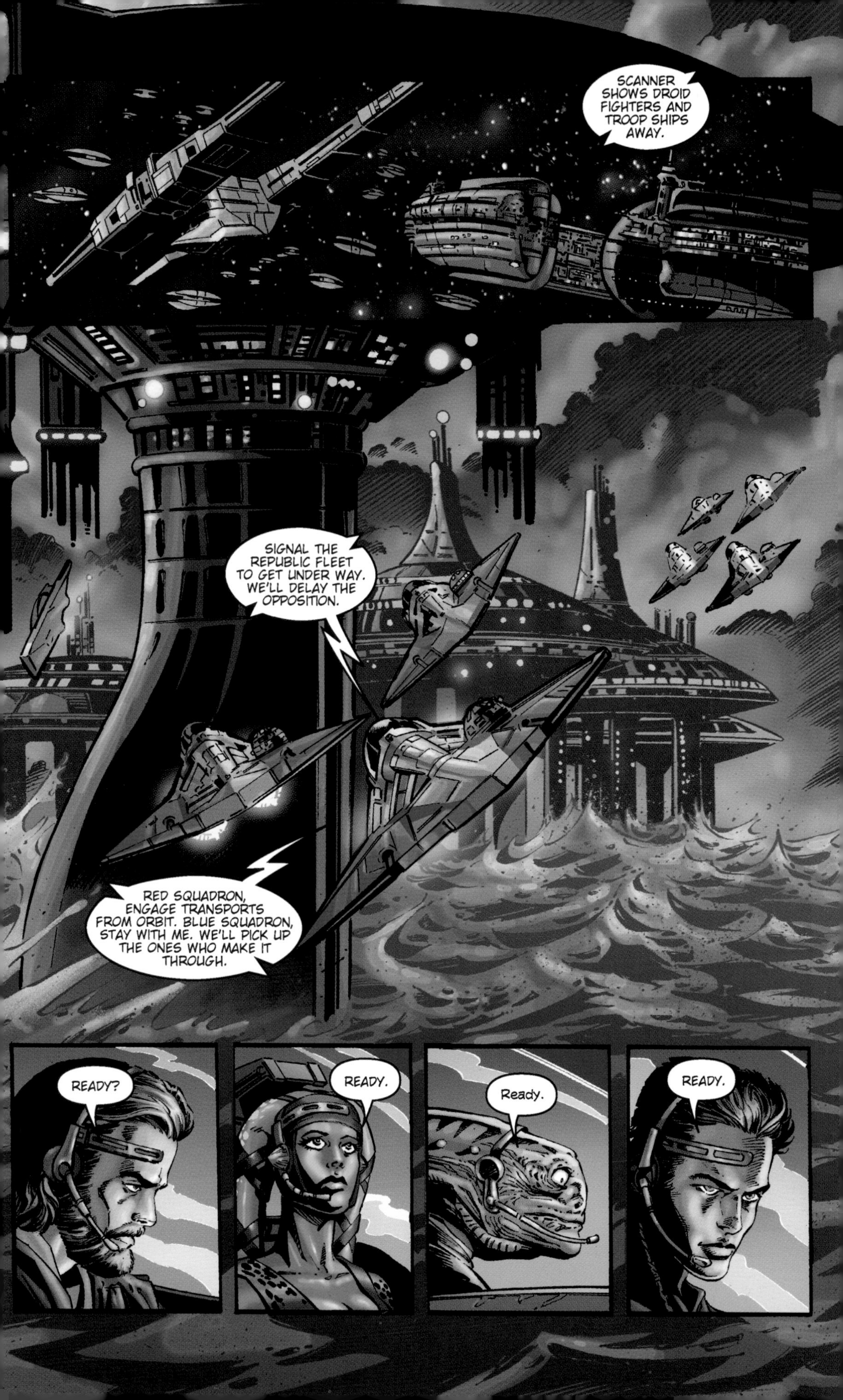
SCANNER SHOWS DROID FIGHTERS AND TROOP SHIPS AWAY.
SIGNAL THE REPUBLIC FLEET TO GET UNDER WAY. WE'LL DELAY THE OPPOSITION.
RED SQUADRON, ENGAGE TRANSPORTS FROM ORBIT. BLUE SQUADRON, STAY WITH ME. WE'LL PICK UP THE ONES WHO MAKE IT THROUGH.
READY?
READY.
Ready.
READY.

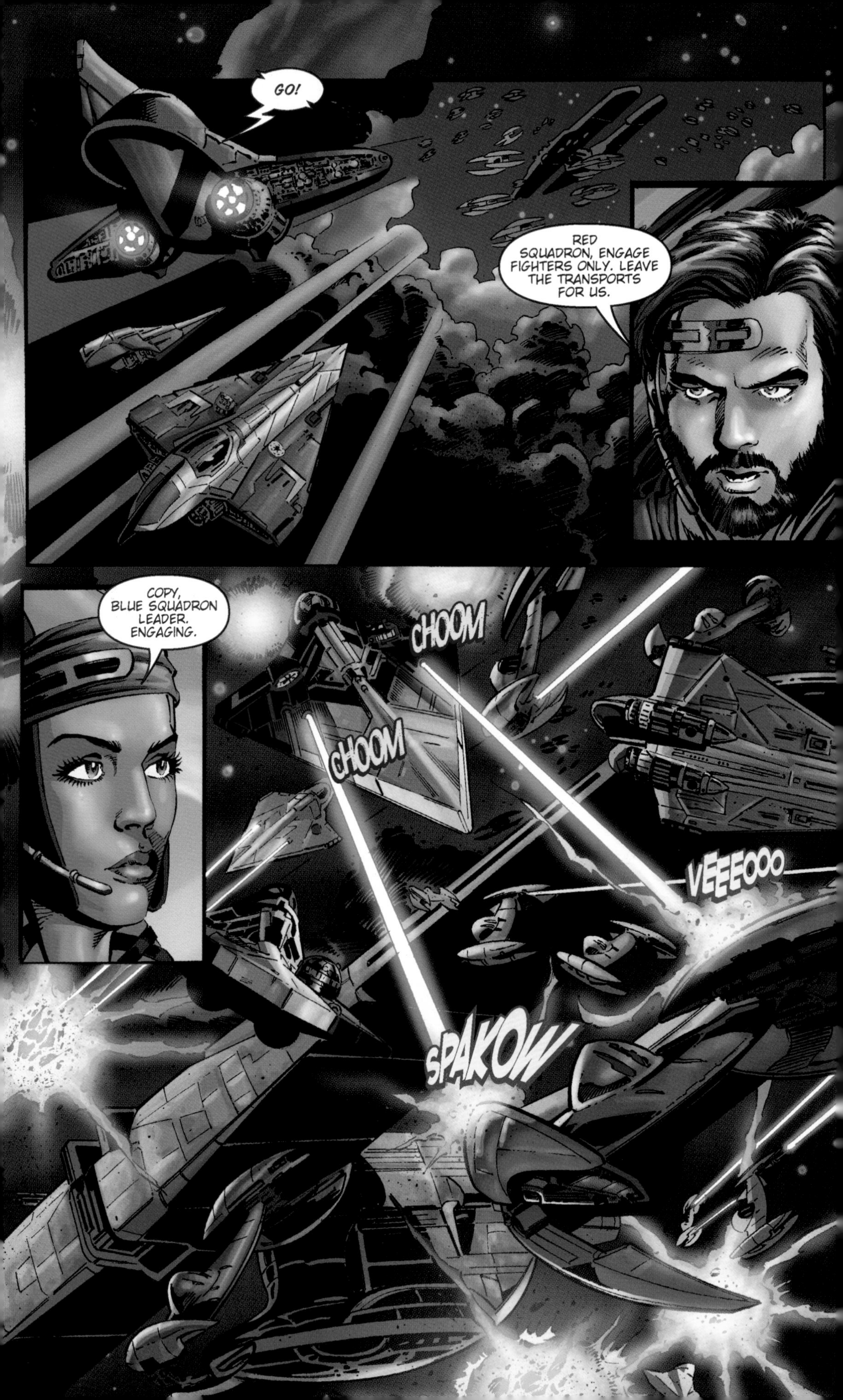
GO!
RED SQUADRON, ENGAGE FIGHTERS ONLY. LEAVE THE TRANSPORTS FOR US.
COPY, BLUE SQUADRON LEADER. ENGAGING.
CHOOM
CHOOM
VEEEOOO
SPAKOW

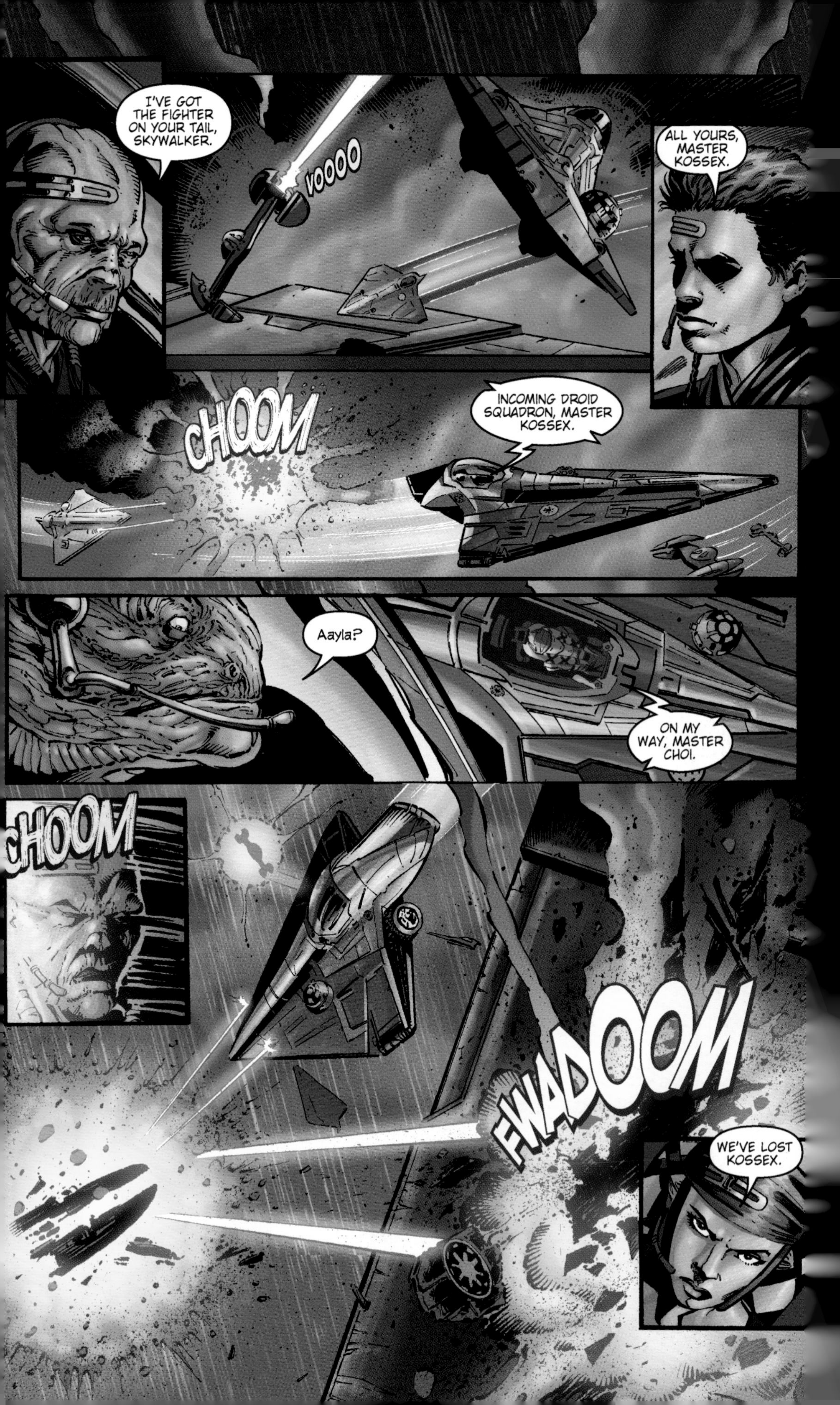
I'VE GOT THE FIGHTER ON YOUR TAIL, SKYWALKER.
VOOOO
ALL YOURS, MASTER KOSSEX.
CHOOM
INCOMING DROID SQUADRON, MASTER KOSSEX.
Aayla?
ON MY WAY, MASTER CHOI.
CHOOM
FWADOOM
WE'VE LOST KOSSEX.

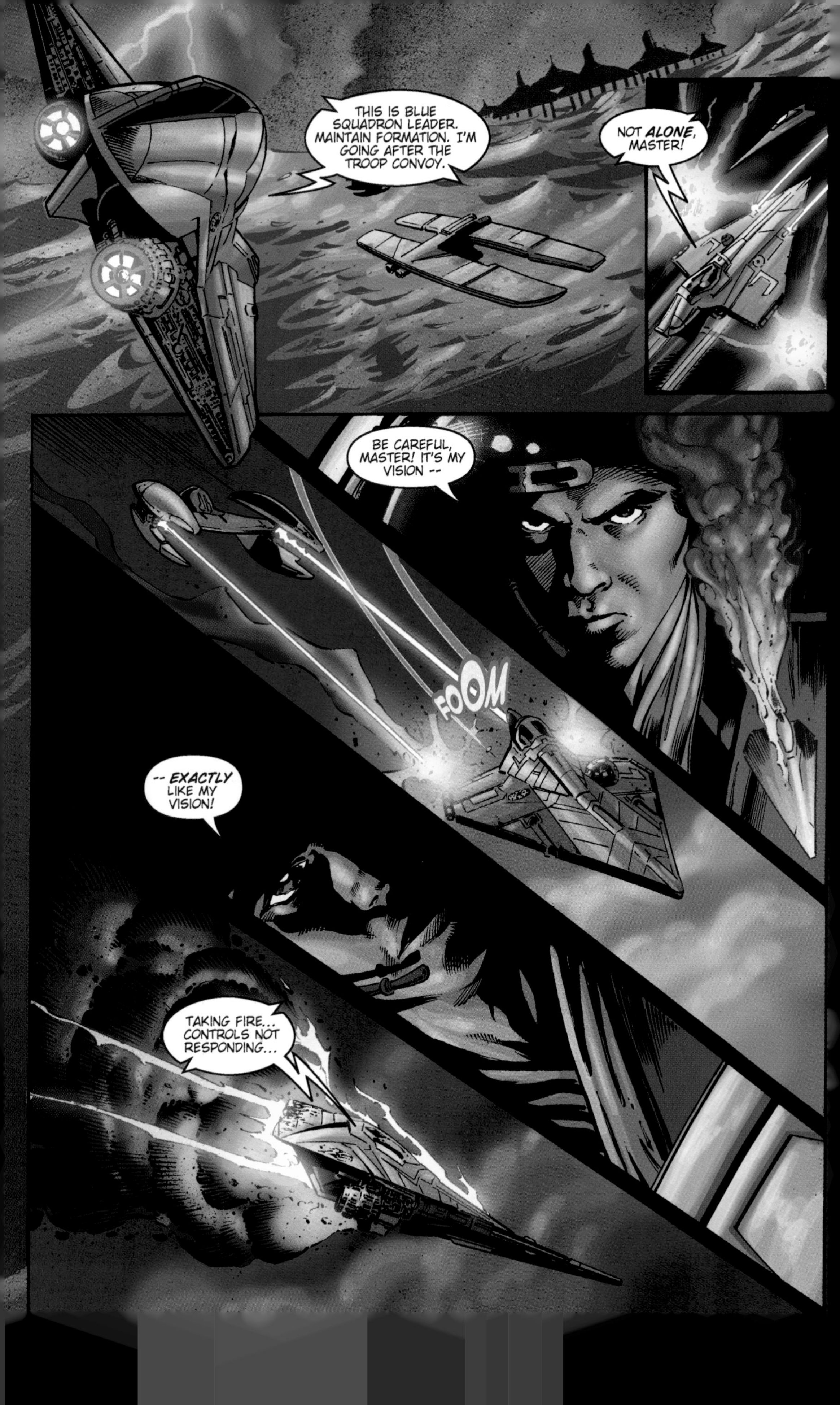

THIS IS BLUE SQUADRON LEADER. MAINTAIN FORMATION. I'M GOING AFTER THE TROOP CONVOY.
NOT *ALONE*, MASTER!
BE CAREFUL, MASTER! IT'S MY VISION --
FOOM
-- *EXACTLY* LIKE MY VISION!
TAKING FIRE... CONTROLS NOT RESPONDING...

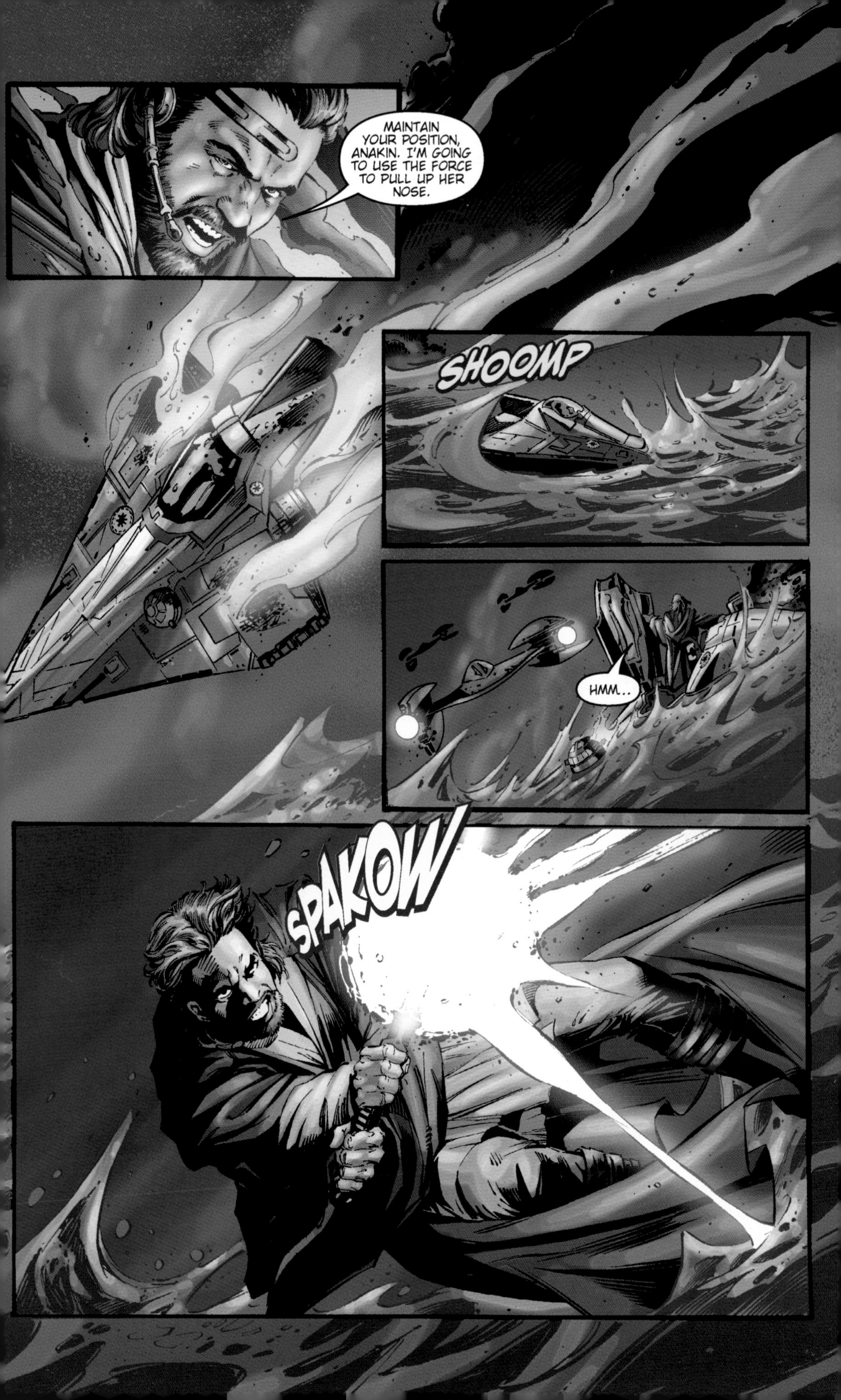
MAINTAIN YOUR POSITION, ANAKIN. I'M GOING TO USE THE FORCE TO PULL UP HER NOSE.
SHOOMP
HMM...
SPAKOW

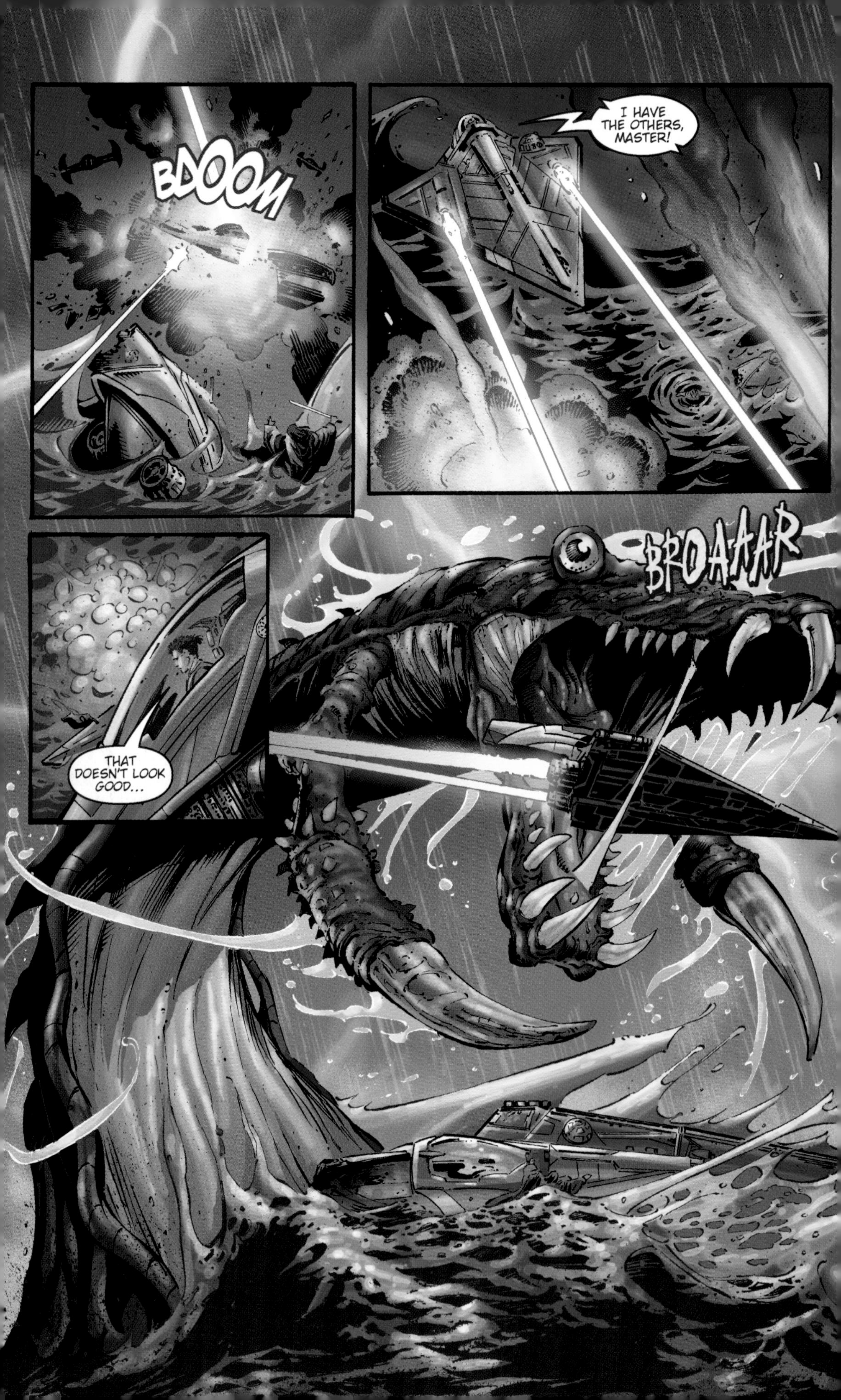
BDOOM
I HAVE THE OTHERS, MASTER!
BROAAAR
THAT DOESN'T LOOK GOOD...

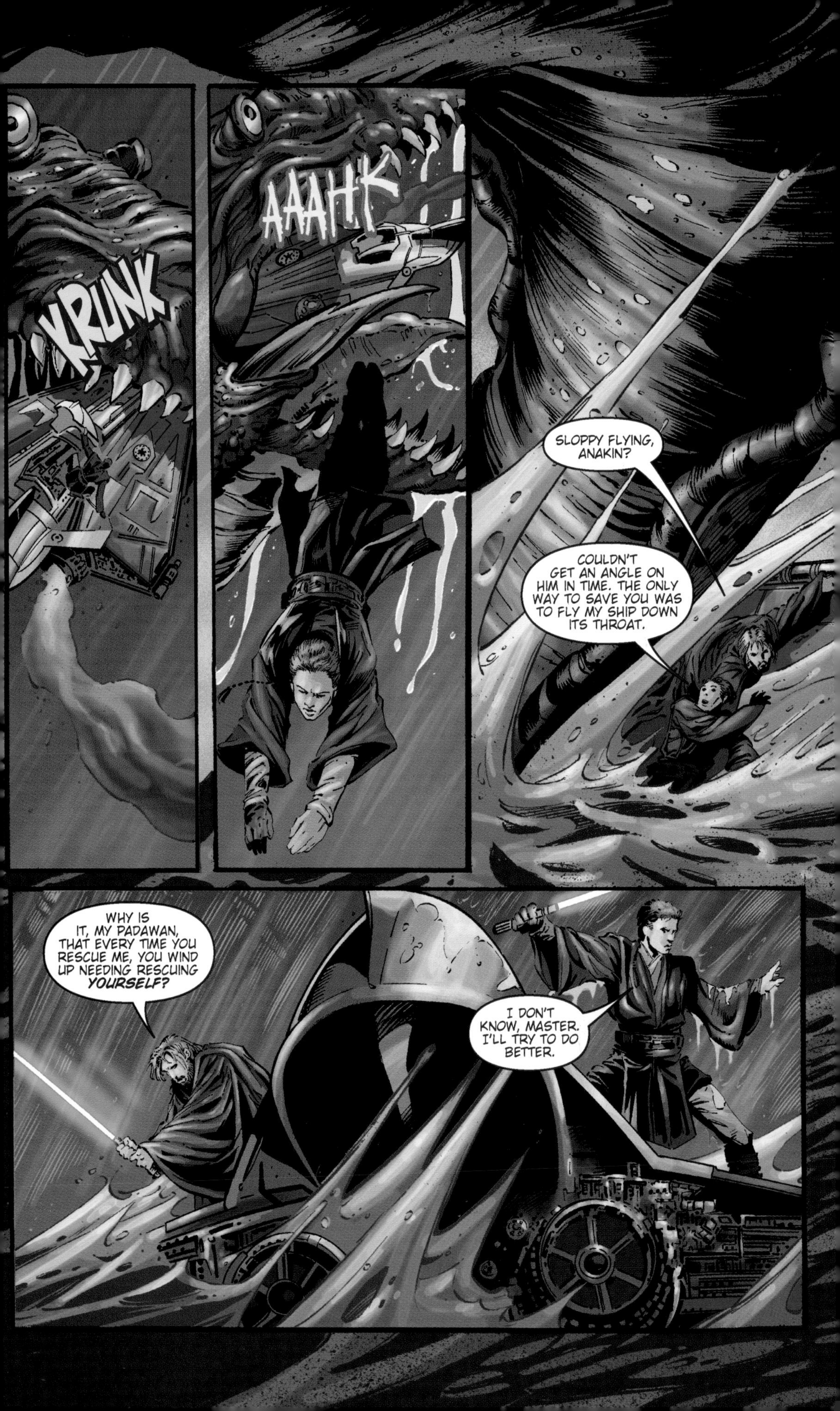
KRUNK
AAAHK
SLOPPY FLYING, ANAKIN?
COULDN'T GET AN ANGLE ON HIM IN TIME. THE ONLY WAY TO SAVE YOU WAS TO FLY MY SHIP DOWN ITS THROAT.
WHY IS IT, MY PADAWAN, THAT EVERY TIME YOU RESCUE ME, YOU WIND UP NEEDING RESCUING *YOURSELF?*
I DON'T KNOW, MASTER. I'LL TRY TO DO BETTER.

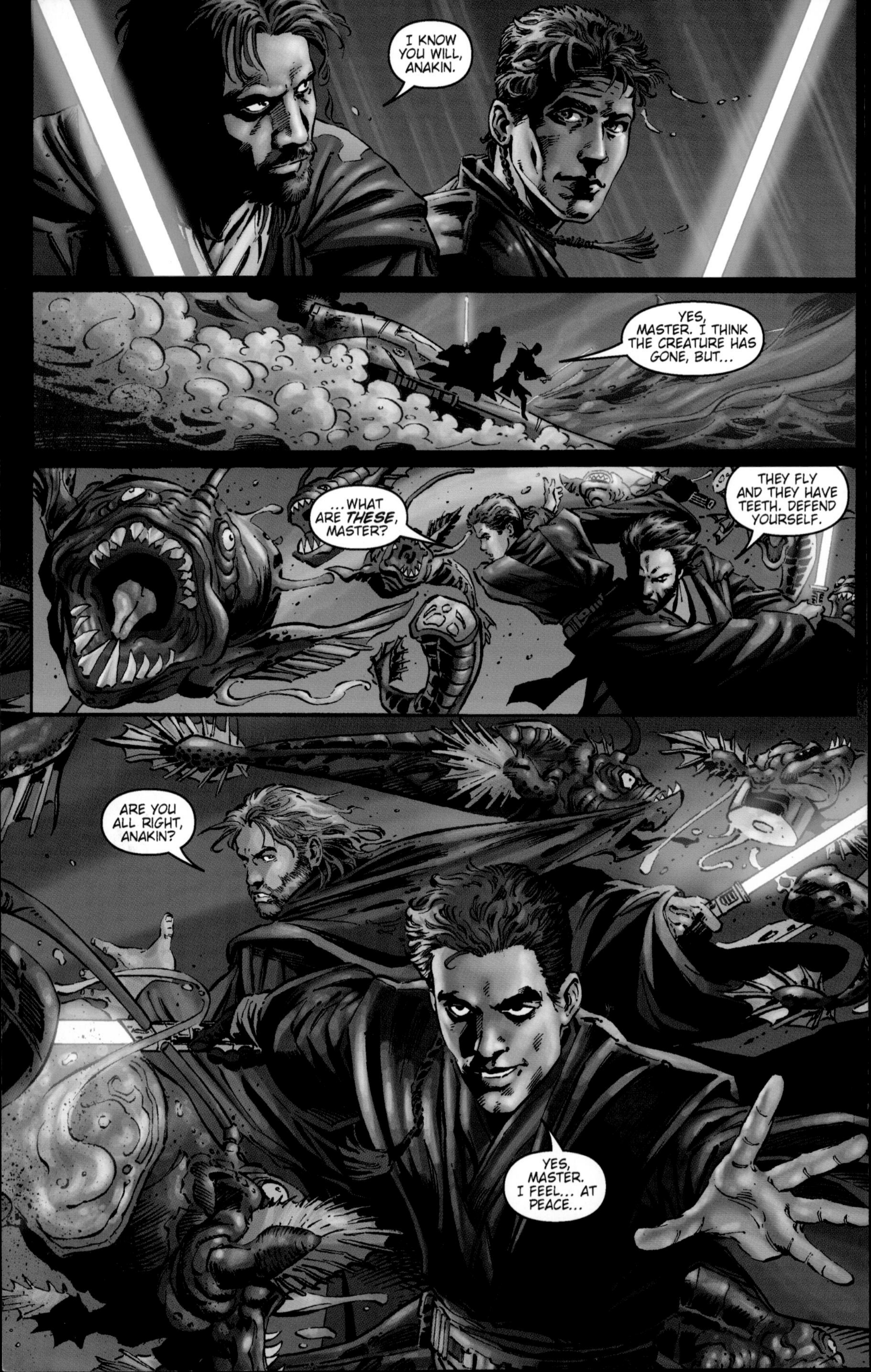
I KNOW YOU WILL, ANAKIN.
YES, MASTER. I THINK THE CREATURE HAS GONE, BUT...
...WHAT ARE *THESE*, MASTER?
THEY FLY AND THEY HAVE TEETH. DEFEND YOURSELF.
ARE YOU ALL RIGHT, ANAKIN?
YES, MASTER. I FEEL... AT PEACE...

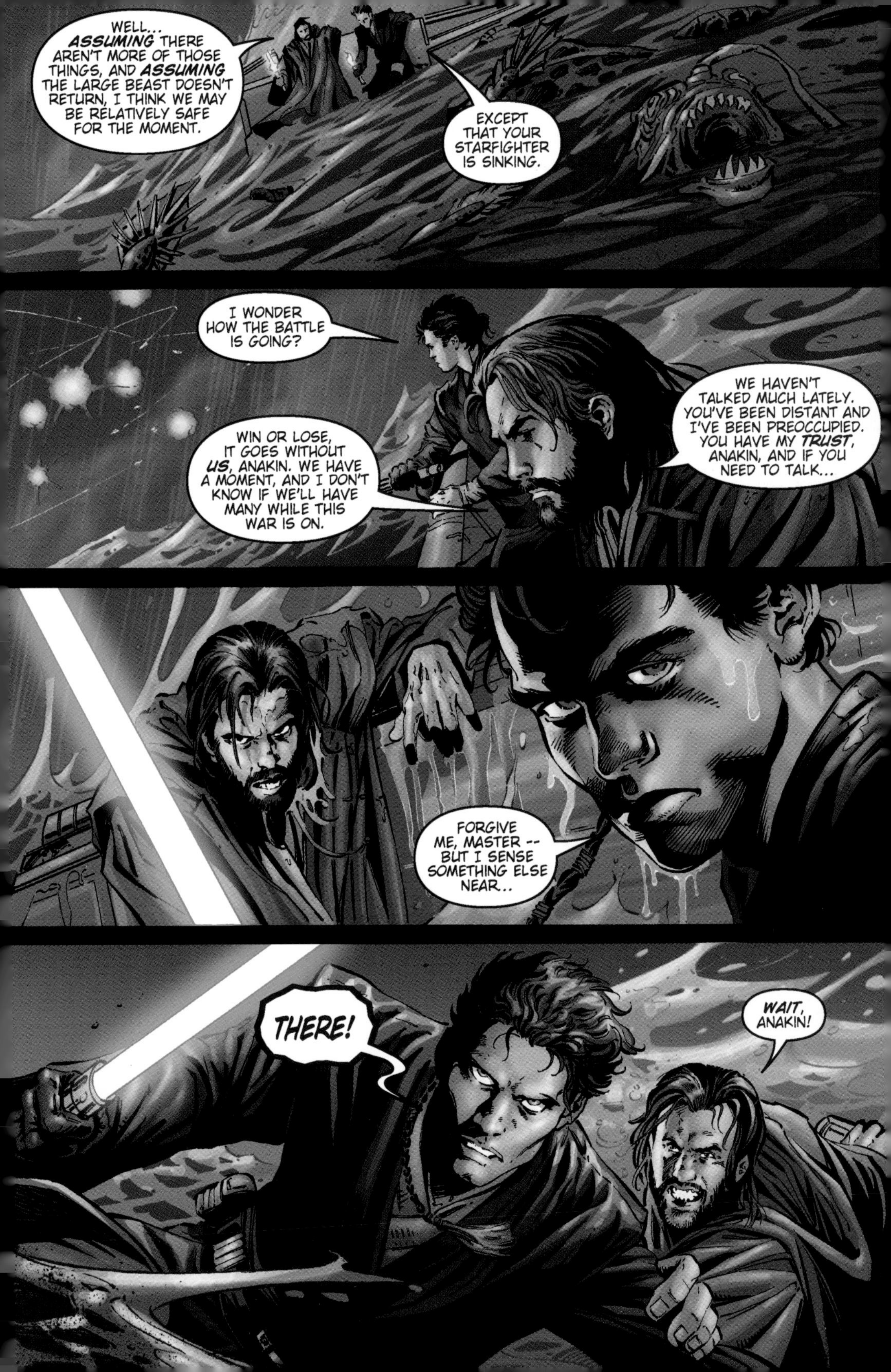
WELL... ASSUMING THERE AREN'T MORE OF THOSE THINGS, AND ASSUMING THE LARGE BEAST DOESN'T RETURN, I THINK WE MAY BE RELATIVELY SAFE FOR THE MOMENT.
EXCEPT THAT YOUR STARFIGHTER IS SINKING.
I WONDER HOW THE BATTLE IS GOING?
WIN OR LOSE, IT GOES WITHOUT US, ANAKIN. WE HAVE A MOMENT, AND I DON'T KNOW IF WE'LL HAVE MANY WHILE THIS WAR IS ON.
WE HAVEN'T TALKED MUCH LATELY. YOU'VE BEEN DISTANT AND I'VE BEEN PREOCCUPIED. YOU HAVE MY TRUST, ANAKIN, AND IF YOU NEED TO TALK...
FORGIVE ME, MASTER -- BUT I SENSE SOMETHING ELSE NEAR..
THERE!
WAIT, ANAKIN!

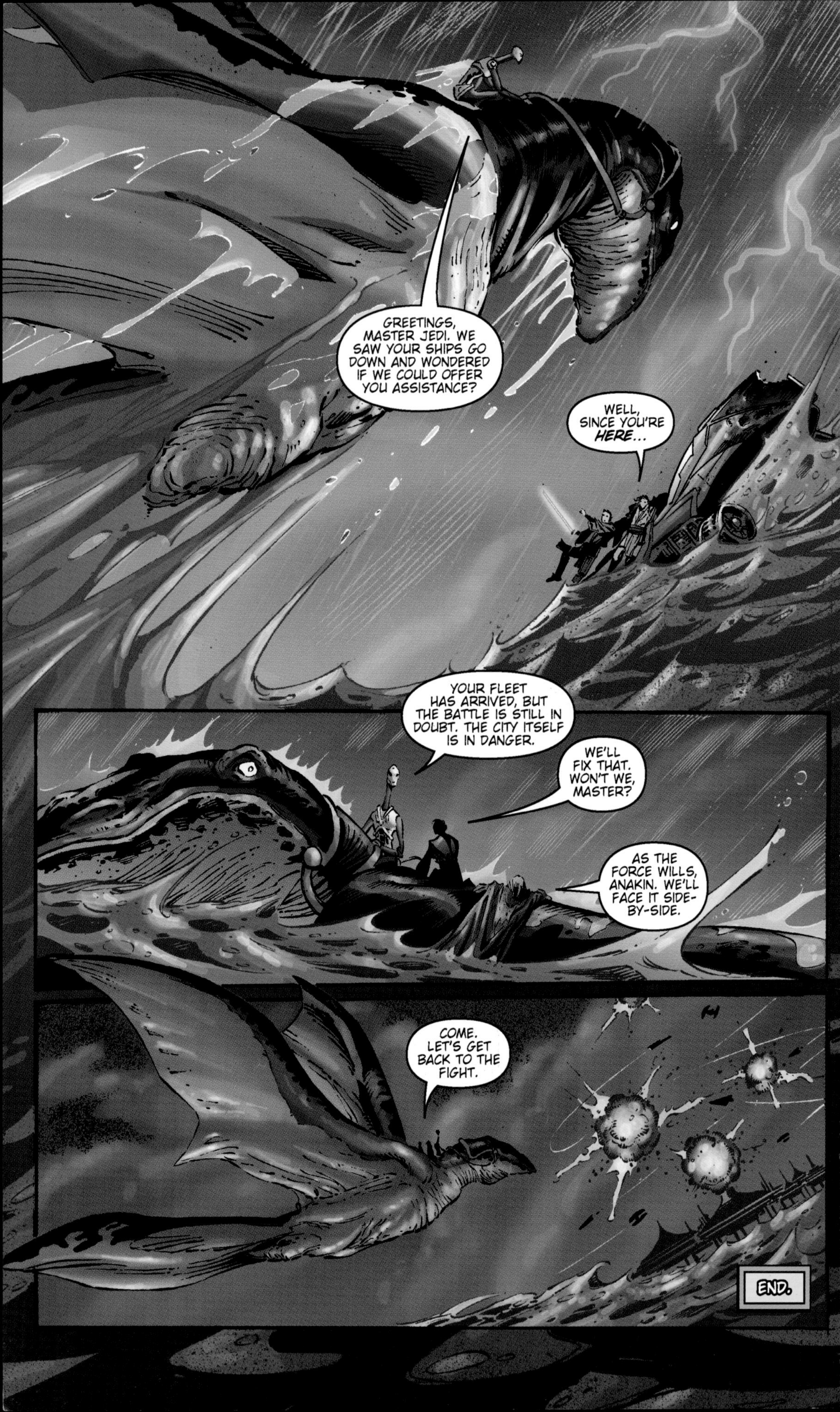
GREETINGS, MASTER JEDI. WE SAW YOUR SHIPS GO DOWN AND WONDERED IF WE COULD OFFER YOU ASSISTANCE?
WELL, SINCE YOU'RE HERE...
YOUR FLEET HAS ARRIVED, BUT THE BATTLE IS STILL IN DOUBT. THE CITY ITSELF IS IN DANGER.
WE'LL FIX THAT. WON'T WE, MASTER?
AS THE FORCE WILLS, ANAKIN. WE'LL FACE IT SIDE-BY-SIDE.
COME. LET'S GET BACK TO THE FIGHT.
END.

"JANGO'S LEGACY"

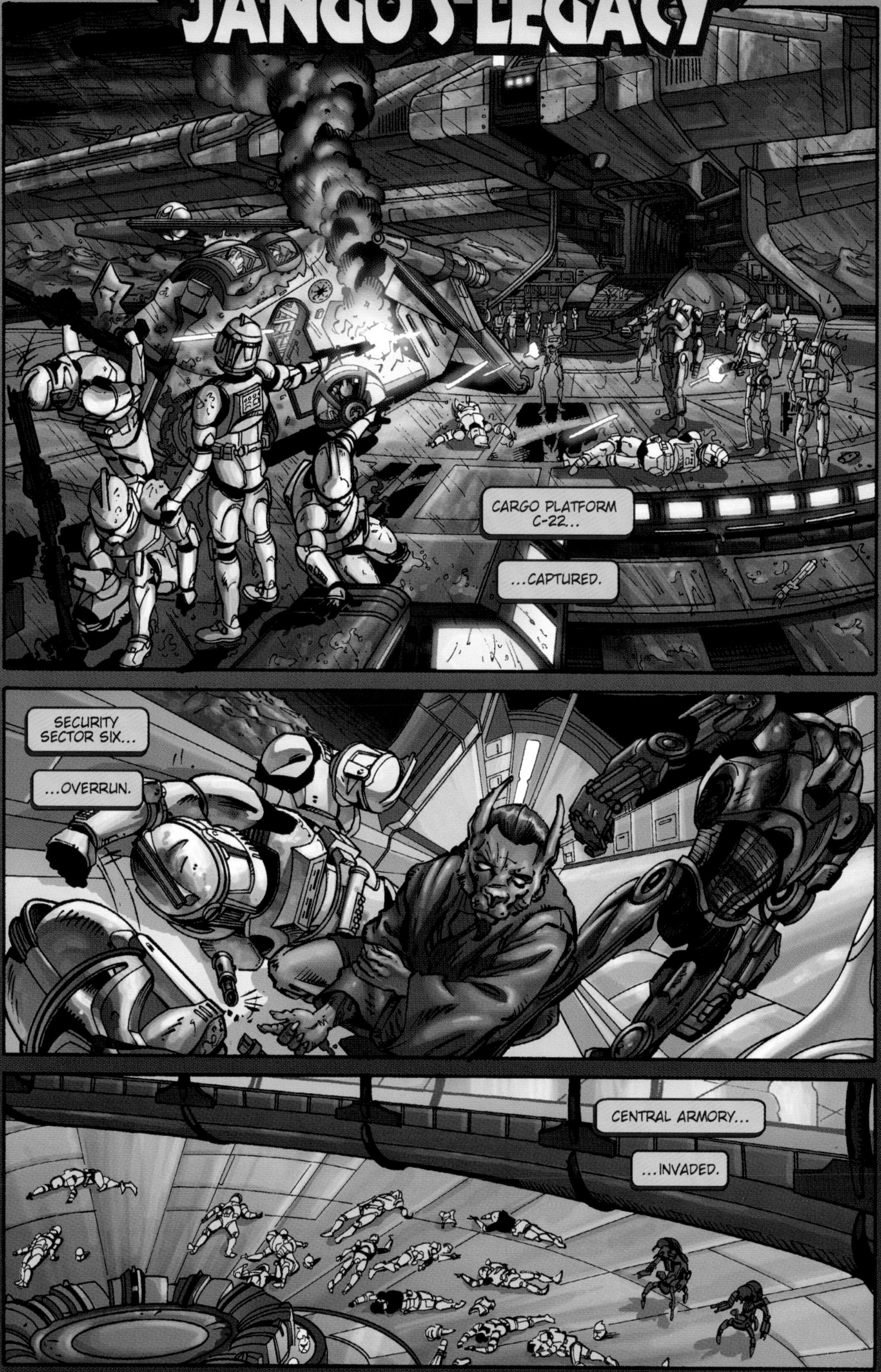

CARGO PLATFORM C-22...
...CAPTURED.
SECURITY SECTOR SIX...
...OVERRUN.
CENTRAL ARMORY...
...INVADED.

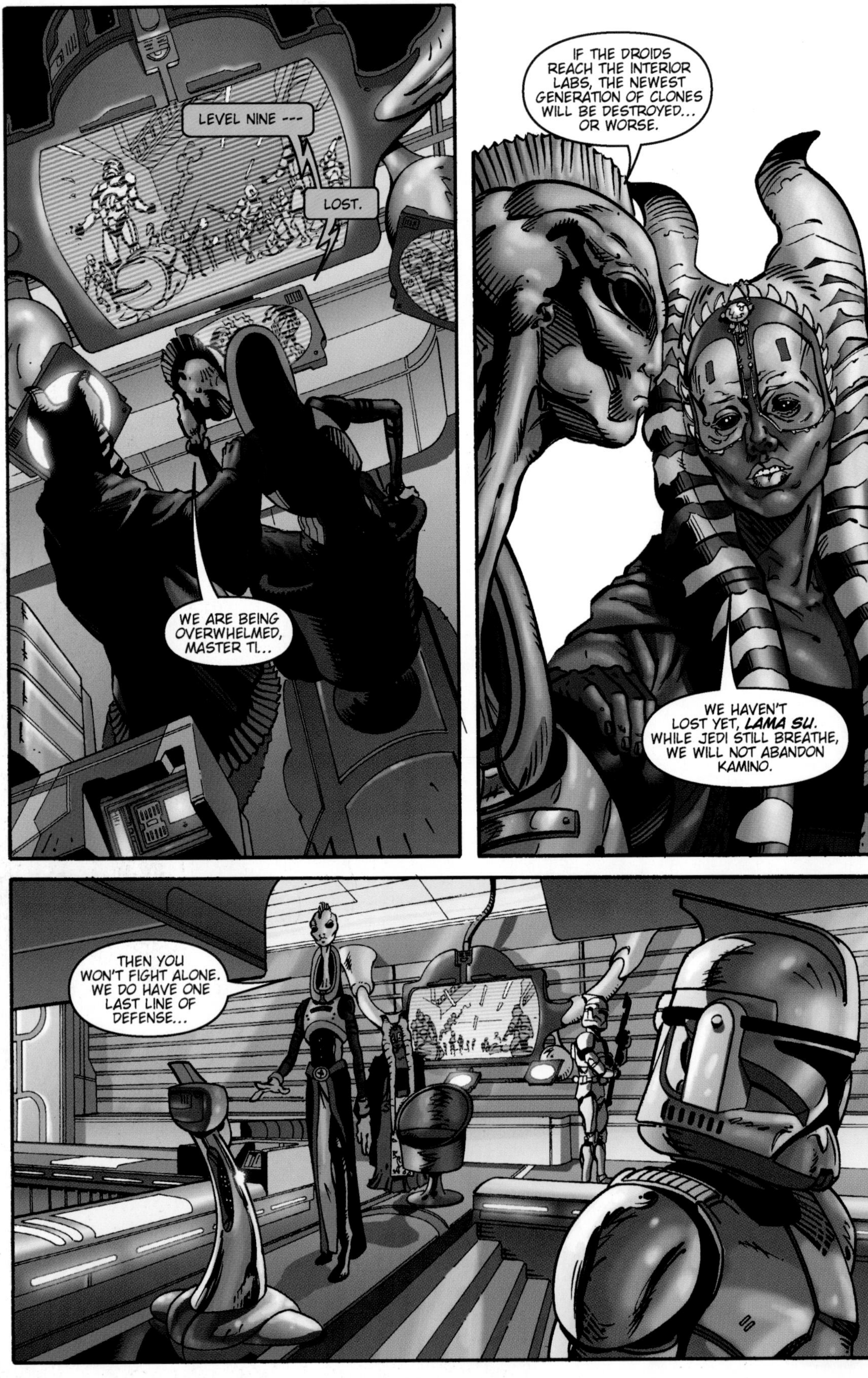
LEVEL NINE ---
LOST.
WE ARE BEING OVERWHELMED, MASTER TI...
IF THE DROIDS REACH THE INTERIOR LABS, THE NEWEST GENERATION OF CLONES WILL BE DESTROYED... OR WORSE.
WE HAVEN'T LOST YET, LAMA SU. WHILE JEDI STILL BREATHE, WE WILL NOT ABANDON KAMINO.
THEN YOU WON'T FIGHT ALONE. WE DO HAVE ONE LAST LINE OF DEFENSE...

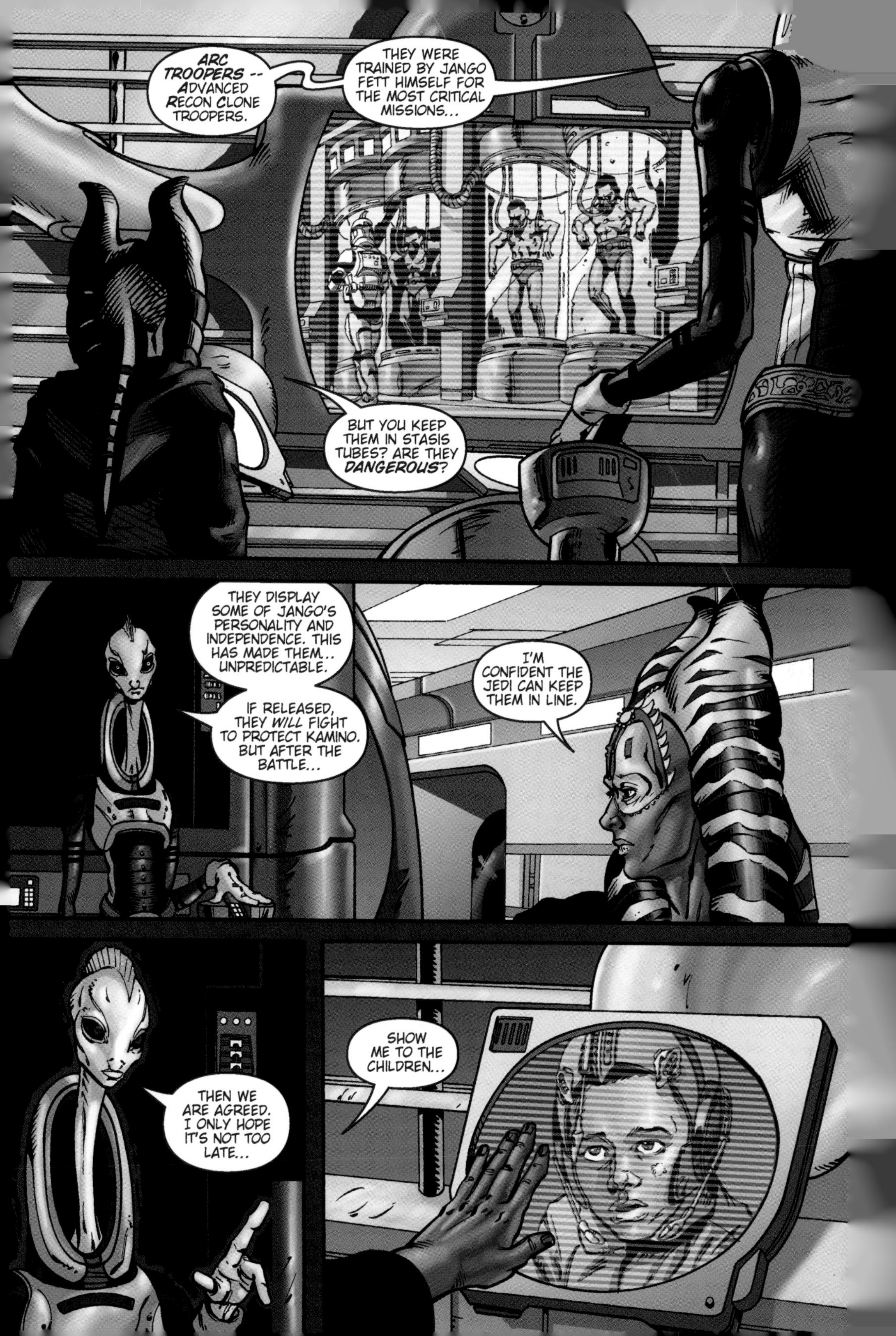
ARC TROOPERS -- ADVANCED RECON CLONE TROOPERS.
THEY WERE TRAINED BY JANGO FETT HIMSELF FOR THE MOST CRITICAL MISSIONS...
BUT YOU KEEP THEM IN STASIS TUBES? ARE THEY DANGEROUS?
THEY DISPLAY SOME OF JANGO'S PERSONALITY AND INDEPENDENCE. THIS HAS MADE THEM... UNPREDICTABLE.
IF RELEASED, THEY WILL FIGHT TO PROTECT KAMINO. BUT AFTER THE BATTLE...
I'M CONFIDENT THE JEDI CAN KEEP THEM IN LINE.
THEN WE ARE AGREED. I ONLY HOPE IT'S NOT TOO LATE...
SHOW ME TO THE CHILDREN...

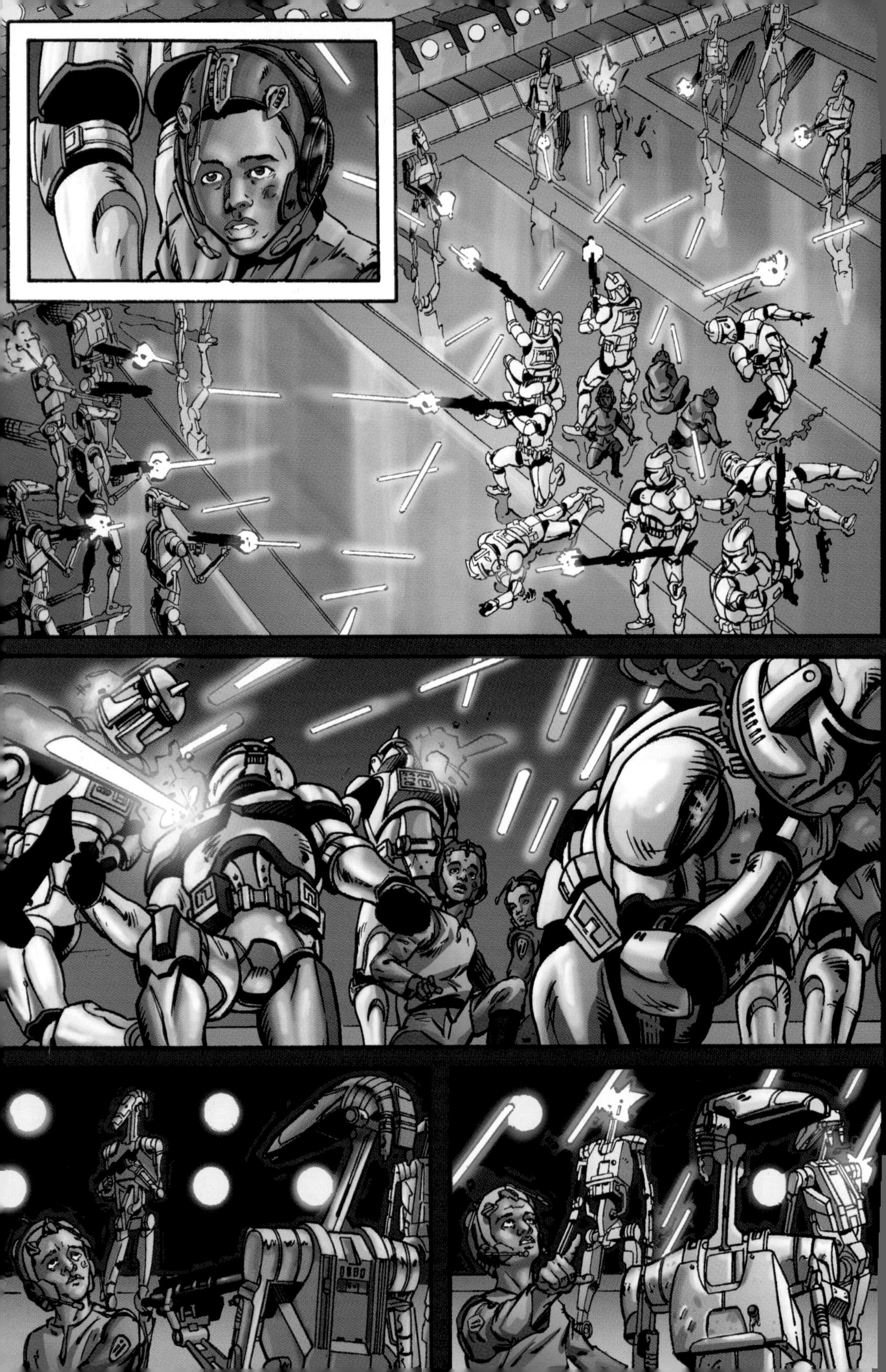

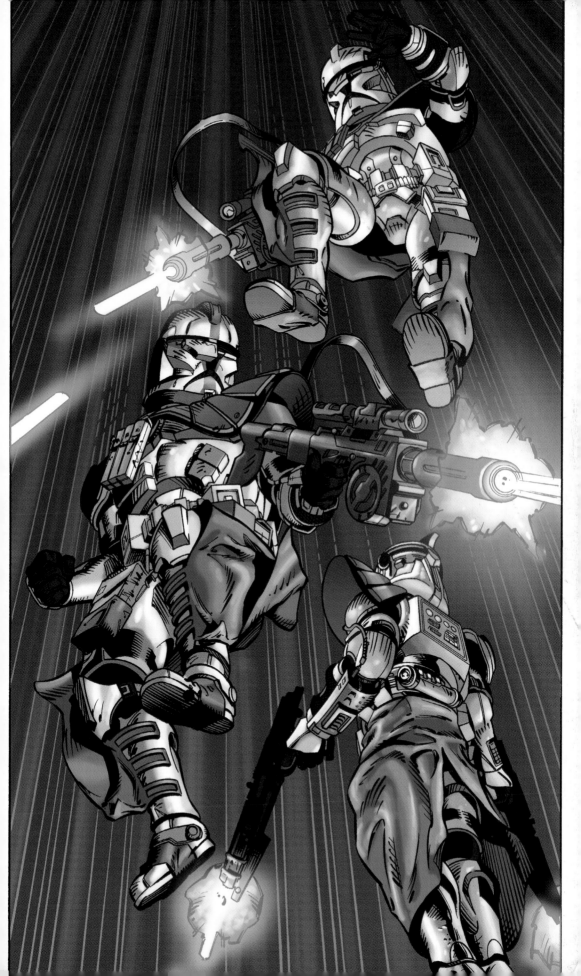

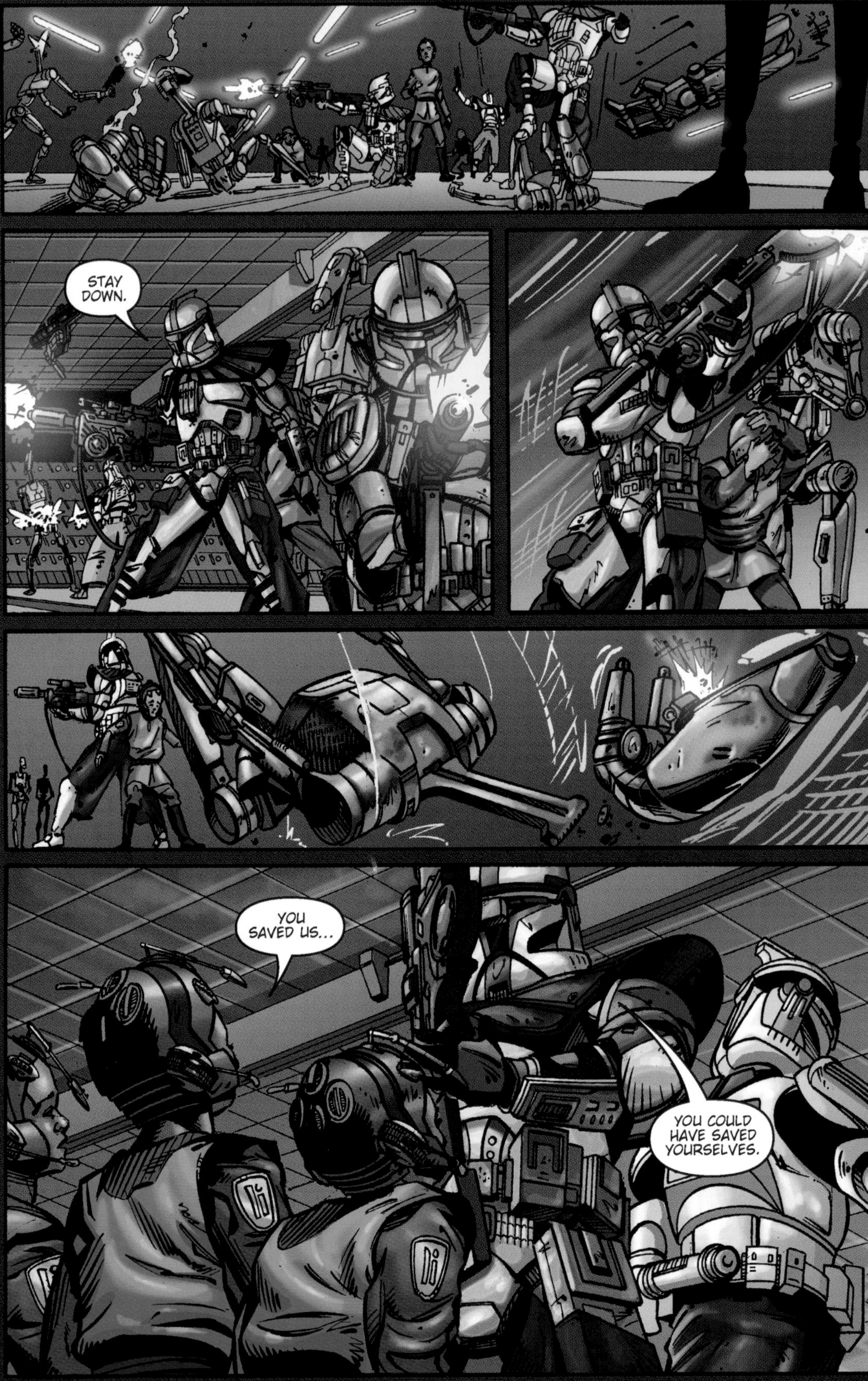
STAY DOWN.
YOU SAVED US...
YOU COULD HAVE SAVED YOURSELVES.

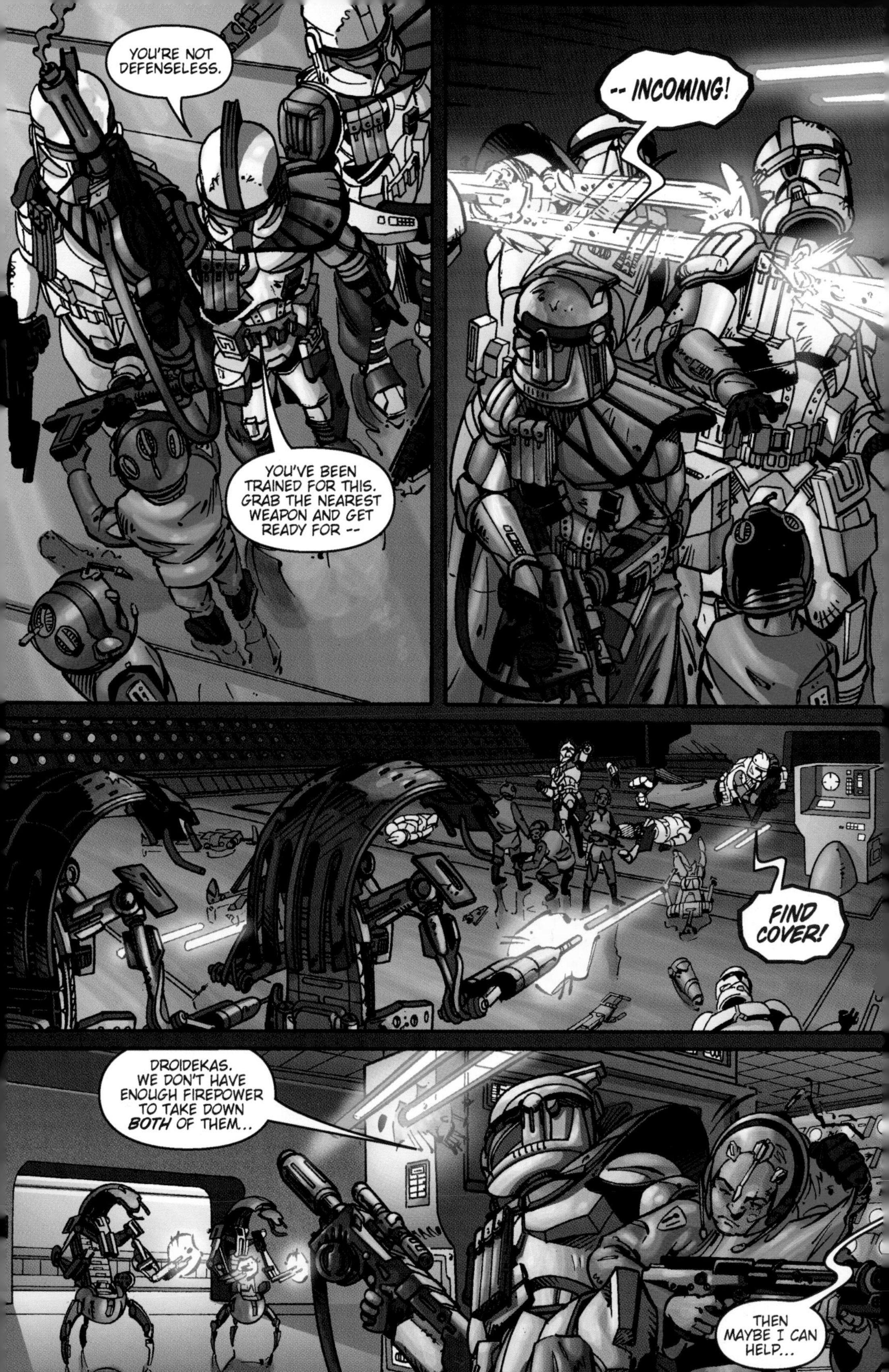
YOU'RE NOT DEFENSELESS.
YOU'VE BEEN TRAINED FOR THIS. GRAB THE NEAREST WEAPON AND GET READY FOR --
-- INCOMING!
FIND COVER!
DROIDEKAS. WE DON'T HAVE ENOUGH FIREPOWER TO TAKE DOWN BOTH OF THEM..
THEN MAYBE I CAN HELP...

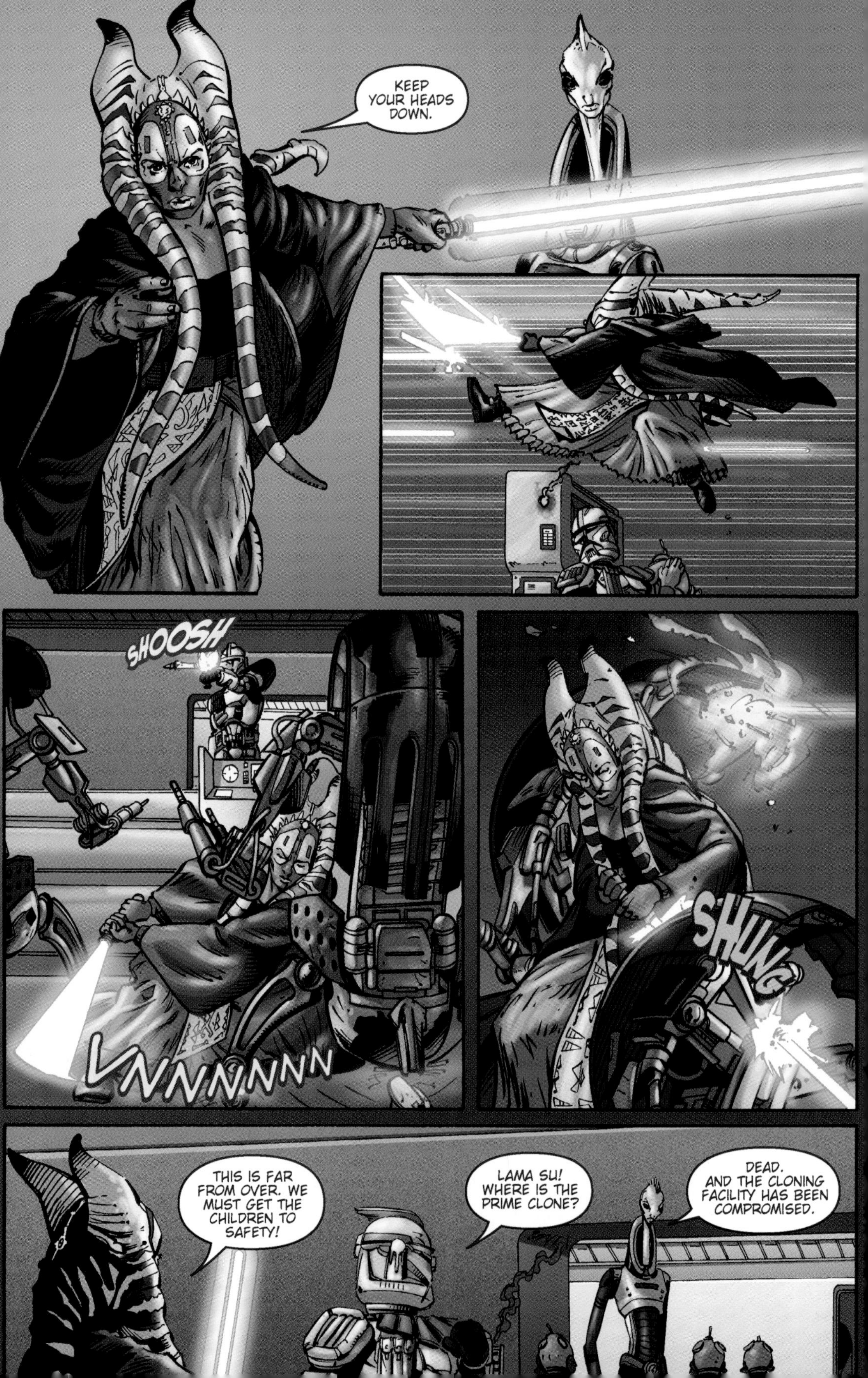
KEEP YOUR HEADS DOWN.
SHOOSH
VNNNNNN
SHUNG
THIS IS FAR FROM OVER. WE MUST GET THE CHILDREN TO SAFETY!
LAMA SU! WHERE IS THE PRIME CLONE?
DEAD. AND THE CLONING FACILITY HAS BEEN COMPROMISED.

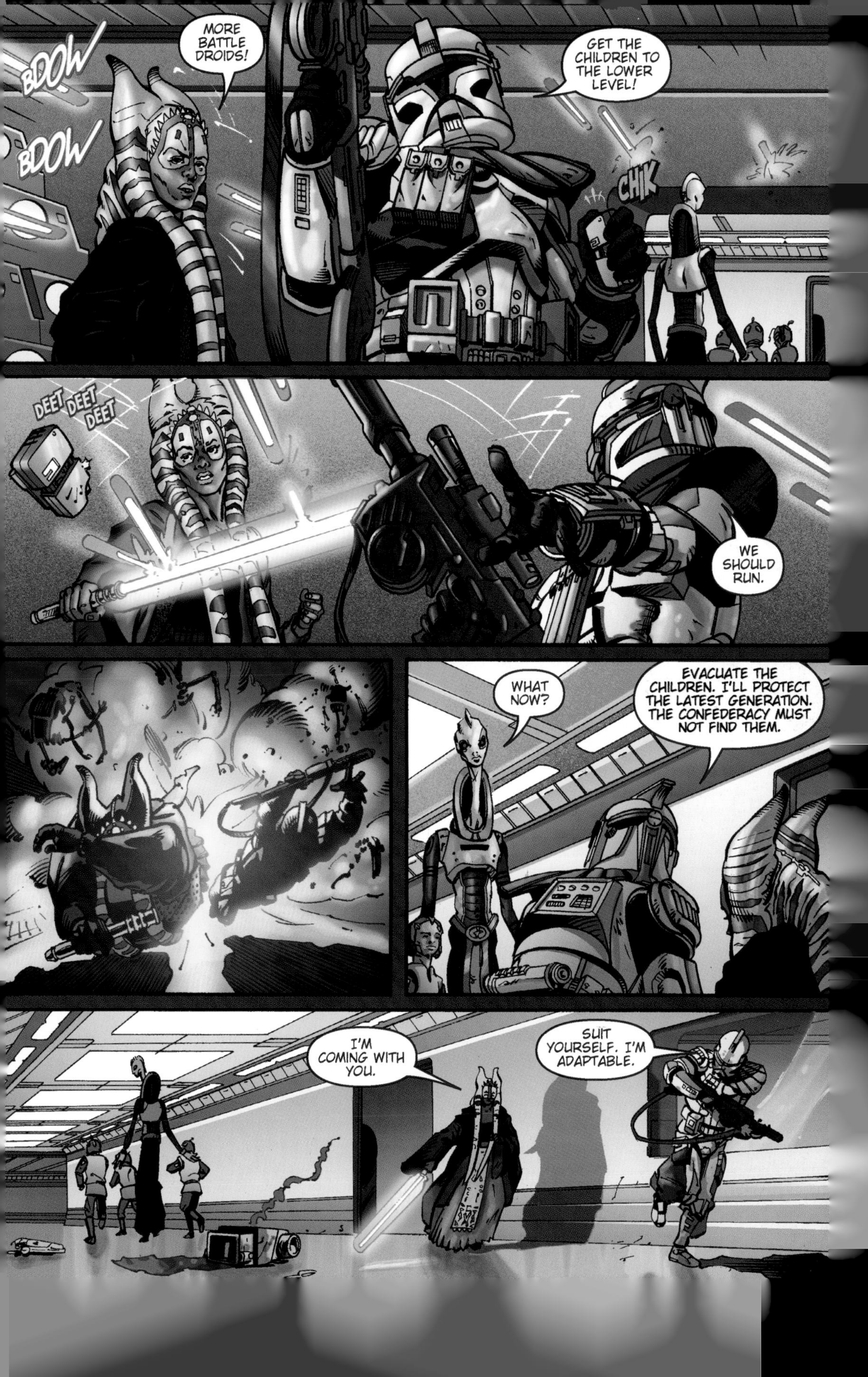
BDOW
BDOW
MORE BATTLE DROIDS!
GET THE CHILDREN TO THE LOWER LEVEL!
CHIK
DEET DEET DEET
WE SHOULD RUN.
WHAT NOW?
EVACUATE THE CHILDREN. I'LL PROTECT THE LATEST GENERATION. THE CONFEDERACY MUST NOT FIND THEM.
I'M COMING WITH YOU.
SUIT YOURSELF. I'M ADAPTABLE.

WHERE ARE WE GOING?

TO THE CLONING LABS. JUST STAY CLOSE.

I'LL HANDLE THIS.

NICE WORK.

THIS WILL FINISH THEM.

MMMMM

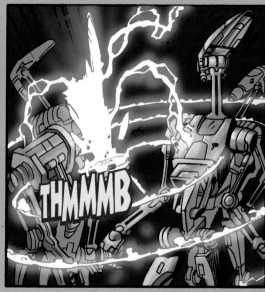

THMMMB

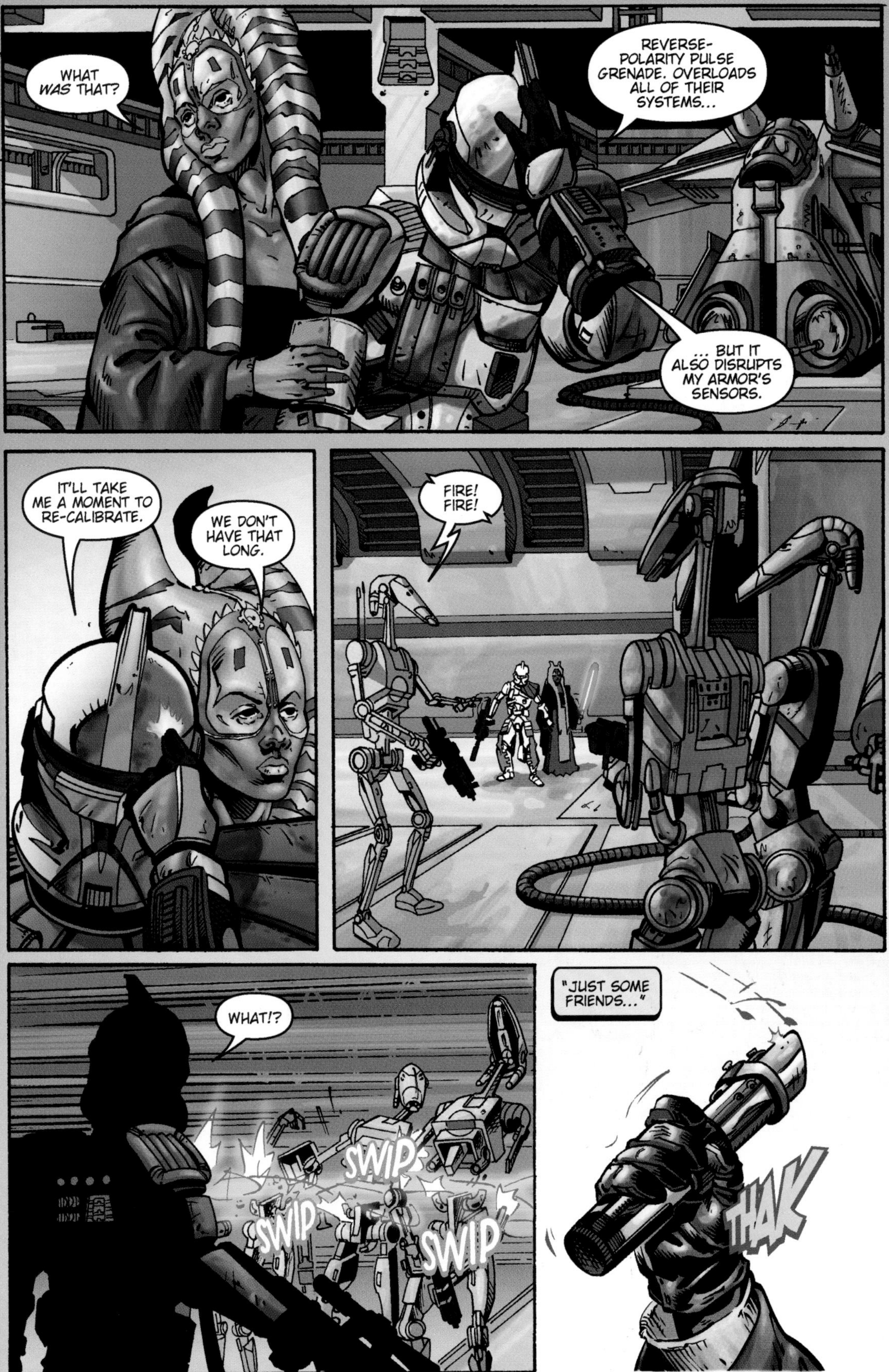
WHAT WAS THAT?
REVERSE-POLARITY PULSE GRENADE. OVERLOADS ALL OF THEIR SYSTEMS...
... BUT IT ALSO DISRUPTS MY ARMOR'S SENSORS.
IT'LL TAKE ME A MOMENT TO RE-CALIBRATE.
WE DON'T HAVE THAT LONG.
FIRE! FIRE!
WHAT!?
SWIP
SWIP
SWIP
"JUST SOME FRIENDS..."
THAK

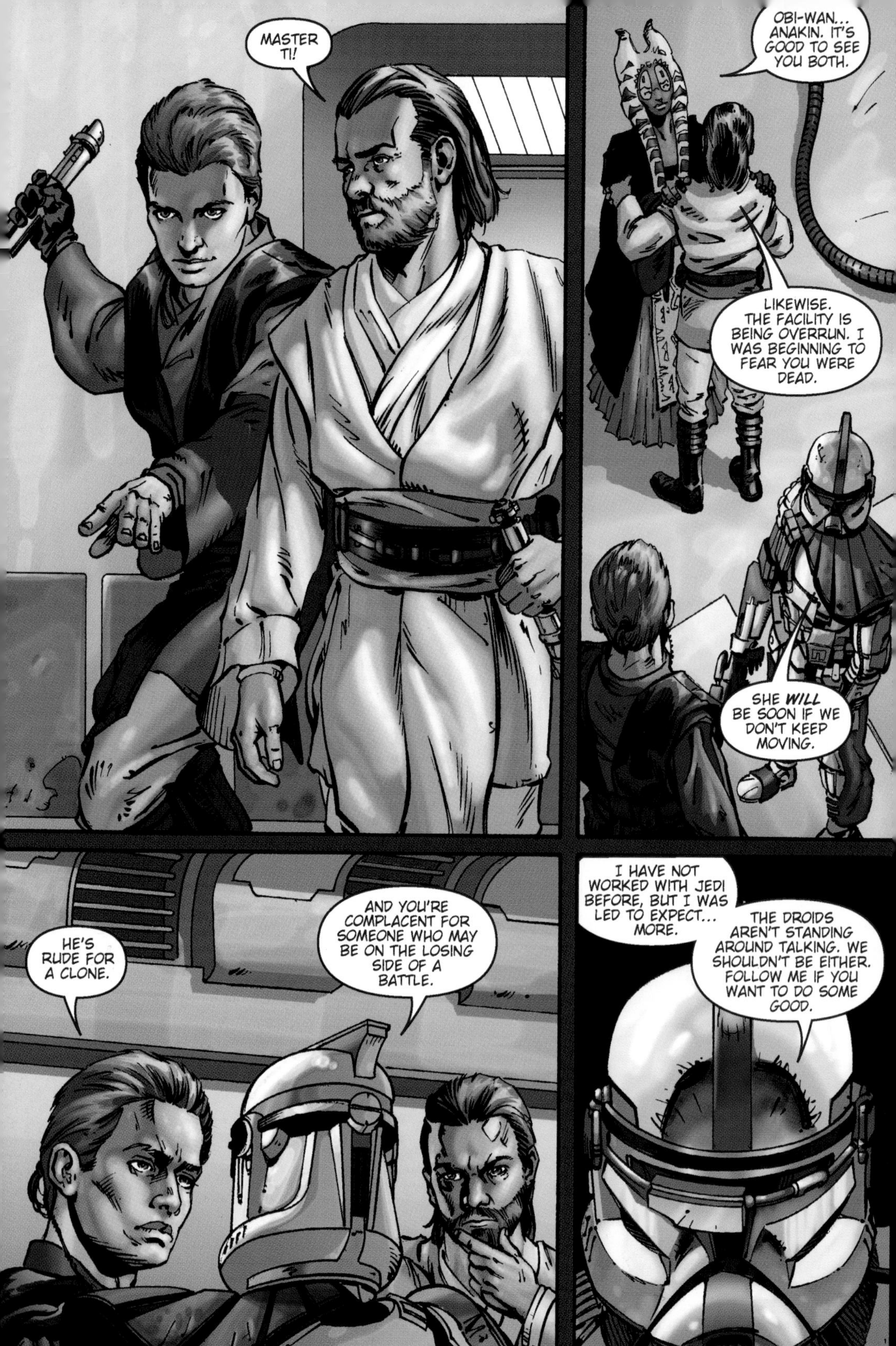
MASTER TI!
OBI-WAN... ANAKIN. IT'S GOOD TO SEE YOU BOTH.
LIKEWISE. THE FACILITY IS BEING OVERRUN. I WAS BEGINNING TO FEAR YOU WERE DEAD.
SHE *WILL* BE SOON IF WE DON'T KEEP MOVING.
HE'S RUDE FOR A CLONE.
AND YOU'RE COMPLACENT FOR SOMEONE WHO MAY BE ON THE LOSING SIDE OF A BATTLE.
I HAVE NOT WORKED WITH JEDI BEFORE, BUT I WAS LED TO EXPECT... MORE.
THE DROIDS AREN'T STANDING AROUND TALKING. WE SHOULDN'T BE EITHER. FOLLOW ME IF YOU WANT TO DO SOME GOOD.

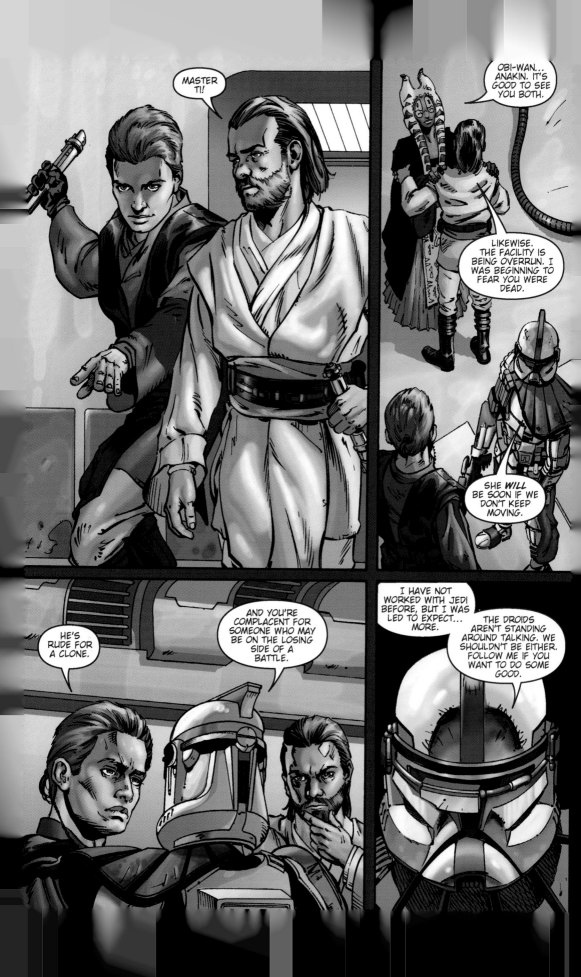

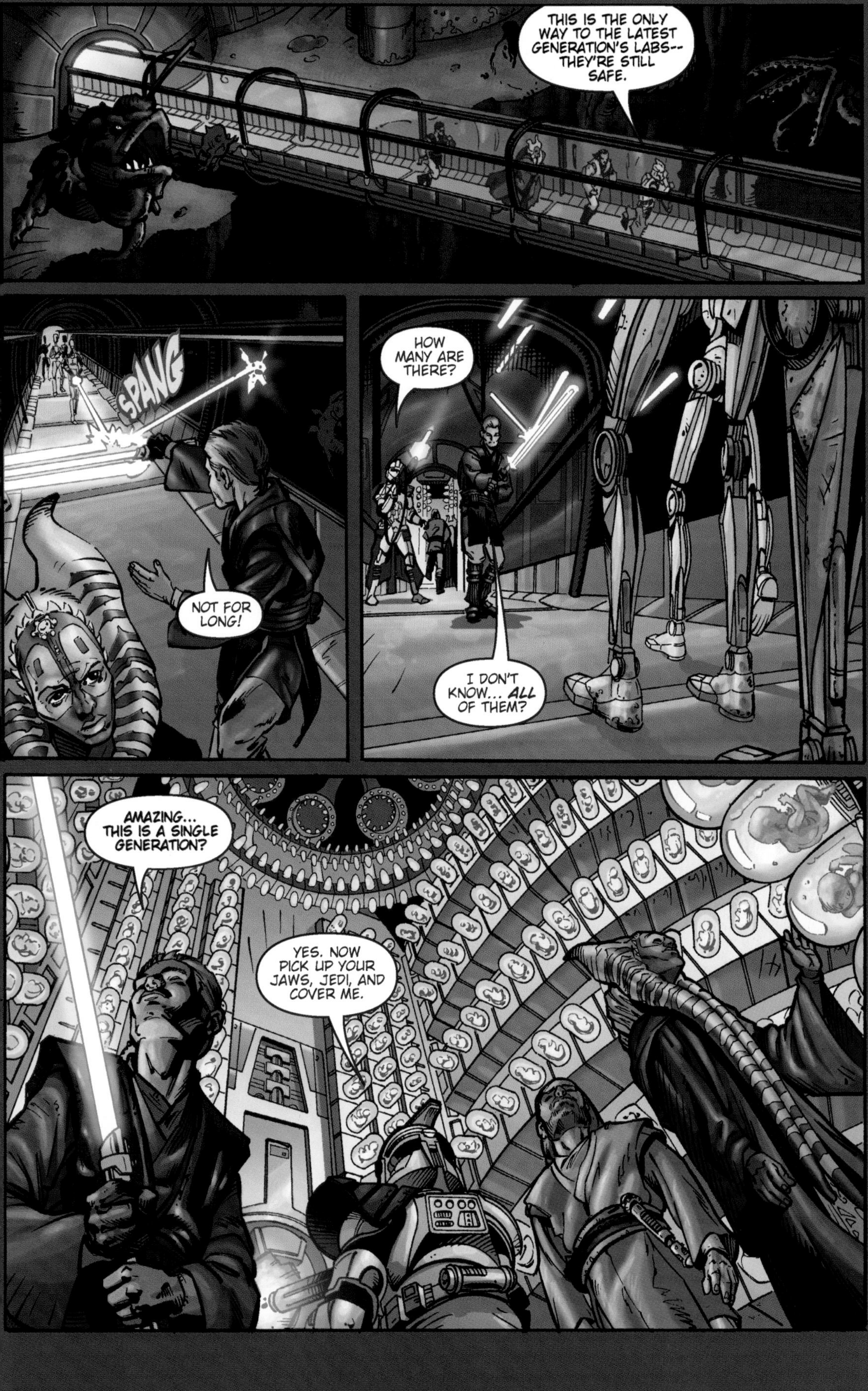

THIS IS THE ONLY WAY TO THE LATEST GENERATION'S LABS-- THEY'RE STILL SAFE.
SPANG
NOT FOR LONG!
HOW MANY ARE THERE?
I DON'T KNOW... ALL OF THEM?
AMAZING... THIS IS A SINGLE GENERATION?
YES. NOW PICK UP YOUR JAWS, JEDI, AND COVER ME.

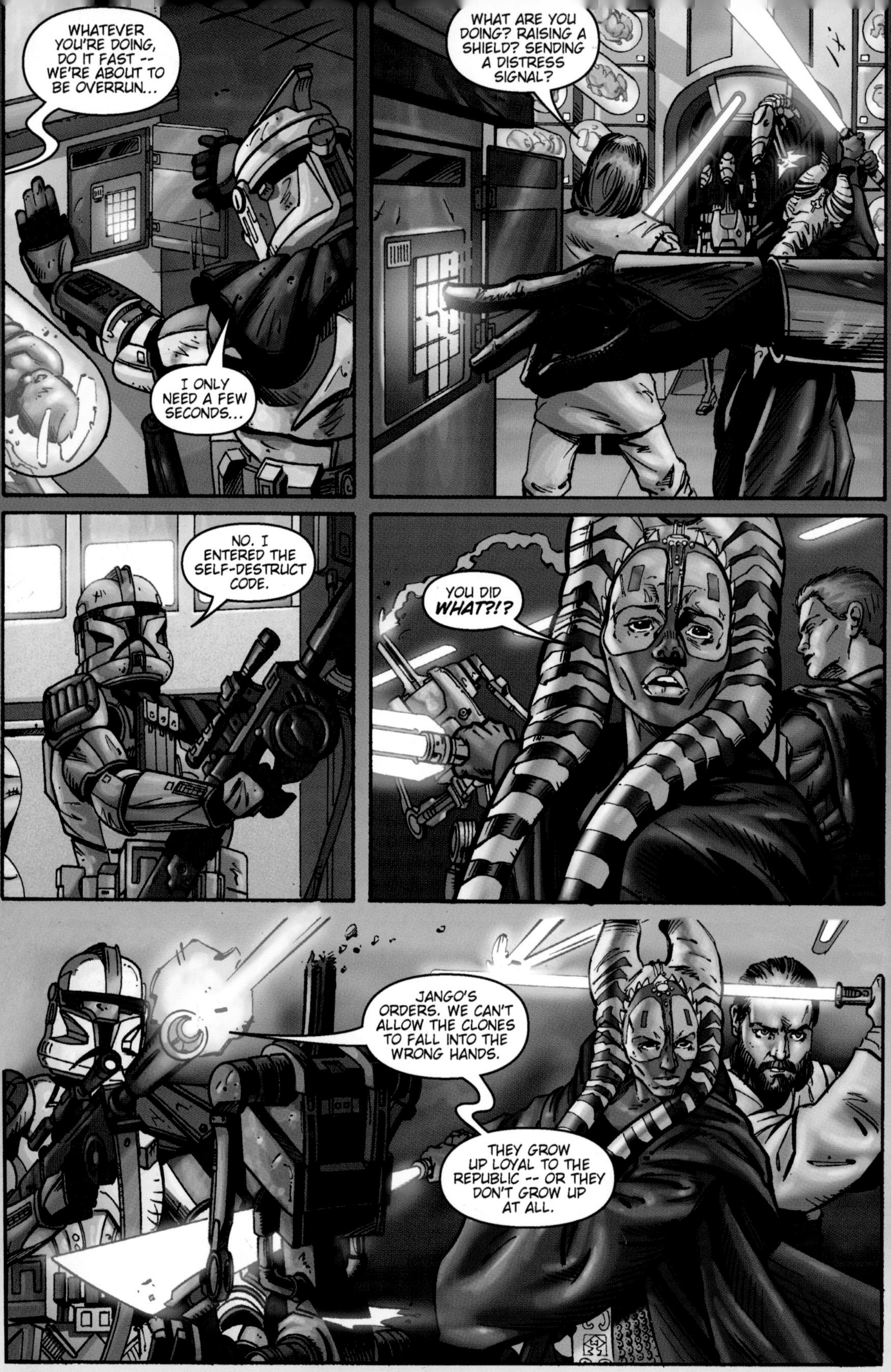
WHATEVER YOU'RE DOING, DO IT FAST -- WE'RE ABOUT TO BE OVERRUN...
I ONLY NEED A FEW SECONDS...
WHAT ARE YOU DOING? RAISING A SHIELD? SENDING A DISTRESS SIGNAL?
NO. I ENTERED THE SELF-DESTRUCT CODE.
YOU DID *WHAT?!?*
JANGO'S ORDERS. WE CAN'T ALLOW THE CLONES TO FALL INTO THE WRONG HANDS.
THEY GROW UP LOYAL TO THE REPUBLIC -- OR THEY DON'T GROW UP AT ALL.

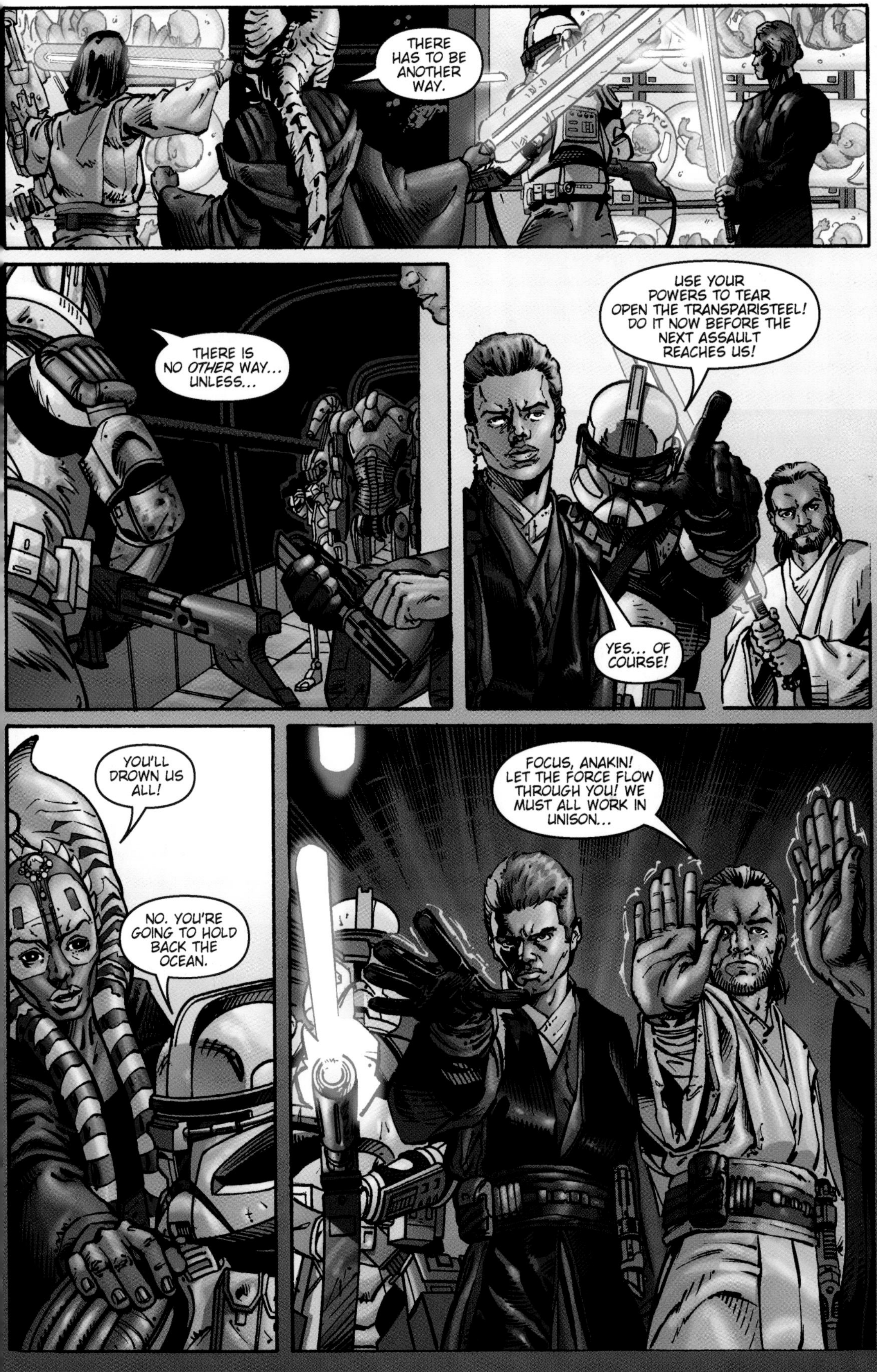
THERE HAS TO BE ANOTHER WAY.
THERE IS NO *OTHER* WAY... UNLESS...
USE YOUR POWERS TO TEAR OPEN THE TRANSPARISTEEL! DO IT NOW BEFORE THE NEXT ASSAULT REACHES US!
YES... OF COURSE!
YOU'LL DROWN US ALL!
NO. YOU'RE GOING TO HOLD BACK THE OCEAN.
FOCUS, ANAKIN! LET THE FORCE FLOW THROUGH YOU! WE MUST ALL WORK IN UNISON...

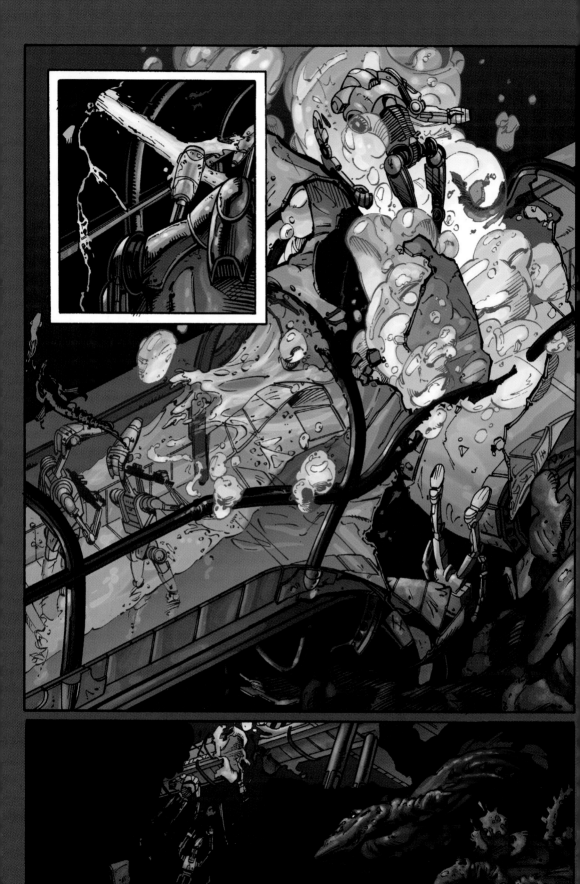

I HOPE WE DIDN'T JUST COMMIT SUICIDE...
WE NEED TO CLOSE THE TUNNEL...
IT'S WORKING, JEDI.
INCREDIBLE...

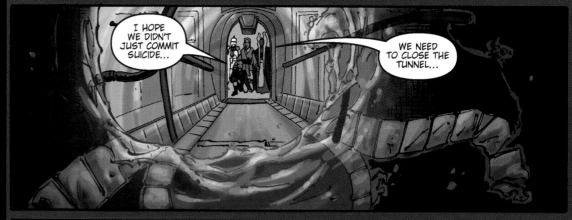

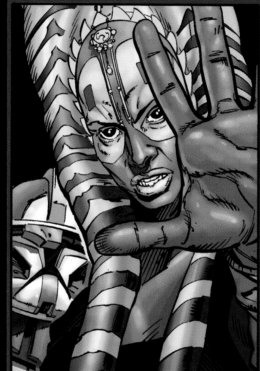

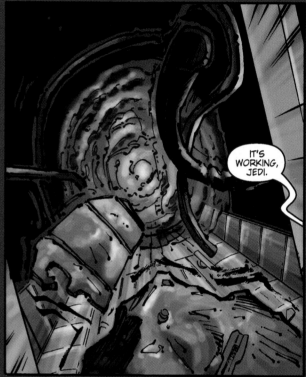

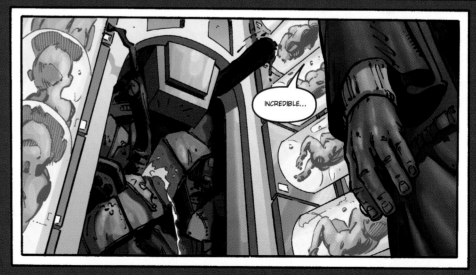

WHAT NOW?
FIRST, I DEACTIVATE THE SELF-DESTRUCT BEFORE WE'RE ALL BLOWN TO CORELLIA.
THEN WE HOLD THIS POSITION UNTIL THE BATTLE IS OVER ... OR WE'RE DEAD.
TAK TAK-TAK
THANK YOU FOR SAVING THEM.
HNH. YOU'RE WELCOME. BUT I DIDN'T DO IT FOR YOU.
I WAS JUST FOLLOWING JANGO'S ORDERS...
END.

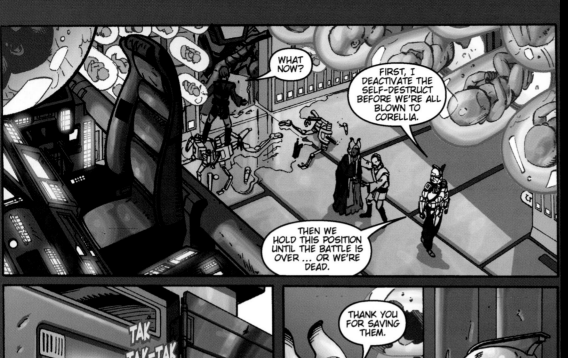

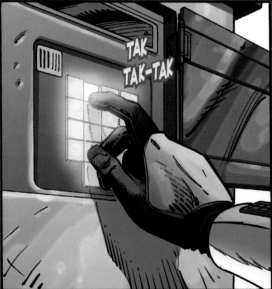

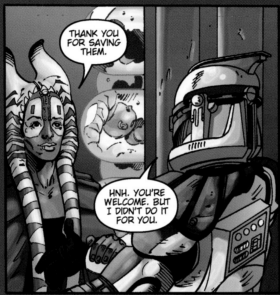

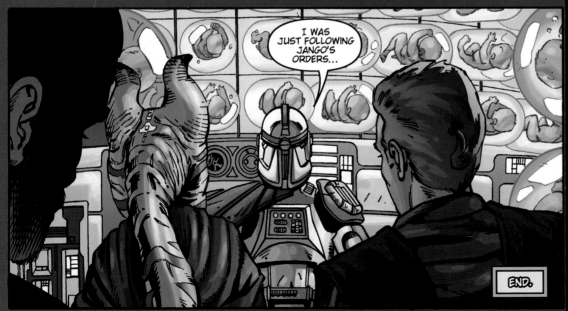

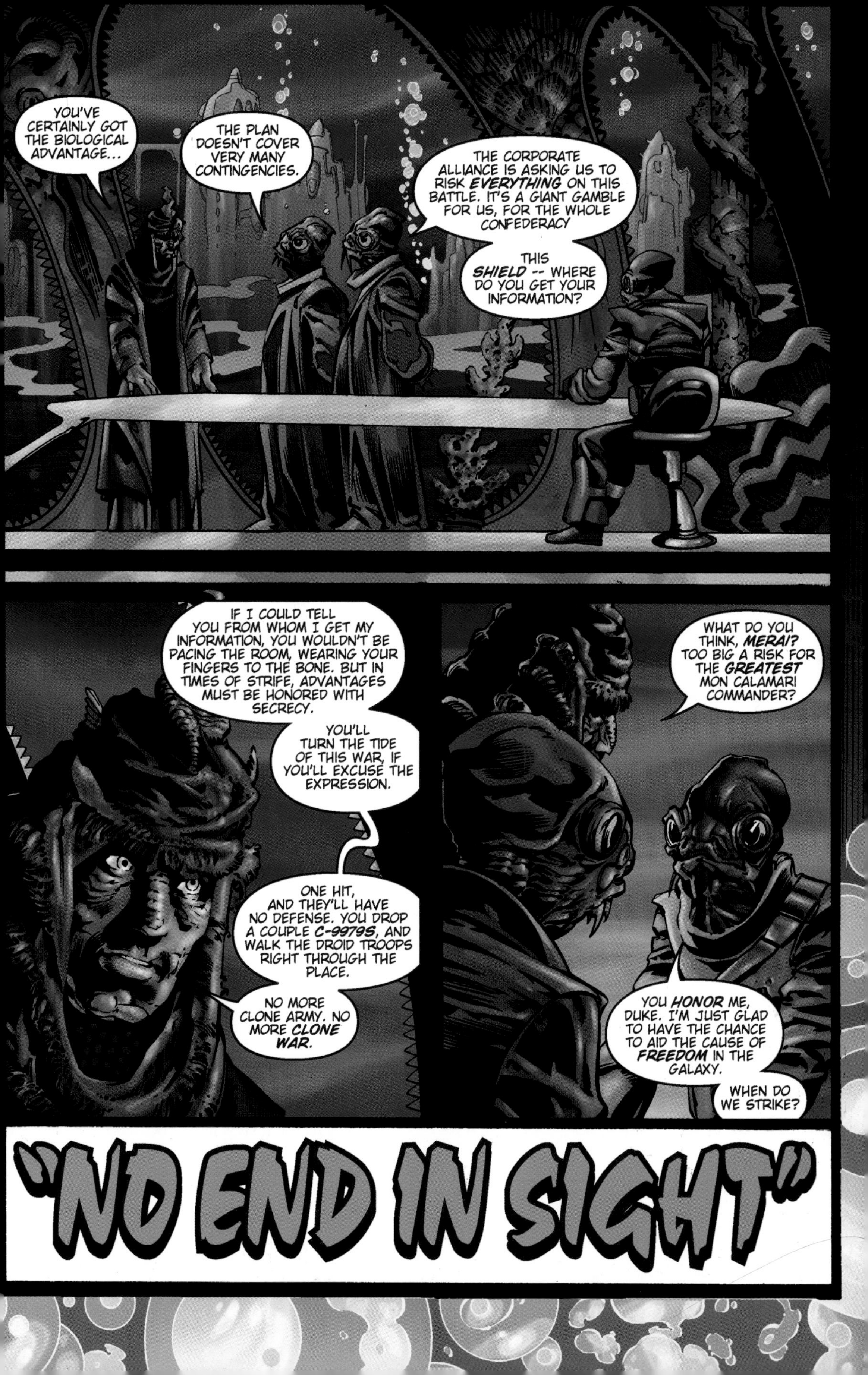
YOU'VE CERTAINLY GOT THE BIOLOGICAL ADVANTAGE...
THE PLAN DOESN'T COVER VERY MANY CONTINGENCIES.
THE CORPORATE ALLIANCE IS ASKING US TO RISK EVERYTHING ON THIS BATTLE. IT'S A GIANT GAMBLE FOR US, FOR THE WHOLE CONFEDERACY
THIS SHIELD -- WHERE DO YOU GET YOUR INFORMATION?
IF I COULD TELL YOU FROM WHOM I GET MY INFORMATION, YOU WOULDN'T BE PACING THE ROOM, WEARING YOUR FINGERS TO THE BONE. BUT IN TIMES OF STRIFE, ADVANTAGES MUST BE HONORED WITH SECRECY.
YOU'LL TURN THE TIDE OF THIS WAR, IF YOU'LL EXCUSE THE EXPRESSION.
ONE HIT, AND THEY'LL HAVE NO DEFENSE. YOU DROP A COUPLE C-9979S, AND WALK THE DROID TROOPS RIGHT THROUGH THE PLACE.
NO MORE CLONE ARMY. NO MORE CLONE WAR.
WHAT DO YOU THINK, MERAI? TOO BIG A RISK FOR THE GREATEST MON CALAMARI COMMANDER?
YOU HONOR ME, DUKE. I'M JUST GLAD TO HAVE THE CHANCE TO AID THE CAUSE OF FREEDOM IN THE GALAXY.
WHEN DO WE STRIKE?
"NO END IN SIGHT"

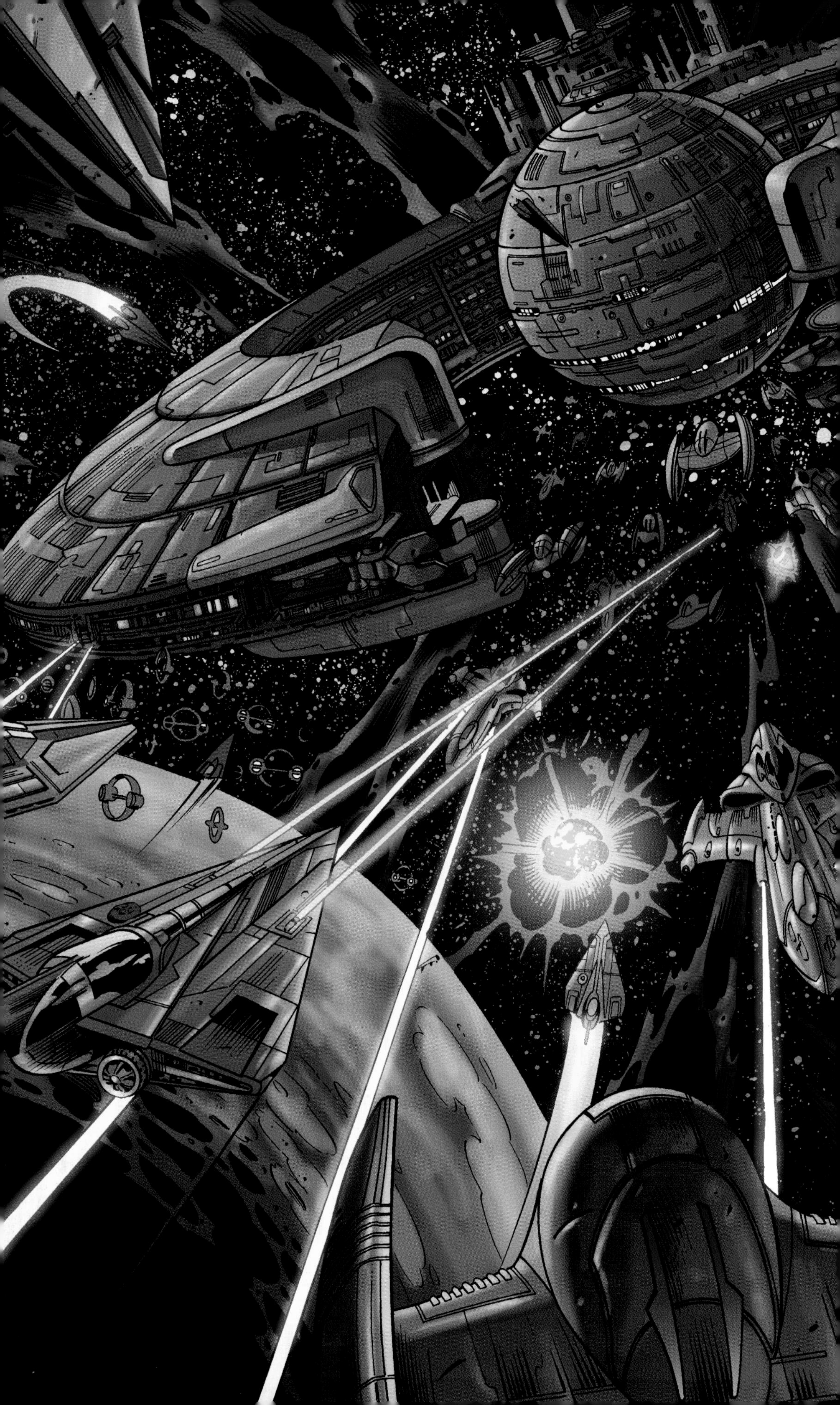

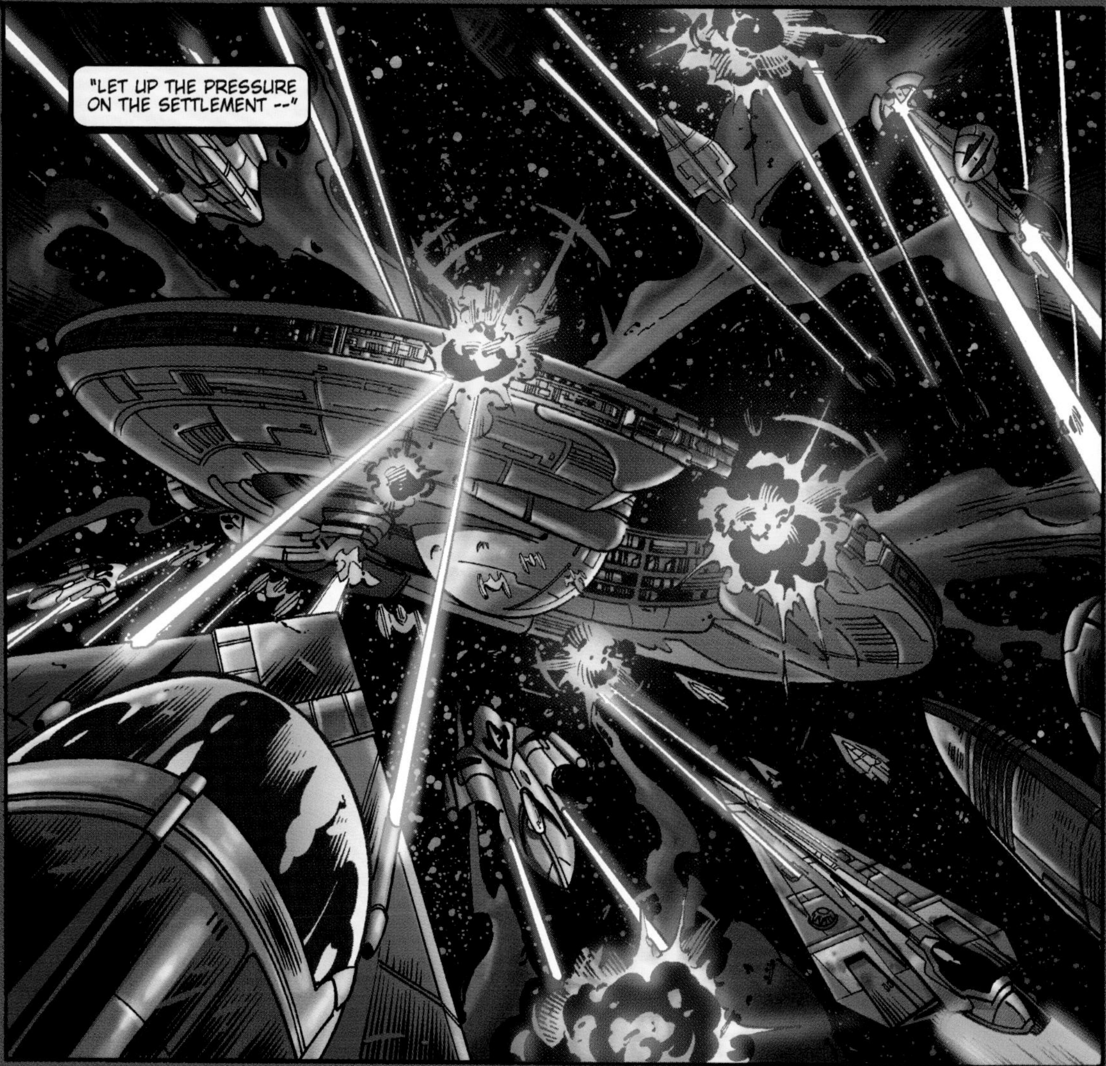
"LET UP THE PRESSURE ON THE SETTLEMENT --"

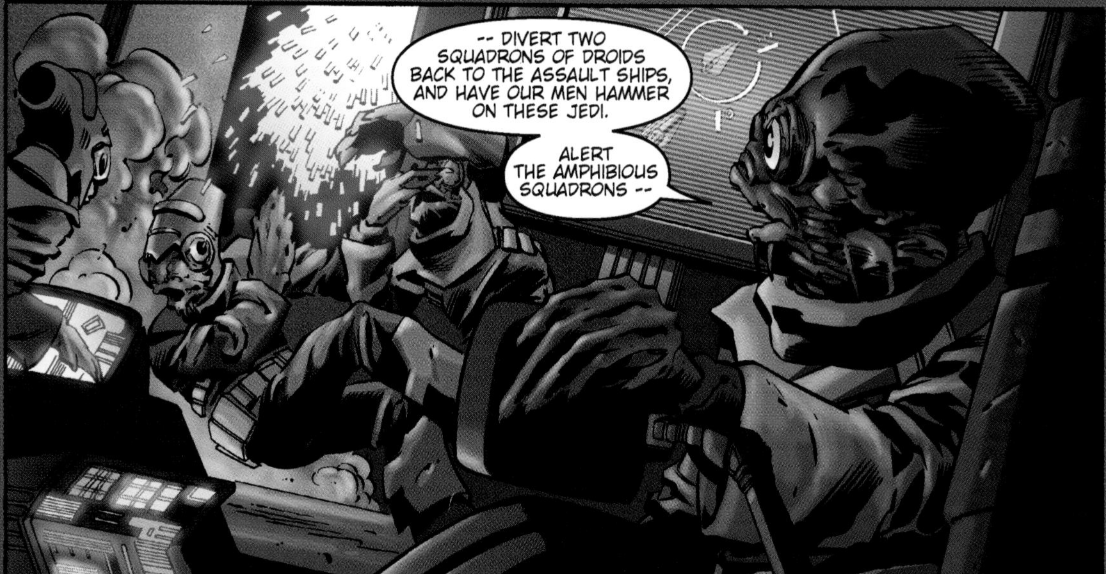
-- DIVERT TWO SQUADRONS OF DROIDS BACK TO THE ASSAULT SHIPS, AND HAVE OUR MEN HAMMER ON THESE JEDI.
ALERT THE AMPHIBIOUS SQUADRONS --

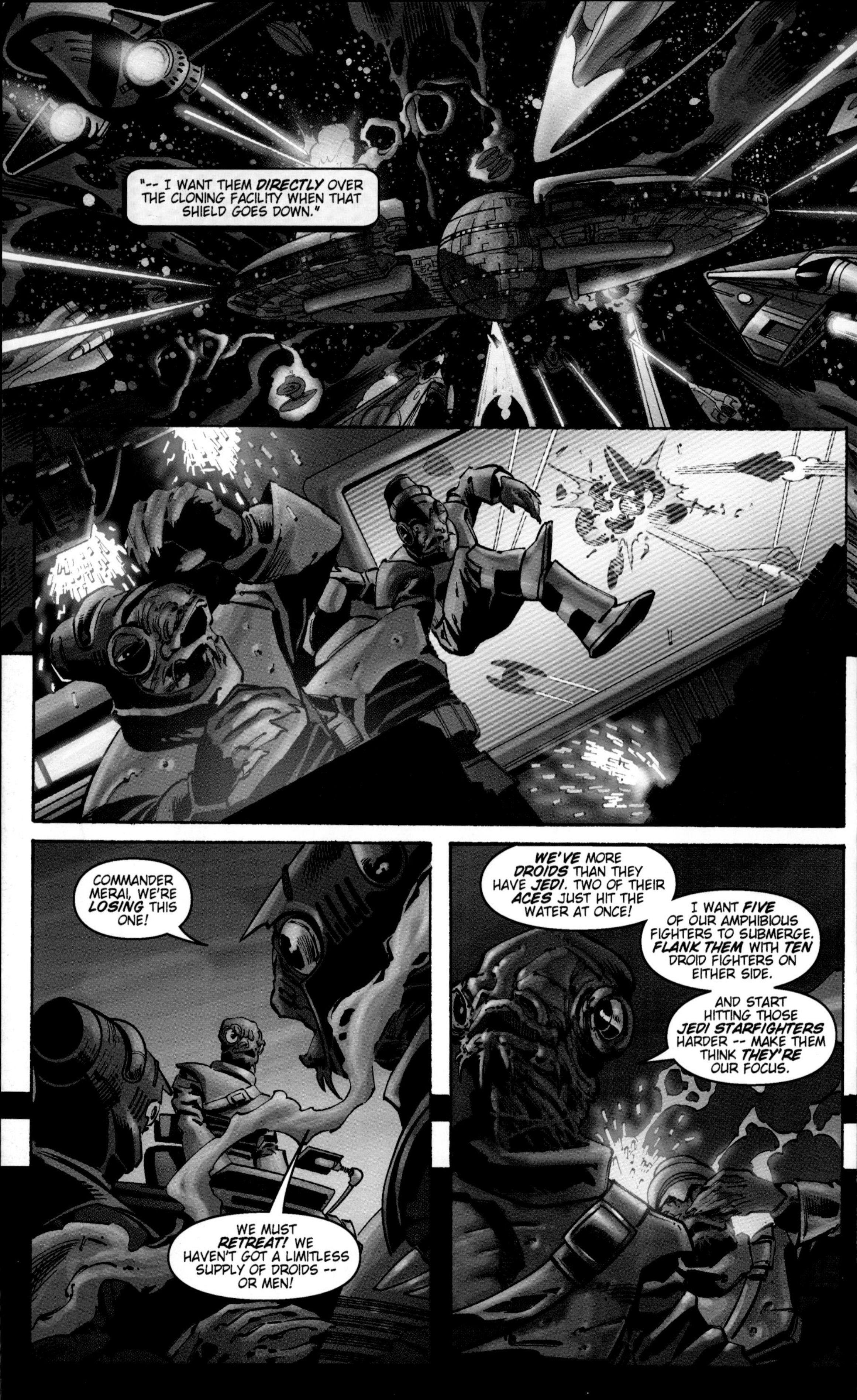
"-- I WANT THEM DIRECTLY OVER THE CLONING FACILITY WHEN THAT SHIELD GOES DOWN."
COMMANDER MERAI, WE'RE LOSING THIS ONE!
WE MUST RETREAT! WE HAVEN'T GOT A LIMITLESS SUPPLY OF DROIDS -- OR MEN!
WE'VE MORE DROIDS THAN THEY HAVE JEDI. TWO OF THEIR ACES JUST HIT THE WATER AT ONCE!
I WANT FIVE OF OUR AMPHIBIOUS FIGHTERS TO SUBMERGE. FLANK THEM WITH TEN DROID FIGHTERS ON EITHER SIDE.
AND START HITTING THOSE JEDI STARFIGHTERS HARDER -- MAKE THEM THINK THEY'RE OUR FOCUS.

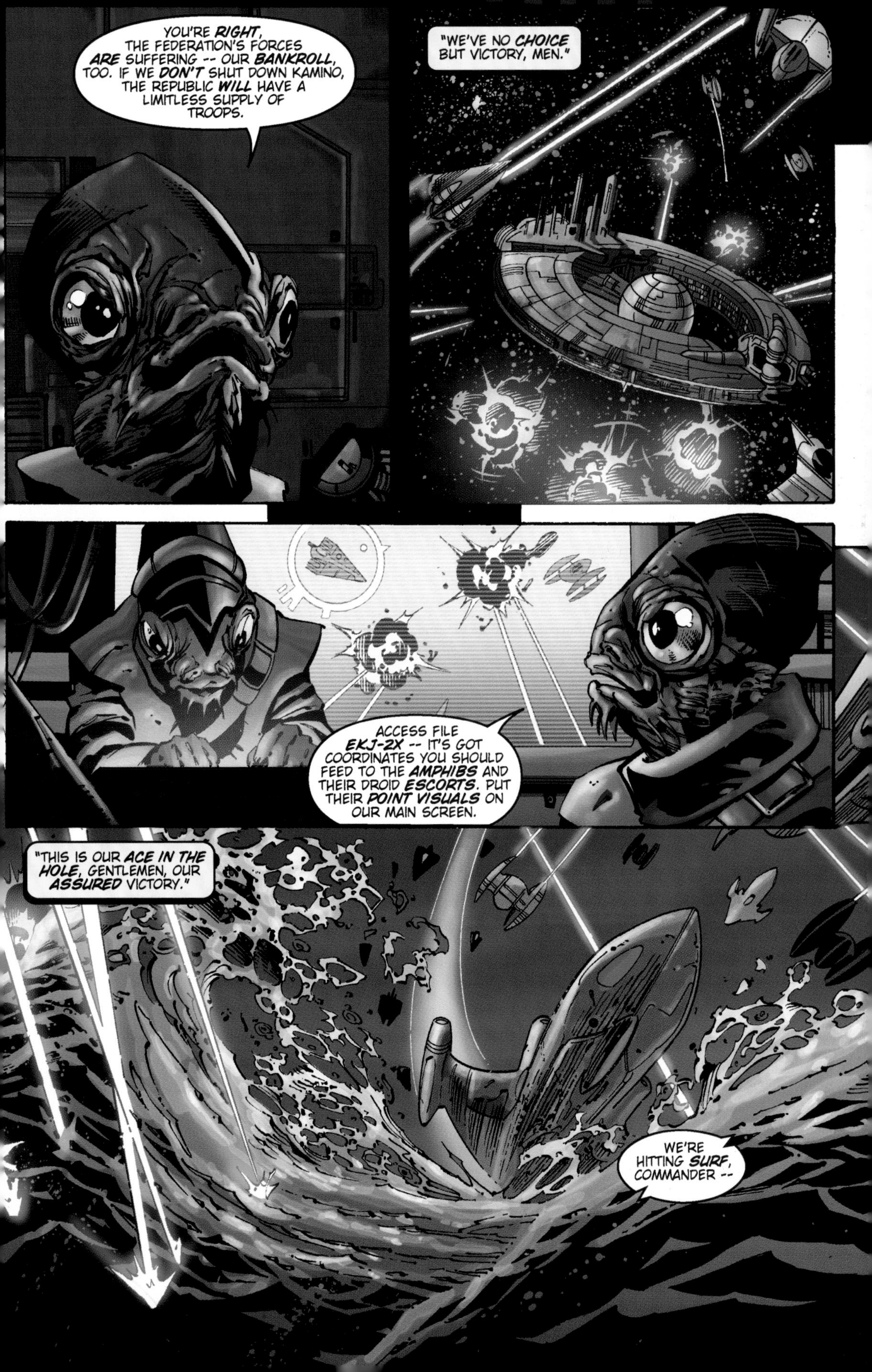
YOU'RE RIGHT, THE FEDERATION'S FORCES ARE SUFFERING -- OUR BANKROLL, TOO. IF WE DON'T SHUT DOWN KAMINO, THE REPUBLIC WILL HAVE A LIMITLESS SUPPLY OF TROOPS.
"WE'VE NO CHOICE BUT VICTORY, MEN."
ACCESS FILE EKJ-2X -- IT'S GOT COORDINATES YOU SHOULD FEED TO THE AMPHIBS AND THEIR DROID ESCORTS. PUT THEIR POINT VISUALS ON OUR MAIN SCREEN.
"THIS IS OUR ACE IN THE HOLE, GENTLEMEN, OUR ASSURED VICTORY."
WE'RE HITTING SURF, COMMANDER --

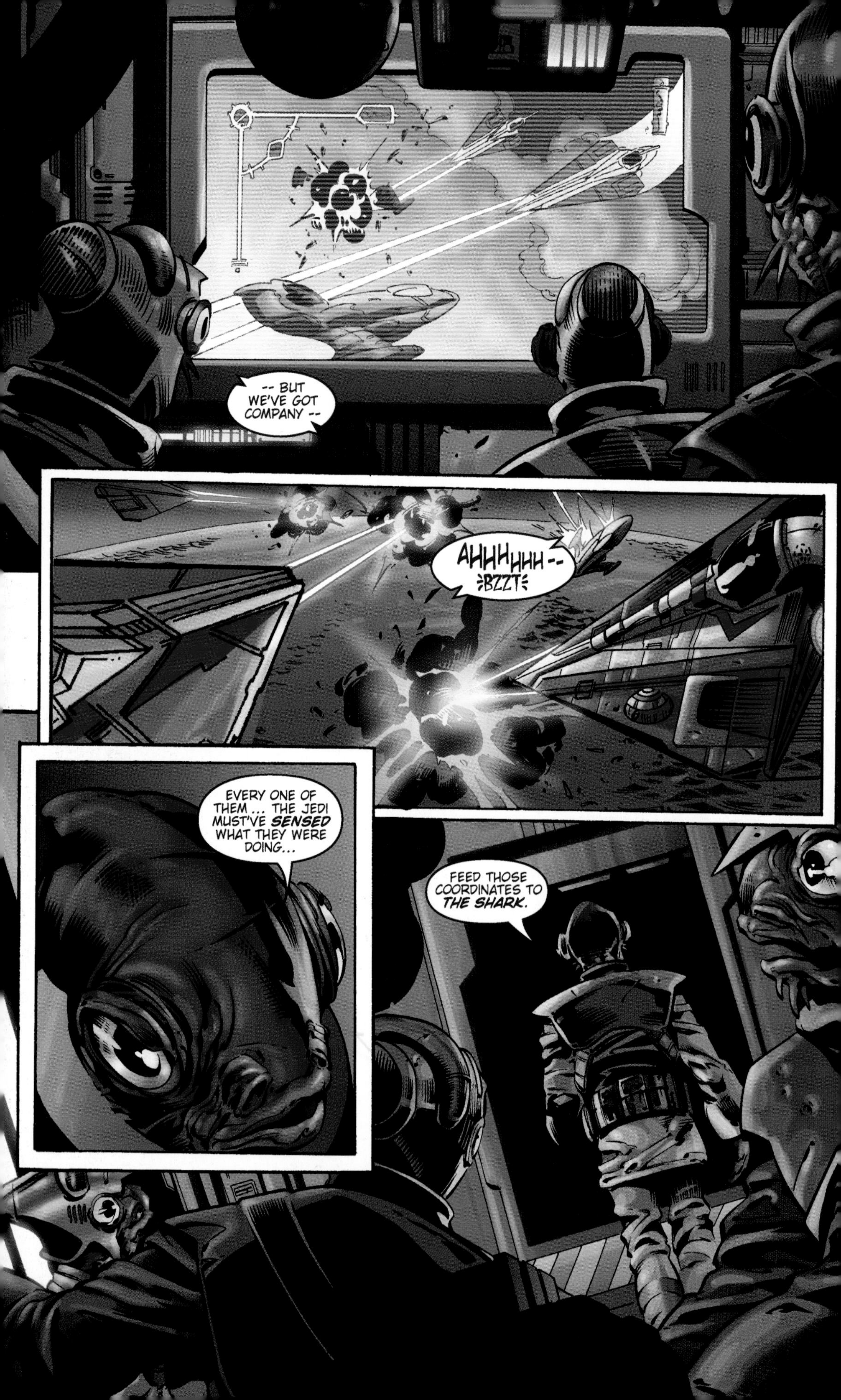
-- BUT WE'VE GOT COMPANY --
AHHHHHH -- BZZT
EVERY ONE OF THEM ... THE JEDI MUST'VE SENSED WHAT THEY WERE DOING...
FEED THOSE COORDINATES TO THE SHARK.

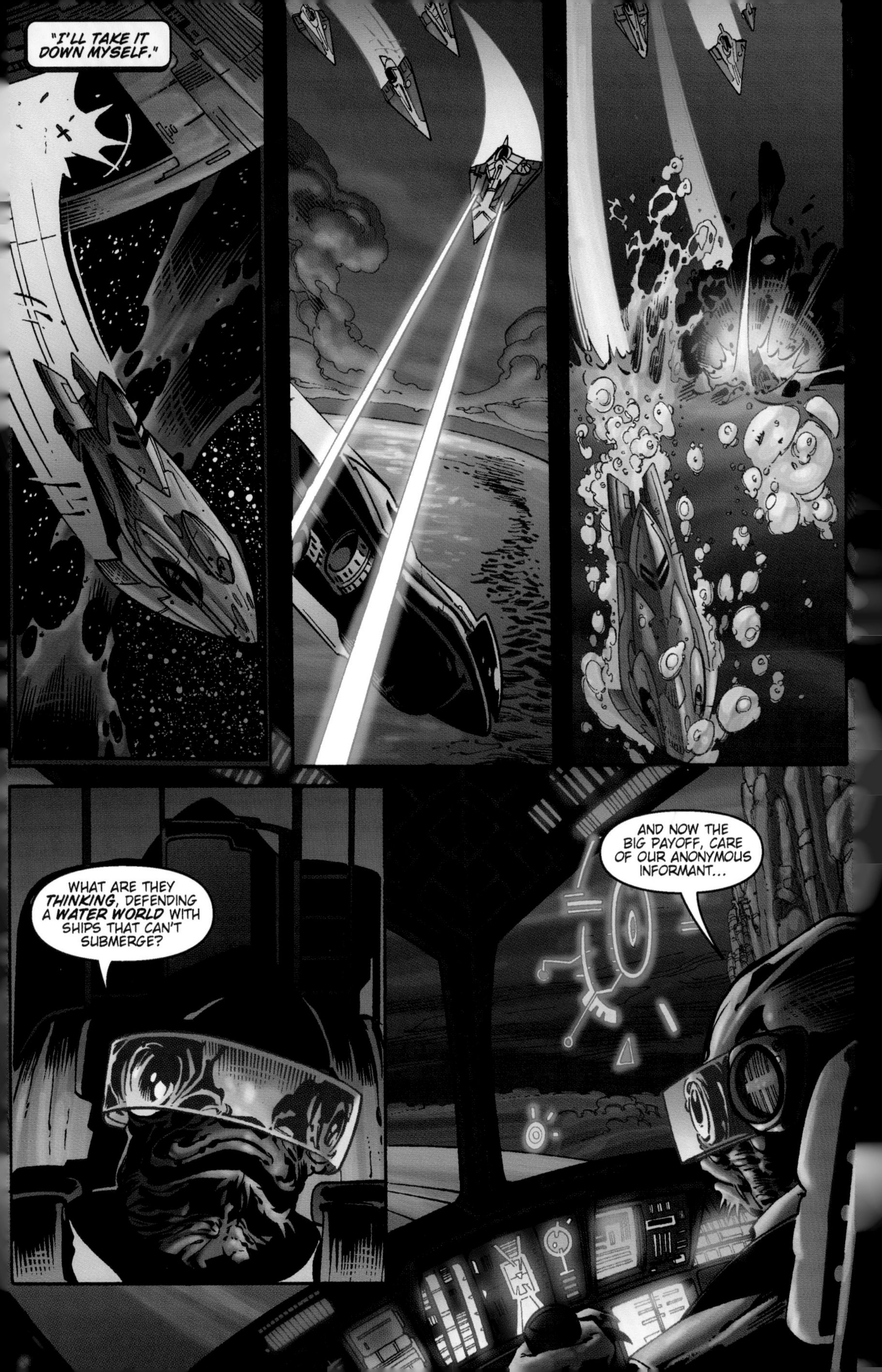
"I'LL TAKE IT DOWN MYSELF."
WHAT ARE THEY *THINKING*, DEFENDING A *WATER WORLD* WITH SHIPS THAT CAN'T SUBMERGE?
AND NOW THE BIG PAYOFF, CARE OF OUR ANONYMOUS INFORMANT...

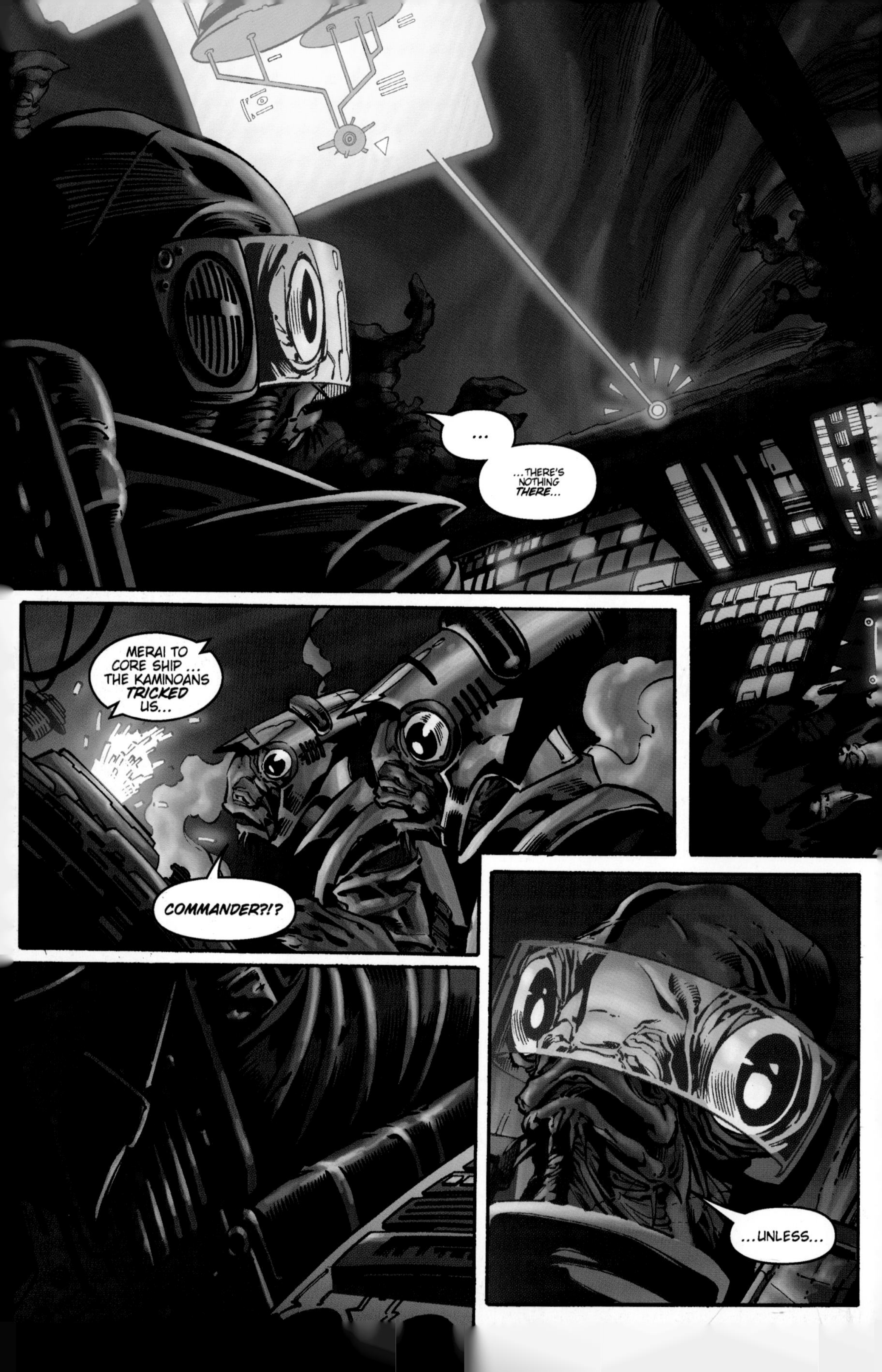
...
...THERE'S NOTHING THERE...
MERAI TO CORE SHIP... THE KAMINOANS TRICKED US...
COMMANDER?!?
...UNLESS...

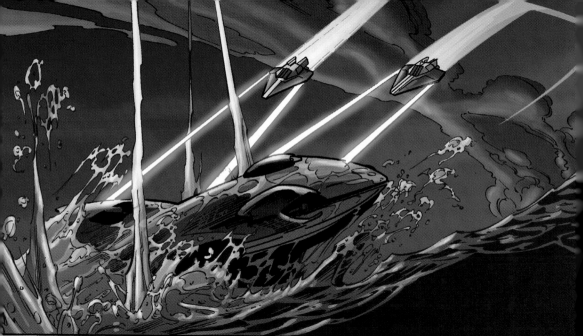

...THERE IS *NO POWER* SOURCE DOWN THERE.

I'M GOING TO TRY TO BLAST THROUGH THE SHIELD MYSELF.

COMMANDER! YOUR *POWER'S* COMPROMISED! THE *SHARK* CAN'T *CHANGE ENVIRONS* SO QUICKLY --

"-- LET US PULL YOU BACK UP INTO THE *CORE SHIP* WITH OUR TRACTOR BEAMS!"

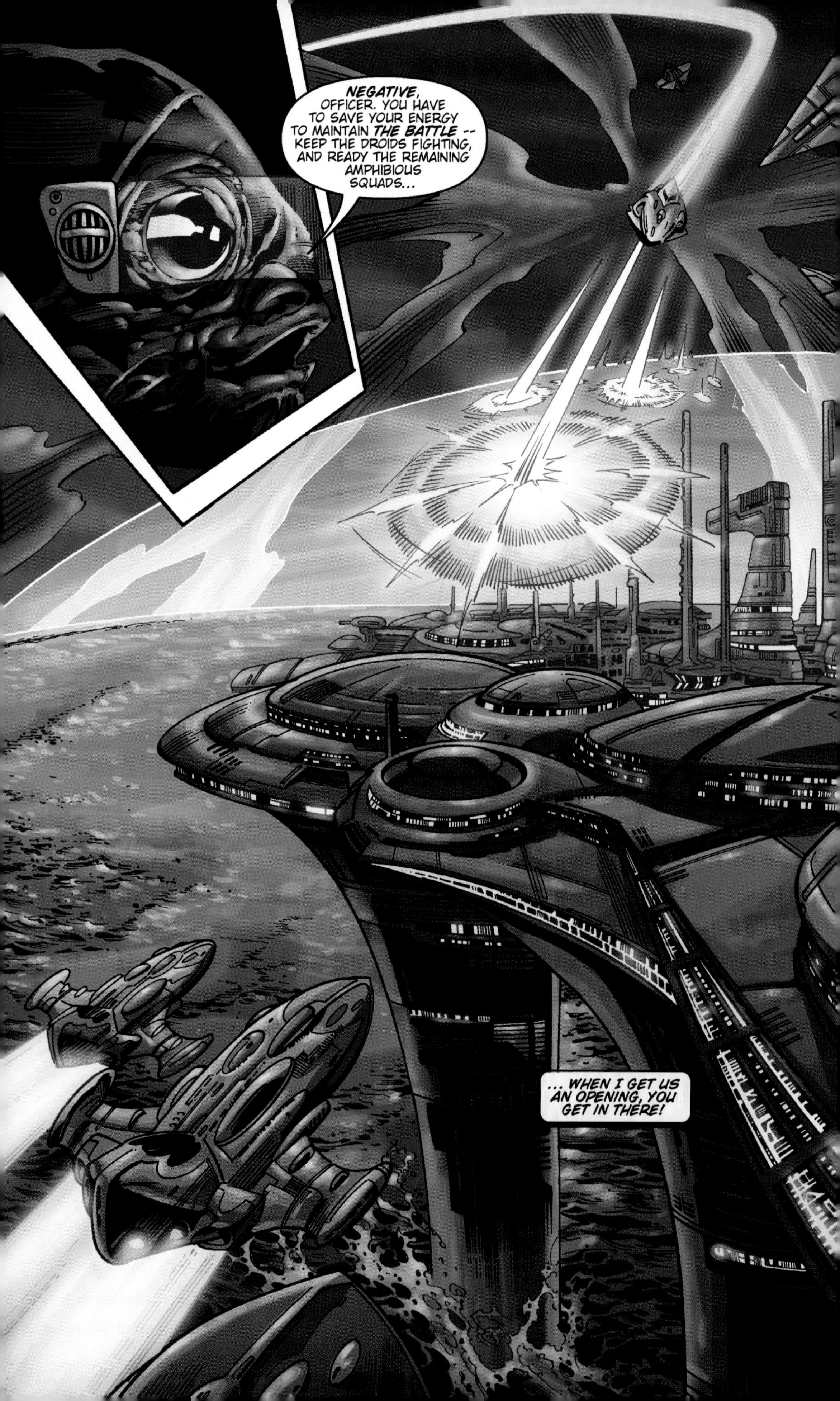
NEGATIVE, OFFICER. YOU HAVE TO SAVE YOUR ENERGY TO MAINTAIN THE BATTLE -- KEEP THE DROIDS FIGHTING, AND READY THE REMAINING AMPHIBIOUS SQUADS...
... WHEN I GET US AN OPENING, YOU GET IN THERE!

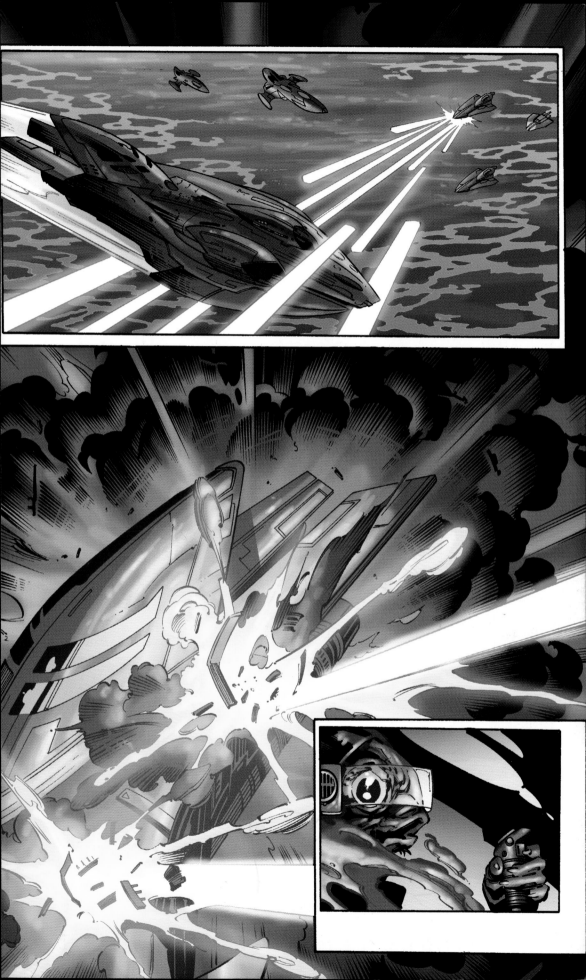

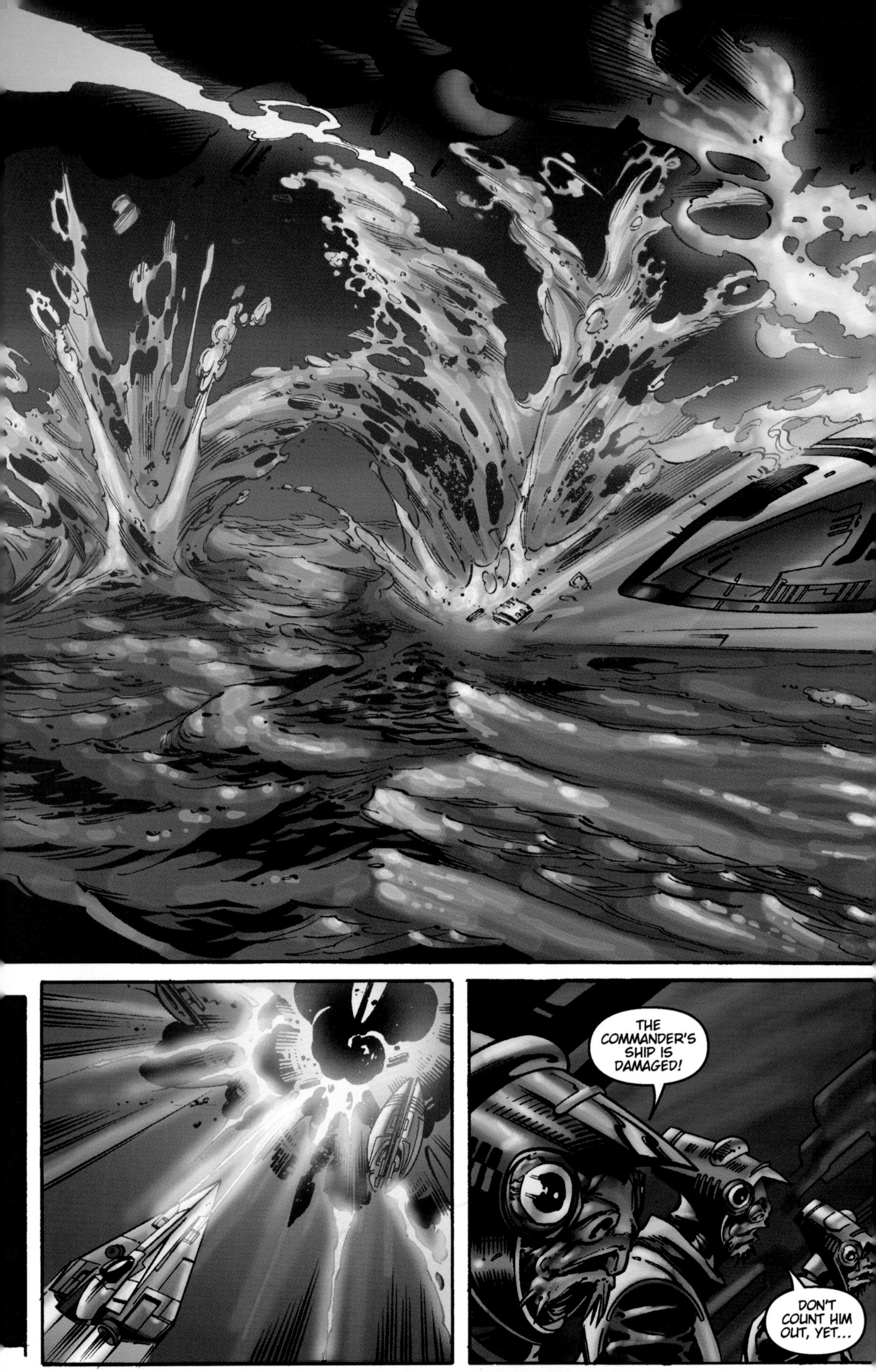
THE COMMANDER'S SHIP IS DAMAGED!
DON'T COUNT HIM OUT, YET...

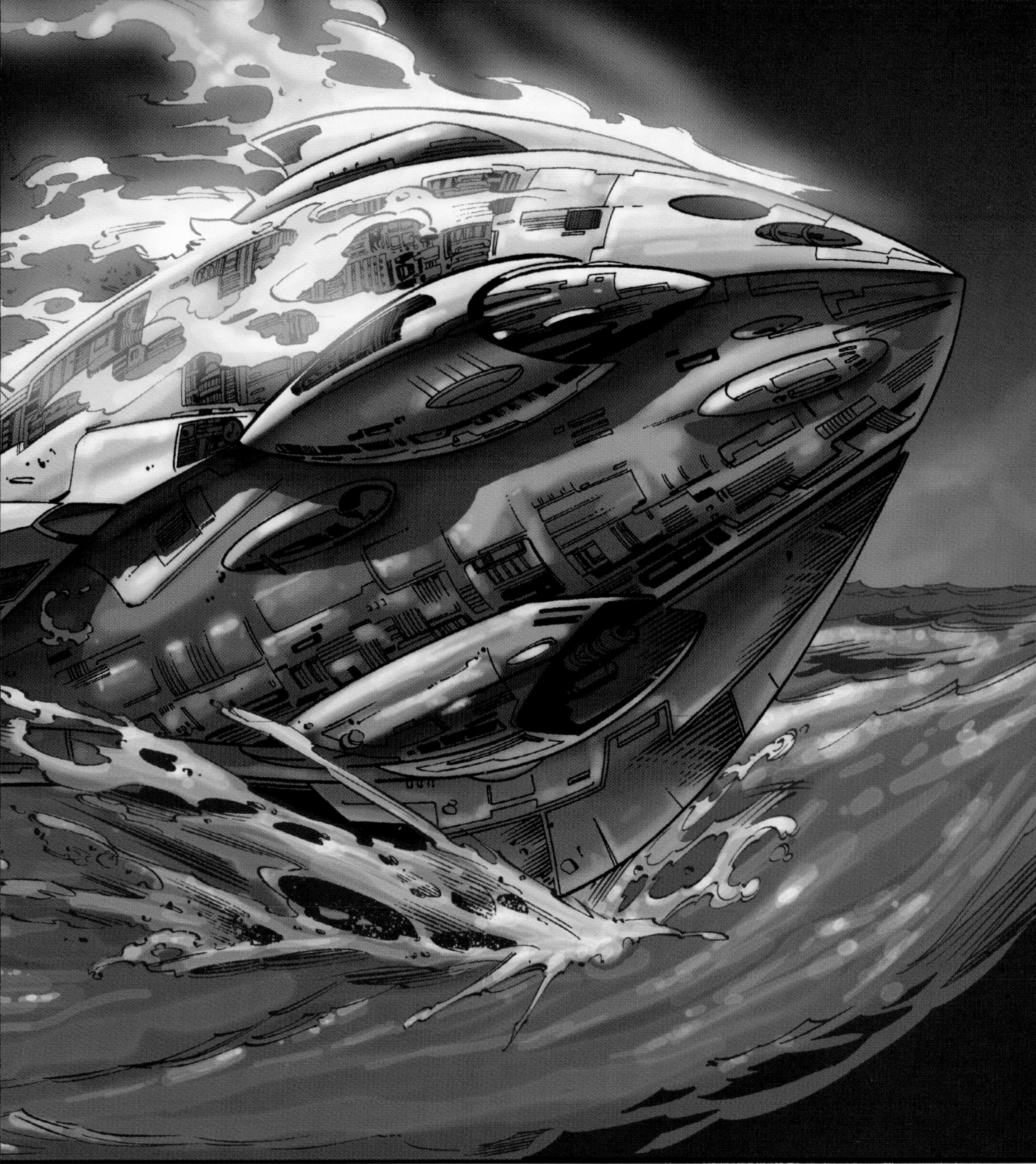

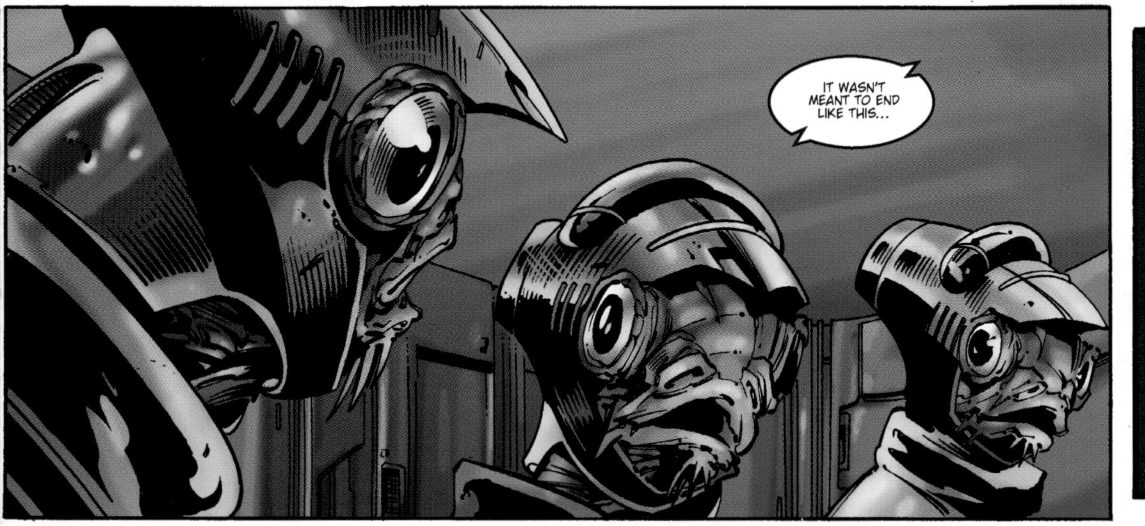
IT WASN'T MEANT TO END LIKE THIS...

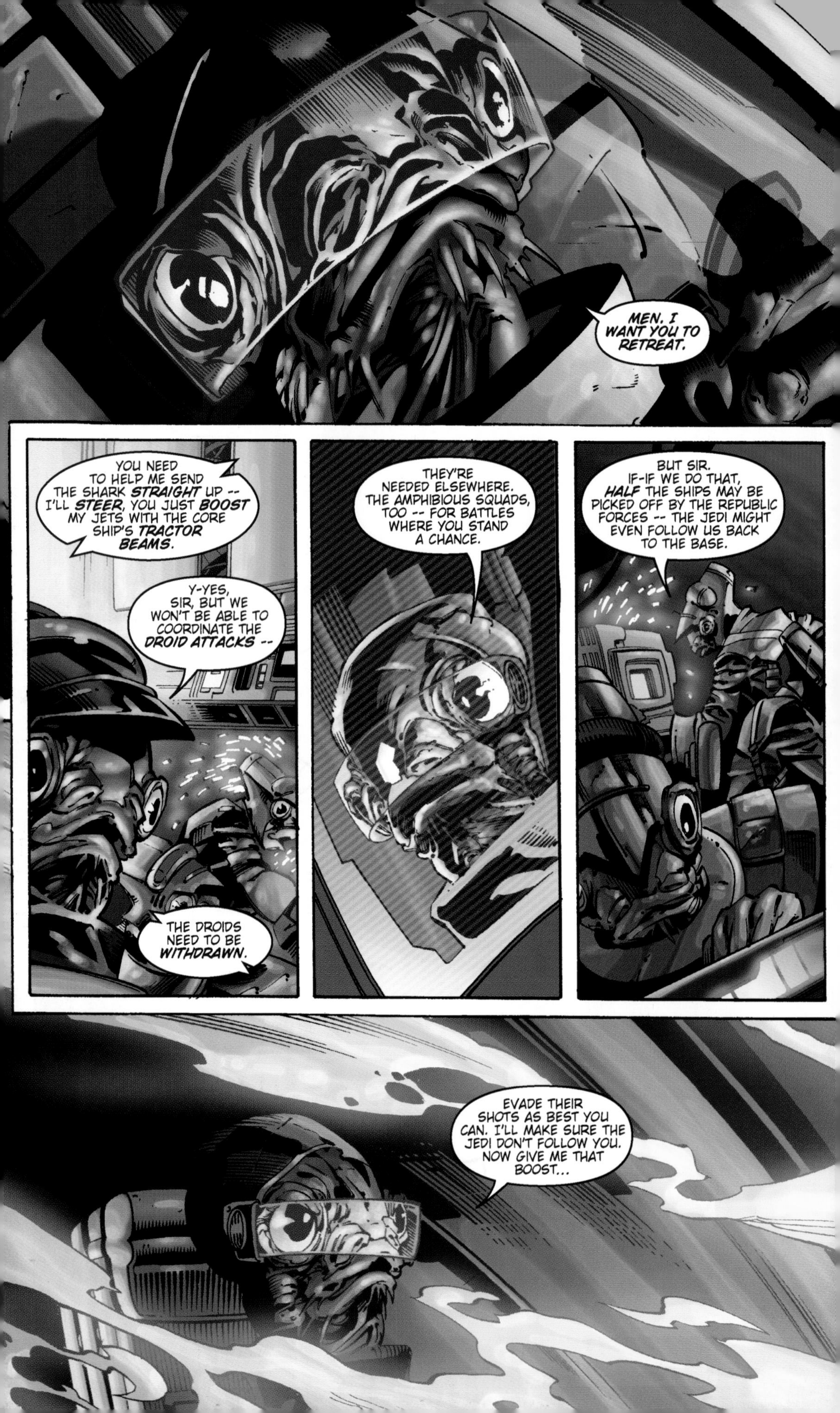
MEN. I WANT YOU TO RETREAT.
YOU NEED TO HELP ME SEND THE SHARK STRAIGHT UP -- I'LL STEER, YOU JUST BOOST MY JETS WITH THE CORE SHIP'S TRACTOR BEAMS.
Y-YES, SIR, BUT WE WON'T BE ABLE TO COORDINATE THE DROID ATTACKS --
THE DROIDS NEED TO BE WITHDRAWN.
THEY'RE NEEDED ELSEWHERE. THE AMPHIBIOUS SQUADS, TOO -- FOR BATTLES WHERE YOU STAND A CHANCE.
BUT SIR. IF-IF WE DO THAT, HALF THE SHIPS MAY BE PICKED OFF BY THE REPUBLIC FORCES -- THE JEDI MIGHT EVEN FOLLOW US BACK TO THE BASE.
EVADE THEIR SHOTS AS BEST YOU CAN. I'LL MAKE SURE THE JEDI DON'T FOLLOW YOU. NOW GIVE ME THAT BOOST...

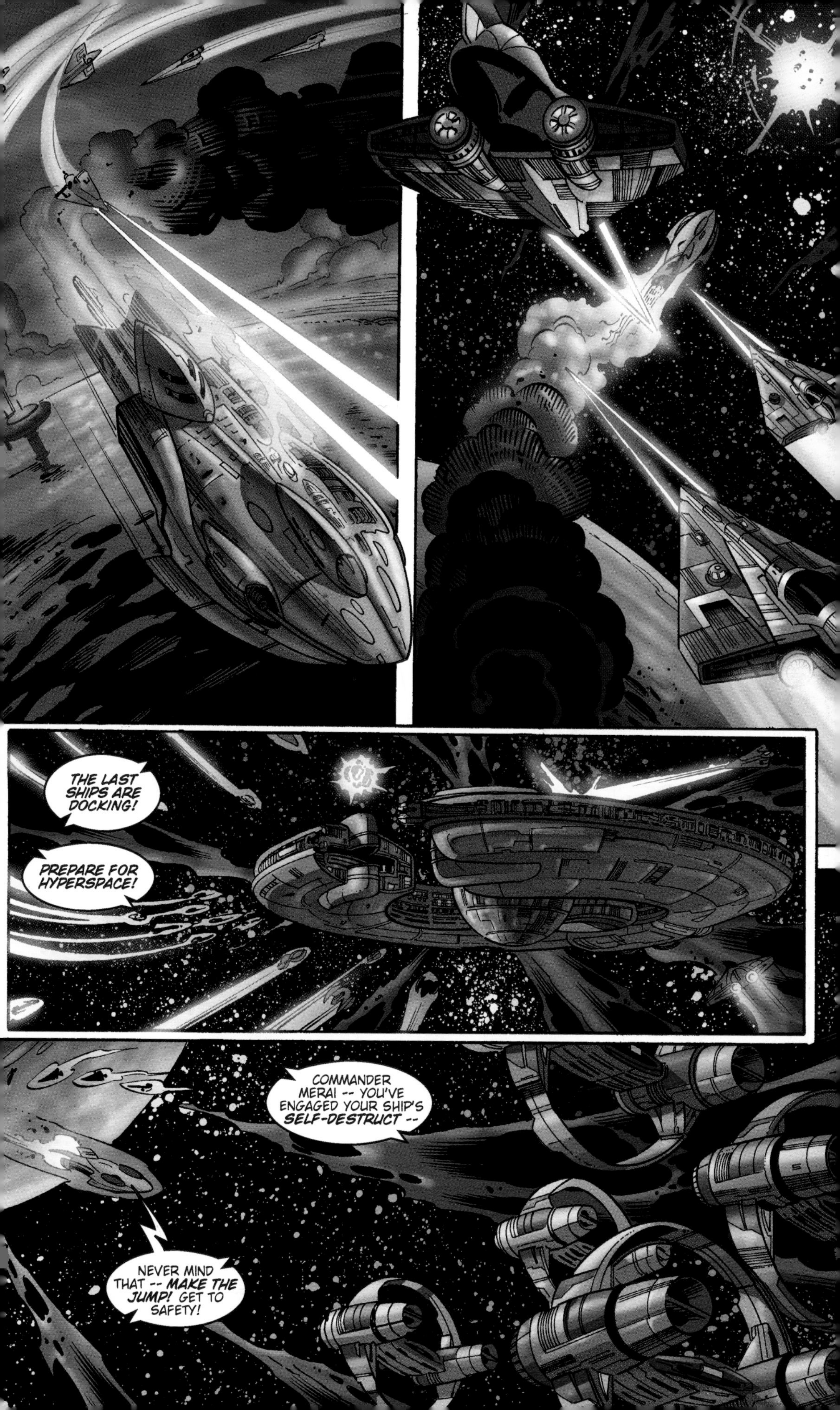

THE LAST SHIPS ARE DOCKING!
PREPARE FOR HYPERSPACE!
COMMANDER MERAI -- YOU'VE ENGAGED YOUR SHIP'S SELF-DESTRUCT --
NEVER MIND THAT -- MAKE THE JUMP! GET TO SAFETY!

DO YOU SENSE IT? HE'S GOING TO SELF-DESTRUCT! PULL UP!

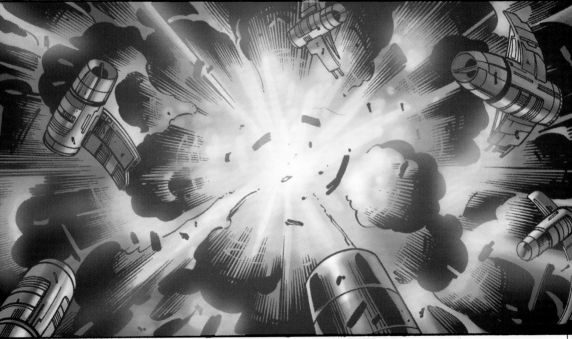

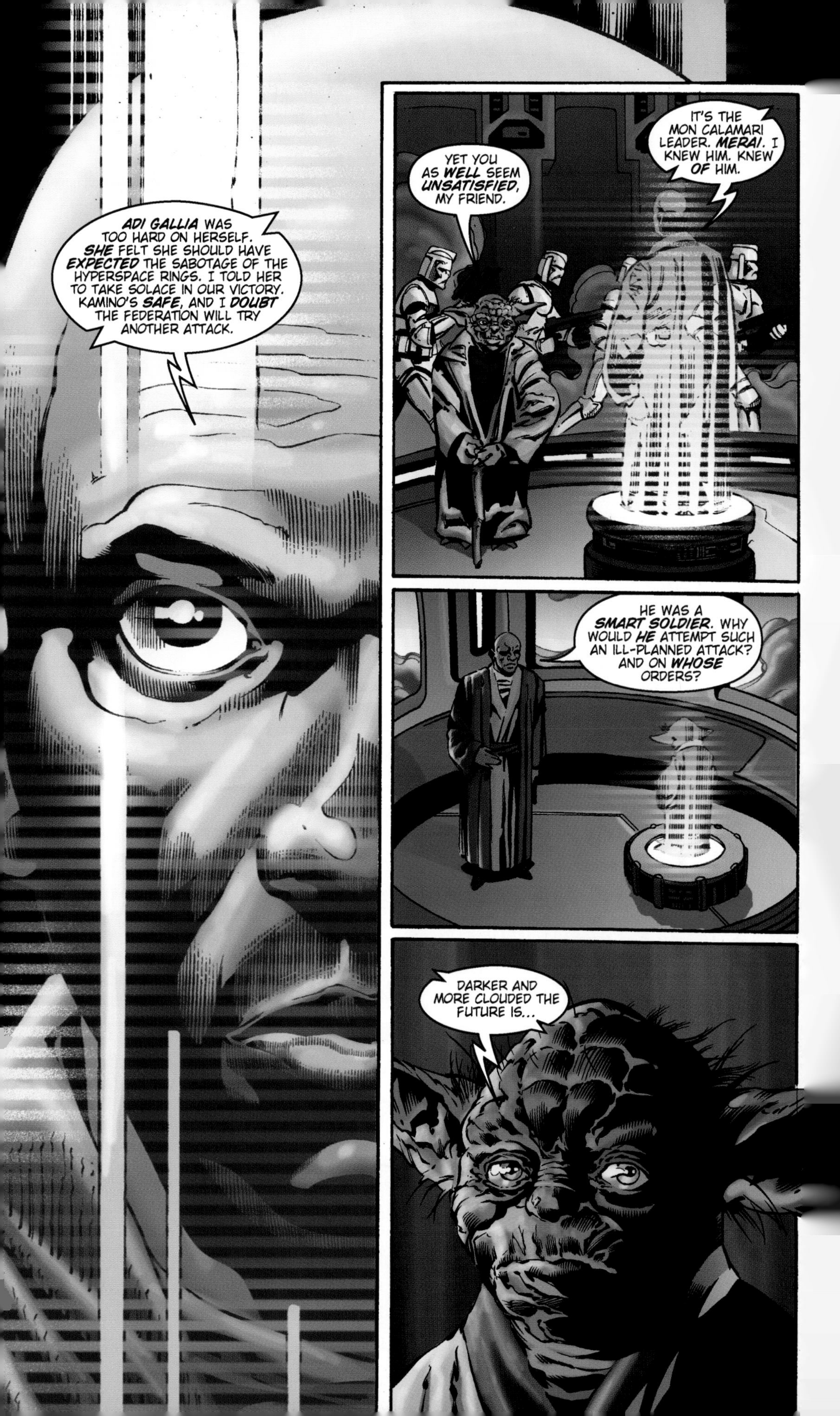
ADI GALLIA WAS TOO HARD ON HERSELF. SHE FELT SHE SHOULD HAVE EXPECTED THE SABOTAGE OF THE HYPERSPACE RINGS. I TOLD HER TO TAKE SOLACE IN OUR VICTORY. KAMINO'S SAFE, AND I DOUBT THE FEDERATION WILL TRY ANOTHER ATTACK.
YET YOU AS WELL SEEM UNSATISFIED, MY FRIEND.
IT'S THE MON CALAMARI LEADER. MERAI. I KNEW HIM. KNEW OF HIM.
HE WAS A SMART SOLDIER. WHY WOULD HE ATTEMPT SUCH AN ILL-PLANNED ATTACK? AND ON WHOSE ORDERS?
DARKER AND MORE CLOUDED THE FUTURE IS...

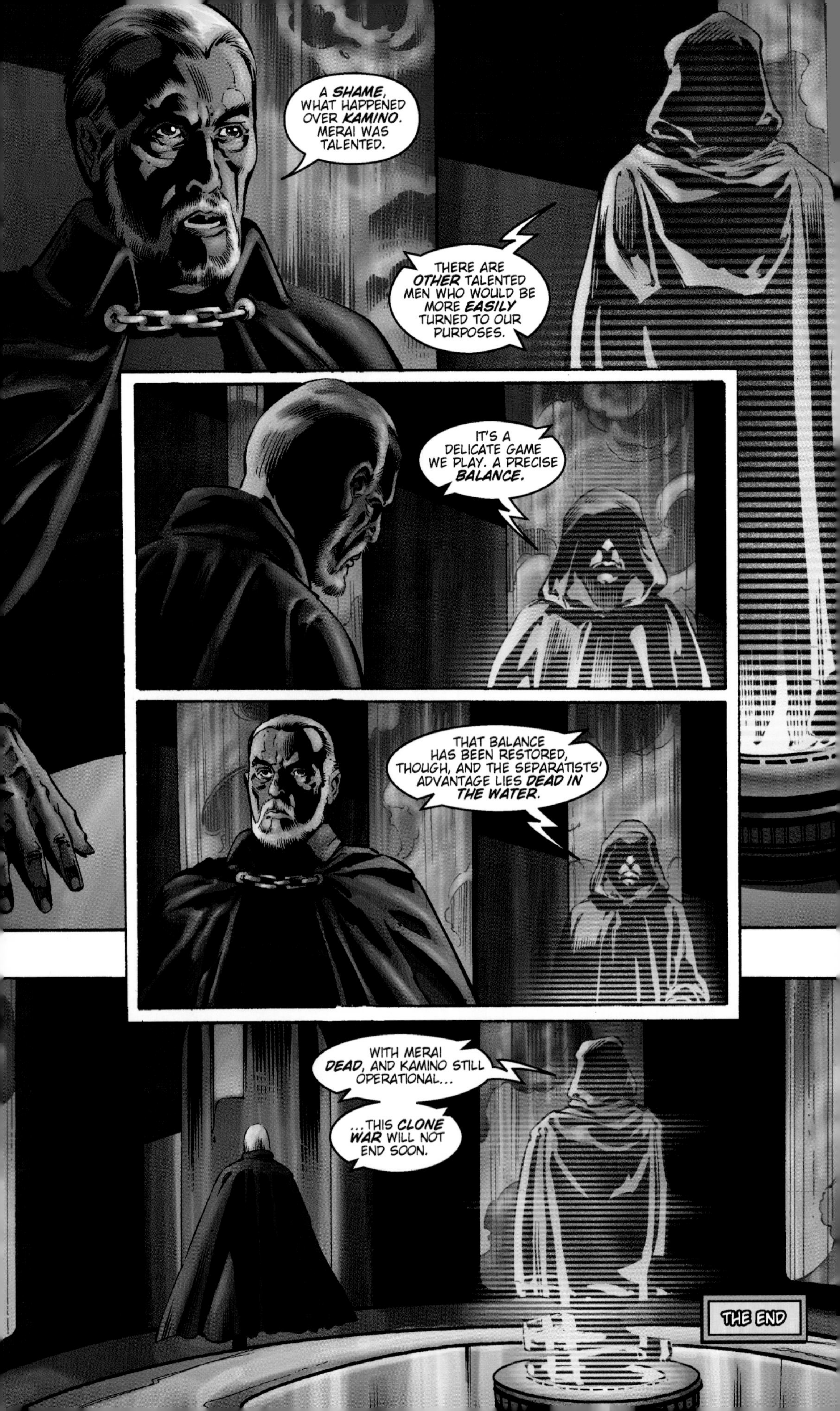
A SHAME, WHAT HAPPENED OVER KAMINO. MERAI WAS TALENTED.
THERE ARE OTHER TALENTED MEN WHO WOULD BE MORE EASILY TURNED TO OUR PURPOSES.
IT'S A DELICATE GAME WE PLAY. A PRECISE BALANCE.
THAT BALANCE HAS BEEN RESTORED, THOUGH, AND THE SEPARATISTS' ADVANTAGE LIES DEAD IN THE WATER.
WITH MERAI DEAD, AND KAMINO STILL OPERATIONAL...
...THIS CLONE WAR WILL NOT END SOON.
THE END

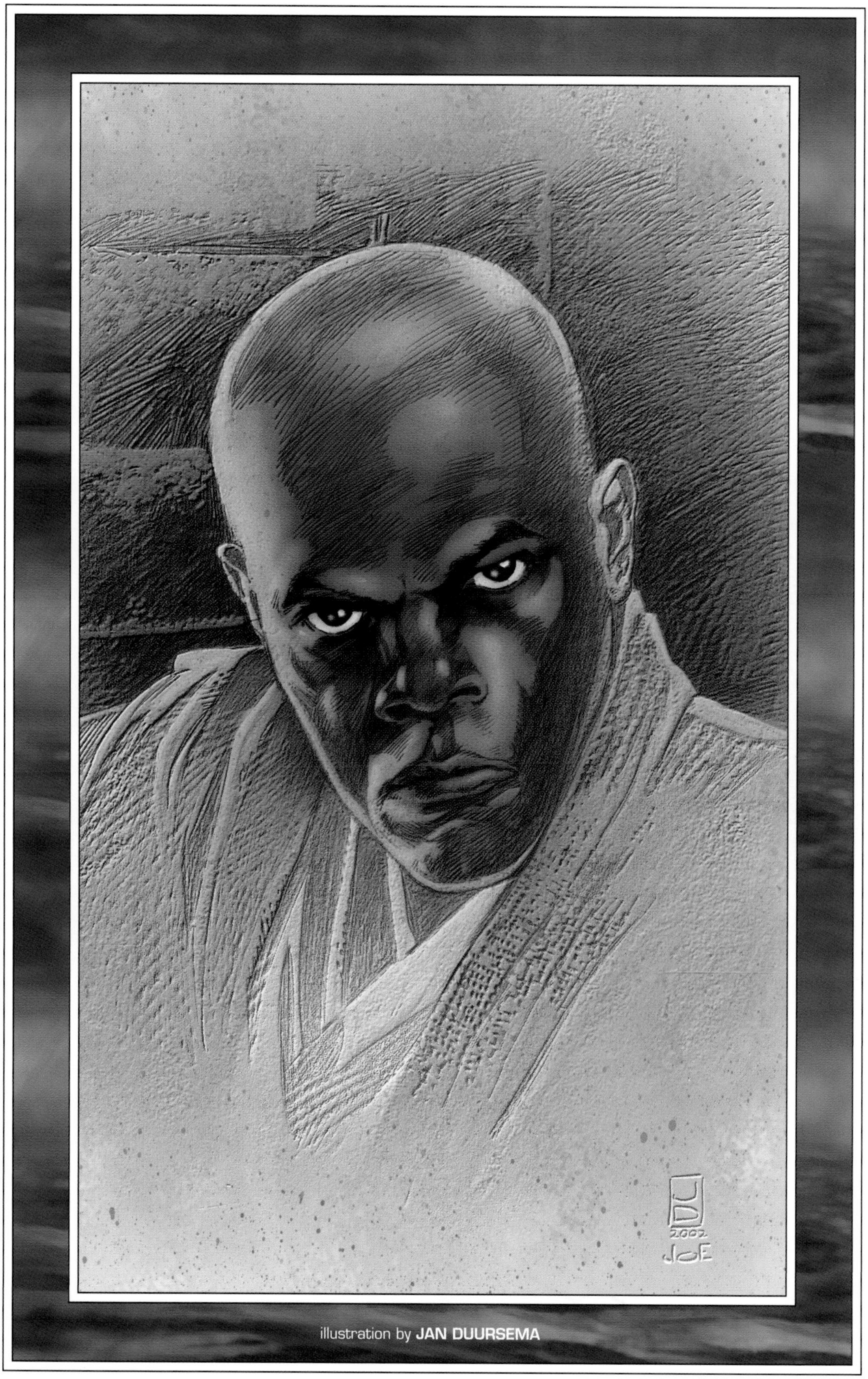
JD
2002
JOE
illustration by **JAN DUURSEMA**

SCHISM

"Schism"
written by **John Ostrander**
pencilled by **Jan Duursema**
inked by **Dan Parsons**

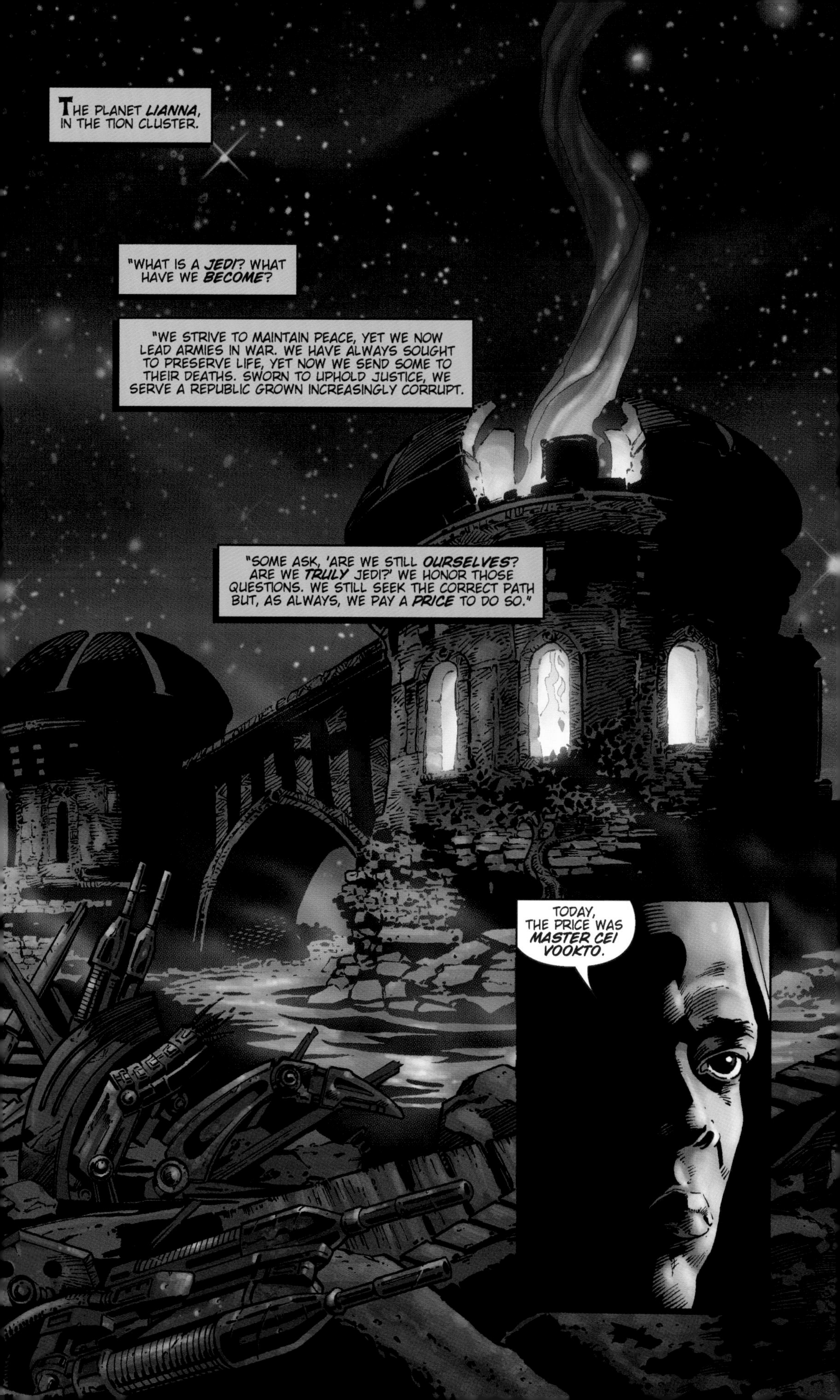
THE PLANET LIANNA, IN THE TION CLUSTER.
"WHAT IS A JEDI? WHAT HAVE WE BECOME?
"WE STRIVE TO MAINTAIN PEACE, YET WE NOW LEAD ARMIES IN WAR. WE HAVE ALWAYS SOUGHT TO PRESERVE LIFE, YET NOW WE SEND SOME TO THEIR DEATHS. SWORN TO UPHOLD JUSTICE, WE SERVE A REPUBLIC GROWN INCREASINGLY CORRUPT.
"SOME ASK, 'ARE WE STILL OURSELVES? ARE WE TRULY JEDI?' WE HONOR THOSE QUESTIONS. WE STILL SEEK THE CORRECT PATH BUT, AS ALWAYS, WE PAY A PRICE TO DO SO."
TODAY, THE PRICE WAS MASTER CEI VOOKTO.

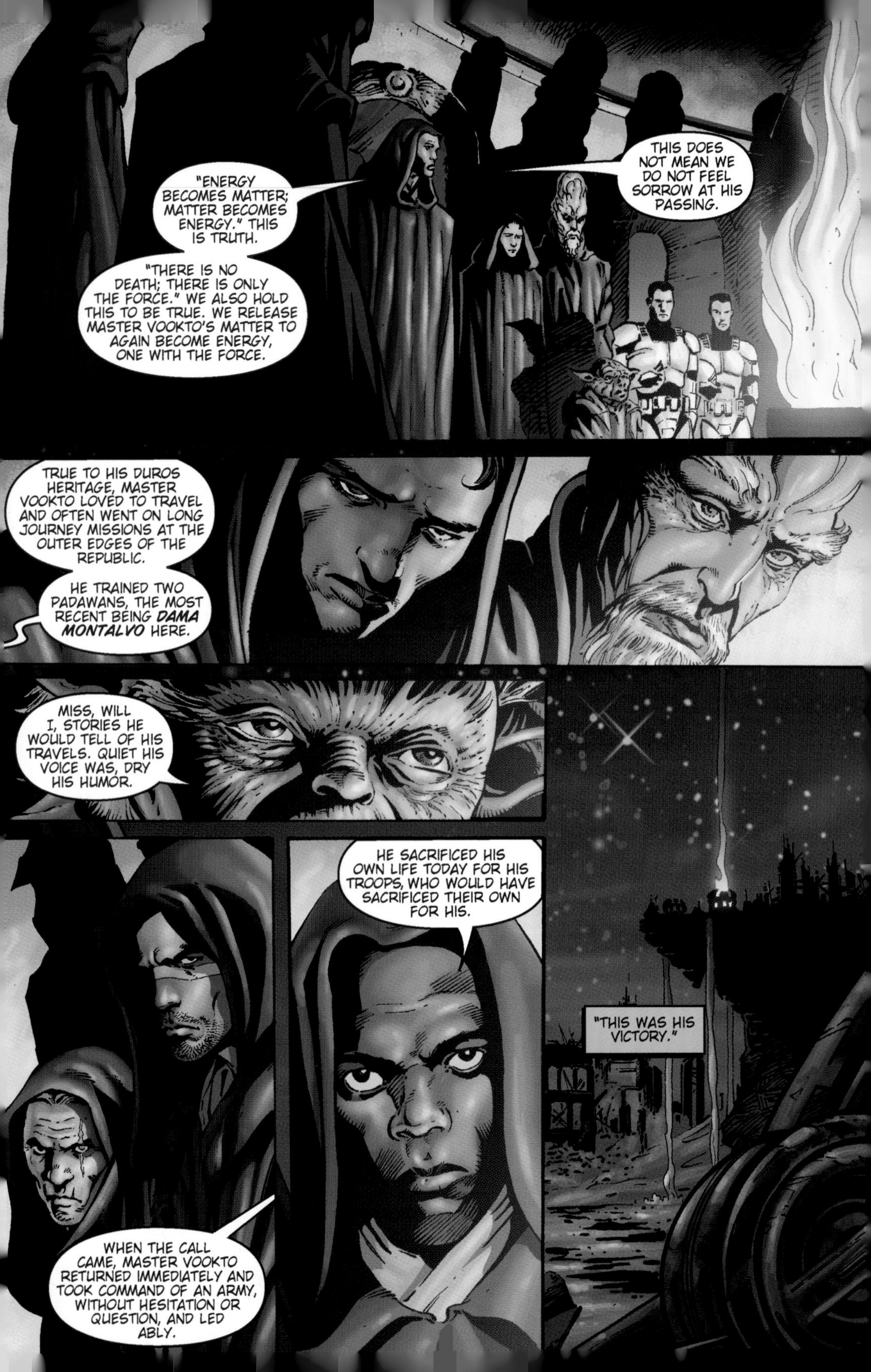

"ENERGY BECOMES MATTER; MATTER BECOMES ENERGY." THIS IS TRUTH.
"THERE IS NO DEATH; THERE IS ONLY THE FORCE." WE ALSO HOLD THIS TO BE TRUE. WE RELEASE MASTER VOOKTO'S MATTER TO AGAIN BECOME ENERGY, ONE WITH THE FORCE.
THIS DOES NOT MEAN WE DO NOT FEEL SORROW AT HIS PASSING.
TRUE TO HIS DUROS HERITAGE, MASTER VOOKTO LOVED TO TRAVEL AND OFTEN WENT ON LONG JOURNEY MISSIONS AT THE OUTER EDGES OF THE REPUBLIC.
HE TRAINED TWO PADAWANS, THE MOST RECENT BEING DAMA MONTALVO HERE.
MISS, WILL I, STORIES HE WOULD TELL OF HIS TRAVELS. QUIET HIS VOICE WAS, DRY HIS HUMOR.
WHEN THE CALL CAME, MASTER VOOKTO RETURNED IMMEDIATELY AND TOOK COMMAND OF AN ARMY, WITHOUT HESITATION OR QUESTION, AND LED ABLY.
HE SACRIFICED HIS OWN LIFE TODAY FOR HIS TROOPS, WHO WOULD HAVE SACRIFICED THEIR OWN FOR HIS.
"THIS WAS HIS VICTORY."

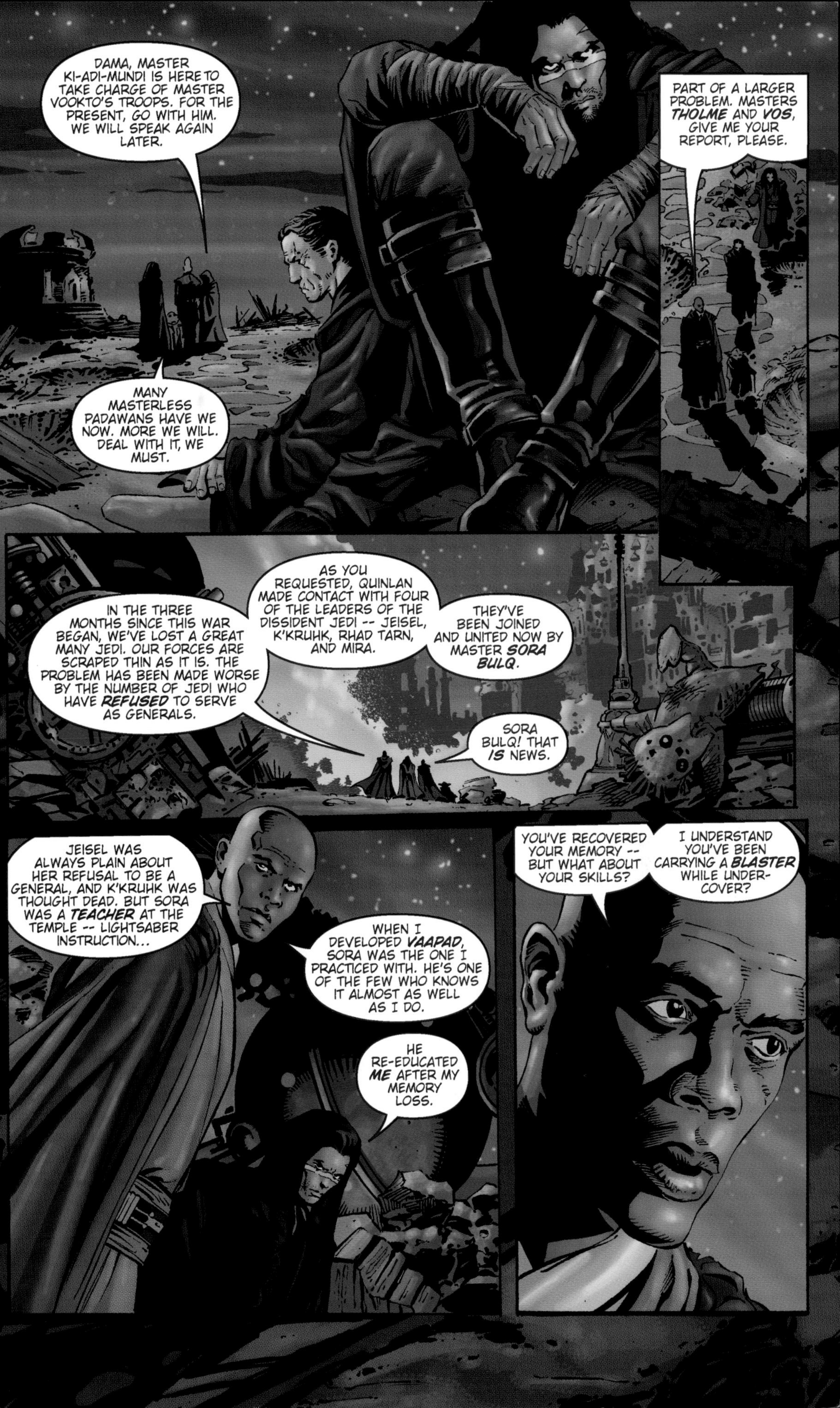
DAMA, MASTER KI-ADI-MUNDI IS HERE TO TAKE CHARGE OF MASTER VOOKTO'S TROOPS. FOR THE PRESENT, GO WITH HIM. WE WILL SPEAK AGAIN LATER.
MANY MASTERLESS PADAWANS HAVE WE NOW. MORE WE WILL. DEAL WITH IT, WE MUST.
PART OF A LARGER PROBLEM. MASTERS THOLME AND VOS, GIVE ME YOUR REPORT, PLEASE.
IN THE THREE MONTHS SINCE THIS WAR BEGAN, WE'VE LOST A GREAT MANY JEDI. OUR FORCES ARE SCRAPED THIN AS IT IS. THE PROBLEM HAS BEEN MADE WORSE BY THE NUMBER OF JEDI WHO HAVE REFUSED TO SERVE AS GENERALS.
AS YOU REQUESTED, QUINLAN MADE CONTACT WITH FOUR OF THE LEADERS OF THE DISSIDENT JEDI -- JEISEL, K'KRUHK, RHAD TARN, AND MIRA.
THEY'VE BEEN JOINED AND UNITED NOW BY MASTER SORA BULQ.
SORA BULQ! THAT IS NEWS.
JEISEL WAS ALWAYS PLAIN ABOUT HER REFUSAL TO BE A GENERAL, AND K'KRUHK WAS THOUGHT DEAD. BUT SORA WAS A TEACHER AT THE TEMPLE -- LIGHTSABER INSTRUCTION...
WHEN I DEVELOPED VAAPAD, SORA WAS THE ONE I PRACTICED WITH. HE'S ONE OF THE FEW WHO KNOWS IT ALMOST AS WELL AS I DO.
HE RE-EDUCATED ME AFTER MY MEMORY LOSS.
YOU'VE RECOVERED YOUR MEMORY -- BUT WHAT ABOUT YOUR SKILLS?
I UNDERSTAND YOU'VE BEEN CARRYING A BLASTER WHILE UNDER-COVER?

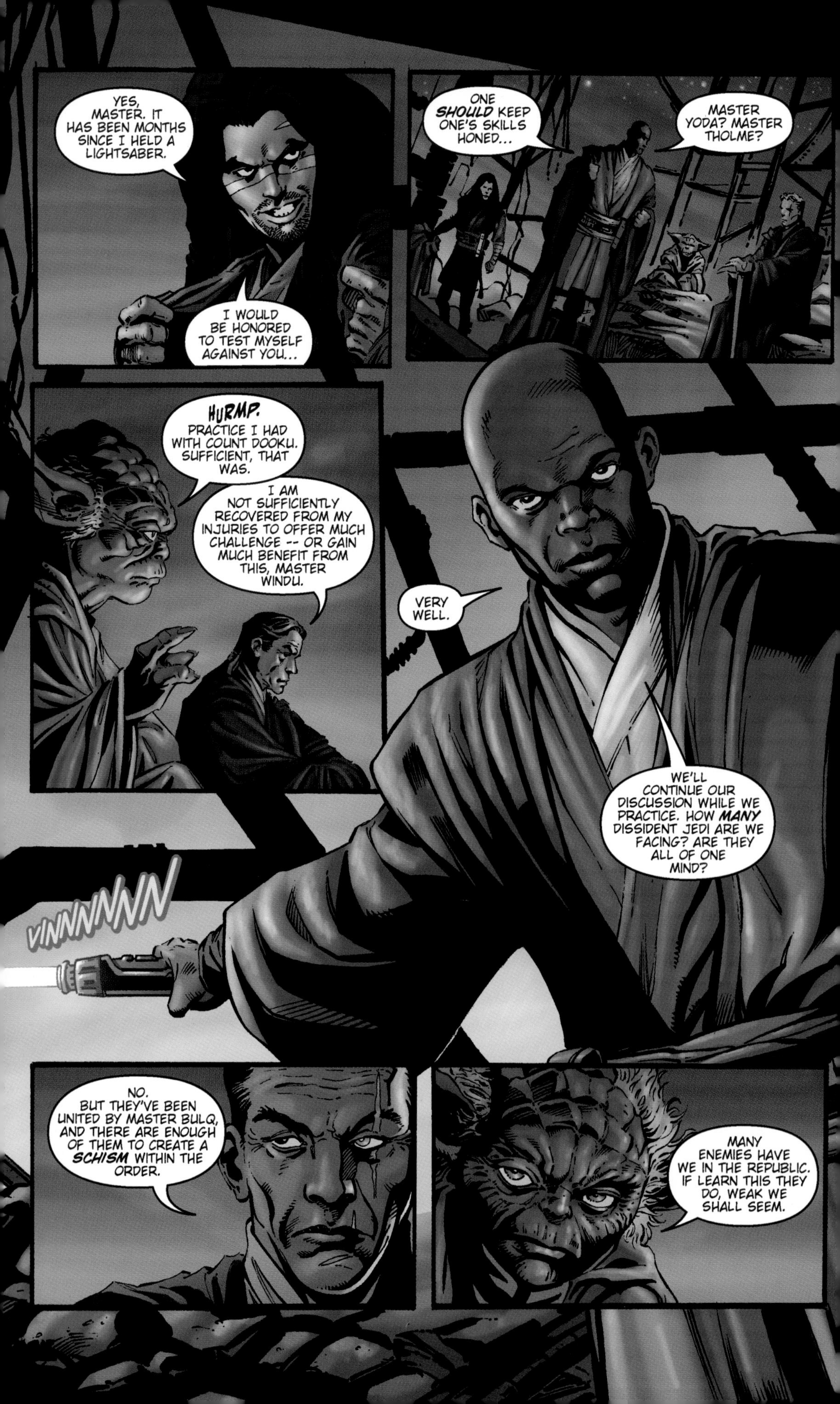
YES, MASTER. IT HAS BEEN MONTHS SINCE I HELD A LIGHTSABER.
I WOULD BE HONORED TO TEST MYSELF AGAINST YOU...
ONE SHOULD KEEP ONE'S SKILLS HONED...
MASTER YODA? MASTER THOLME?
HURMP. PRACTICE I HAD WITH COUNT DOOKU. SUFFICIENT, THAT WAS.
I AM NOT SUFFICIENTLY RECOVERED FROM MY INJURIES TO OFFER MUCH CHALLENGE -- OR GAIN MUCH BENEFIT FROM THIS, MASTER WINDU.
VERY WELL.
WE'LL CONTINUE OUR DISCUSSION WHILE WE PRACTICE. HOW MANY DISSIDENT JEDI ARE WE FACING? ARE THEY ALL OF ONE MIND?
VINNNNNN
NO. BUT THEY'VE BEEN UNITED BY MASTER BULQ, AND THERE ARE ENOUGH OF THEM TO CREATE A SCHISM WITHIN THE ORDER.
MANY ENEMIES HAVE WE IN THE REPUBLIC. IF LEARN THIS THEY DO, WEAK WE SHALL SEEM.

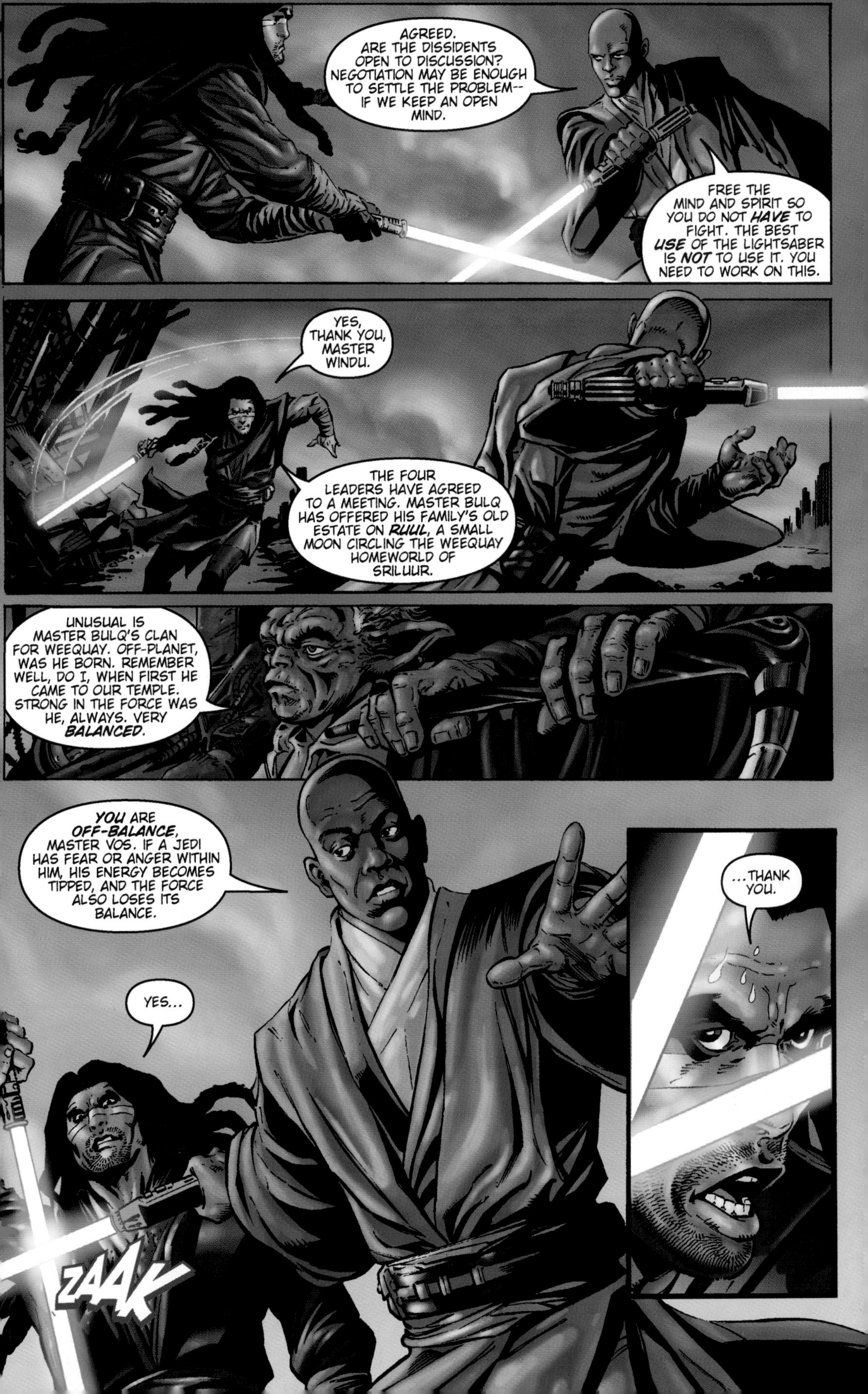
AGREED. ARE THE DISSIDENTS OPEN TO DISCUSSION? NEGOTIATION MAY BE ENOUGH TO SETTLE THE PROBLEM-- IF WE KEEP AN OPEN MIND.
FREE THE MIND AND SPIRIT SO YOU DO NOT *HAVE* TO FIGHT. THE BEST *USE* OF THE LIGHTSABER IS *NOT* TO USE IT. YOU NEED TO WORK ON THIS.
YES, THANK YOU, MASTER WINDU.
THE FOUR LEADERS HAVE AGREED TO A MEETING. MASTER BULQ HAS OFFERED HIS FAMILY'S OLD ESTATE ON *RUUL*, A SMALL MOON CIRCLING THE WEEQUAY HOMEWORLD OF SRILUUR.
UNUSUAL IS MASTER BULQ'S CLAN FOR WEEQUAY. OFF-PLANET, WAS HE BORN. REMEMBER WELL, DO I, WHEN FIRST HE CAME TO OUR TEMPLE. STRONG IN THE FORCE WAS HE, ALWAYS. VERY *BALANCED*.
YOU ARE *OFF-BALANCE*, MASTER VOS. IF A JEDI HAS FEAR OR ANGER WITHIN HIM, HIS ENERGY BECOMES TIPPED, AND THE FORCE ALSO LOSES ITS BALANCE.
YES...
...THANK YOU.
ZAAK

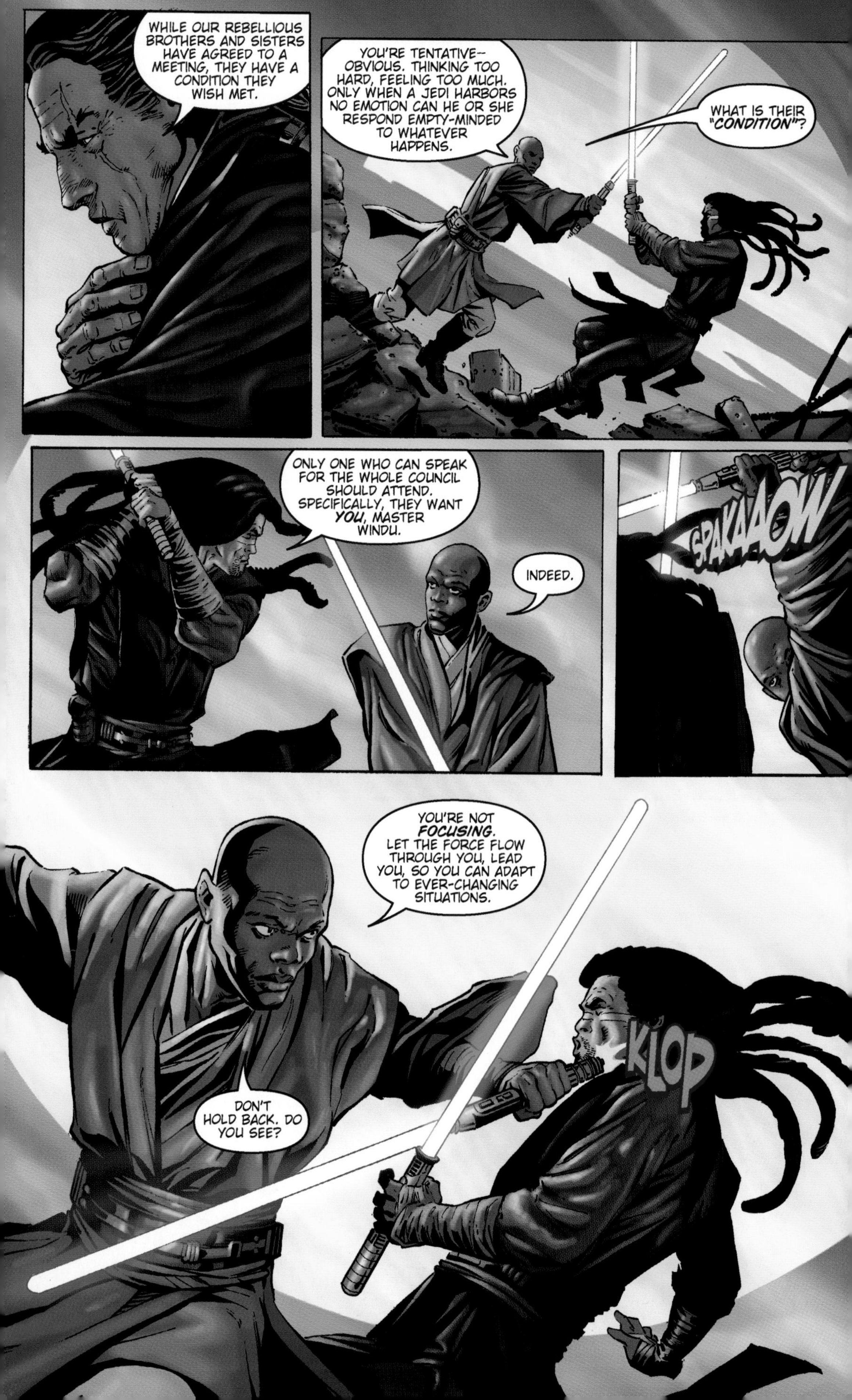
WHILE OUR REBELLIOUS BROTHERS AND SISTERS HAVE AGREED TO A MEETING, THEY HAVE A CONDITION THEY WISH MET.
YOU'RE TENTATIVE-- OBVIOUS. THINKING TOO HARD, FEELING TOO MUCH. ONLY WHEN A JEDI HARBORS NO EMOTION CAN HE OR SHE RESPOND EMPTY-MINDED TO WHATEVER HAPPENS.
WHAT IS THEIR "CONDITION"?
ONLY ONE WHO CAN SPEAK FOR THE WHOLE COUNCIL SHOULD ATTEND. SPECIFICALLY, THEY WANT YOU, MASTER WINDU.
INDEED.
SPAKAAOW
YOU'RE NOT FOCUSING. LET THE FORCE FLOW THROUGH YOU, LEAD YOU, SO YOU CAN ADAPT TO EVER-CHANGING SITUATIONS.
KLOP
DON'T HOLD BACK. DO YOU SEE?

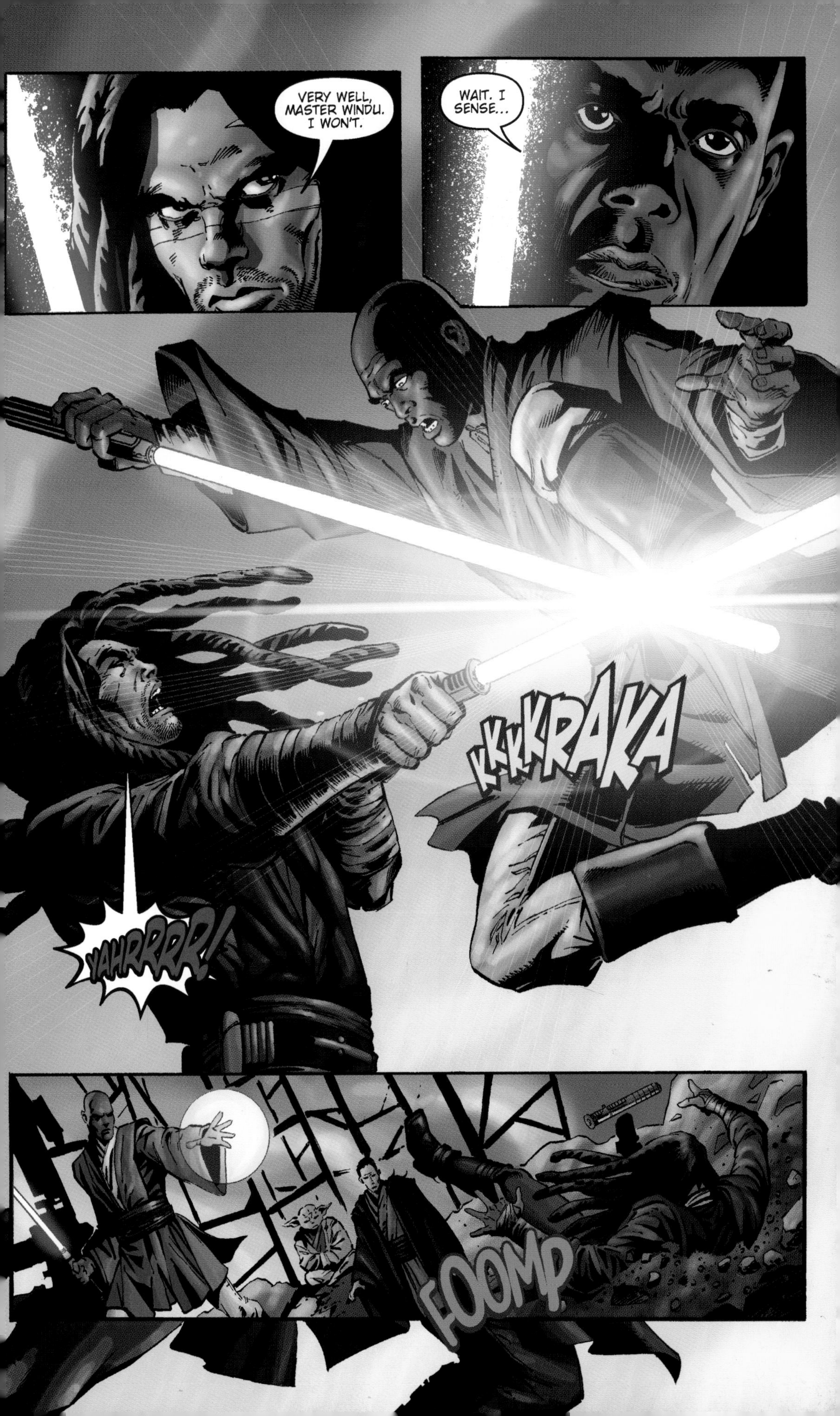
VERY WELL, MASTER WINDU. I WON'T.
WAIT. I SENSE...
KKKKRAKA
YAHRRRR!
FOOMP

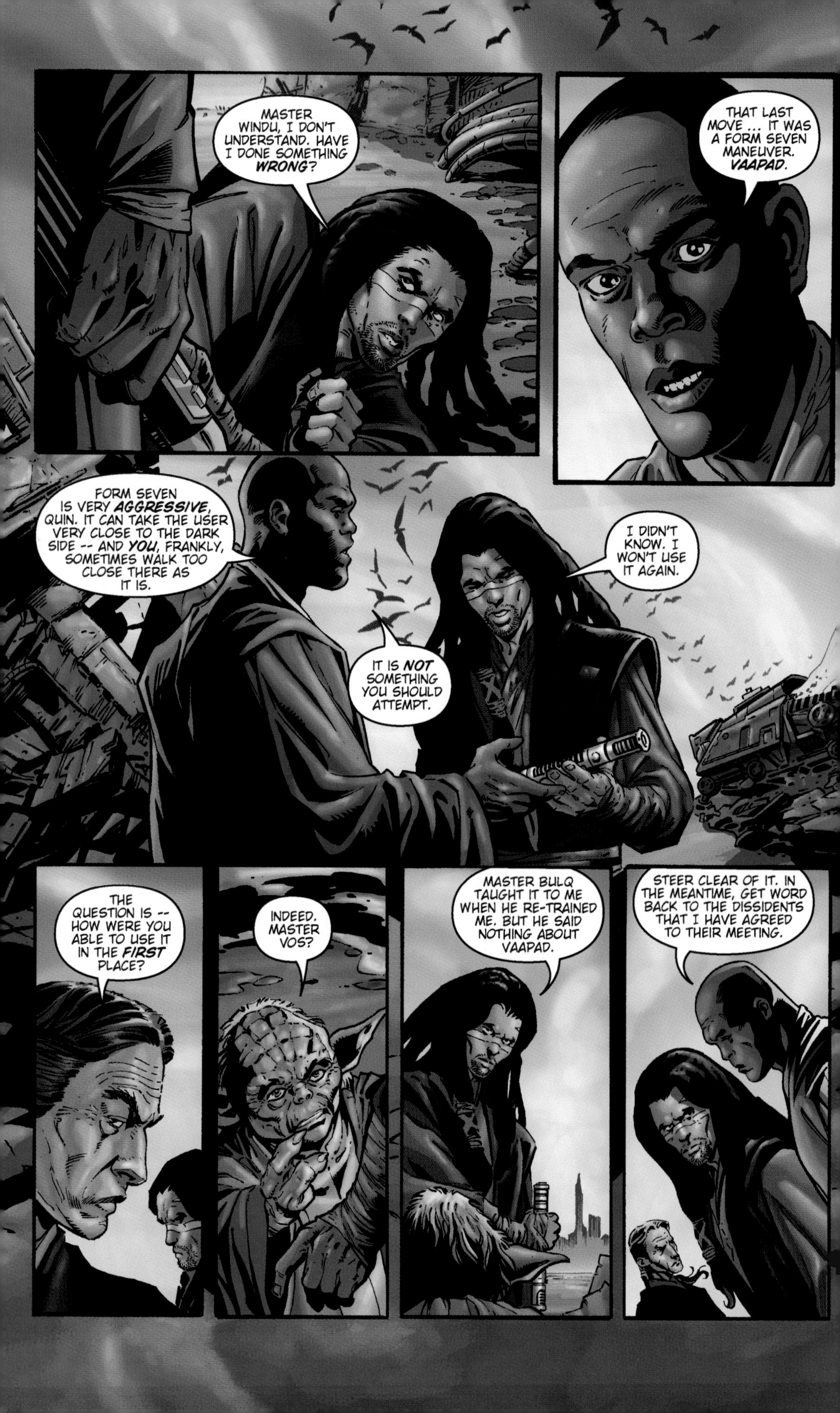
MASTER WINDU, I DON'T UNDERSTAND. HAVE I DONE SOMETHING WRONG?
THAT LAST MOVE ... IT WAS A FORM SEVEN MANEUVER. VAAPAD.
FORM SEVEN IS VERY AGGRESSIVE, QUIN. IT CAN TAKE THE USER VERY CLOSE TO THE DARK SIDE -- AND YOU, FRANKLY, SOMETIMES WALK TOO CLOSE THERE AS IT IS.
I DIDN'T KNOW. I WON'T USE IT AGAIN.
IT IS NOT SOMETHING YOU SHOULD ATTEMPT.
THE QUESTION IS -- HOW WERE YOU ABLE TO USE IT IN THE FIRST PLACE?
INDEED. MASTER VOS?
MASTER BULQ TAUGHT IT TO ME WHEN HE RE-TRAINED ME. BUT HE SAID NOTHING ABOUT VAAPAD.
STEER CLEAR OF IT. IN THE MEANTIME, GET WORD BACK TO THE DISSIDENTS THAT I HAVE AGREED TO THEIR MEETING.

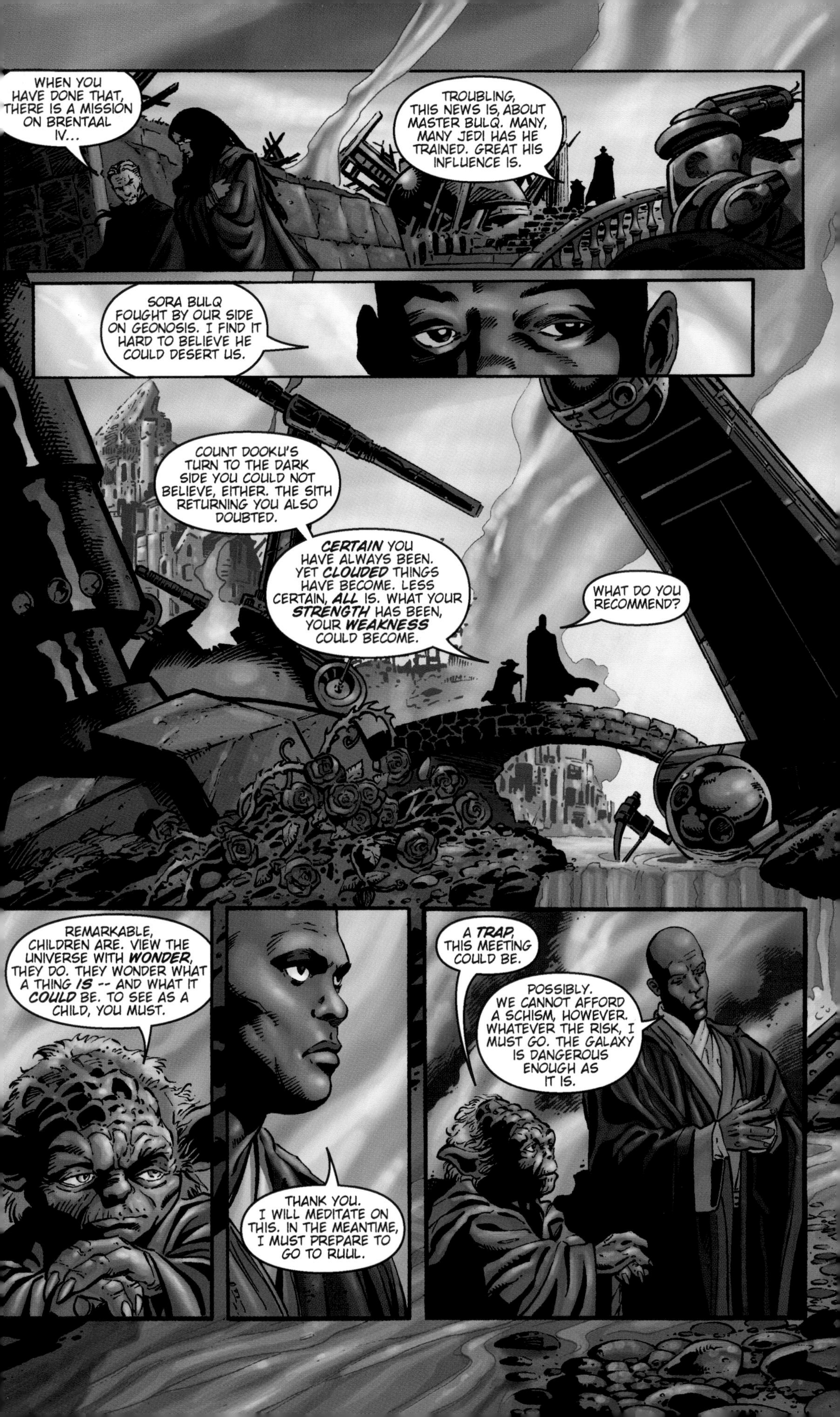
WHEN YOU HAVE DONE THAT, THERE IS A MISSION ON BRENTAAL IV...
TROUBLING, THIS NEWS IS, ABOUT MASTER BULQ. MANY, MANY JEDI HAS HE TRAINED. GREAT HIS INFLUENCE IS.
SORA BULQ FOUGHT BY OUR SIDE ON GEONOSIS. I FIND IT HARD TO BELIEVE HE COULD DESERT US.
COUNT DOOKU'S TURN TO THE DARK SIDE YOU COULD NOT BELIEVE, EITHER. THE SITH RETURNING YOU ALSO DOUBTED.
CERTAIN YOU HAVE ALWAYS BEEN. YET CLOUDED THINGS HAVE BECOME. LESS CERTAIN, ALL IS. WHAT YOUR STRENGTH HAS BEEN, YOUR WEAKNESS COULD BECOME.
WHAT DO YOU RECOMMEND?
REMARKABLE, CHILDREN ARE. VIEW THE UNIVERSE WITH WONDER, THEY DO. THEY WONDER WHAT A THING IS -- AND WHAT IT COULD BE. TO SEE AS A CHILD, YOU MUST.
THANK YOU. I WILL MEDITATE ON THIS. IN THE MEANTIME, I MUST PREPARE TO GO TO RUUL.
A TRAP, THIS MEETING COULD BE.
POSSIBLY. WE CANNOT AFFORD A SCHISM, HOWEVER. WHATEVER THE RISK, I MUST GO. THE GALAXY IS DANGEROUS ENOUGH AS IT IS.

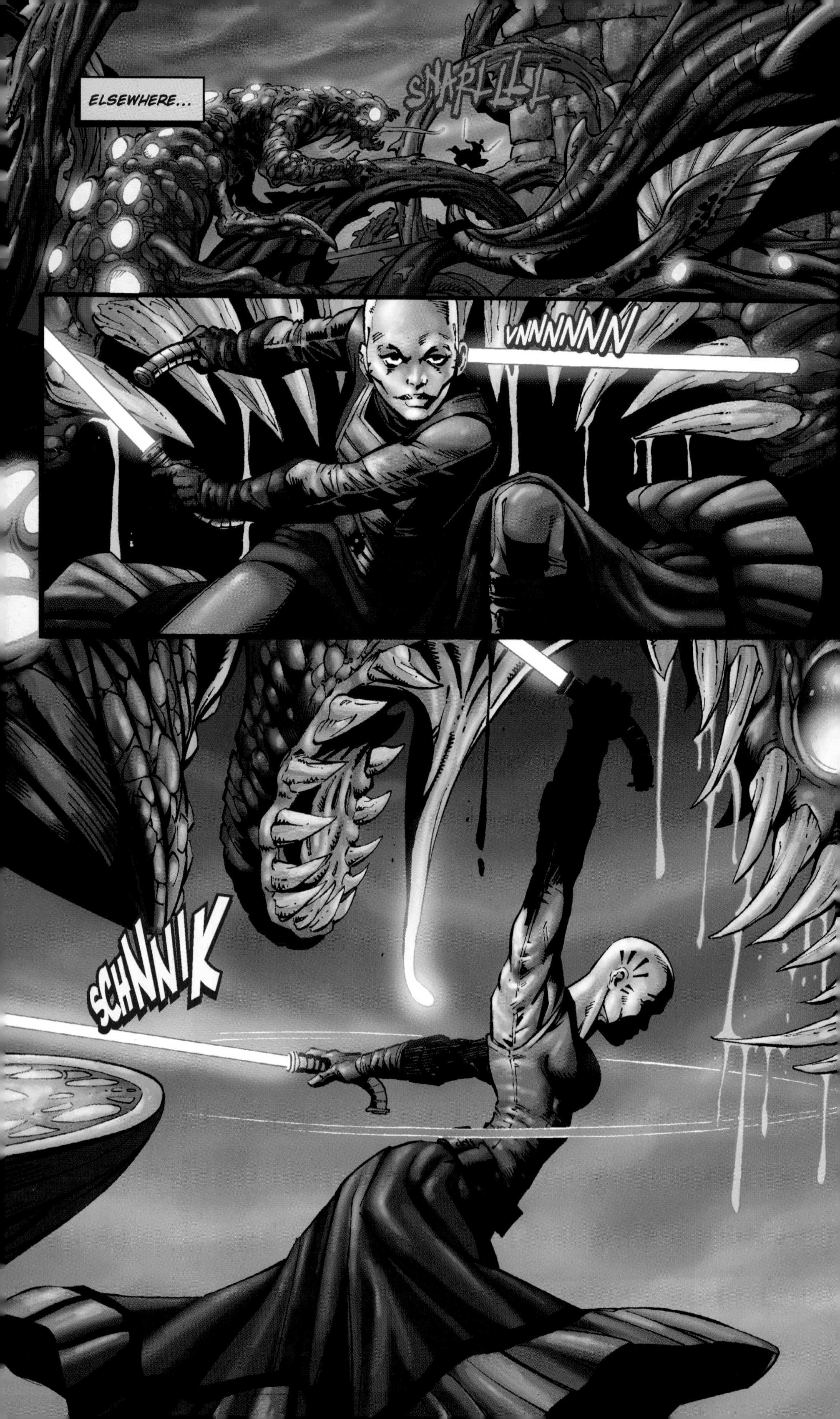
ELSEWHERE...
SNARLLLL
VNNNNNN
SCHNNIK

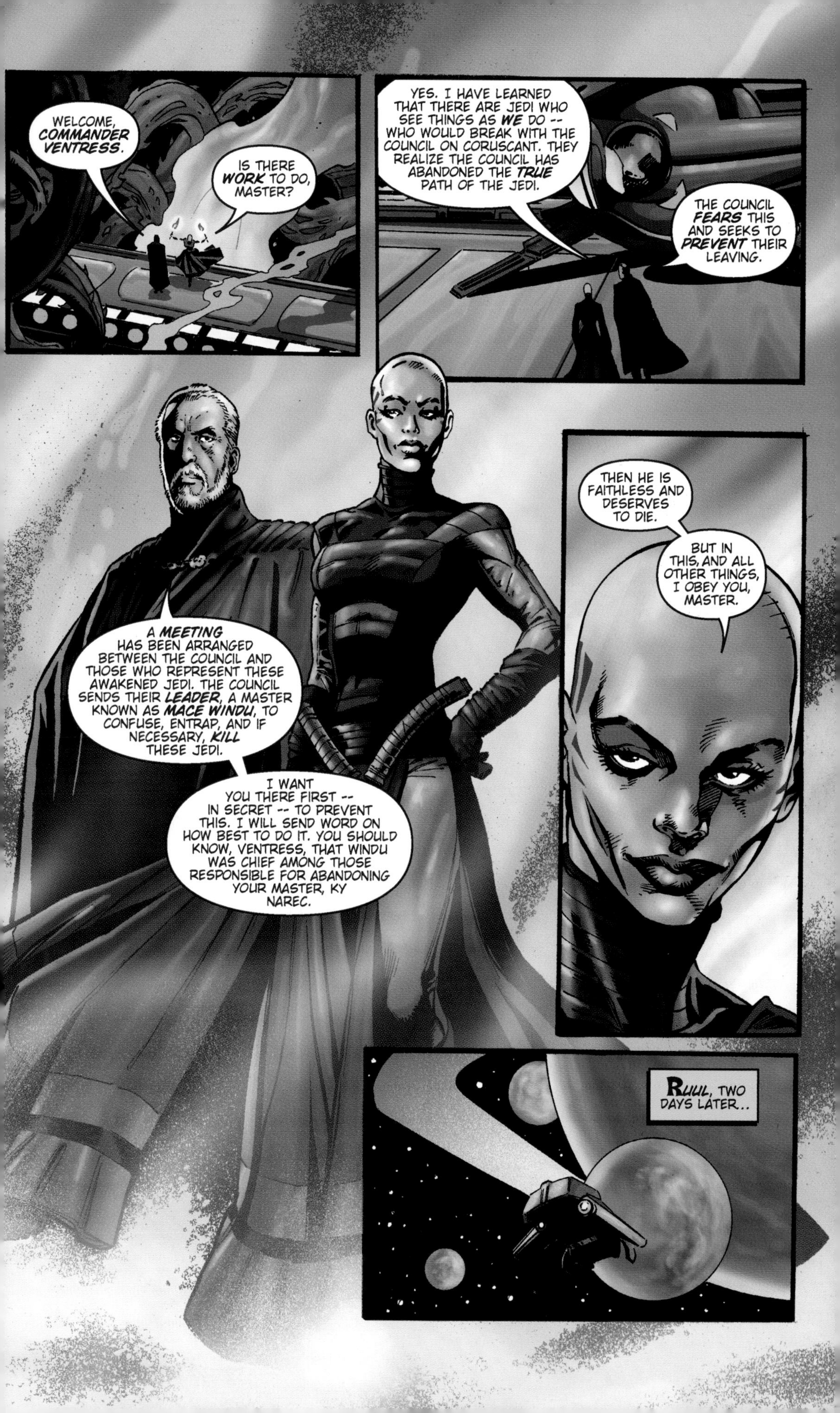

WELCOME, COMMANDER VENTRESS.
IS THERE WORK TO DO, MASTER?
YES. I HAVE LEARNED THAT THERE ARE JEDI WHO SEE THINGS AS WE DO -- WHO WOULD BREAK WITH THE COUNCIL ON CORUSCANT. THEY REALIZE THE COUNCIL HAS ABANDONED THE TRUE PATH OF THE JEDI.
THE COUNCIL FEARS THIS AND SEEKS TO PREVENT THEIR LEAVING.
A MEETING HAS BEEN ARRANGED BETWEEN THE COUNCIL AND THOSE WHO REPRESENT THESE AWAKENED JEDI. THE COUNCIL SENDS THEIR LEADER, A MASTER KNOWN AS MACE WINDU, TO CONFUSE, ENTRAP, AND IF NECESSARY, KILL THESE JEDI.
I WANT YOU THERE FIRST -- IN SECRET -- TO PREVENT THIS. I WILL SEND WORD ON HOW BEST TO DO IT. YOU SHOULD KNOW, VENTRESS, THAT WINDU WAS CHIEF AMONG THOSE RESPONSIBLE FOR ABANDONING YOUR MASTER, KY NAREC.
THEN HE IS FAITHLESS AND DESERVES TO DIE.
BUT IN THIS, AND ALL OTHER THINGS, I OBEY YOU, MASTER.
RUUL, TWO DAYS LATER...

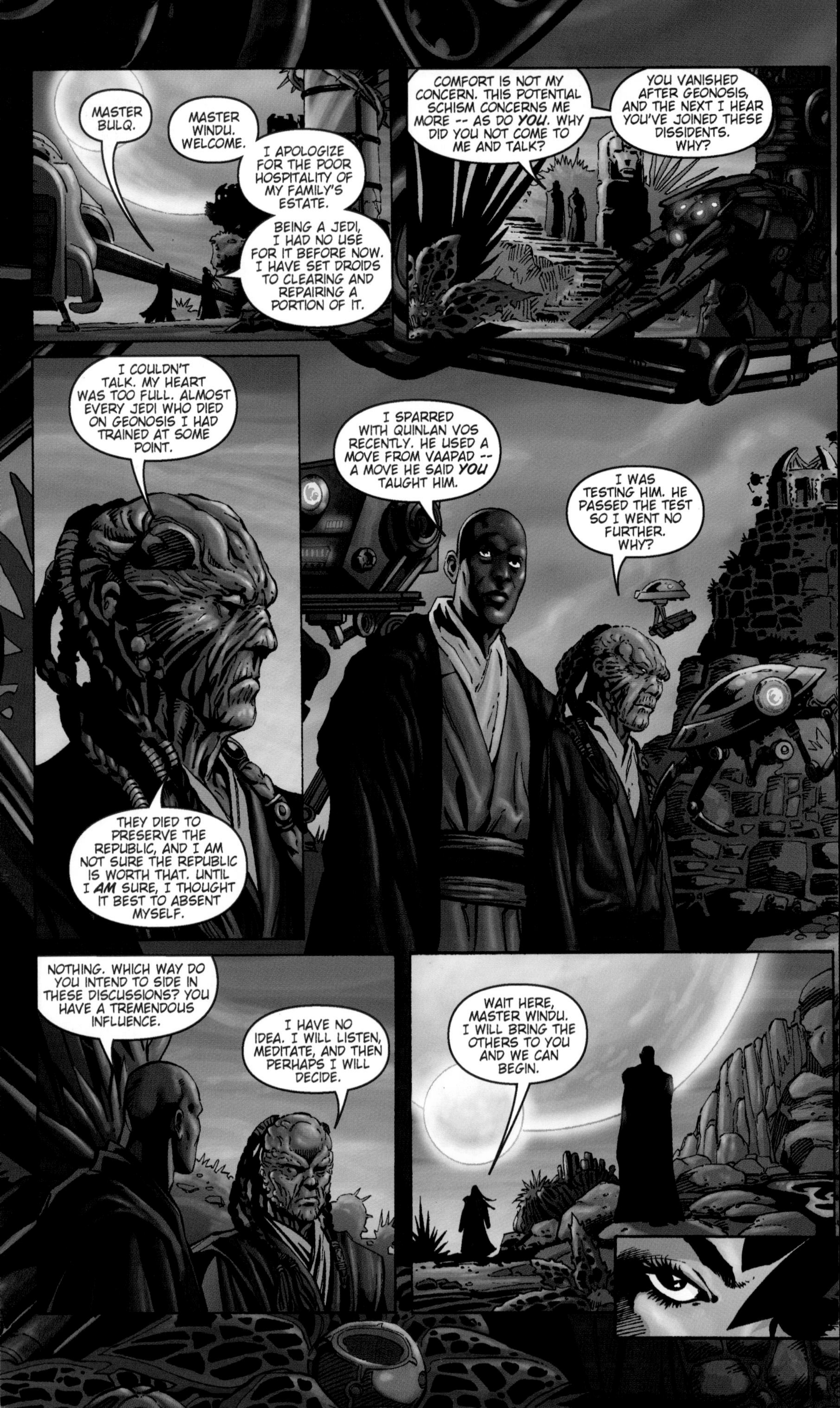
MASTER BULQ.
MASTER WINDU. WELCOME.
I APOLOGIZE FOR THE POOR HOSPITALITY OF MY FAMILY'S ESTATE.
BEING A JEDI, I HAD NO USE FOR IT BEFORE NOW. I HAVE SET DROIDS TO CLEARING AND REPAIRING A PORTION OF IT.
COMFORT IS NOT MY CONCERN. THIS POTENTIAL SCHISM CONCERNS ME MORE -- AS DO YOU. WHY DID YOU NOT COME TO ME AND TALK?
YOU VANISHED AFTER GEONOSIS, AND THE NEXT I HEAR YOU'VE JOINED THESE DISSIDENTS. WHY?
I COULDN'T TALK. MY HEART WAS TOO FULL. ALMOST EVERY JEDI WHO DIED ON GEONOSIS I HAD TRAINED AT SOME POINT.
THEY DIED TO PRESERVE THE REPUBLIC, AND I AM NOT SURE THE REPUBLIC IS WORTH THAT. UNTIL I AM SURE, I THOUGHT IT BEST TO ABSENT MYSELF.
I SPARRED WITH QUINLAN VOS RECENTLY. HE USED A MOVE FROM VAAPAD -- A MOVE HE SAID YOU TAUGHT HIM.
I WAS TESTING HIM. HE PASSED THE TEST SO I WENT NO FURTHER. WHY?
NOTHING. WHICH WAY DO YOU INTEND TO SIDE IN THESE DISCUSSIONS? YOU HAVE A TREMENDOUS INFLUENCE.
I HAVE NO IDEA. I WILL LISTEN, MEDITATE, AND THEN PERHAPS I WILL DECIDE.
WAIT HERE, MASTER WINDU. I WILL BRING THE OTHERS TO YOU AND WE CAN BEGIN.

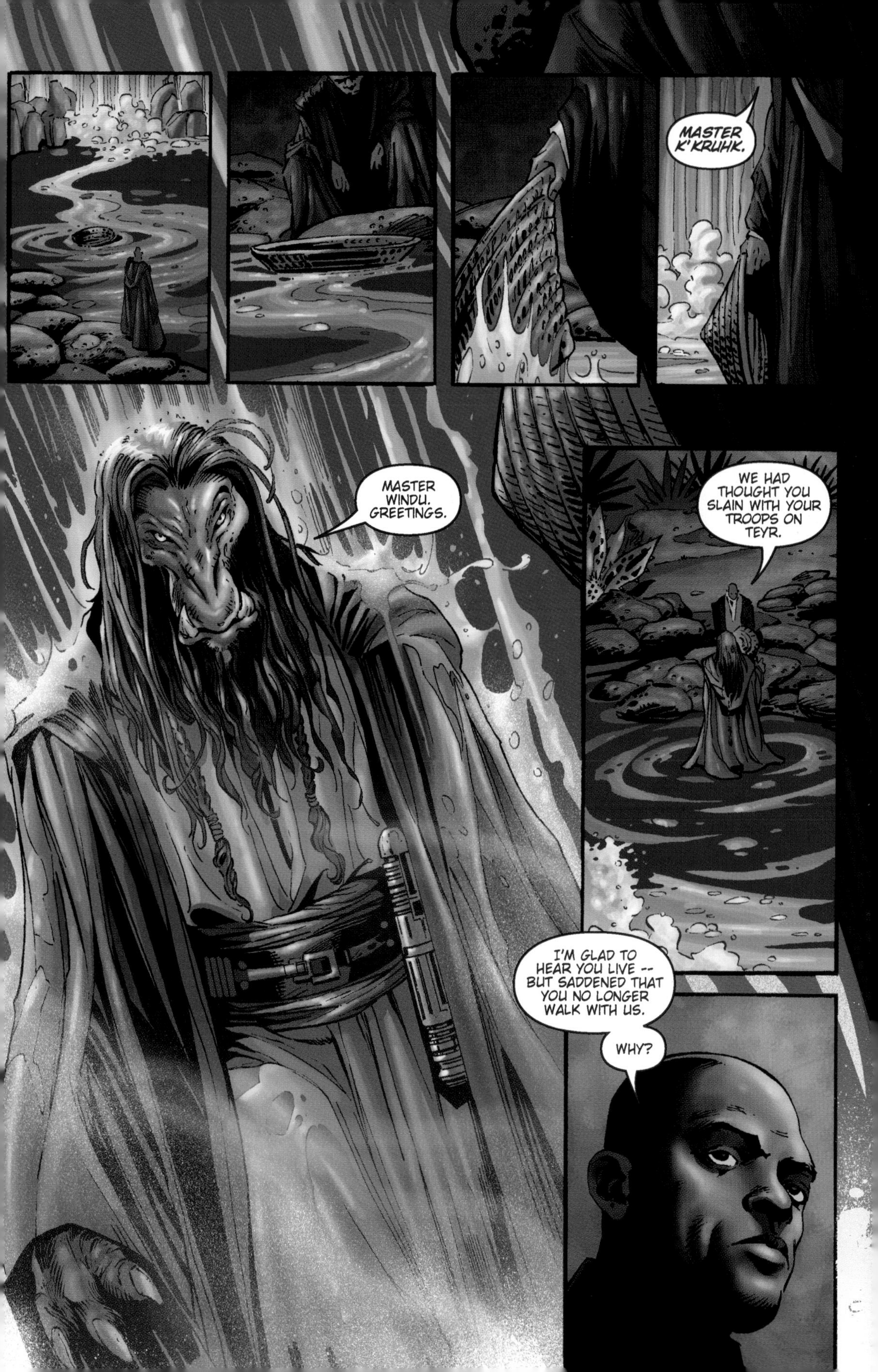
MASTER K'KRUHK.
MASTER WINDU. GREETINGS.
WE HAD THOUGHT YOU SLAIN WITH YOUR TROOPS ON TEYR.
I'M GLAD TO HEAR YOU LIVE -- BUT SADDENED THAT YOU NO LONGER WALK WITH US.
WHY?

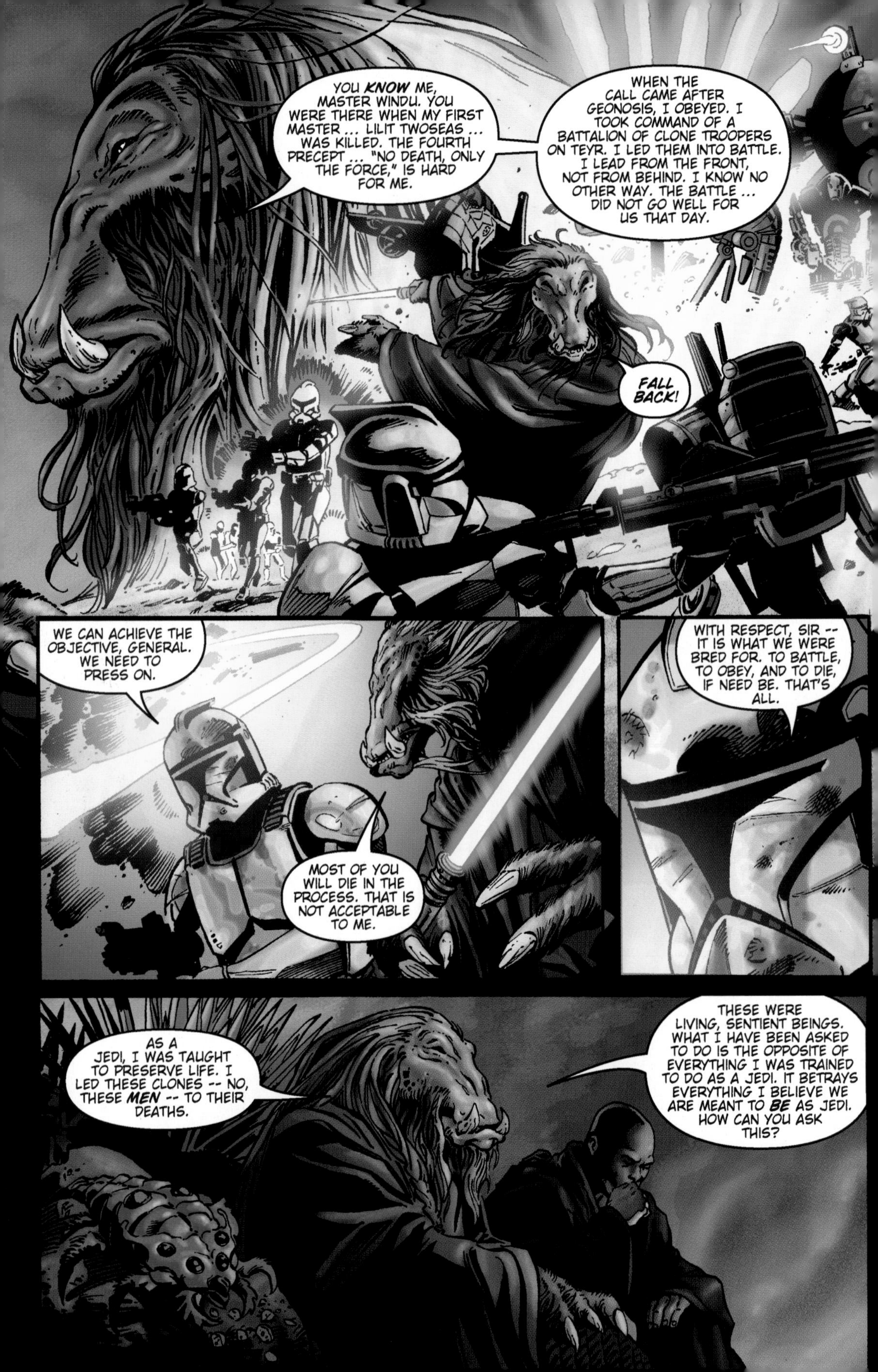
YOU *KNOW* ME, MASTER WINDU. YOU WERE THERE WHEN MY FIRST MASTER ... LILIT TWOSEAS ... WAS KILLED. THE FOURTH PRECEPT ... "NO DEATH, ONLY THE FORCE," IS HARD FOR ME.
WHEN THE CALL CAME AFTER GEONOSIS, I OBEYED. I TOOK COMMAND OF A BATTALION OF CLONE TROOPERS ON TEYR. I LED THEM INTO BATTLE. I LEAD FROM THE FRONT, NOT FROM BEHIND. I KNOW NO OTHER WAY. THE BATTLE ... DID NOT GO WELL FOR US THAT DAY.
FALL BACK!
WE CAN ACHIEVE THE OBJECTIVE, GENERAL. WE NEED TO PRESS ON.
MOST OF YOU WILL DIE IN THE PROCESS. THAT IS NOT ACCEPTABLE TO ME.
WITH RESPECT, SIR -- IT IS WHAT WE WERE BRED FOR. TO BATTLE, TO OBEY, AND TO DIE, IF NEED BE. THAT'S ALL.
AS A JEDI, I WAS TAUGHT TO PRESERVE LIFE. I LED THESE CLONES -- NO, THESE *MEN* -- TO THEIR DEATHS.
THESE WERE LIVING, SENTIENT BEINGS. WHAT I HAVE BEEN ASKED TO DO IS THE OPPOSITE OF EVERYTHING I WAS TRAINED TO DO AS A JEDI. IT BETRAYS EVERYTHING I BELIEVE WE ARE MEANT TO *BE* AS JEDI. HOW CAN YOU ASK THIS?

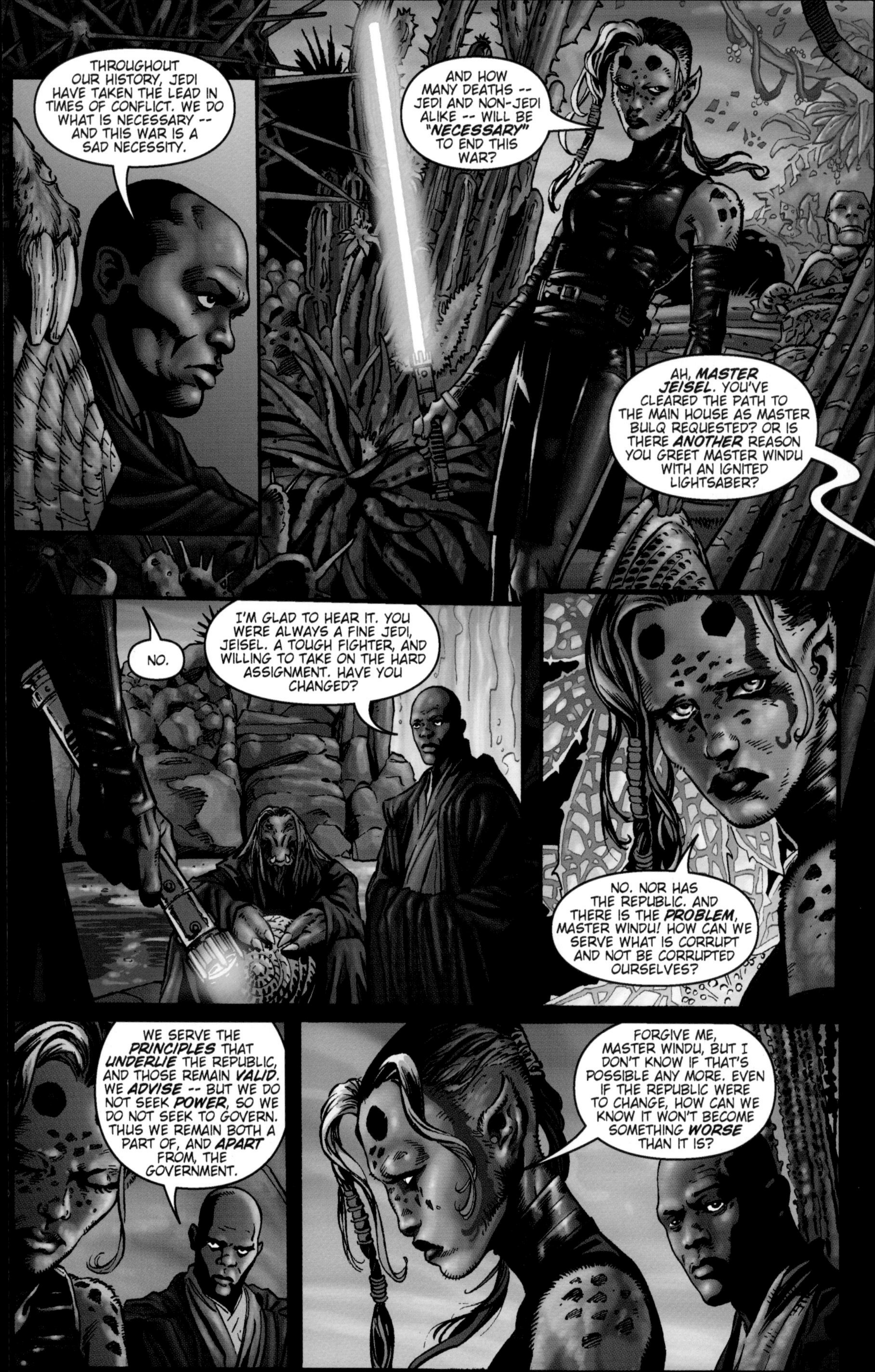
THROUGHOUT OUR HISTORY, JEDI HAVE TAKEN THE LEAD IN TIMES OF CONFLICT. WE DO WHAT IS NECESSARY -- AND THIS WAR IS A SAD NECESSITY.
AND HOW MANY DEATHS -- JEDI AND NON-JEDI ALIKE -- WILL BE "NECESSARY" TO END THIS WAR?
AH, MASTER JEISEL. YOU'VE CLEARED THE PATH TO THE MAIN HOUSE AS MASTER BULQ REQUESTED? OR IS THERE ANOTHER REASON YOU GREET MASTER WINDU WITH AN IGNITED LIGHTSABER?
NO.
I'M GLAD TO HEAR IT. YOU WERE ALWAYS A FINE JEDI, JEISEL. A TOUGH FIGHTER, AND WILLING TO TAKE ON THE HARD ASSIGNMENT. HAVE YOU CHANGED?
NO. NOR HAS THE REPUBLIC. AND THERE IS THE PROBLEM, MASTER WINDU! HOW CAN WE SERVE WHAT IS CORRUPT AND NOT BE CORRUPTED OURSELVES?
WE SERVE THE PRINCIPLES THAT UNDERLIE THE REPUBLIC, AND THOSE REMAIN VALID. WE ADVISE -- BUT WE DO NOT SEEK POWER, SO WE DO NOT SEEK TO GOVERN. THUS WE REMAIN BOTH A PART OF, AND APART FROM, THE GOVERNMENT.
FORGIVE ME, MASTER WINDU, BUT I DON'T KNOW IF THAT'S POSSIBLE ANY MORE. EVEN IF THE REPUBLIC WERE TO CHANGE, HOW CAN WE KNOW IT WON'T BECOME SOMETHING WORSE THAN IT IS?

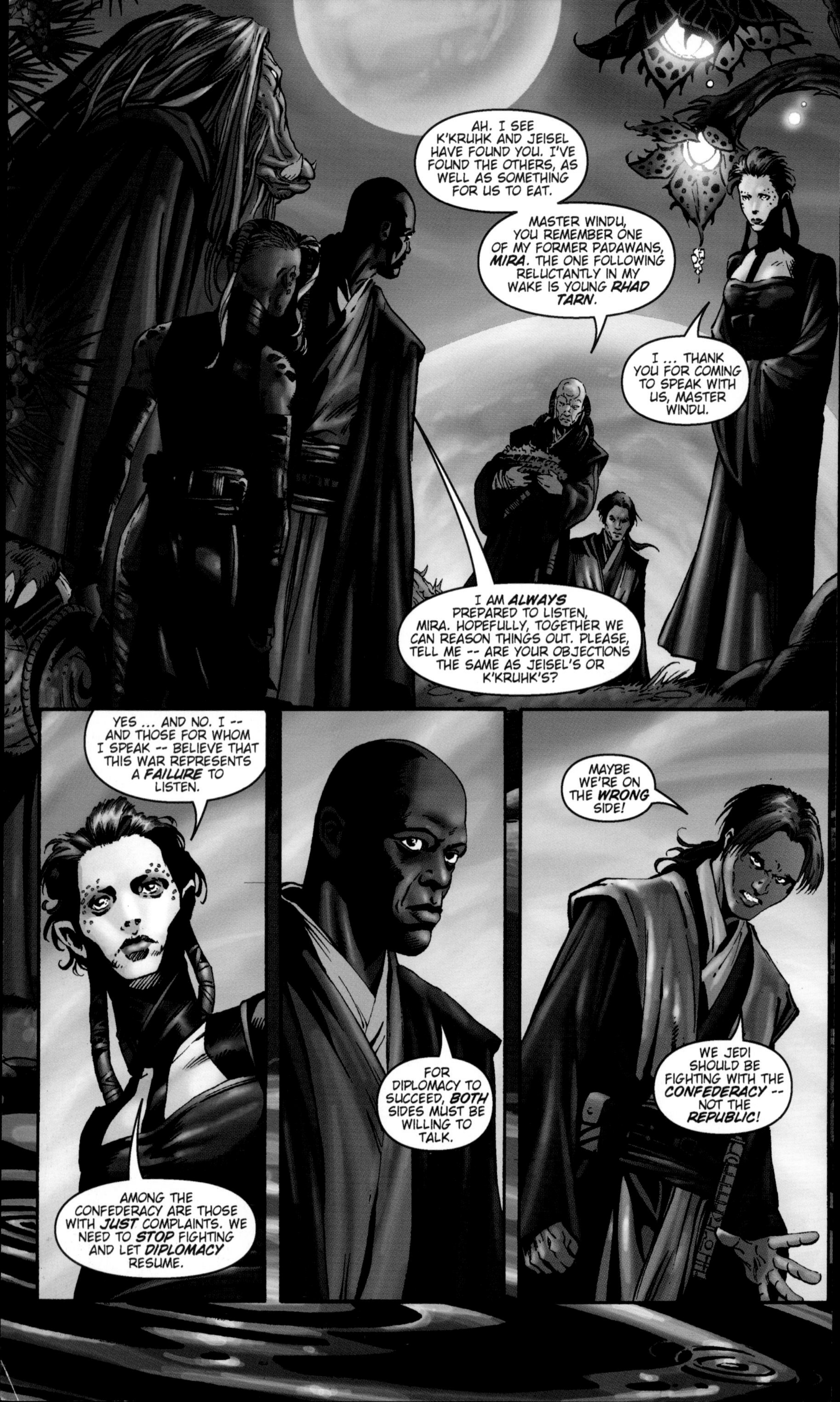
AH. I SEE K'KRUHK AND JEISEL HAVE FOUND YOU. I'VE FOUND THE OTHERS, AS WELL AS SOMETHING FOR US TO EAT.
MASTER WINDU, YOU REMEMBER ONE OF MY FORMER PADAWANS, MIRA. THE ONE FOLLOWING RELUCTANTLY IN MY WAKE IS YOUNG RHAD TARN.
I ... THANK YOU FOR COMING TO SPEAK WITH US, MASTER WINDU.
I AM ALWAYS PREPARED TO LISTEN, MIRA. HOPEFULLY, TOGETHER WE CAN REASON THINGS OUT. PLEASE, TELL ME -- ARE YOUR OBJECTIONS THE SAME AS JEISEL'S OR K'KRUHK'S?
YES ... AND NO. I -- AND THOSE FOR WHOM I SPEAK -- BELIEVE THAT THIS WAR REPRESENTS A FAILURE TO LISTEN.
AMONG THE CONFEDERACY ARE THOSE WITH JUST COMPLAINTS. WE NEED TO STOP FIGHTING AND LET DIPLOMACY RESUME.
FOR DIPLOMACY TO SUCCEED, BOTH SIDES MUST BE WILLING TO TALK.
MAYBE WE'RE ON THE WRONG SIDE!
WE JEDI SHOULD BE FIGHTING WITH THE CONFEDERACY -- NOT THE REPUBLIC!

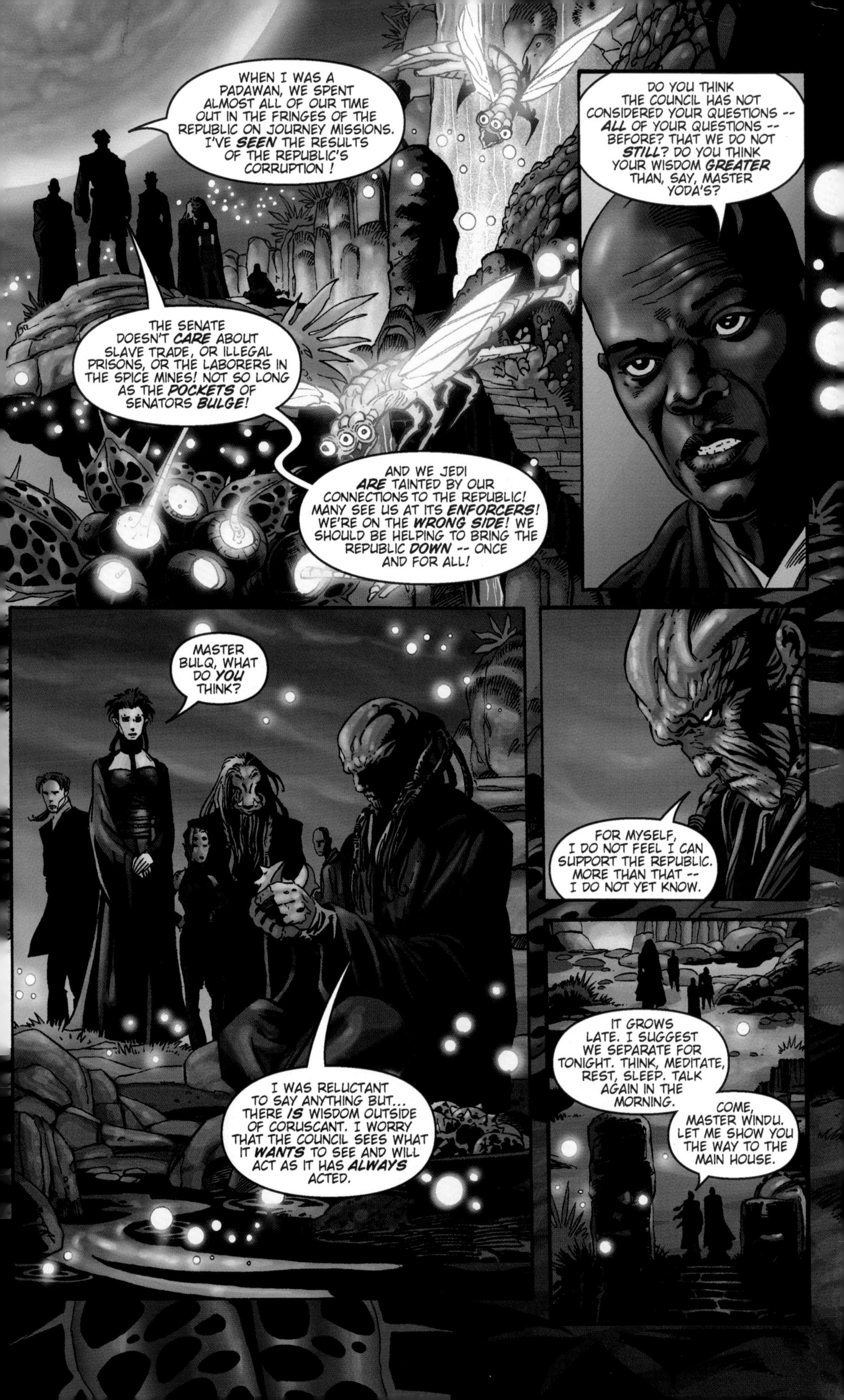
WHEN I WAS A PADAWAN, WE SPENT ALMOST ALL OF OUR TIME OUT IN THE FRINGES OF THE REPUBLIC ON JOURNEY MISSIONS. I'VE SEEN THE RESULTS OF THE REPUBLIC'S CORRUPTION !
THE SENATE DOESN'T CARE ABOUT SLAVE TRADE, OR ILLEGAL PRISONS, OR THE LABORERS IN THE SPICE MINES! NOT SO LONG AS THE POCKETS OF SENATORS BULGE!
AND WE JEDI ARE TAINTED BY OUR CONNECTIONS TO THE REPUBLIC! MANY SEE US AT ITS ENFORCERS! WE'RE ON THE WRONG SIDE! WE SHOULD BE HELPING TO BRING THE REPUBLIC DOWN -- ONCE AND FOR ALL!
DO YOU THINK THE COUNCIL HAS NOT CONSIDERED YOUR QUESTIONS -- ALL OF YOUR QUESTIONS -- BEFORE? THAT WE DO NOT STILL? DO YOU THINK YOUR WISDOM GREATER THAN, SAY, MASTER YODA'S?
MASTER BULQ, WHAT DO YOU THINK?
I WAS RELUCTANT TO SAY ANYTHING BUT... THERE IS WISDOM OUTSIDE OF CORUSCANT. I WORRY THAT THE COUNCIL SEES WHAT IT WANTS TO SEE AND WILL ACT AS IT HAS ALWAYS ACTED.
FOR MYSELF, I DO NOT FEEL I CAN SUPPORT THE REPUBLIC. MORE THAN THAT -- I DO NOT YET KNOW.
IT GROWS LATE. I SUGGEST WE SEPARATE FOR TONIGHT. THINK, MEDITATE, REST, SLEEP. TALK AGAIN IN THE MORNING.
COME, MASTER WINDU. LET ME SHOW YOU THE WAY TO THE MAIN HOUSE.

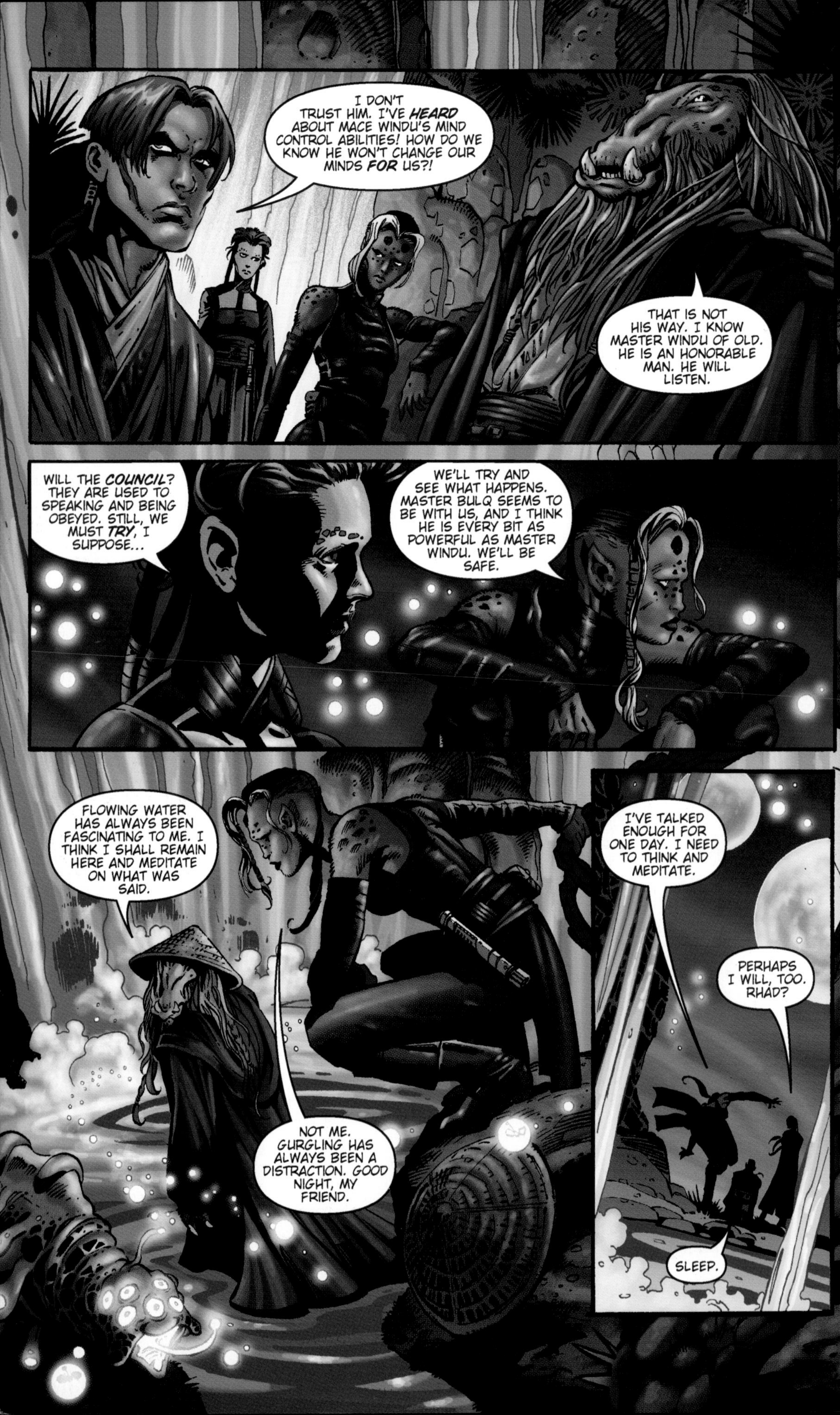
I DON'T TRUST HIM. I'VE HEARD ABOUT MACE WINDU'S MIND CONTROL ABILITIES! HOW DO WE KNOW HE WON'T CHANGE OUR MINDS FOR US?!
THAT IS NOT HIS WAY. I KNOW MASTER WINDU OF OLD. HE IS AN HONORABLE MAN. HE WILL LISTEN.
WILL THE COUNCIL? THEY ARE USED TO SPEAKING AND BEING OBEYED. STILL, WE MUST TRY, I SUPPOSE...
WE'LL TRY AND SEE WHAT HAPPENS. MASTER BULQ SEEMS TO BE WITH US, AND I THINK HE IS EVERY BIT AS POWERFUL AS MASTER WINDU. WE'LL BE SAFE.
FLOWING WATER HAS ALWAYS BEEN FASCINATING TO ME. I THINK I SHALL REMAIN HERE AND MEDITATE ON WHAT WAS SAID.
NOT ME. GURGLING HAS ALWAYS BEEN A DISTRACTION. GOOD NIGHT, MY FRIEND.
I'VE TALKED ENOUGH FOR ONE DAY. I NEED TO THINK AND MEDITATE.
PERHAPS I WILL, TOO. RHAD?
SLEEP.

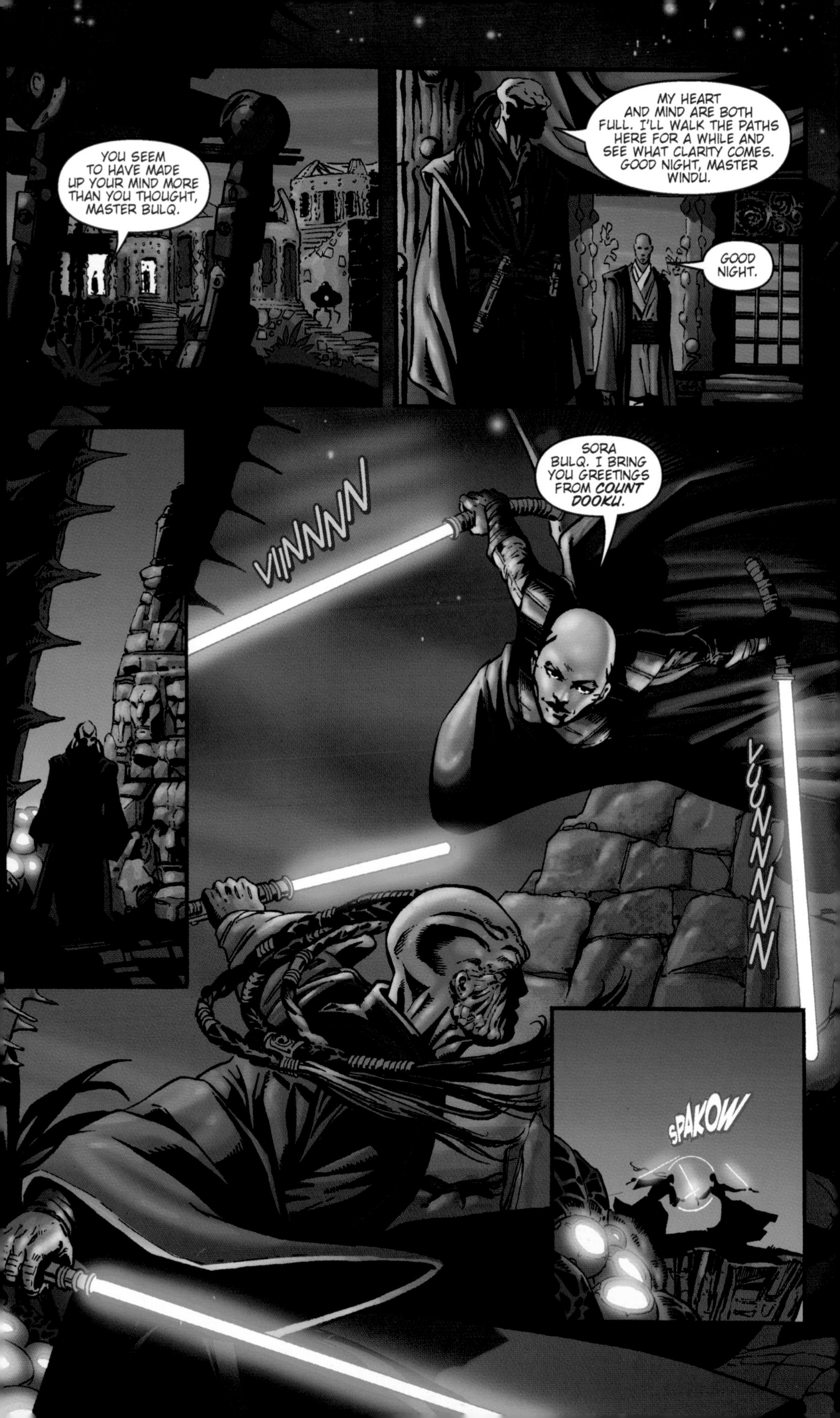
YOU SEEM TO HAVE MADE UP YOUR MIND MORE THAN YOU THOUGHT, MASTER BULQ.
MY HEART AND MIND ARE BOTH FULL. I'LL WALK THE PATHS HERE FOR A WHILE AND SEE WHAT CLARITY COMES. GOOD NIGHT, MASTER WINDU.
GOOD NIGHT.
SORA BULQ. I BRING YOU GREETINGS FROM COUNT DOOKU.
VIINNNN
VUNNNNNNN
SPAKOW

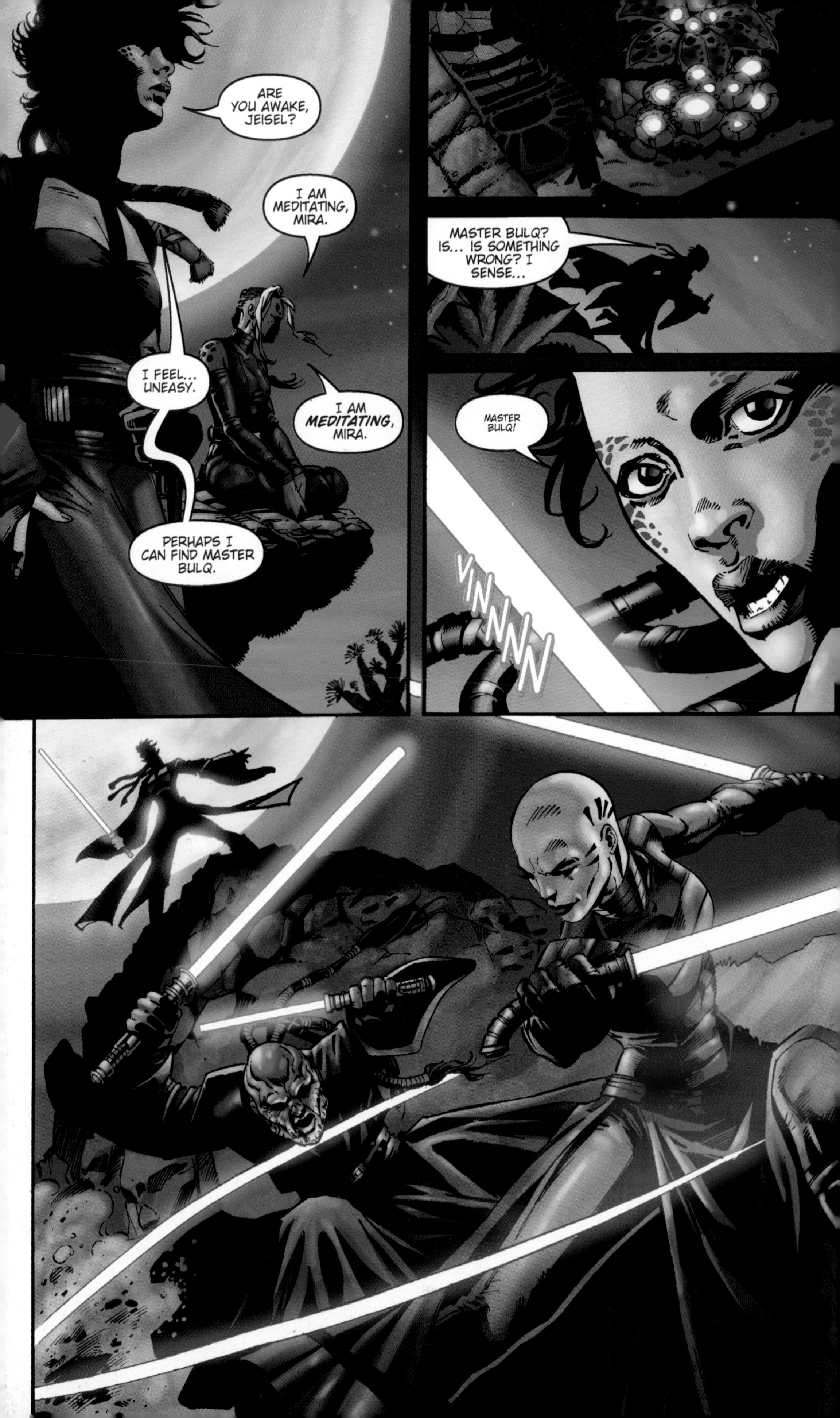
ARE YOU AWAKE, JEISEL?
I AM MEDITATING, MIRA.
I FEEL... UNEASY.
I AM MEDITATING, MIRA.
PERHAPS I CAN FIND MASTER BULQ.
MASTER BULQ? IS... IS SOMETHING WRONG? I SENSE...
MASTER BULQ!
VINNNNN

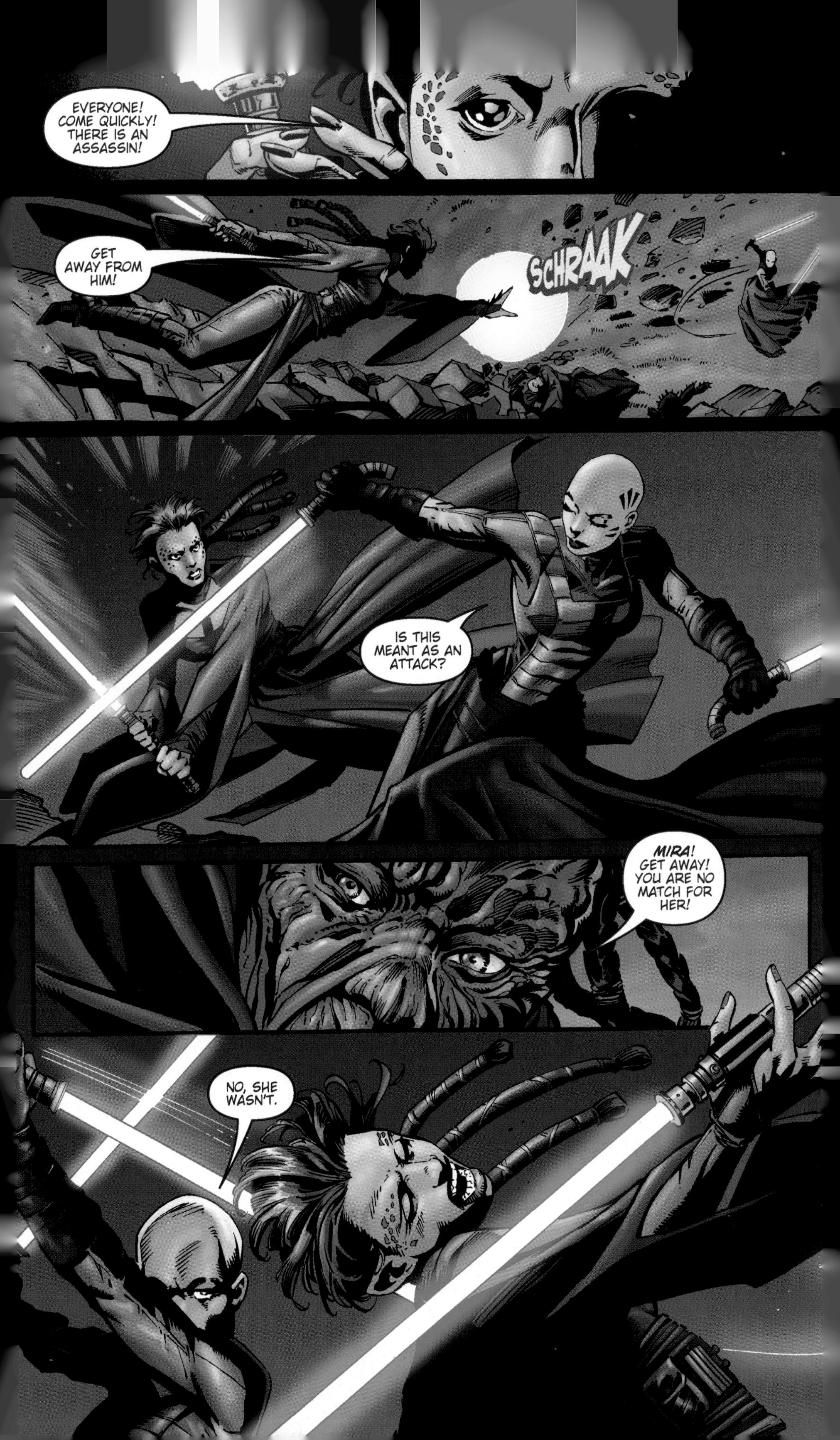
EVERYONE! COME QUICKLY! THERE IS AN ASSASSIN!
GET AWAY FROM HIM!
SCHRAAK
IS THIS MEANT AS AN ATTACK?
MIRA! GET AWAY! YOU ARE NO MATCH FOR HER!
NO, SHE WASN'T.

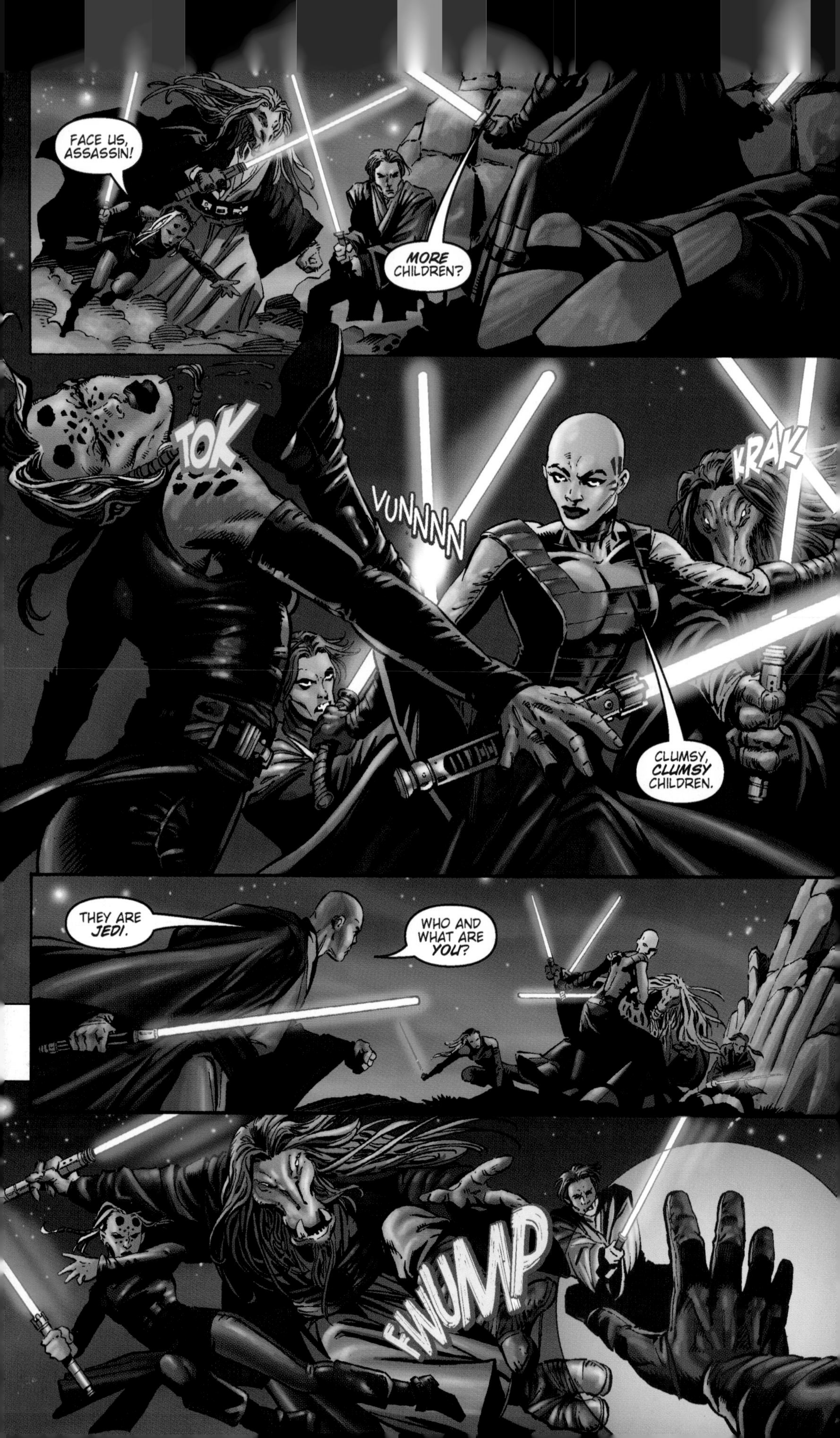

FACE US, ASSASSIN!
MORE CHILDREN?
TOK
VUNNNN
KRAK
CLUMSY, CLUMSY CHILDREN.
THEY ARE JEDI.
WHO AND WHAT ARE YOU?
FWUMP

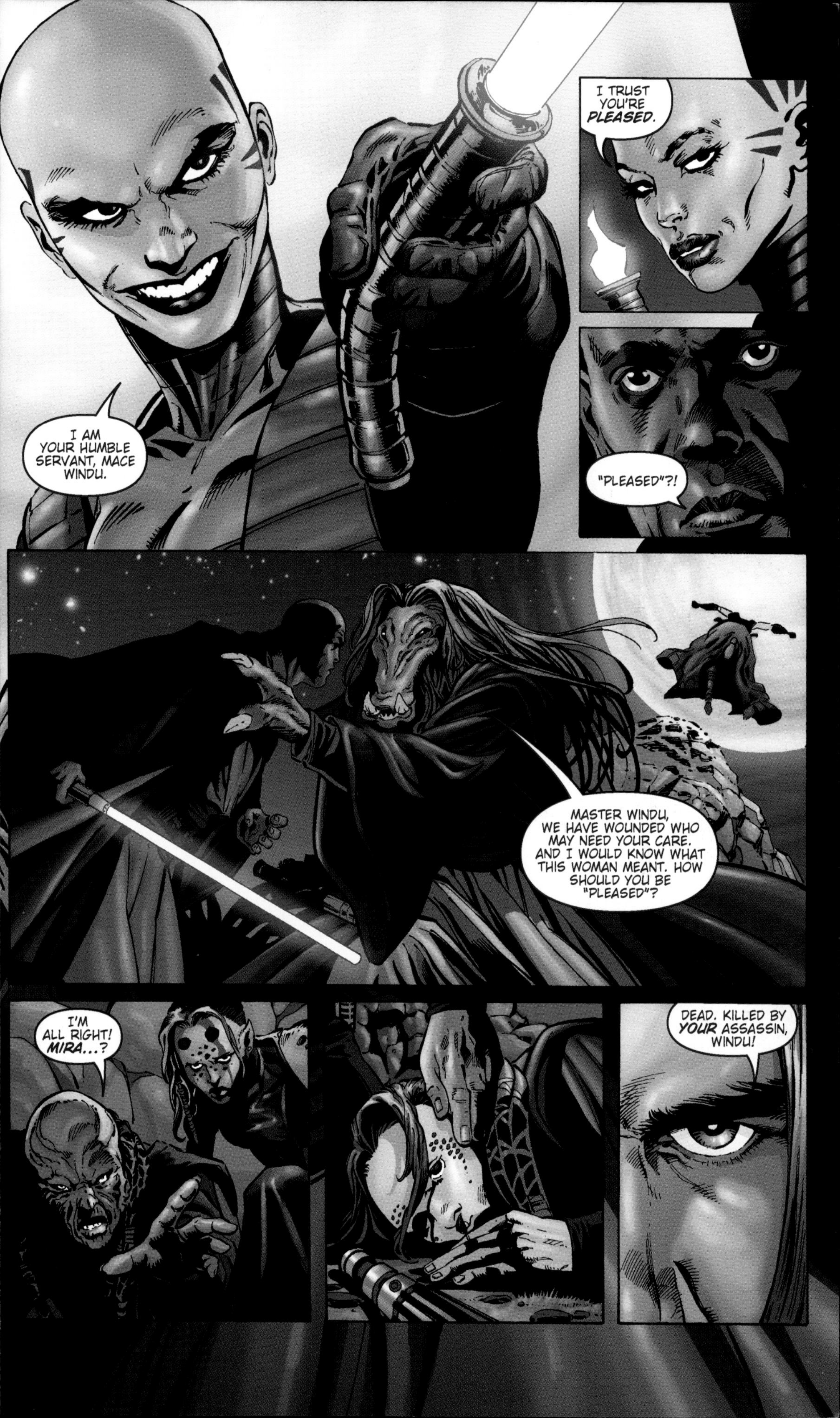
I TRUST YOU'RE *PLEASED*.
I AM YOUR HUMBLE SERVANT, MACE WINDU.
"PLEASED"?!
MASTER WINDU, WE HAVE WOUNDED WHO MAY NEED YOUR CARE. AND I WOULD KNOW WHAT THIS WOMAN MEANT. HOW SHOULD YOU BE "PLEASED"?
I'M ALL RIGHT! *MIRA*...?
DEAD. KILLED BY *YOUR* ASSASSIN, WINDU!

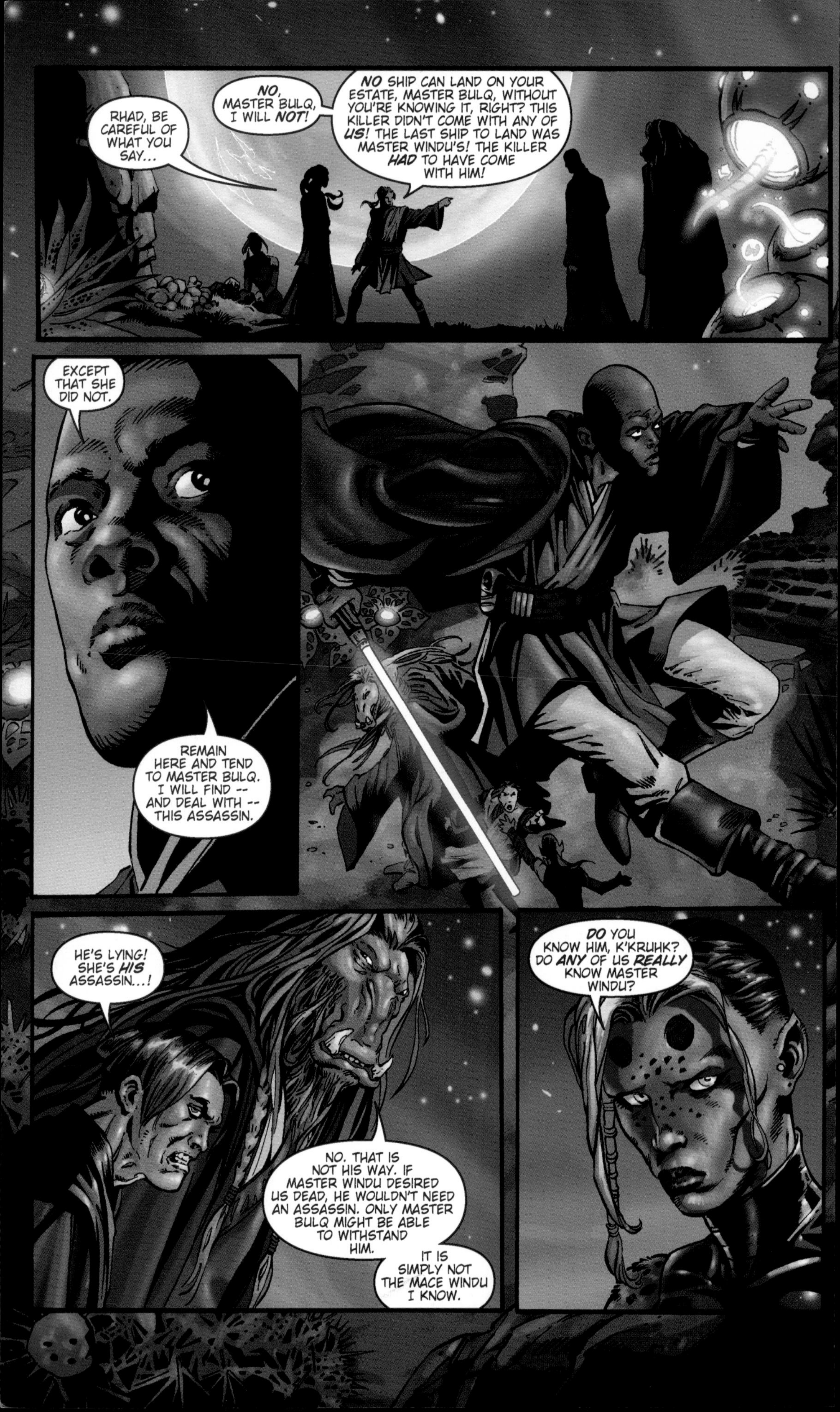
RHAD, BE CAREFUL OF WHAT YOU SAY...
NO, MASTER BULQ, I WILL NOT!
NO SHIP CAN LAND ON YOUR ESTATE, MASTER BULQ, WITHOUT YOU'RE KNOWING IT, RIGHT? THIS KILLER DIDN'T COME WITH ANY OF US! THE LAST SHIP TO LAND WAS MASTER WINDU'S! THE KILLER HAD TO HAVE COME WITH HIM!
EXCEPT THAT SHE DID NOT.
REMAIN HERE AND TEND TO MASTER BULQ. I WILL FIND -- AND DEAL WITH -- THIS ASSASSIN.
HE'S LYING! SHE'S HIS ASSASSIN...!
NO. THAT IS NOT HIS WAY. IF MASTER WINDU DESIRED US DEAD, HE WOULDN'T NEED AN ASSASSIN. ONLY MASTER BULQ MIGHT BE ABLE TO WITHSTAND HIM.
IT IS SIMPLY NOT THE MACE WINDU I KNOW.
DO YOU KNOW HIM, K'KRUHK? DO ANY OF US REALLY KNOW MASTER WINDU?

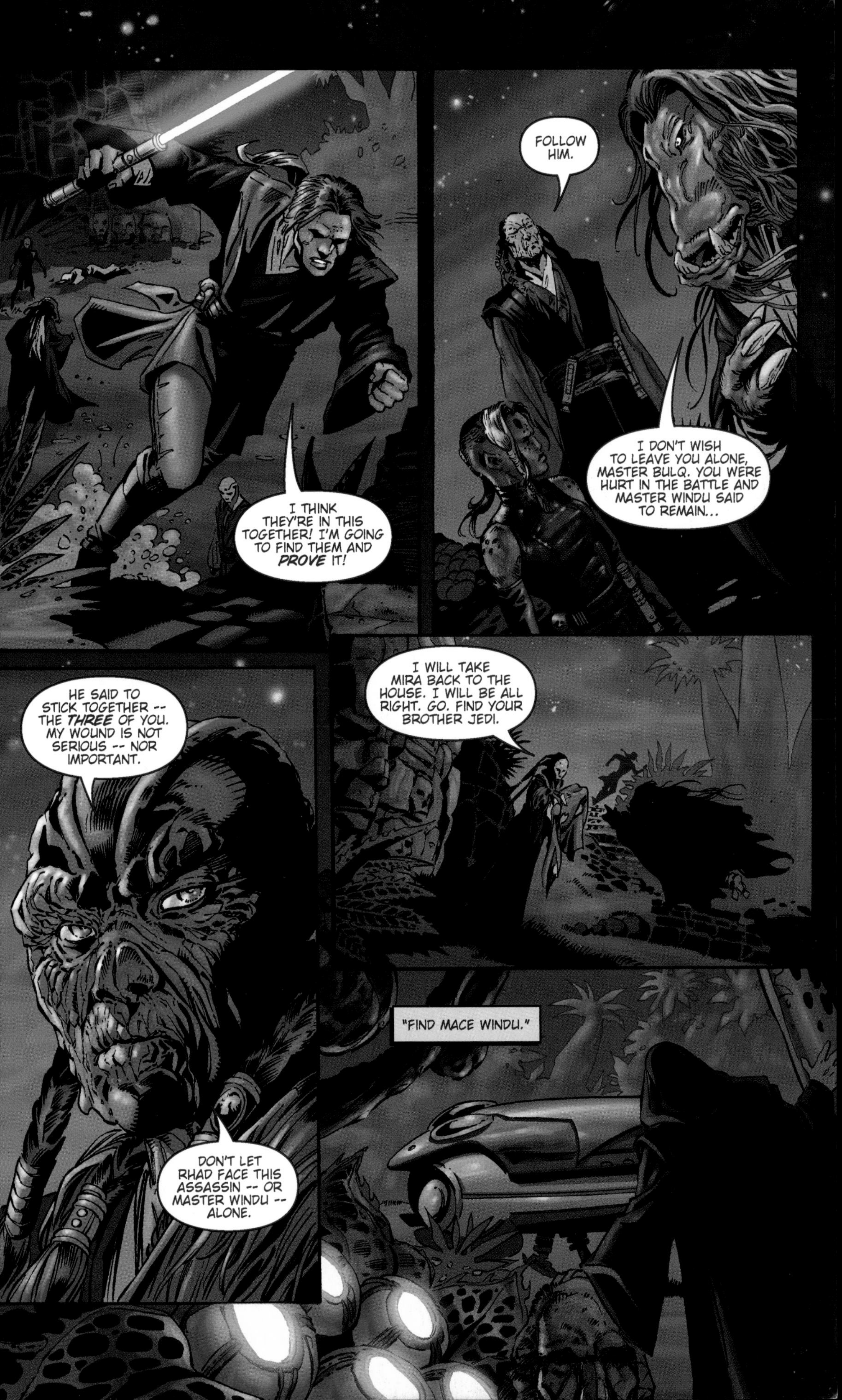
I THINK THEY'RE IN THIS TOGETHER! I'M GOING TO FIND THEM AND *PROVE* IT!
FOLLOW HIM.
I DON'T WISH TO LEAVE YOU ALONE, MASTER BULQ. YOU WERE HURT IN THE BATTLE AND MASTER WINDU SAID TO REMAIN...
HE SAID TO STICK TOGETHER -- THE *THREE* OF YOU. MY WOUND IS NOT SERIOUS -- NOR IMPORTANT.
DON'T LET RHAD FACE THIS ASSASSIN -- OR MASTER WINDU -- ALONE.
I WILL TAKE MIRA BACK TO THE HOUSE. I WILL BE ALL RIGHT. GO. FIND YOUR BROTHER JEDI.
"FIND MACE WINDU."

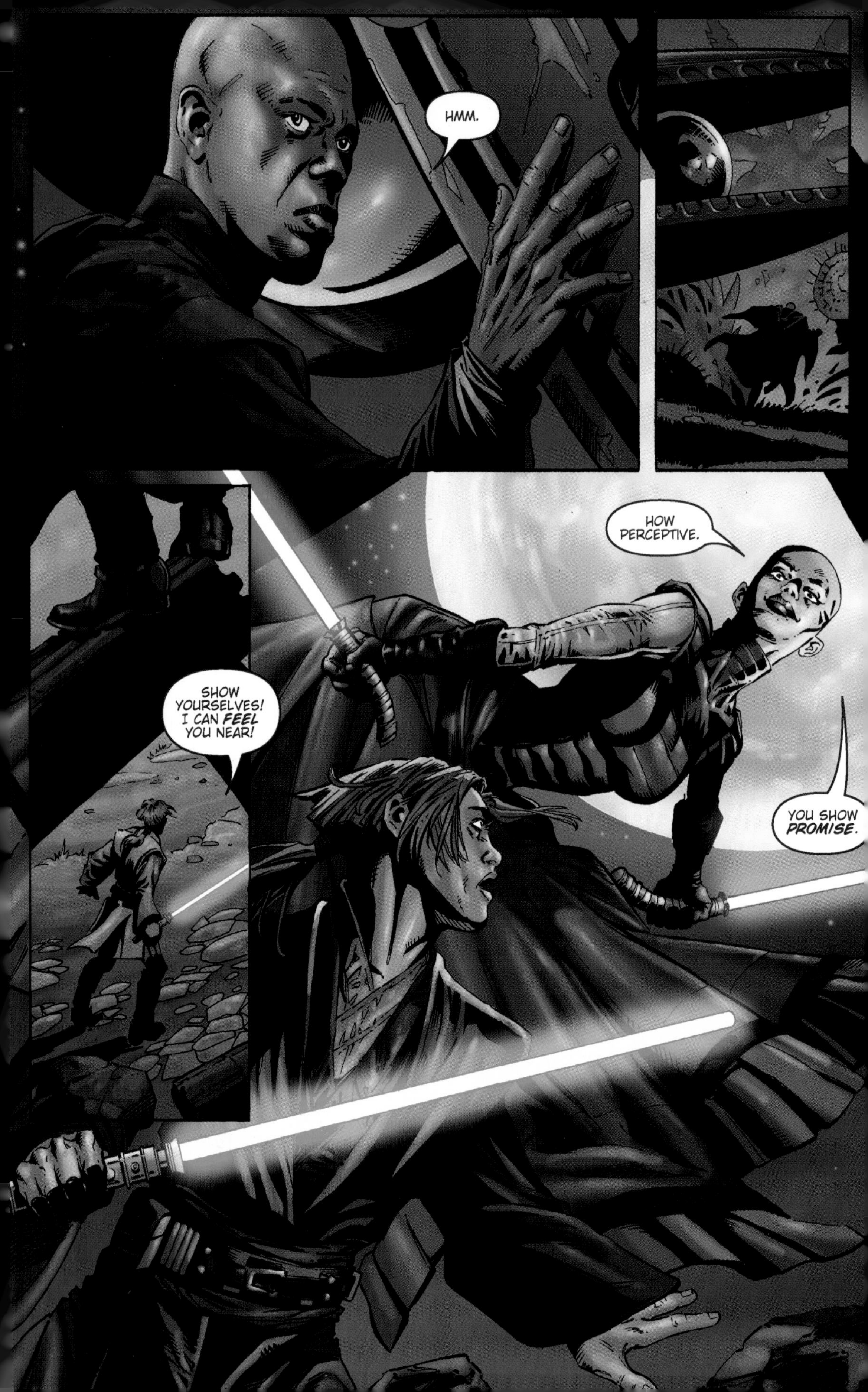
HMM.
HOW PERCEPTIVE.
SHOW YOURSELVES! I CAN FEEL YOU NEAR!
YOU SHOW PROMISE.

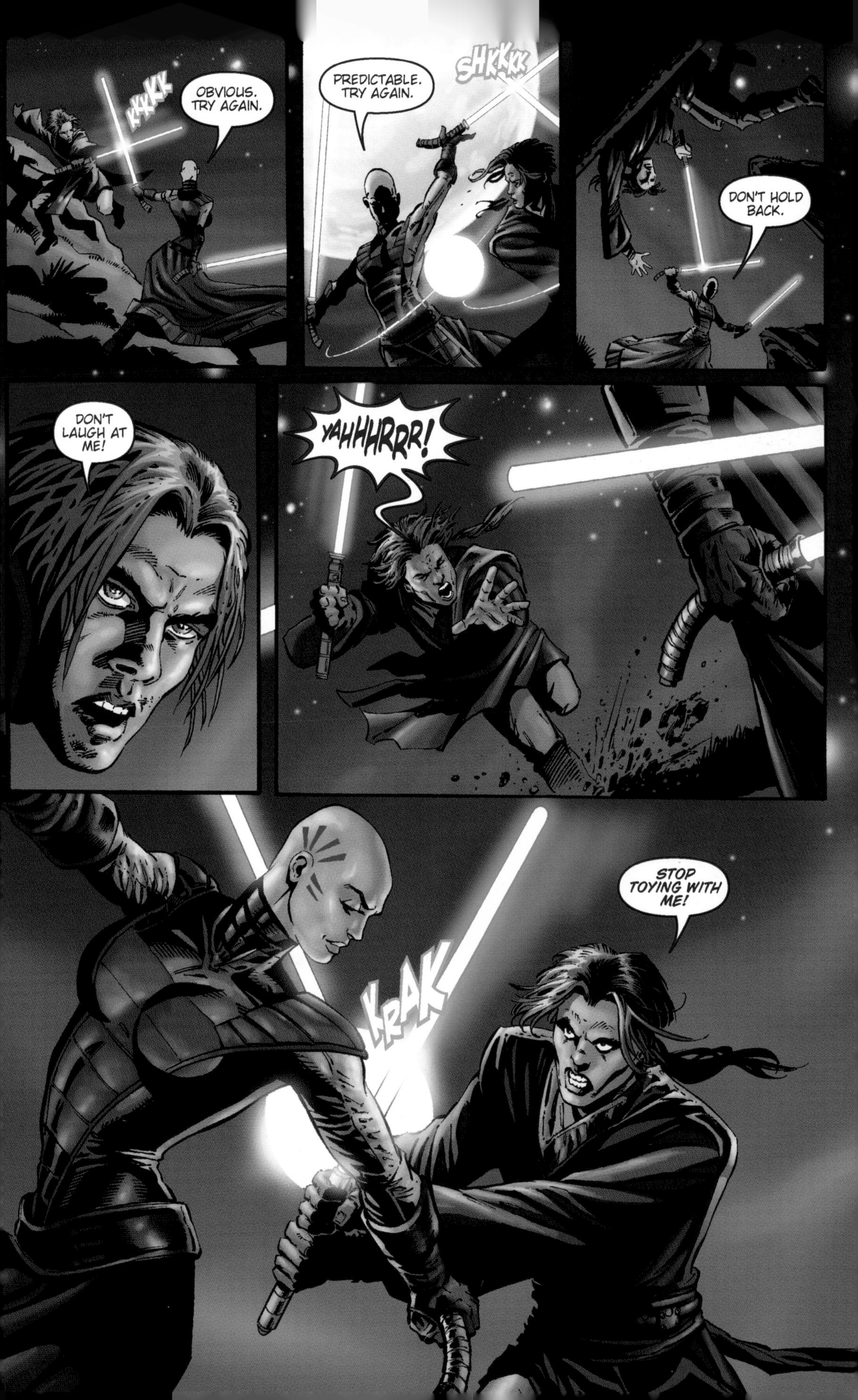
KKKKK
OBVIOUS. TRY AGAIN.
SHKKKK
PREDICTABLE. TRY AGAIN.
DON'T HOLD BACK.
DON'T LAUGH AT ME!
YAHHHRRR!
STOP TOYING WITH ME!
KRAK

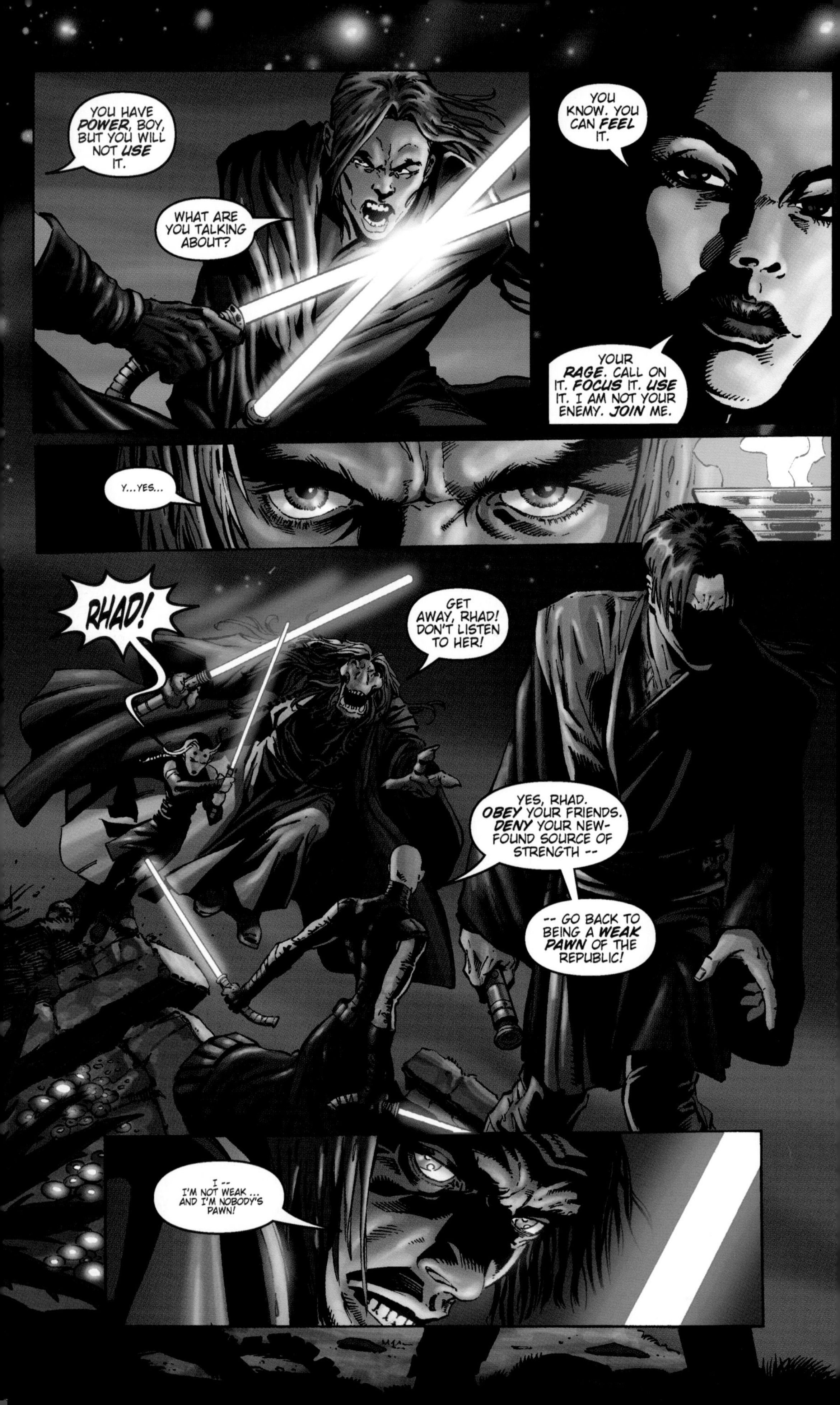
YOU HAVE POWER, BOY, BUT YOU WILL NOT USE IT.
WHAT ARE YOU TALKING ABOUT?
YOU KNOW. YOU CAN FEEL IT.
YOUR RAGE. CALL ON IT. FOCUS IT. USE IT. I AM NOT YOUR ENEMY. JOIN ME.
Y...YES...
RHAD!
GET AWAY, RHAD! DON'T LISTEN TO HER!
YES, RHAD. OBEY YOUR FRIENDS. DENY YOUR NEW-FOUND SOURCE OF STRENGTH --
-- GO BACK TO BEING A WEAK PAWN OF THE REPUBLIC!
I -- I'M NOT WEAK ... AND I'M NOBODY'S PAWN!

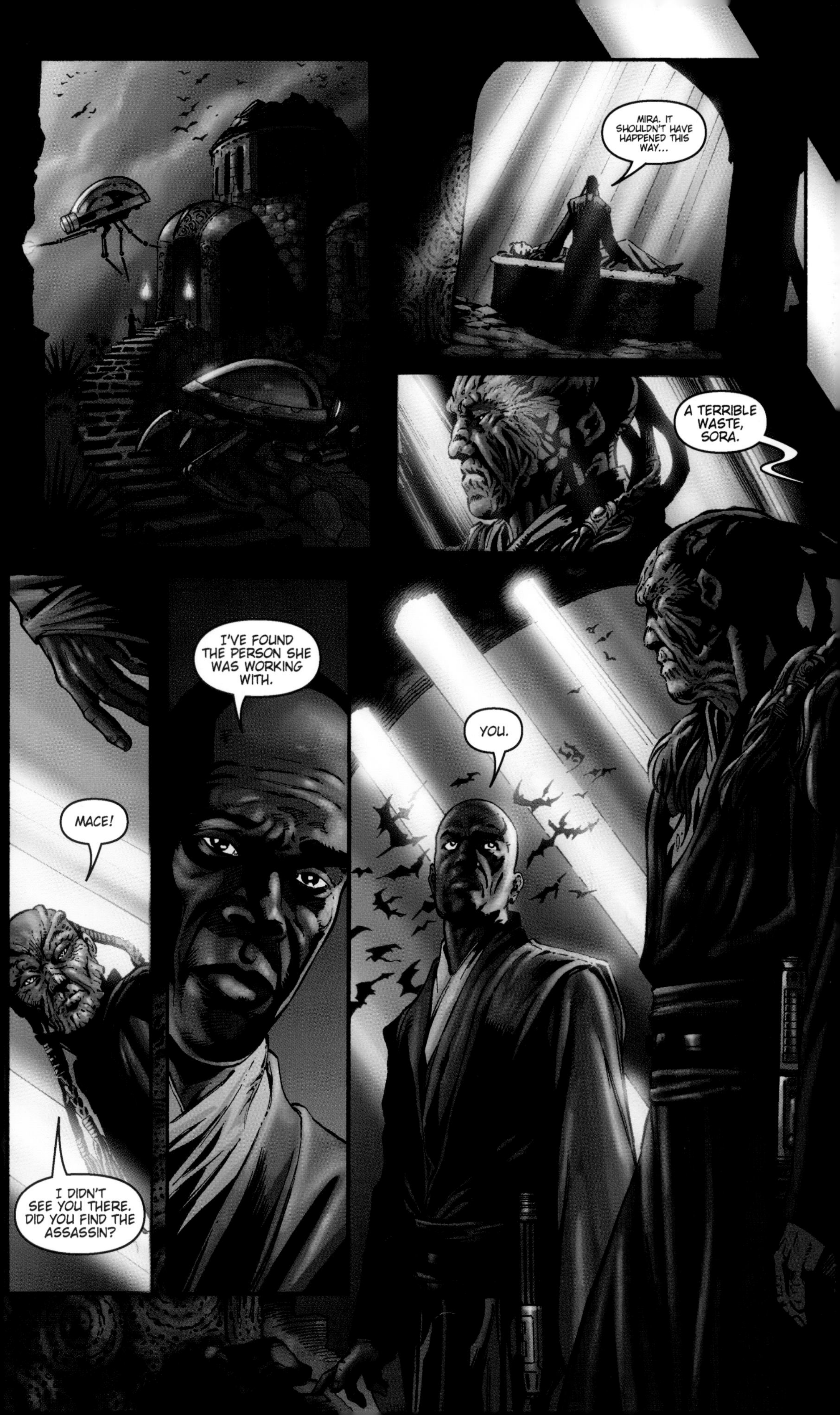
MIRA. IT SHOULDN'T HAVE HAPPENED THIS WAY...
A TERRIBLE WASTE, SORA.
MACE!
I DIDN'T SEE YOU THERE. DID YOU FIND THE ASSASSIN?
I'VE FOUND THE PERSON SHE WAS WORKING WITH.
YOU.

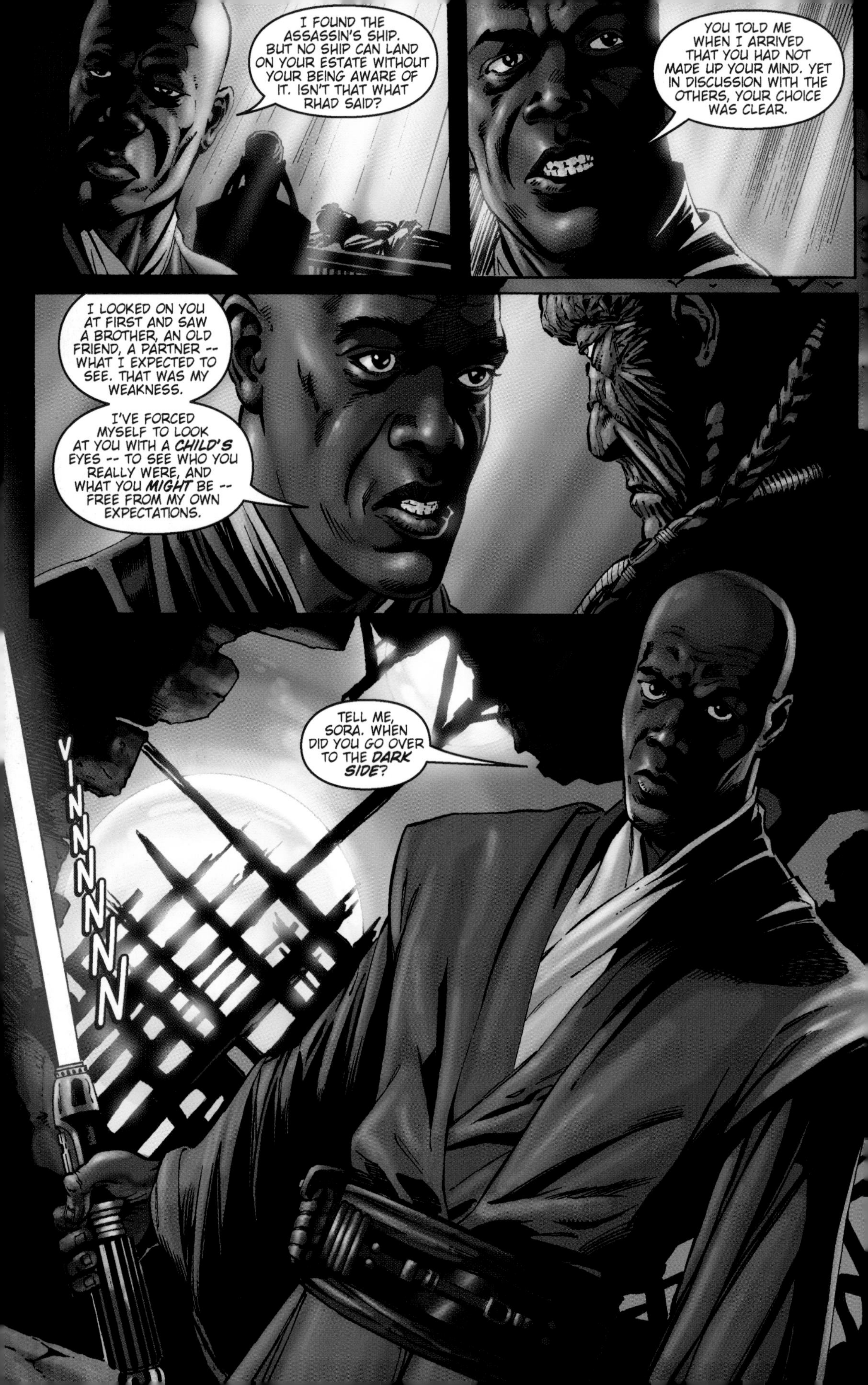
I FOUND THE ASSASSIN'S SHIP. BUT NO SHIP CAN LAND ON YOUR ESTATE WITHOUT YOUR BEING AWARE OF IT. ISN'T THAT WHAT RHAD SAID?
YOU TOLD ME WHEN I ARRIVED THAT YOU HAD NOT MADE UP YOUR MIND. YET IN DISCUSSION WITH THE OTHERS, YOUR CHOICE WAS CLEAR.
I LOOKED ON YOU AT FIRST AND SAW A BROTHER, AN OLD FRIEND, A PARTNER -- WHAT I EXPECTED TO SEE. THAT WAS MY WEAKNESS.
I'VE FORCED MYSELF TO LOOK AT YOU WITH A ***CHILD'S*** EYES -- TO SEE WHO YOU REALLY WERE, AND WHAT YOU ***MIGHT*** BE -- FREE FROM MY OWN EXPECTATIONS.
TELL ME, SORA. WHEN DID YOU GO OVER TO THE ***DARK SIDE***?
VINNNNNNN

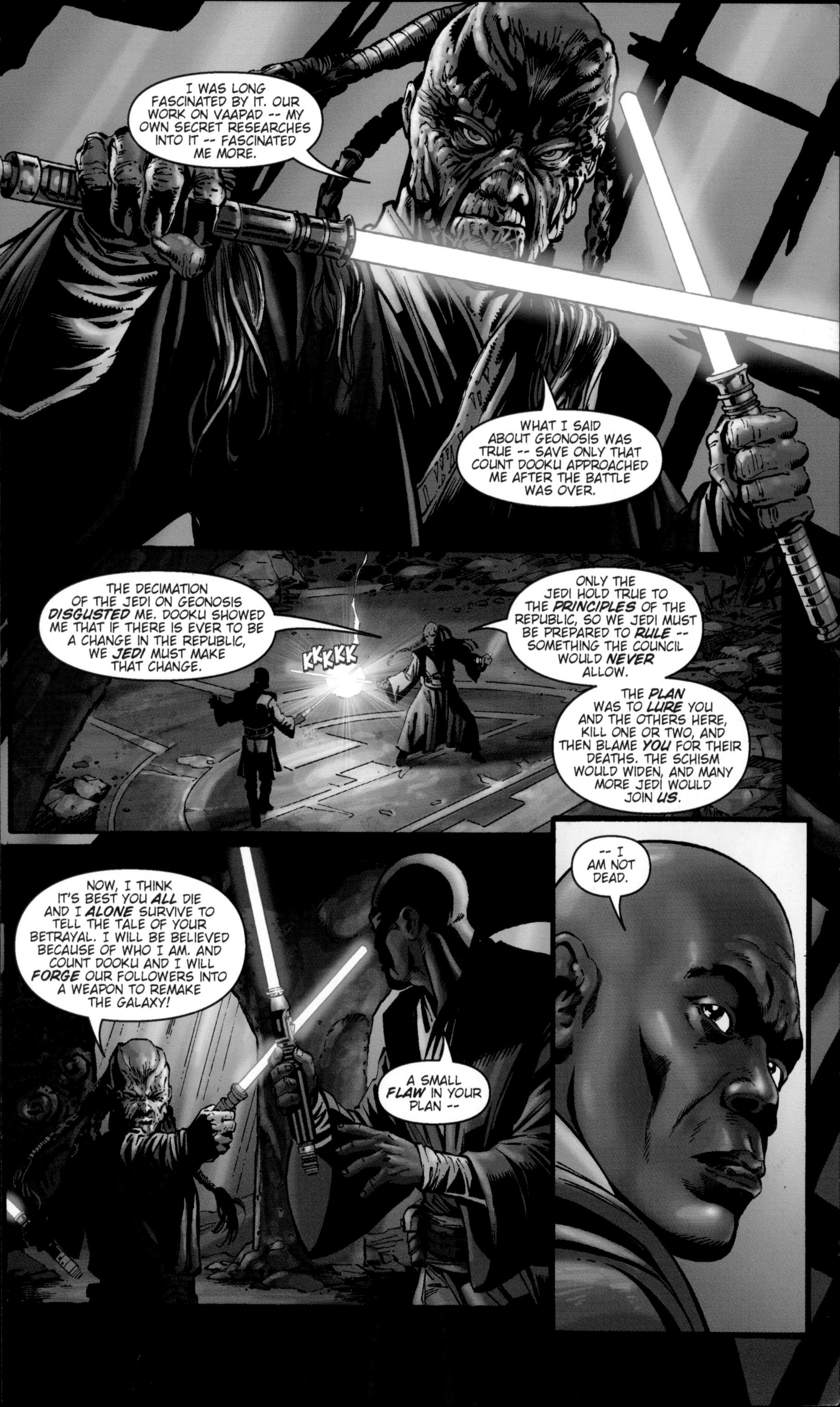
I WAS LONG FASCINATED BY IT. OUR WORK ON VAAPAD -- MY OWN SECRET RESEARCHES INTO IT -- FASCINATED ME MORE.
WHAT I SAID ABOUT GEONOSIS WAS TRUE -- SAVE ONLY THAT COUNT DOOKU APPROACHED ME AFTER THE BATTLE WAS OVER.
THE DECIMATION OF THE JEDI ON GEONOSIS DISGUSTED ME. DOOKU SHOWED ME THAT IF THERE IS EVER TO BE A CHANGE IN THE REPUBLIC, WE JEDI MUST MAKE THAT CHANGE.
KKKKK
ONLY THE JEDI HOLD TRUE TO THE PRINCIPLES OF THE REPUBLIC, SO WE JEDI MUST BE PREPARED TO RULE -- SOMETHING THE COUNCIL WOULD NEVER ALLOW.
THE PLAN WAS TO LURE YOU AND THE OTHERS HERE, KILL ONE OR TWO, AND THEN BLAME YOU FOR THEIR DEATHS. THE SCHISM WOULD WIDEN, AND MANY MORE JEDI WOULD JOIN US.
NOW, I THINK IT'S BEST YOU ALL DIE AND I ALONE SURVIVE TO TELL THE TALE OF YOUR BETRAYAL. I WILL BE BELIEVED BECAUSE OF WHO I AM. AND COUNT DOOKU AND I WILL FORGE OUR FOLLOWERS INTO A WEAPON TO REMAKE THE GALAXY!
A SMALL FLAW IN YOUR PLAN --
-- I AM NOT DEAD.

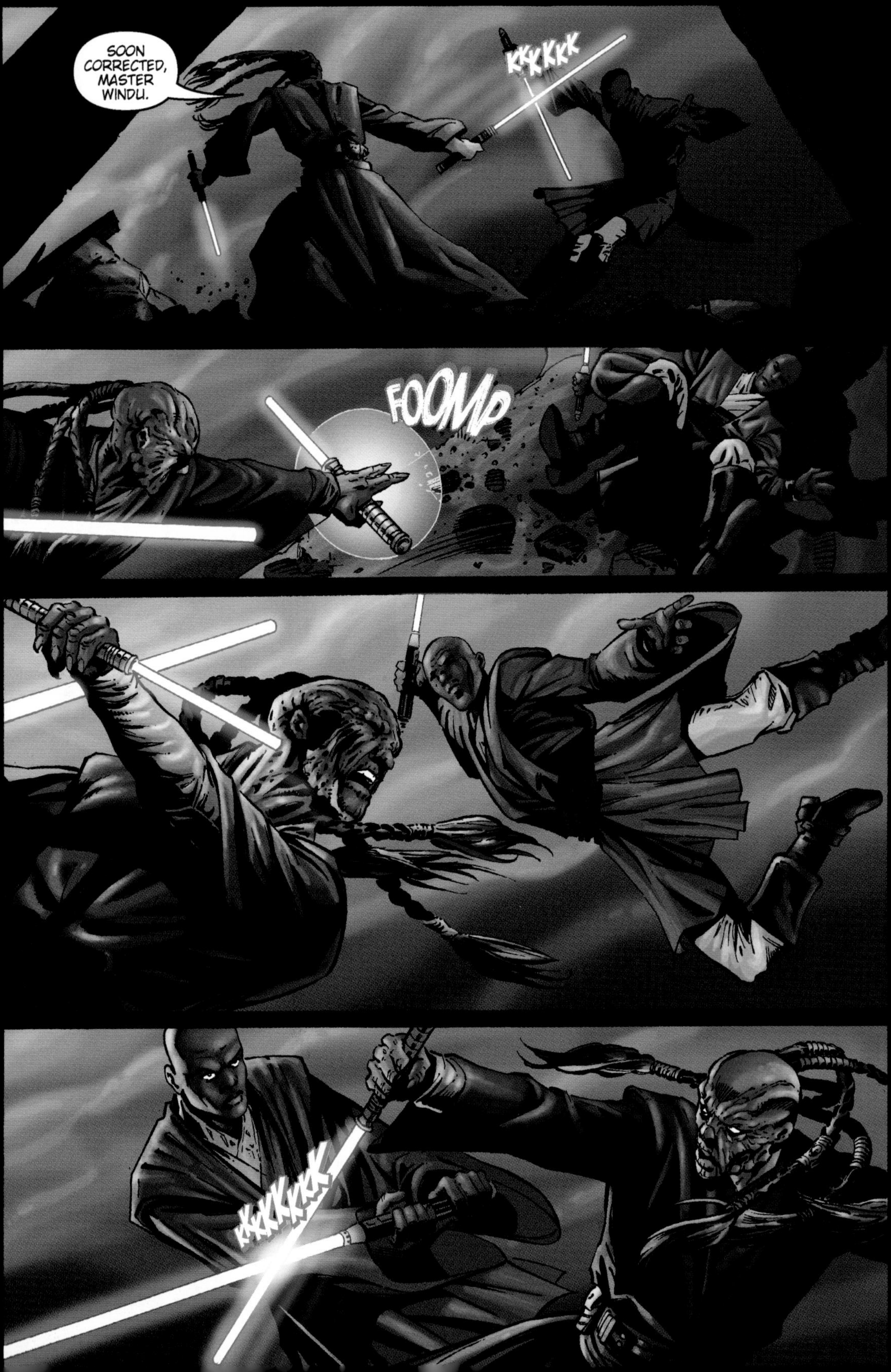
SOON CORRECTED, MASTER WINDU.
KKKKKK
FOOMP
KKKKKKKK

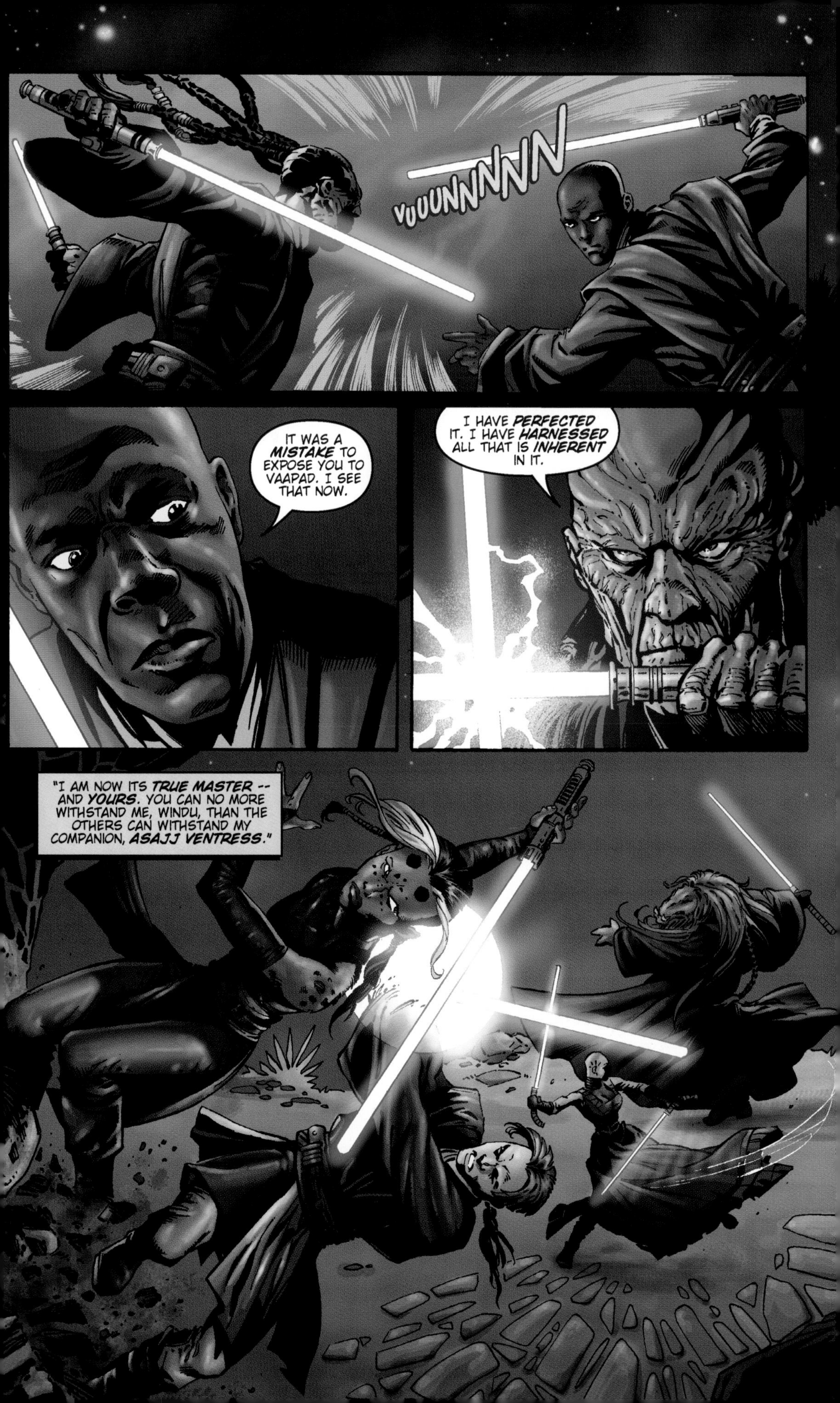

VUUUNNNNNN
IT WAS A MISTAKE TO EXPOSE YOU TO VAAPAD. I SEE THAT NOW.
I HAVE PERFECTED IT. I HAVE HARNESSED ALL THAT IS INHERENT IN IT.
"I AM NOW ITS TRUE MASTER -- AND YOURS. YOU CAN NO MORE WITHSTAND ME, WINDU, THAN THE OTHERS CAN WITHSTAND MY COMPANION, ASAJJ VENTRESS."

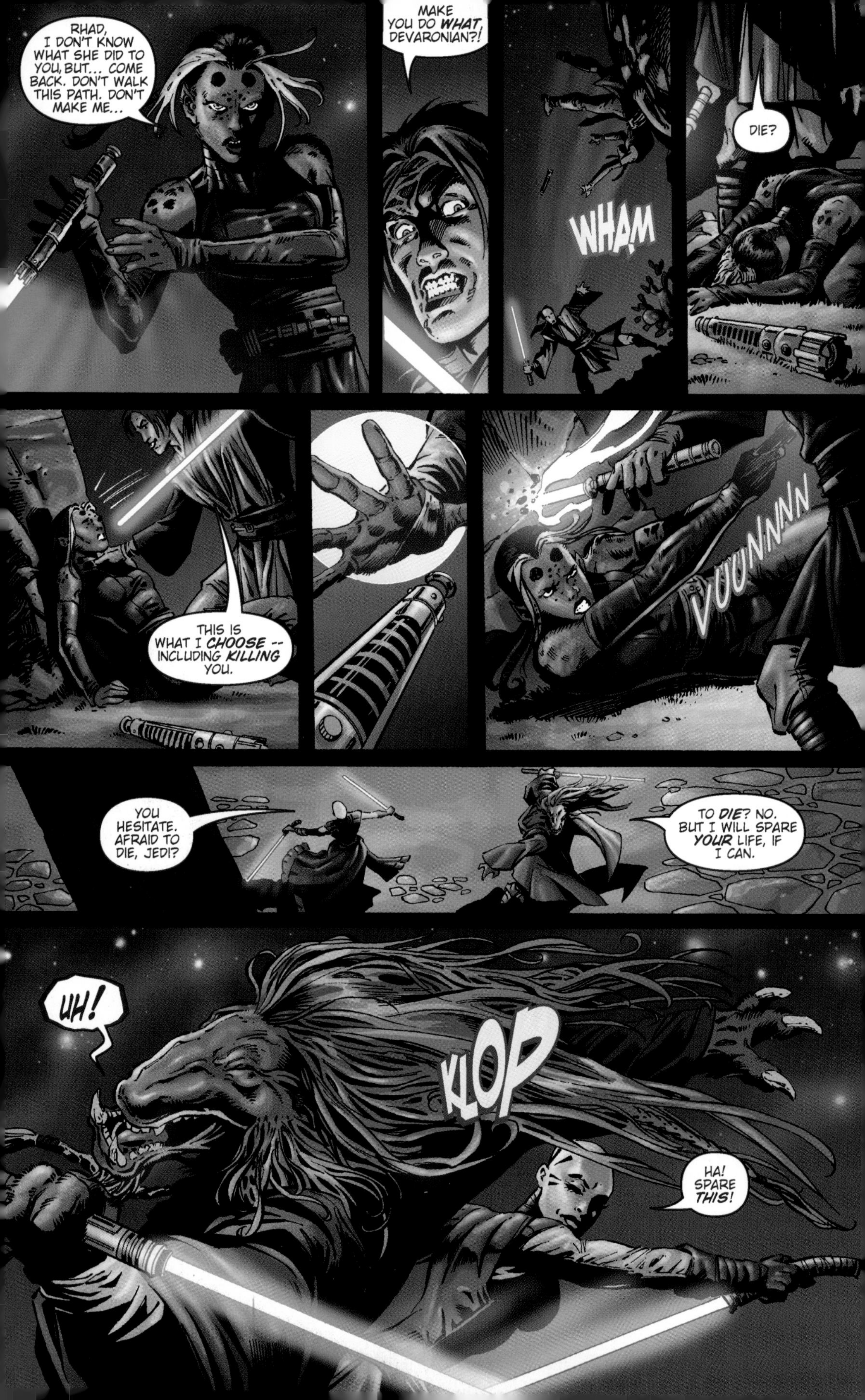
RHAD, I DON'T KNOW WHAT SHE DID TO YOU, BUT... COME BACK. DON'T WALK THIS PATH. DON'T MAKE ME...
MAKE YOU DO *WHAT*, DEVARONIAN?!
WHAM
DIE?
THIS IS WHAT I *CHOOSE* -- INCLUDING *KILLING* YOU.
VUUNNNN
YOU HESITATE. AFRAID TO DIE, JEDI?
TO *DIE*? NO. BUT I WILL SPARE *YOUR* LIFE, IF I CAN.
UH!
KLOP
HA! SPARE *THIS*!

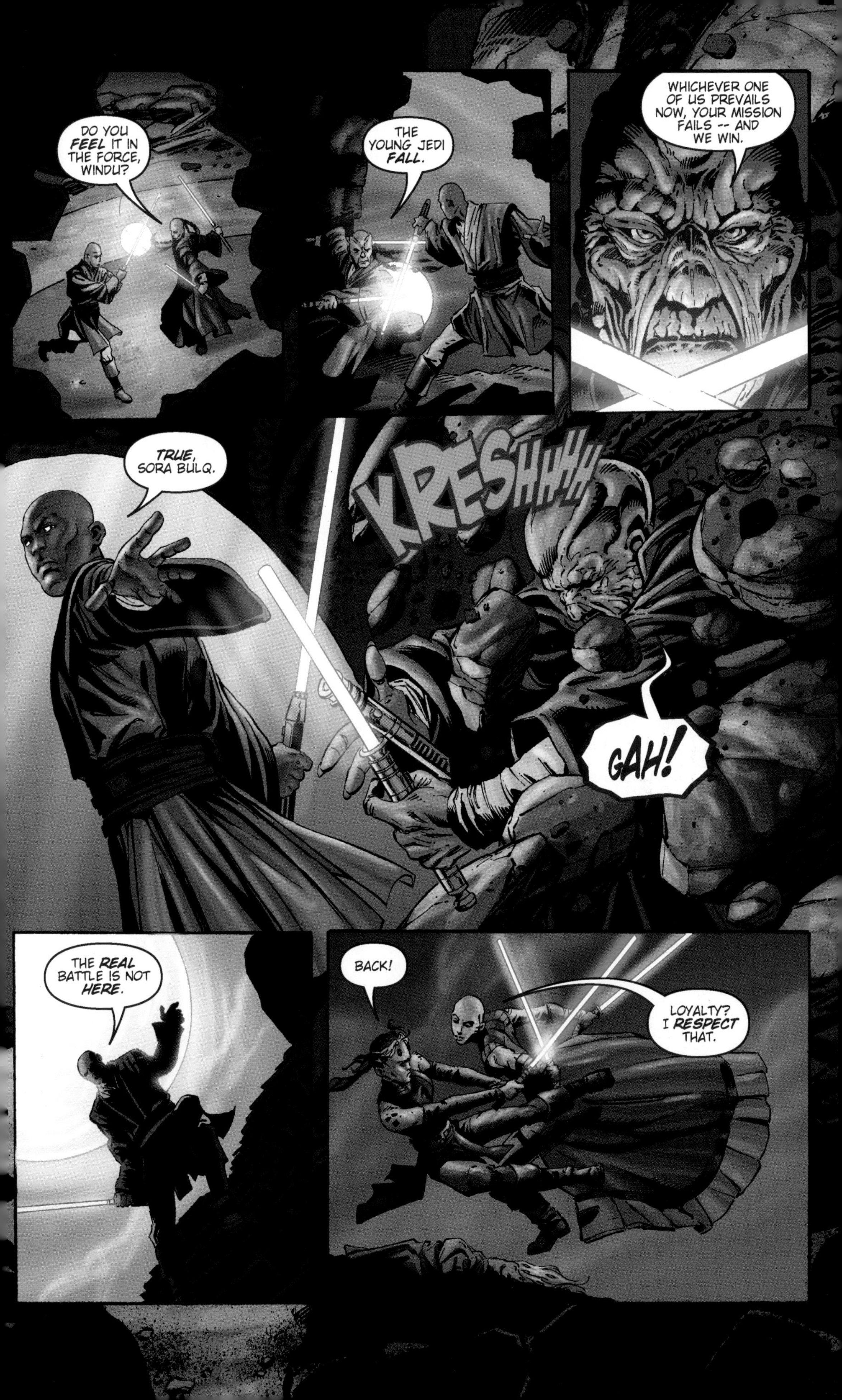

DO YOU FEEL IT IN THE FORCE, WINDU?
THE YOUNG JEDI FALL.
WHICHEVER ONE OF US PREVAILS NOW, YOUR MISSION FAILS -- AND WE WIN.
TRUE, SORA BULQ.
KRESHHHH
GAH!
THE REAL BATTLE IS NOT HERE.
BACK!
LOYALTY? I RESPECT THAT.

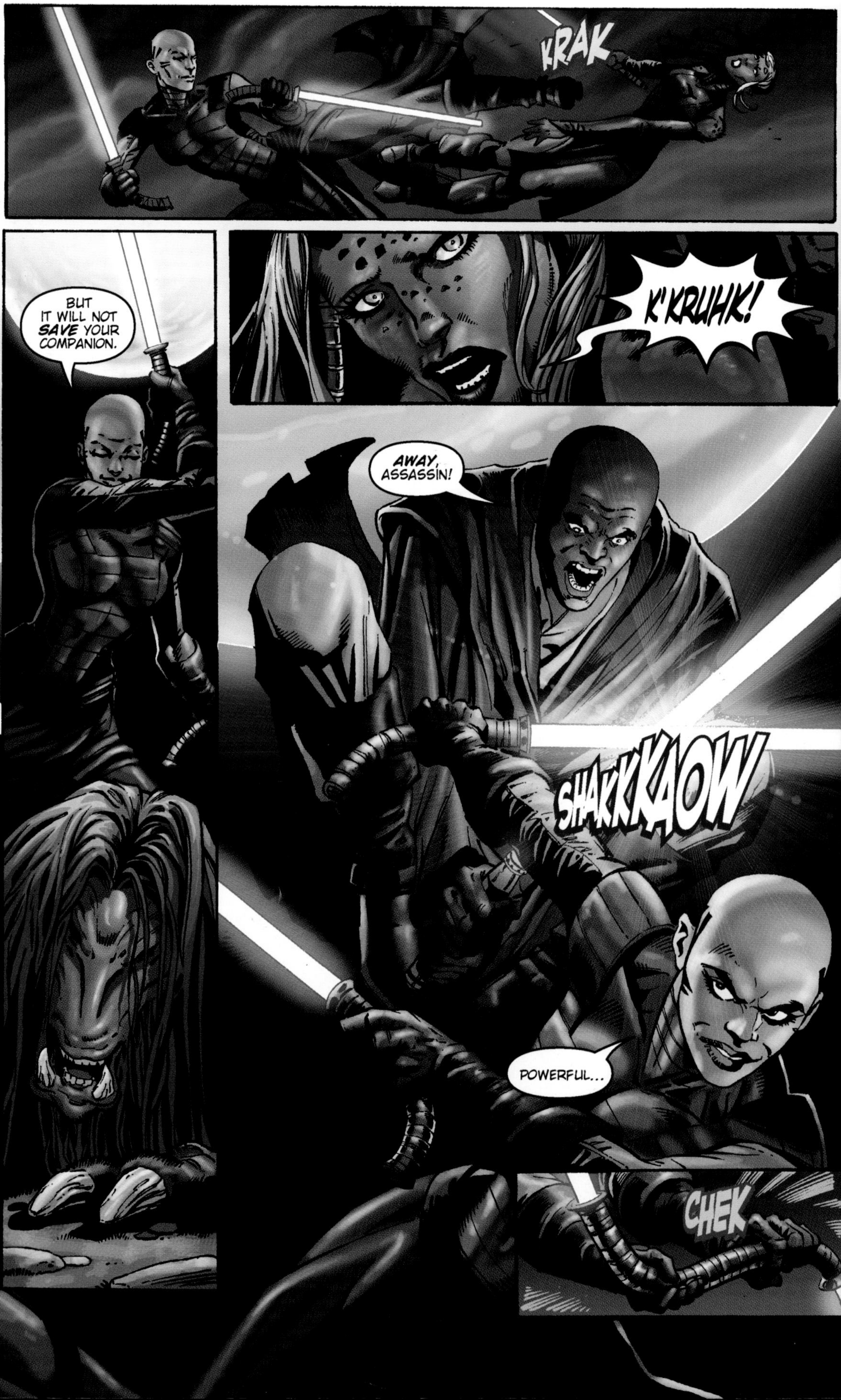
KRAK
BUT IT WILL NOT SAVE YOUR COMPANION.
K'KRUHK!
AWAY, ASSASSIN!
SHAKKKAOW
POWERFUL...
CHEK

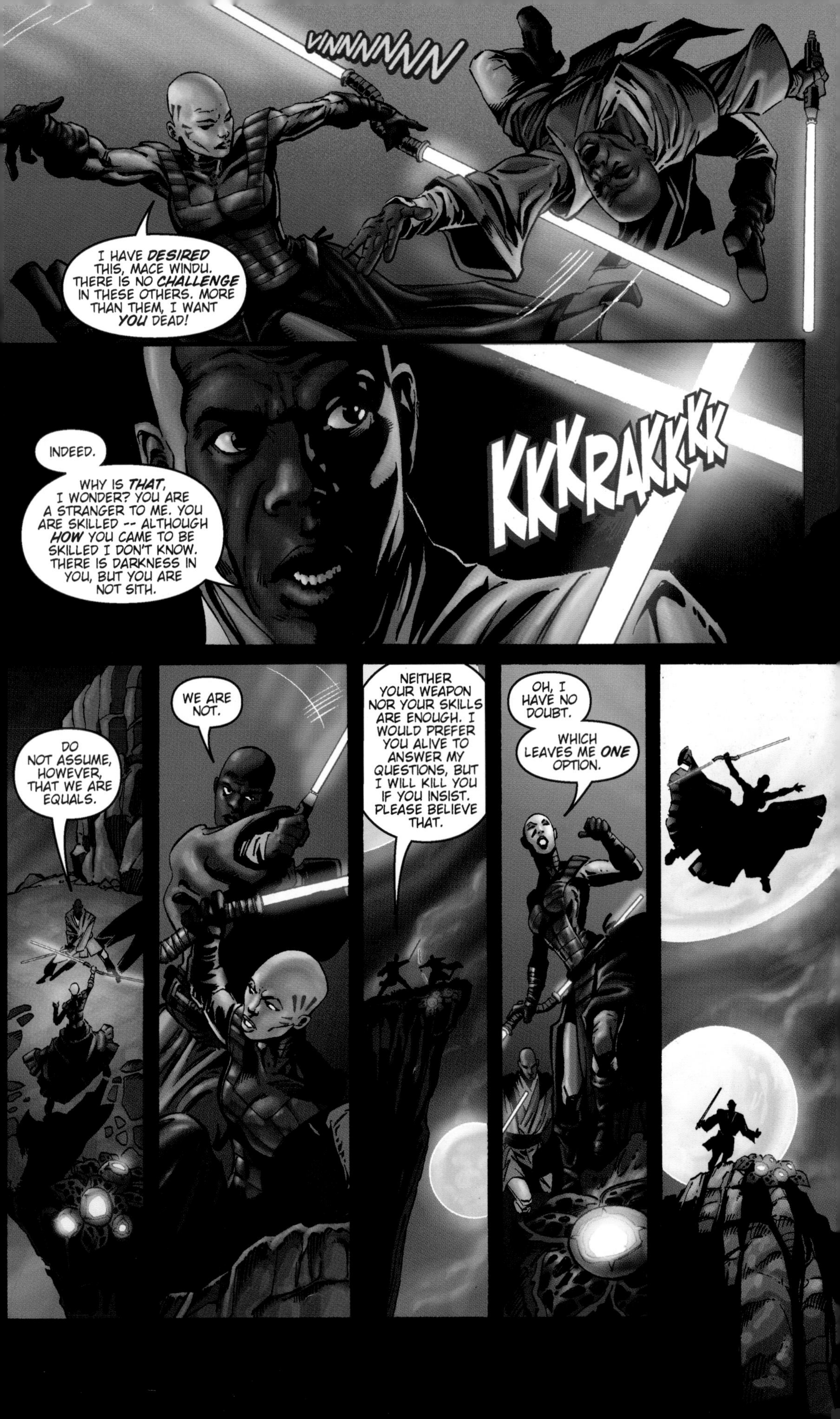
VNNNNNN
I HAVE DESIRED THIS, MACE WINDU. THERE IS NO CHALLENGE IN THESE OTHERS. MORE THAN THEM, I WANT YOU DEAD!
INDEED.
WHY IS THAT, I WONDER? YOU ARE A STRANGER TO ME. YOU ARE SKILLED -- ALTHOUGH HOW YOU CAME TO BE SKILLED I DON'T KNOW. THERE IS DARKNESS IN YOU, BUT YOU ARE NOT SITH.
KKKRAKKKK
DO NOT ASSUME, HOWEVER, THAT WE ARE EQUALS.
WE ARE NOT.
NEITHER YOUR WEAPON NOR YOUR SKILLS ARE ENOUGH. I WOULD PREFER YOU ALIVE TO ANSWER MY QUESTIONS, BUT I WILL KILL YOU IF YOU INSIST. PLEASE BELIEVE THAT.
OH, I HAVE NO DOUBT.
WHICH LEAVES ME ONE OPTION.

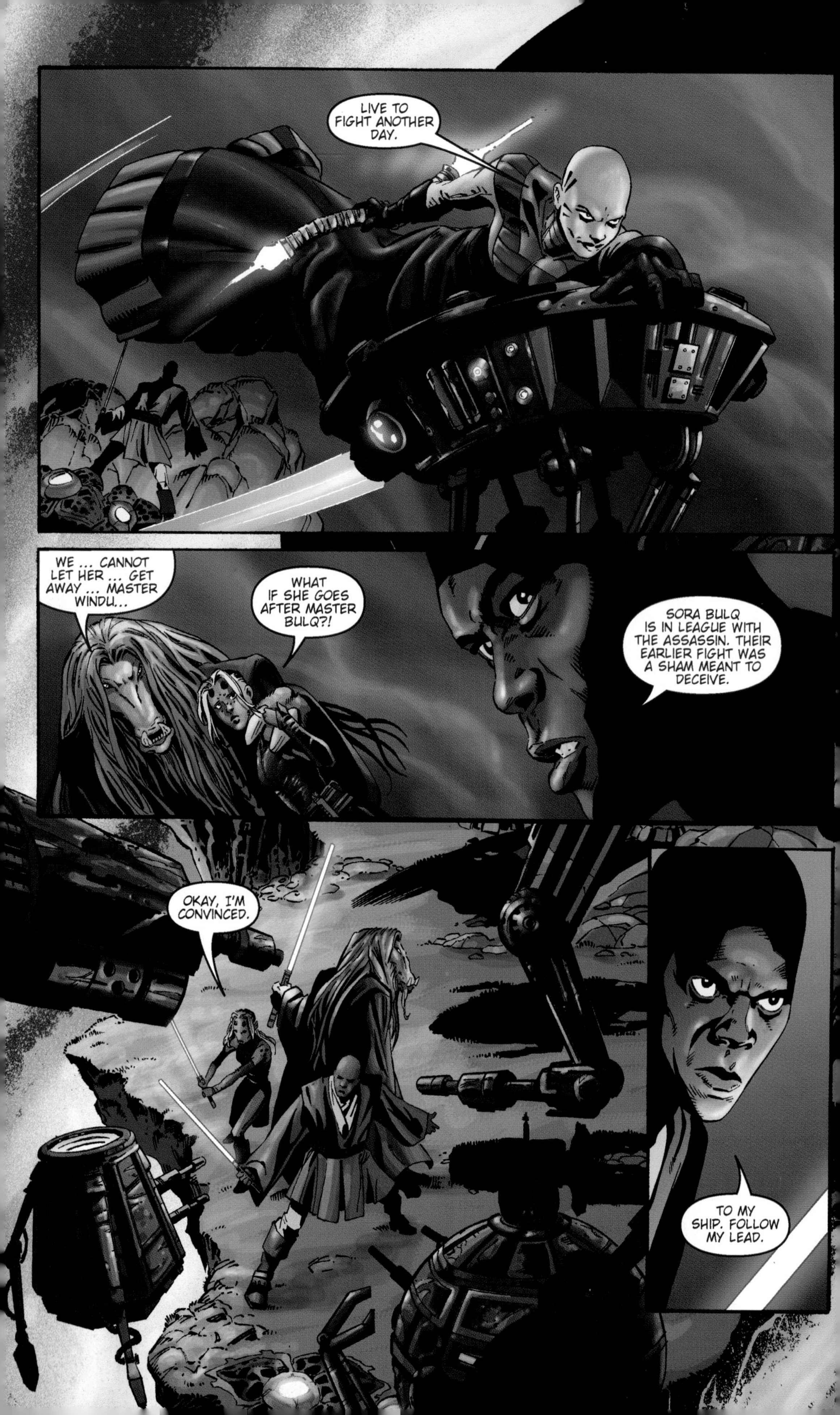
LIVE TO FIGHT ANOTHER DAY.
WE ... CANNOT LET HER ... GET AWAY ... MASTER WINDU...
WHAT IF SHE GOES AFTER MASTER BULQ?!
SORA BULQ IS IN LEAGUE WITH THE ASSASSIN. THEIR EARLIER FIGHT WAS A SHAM MEANT TO DECEIVE.
OKAY, I'M CONVINCED.
TO MY SHIP. FOLLOW MY LEAD.

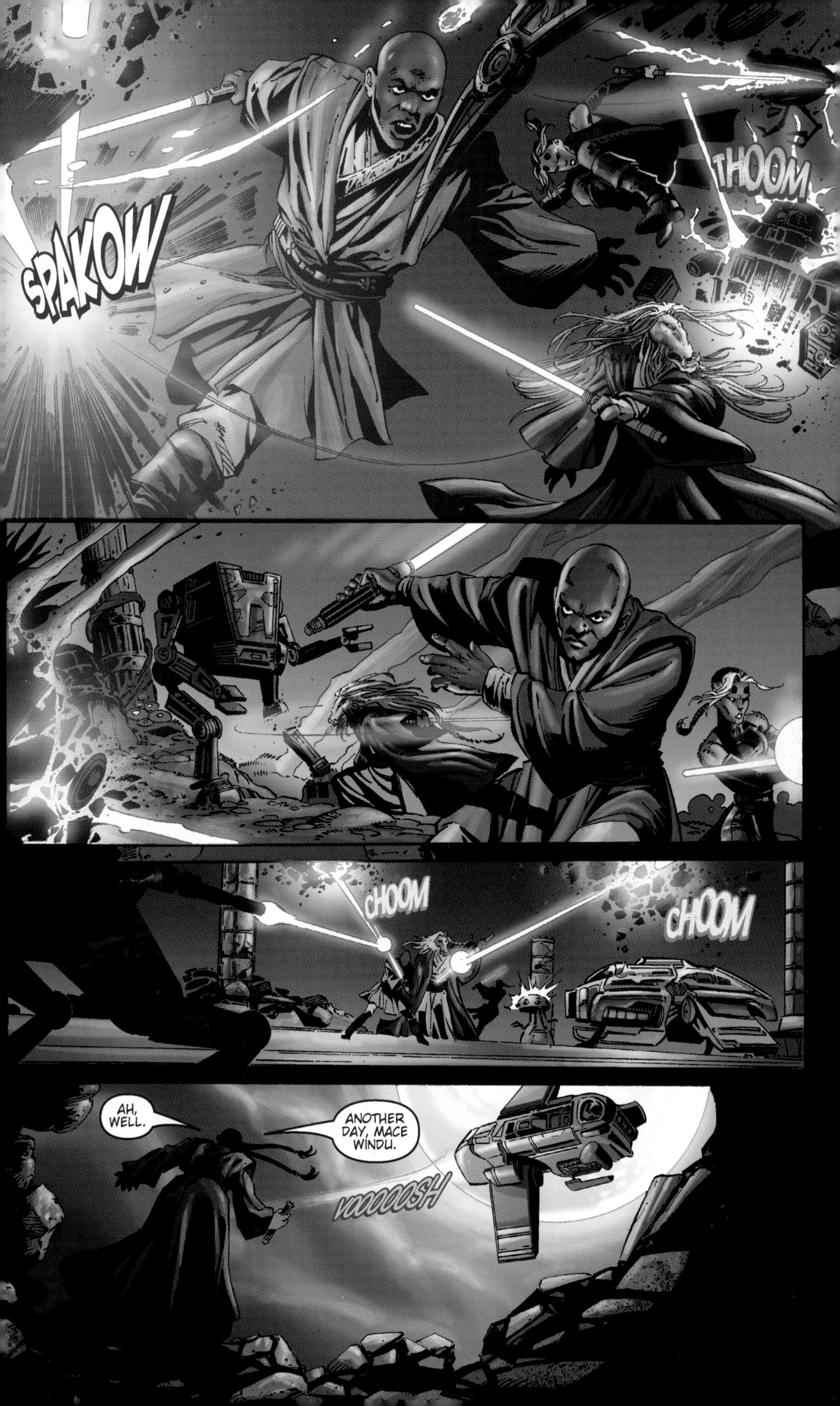
THOOM
SPAKOW
CHOOM
CHOOM
AH, WELL.
ANOTHER DAY, MACE WINDU.
VOOOOOOSH

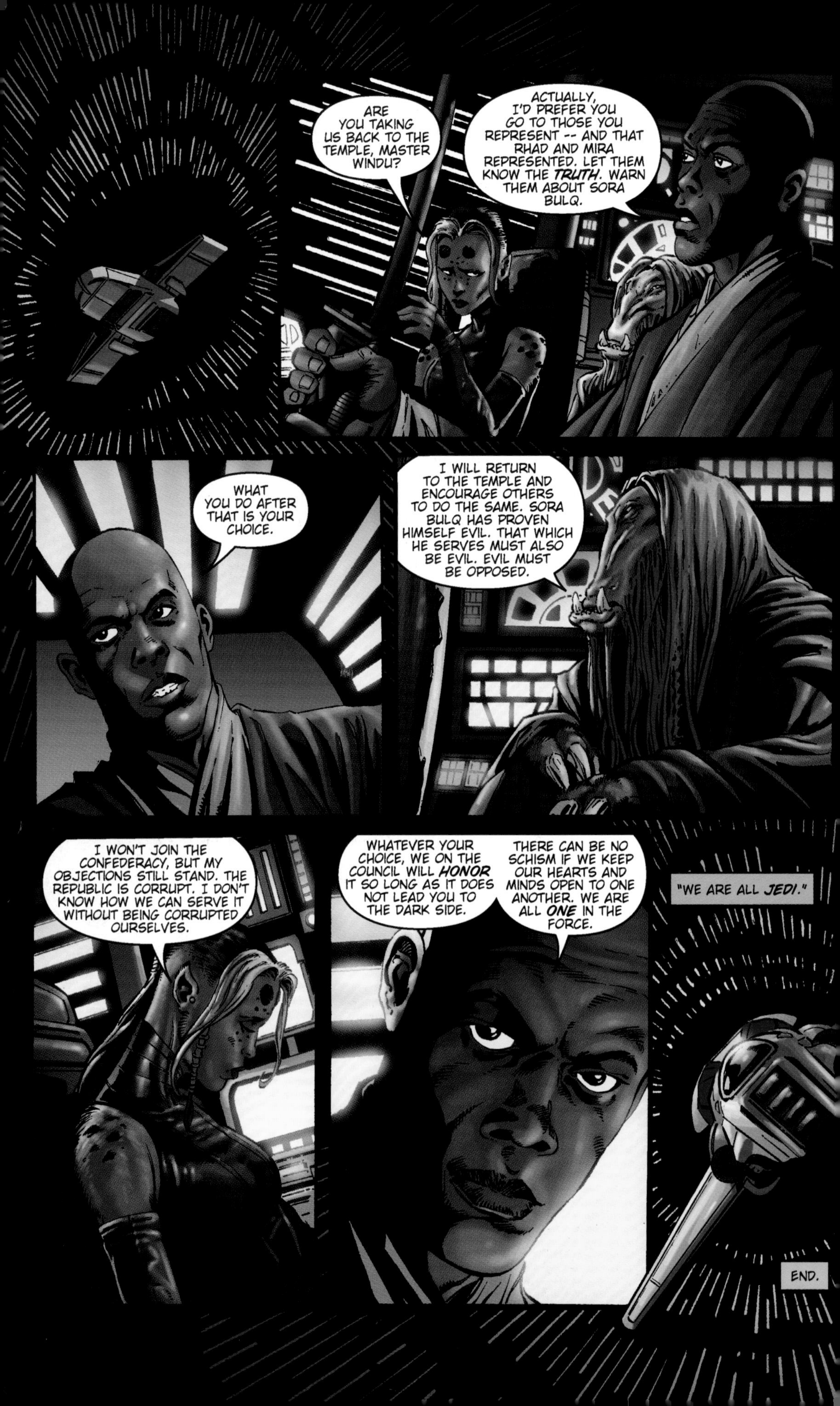
ARE YOU TAKING US BACK TO THE TEMPLE, MASTER WINDU?
ACTUALLY, I'D PREFER YOU GO TO THOSE YOU REPRESENT -- AND THAT RHAD AND MIRA REPRESENTED. LET THEM KNOW THE *TRUTH*. WARN THEM ABOUT SORA BULQ.
WHAT YOU DO AFTER THAT IS YOUR CHOICE.
I WILL RETURN TO THE TEMPLE AND ENCOURAGE OTHERS TO DO THE SAME. SORA BULQ HAS PROVEN HIMSELF EVIL. THAT WHICH HE SERVES MUST ALSO BE EVIL. EVIL MUST BE OPPOSED.
I WON'T JOIN THE CONFEDERACY, BUT MY OBJECTIONS STILL STAND. THE REPUBLIC IS CORRUPT. I DON'T KNOW HOW WE CAN SERVE IT WITHOUT BEING CORRUPTED OURSELVES.
WHATEVER YOUR CHOICE, WE ON THE COUNCIL WILL *HONOR* IT SO LONG AS IT DOES NOT LEAD YOU TO THE DARK SIDE.
THERE CAN BE NO SCHISM IF WE KEEP OUR HEARTS AND MINDS OPEN TO ONE ANOTHER. WE ARE ALL *ONE* IN THE FORCE.
"WE ARE ALL *JEDI*."
END.

CLONE WARS
TIMELINE

With the Battle of Geonosis, the planetary systems of the Republic are plunged into an emerging, galaxy-wide conflict. On one side, the Confederacy of Independent Systems, led by the charismatic Count Dooku and backed by a number of powerful guilds and trade organizations and their droid armies. On the other side, the Republic loyalists and their newly created Clone army, led by the Jedi. It is a war fought on a thousand fronts, with heroism and sacrifices on both sides. Below is a partial list of some of the important events of the Clone Wars and a guide to where those events are chronicled.

MONTHS
(AFTER ATTACK OF THE CLONES)

0	**THE BATTLE OF GEONOSIS** *Star Wars: Episode II — Attack of the Clones* (LF, May '02)
0	**THE SEARCH FOR COUNT DOOKU** *Boba Fett #1: The Fight to Survive* (SB, April '02)
+1	**THE BATTLE OF RAXUS PRIME** *Boba Fett #2: Crossfire* (SB, November '02)
+1	**THE DARK REAPER PROJECT** *The Clone Wars* (LA, May '03)
+1.5	**CONSPIRACY ON AARGAU** *Boba Fett #3: Maze of Deception* (SB, April '03)
+2	**THE BATTLE OF KAMINO** *Clone Wars I: The Defense of Kamino* (DH, June '03)
+3	**THE DEFENSE OF NABOO** *Clone Wars II: Victories and Sacrifices* (DH, September '03)
+6	**THE HARUUN KAL CRISIS** *Shatterpoint* (DR, June '03)
+9	**THE DAGU REVOLT** *Escape from Dagu* (DR, March '04)
+12	**THE BIO-DROID THREAT** *The Cestus Deception* (DR, February '04)
+15	**THE BATTLE OF JABIIM** *Clone Wars III: Last Stand on Jabiim* (DH, February '04)
+30	**THE PRAESITLYN CONQUEST** *Jedi Trial* (DR, November '04)

ABBREVIATION KEY

DH = Dark Horse Comics, graphic novels www.darkhorse.com
DR = Del Rey, hardcover and paperback novels www.delreydigital.com
LA = LucasArts Games, games for XBox, Game Cube, PS2, and PC platforms www.lucasarts.com
LF = Lucasfilm Ltd., motion pictures www.starwars.com
SB = Scholastic Books, juvenile fiction www.scholastic.com/starwars

STAR WARS
TIMELINE OF TRADE PAPERBACKS AND GRAPHIC NOVELS!

TALES OF THE SITH ERA 25,000-1000 YEARS BEFORE STAR WARS: A NEW HOPE

TALES OF THE JEDI
THE GOLDEN AGE OF THE SITH
ISBN: 1-56971-229-8 $16.95
FALL OF THE SITH EMPIRE
ISBN: 1-56971-320-0 $14.95
KNIGHTS OF THE OLD REPUBLIC
ISBN: 1-56971-020-1 $14.95
THE FREEDON NADD UPRISING
ISBN: 1-56971-307-3 $5.95
DARK LORDS OF THE SITH
ISBN: 1-56971-095-3 $17.95
THE SITH WAR
ISBN: 1-56971-173-9 $17.95
**REDEMPTION*
ISBN: 1-56971-535-1 $14.95
**JEDI VS. SITH*
ISBN: 1-56971-649-8 $15.95

PREQUEL ERA 1000-0 YEARS BEFORE STAR WARS: A NEW HOPE

***JEDI COUNCIL**
ACTS OF WAR
ISBN: 1-56971-539-4 $12.95
***DARTH MAUL**
ISBN: 1-56971-542-4 $12.95
PRELUDE TO REBELLION
ISBN: 1-56971-448-7 $14.95
OUTLANDER
ISBN: 1-56971-514-9 $14.95
***JEDI COUNCIL**
EMMISSARIES TO MALASTARE
ISBN: 1-56971-545-9 $15.95
STAR WARS: TWILIGHT
ISBN: 1-56971-558-0 $12.95
***THE HUNT FOR AURRA SING**
ISBN: 1-56971-651-X $12.95
***DARKNESS**
ISBN: 1-56971-659-5 $12.95
EPISODE 1 —
THE PHANTOM MENACE
ISBN: 1-56971-359-6 $12.95
EPISODE 1 —
THE PHANTOM MENACE ADVENTURES
ISBN: 1-56971-443-6 $12.95
MANGA EDITIONS
Translated into English
EPISODE 1 — *THE PHANTOM MENACE*
VOLUME 1
ISBN: 1-56971-483-5 $9.95
VOLUME 2
ISBN: 1-56971-484-3 $9.95
***JANGO FETT**
ISBN: 1-56971-623-4 $5.95
***JANGO FETT: OPEN SEASONS**
ISBN: 1-56971-671-4 $12.95
***ZAM WESELL**
ISBN: 1-56971-624-2 $5.95
EPISODE 2 —
ATTACK OF THE CLONES
ISBN: 1-56971-609-9 $17.95
DROIDS
THE KALARBA ADVENTURES
ISBN: 1-56971-064-3 $17.95
REBELLION
ISBN: 1-56971-224-7 $14.95
JABBA THE HUTT
THE ART OF THE DEAL
ISBN: 1-56971-310-3 $9.95
***UNDERWORLD**
THE YAVIN VASSILIKA
ISBN: 1-56971-618-8 $14.95
CLASSIC STAR WARS
HAN SOLO AT STARS' END
ISBN: 1-56971-254-9 $6.95
BOBA FETT
ENEMY OF THE EMPIRE
ISBN: 1-56971-407-X $12.95

TRILOGY ERA 0-5 YEARS AFTER STAR WARS: A NEW HOPE

A NEW HOPE SPECIAL EDITION
ISBN: 1-56971-213-1 $9.95
MANGA EDITIONS
Translated into English
A NEW HOPE
VOLUME 1
ISBN: 1-56971-362-6 $9.95
VOLUME 2
ISBN: 1-56971-363-4 $9.95
VOLUME 3
ISBN: 1-56971-364-2 $9.95
VOLUME 4
ISBN: 1-56971-365-0 $9.95
VADER'S QUEST
ISBN: 1-56971-415-0 $11.95
***A LONG TIME AGO VOLUME 1—**
ISBN: 1-56971-754-0 $29.95
***A LONG TIME AGO VOLUME 2—**
ISBN: 1-56971-785-0 $29.95
***A LONG TIME AGO VOLUME 3—**
RESURRECTION OF EVIL
ISBN: 1-56971-786-9 $29.95
***A LONG TIME AGO VOLUME 4—**
SCREAMS IN THE VOID
ISBN: 1-56971-787-7 $29.95
CLASSIC STAR WARS
THE EARLY ADVENTURES
ISBN: 1-56971-178-X $19.95
SPLINTER OF THE MIND'S EYE
ISBN: 1-56971-223-9 $14.95
CLASSIC STAR WARS
IN DEADLY PURSUIT
ISBN: 1-56971-109-7 $16.95
***THE EMPIRE STRIKES BACK* SPECIAL EDITION**
ISBN: 1-56971-234-4 $9.95
MANGA EDITIONS
Translated into English
THE EMPIRE STRIKES BACK
VOLUME 1
ISBN: 1-56971-390-1 $9.95
VOLUME 2
ISBN: 1-56971-391-X $9.95
VOLUME 3
ISBN: 1-56971-392-8 $9.95
VOLUME 4
ISBN: 1-56971-393-6 $9.95
CLASSIC STAR WARS
THE REBEL STORM
ISBN: 1-56971-106-2 $16.95
CLASSIC STAR WARS
ESCAPE TO HOTH
ISBN: 1-56971-093-7 $16.95
SHADOWS OF THE EMPIRE
SHADOWS OF THE EMPIRE
ISBN: 1-56971-183-6 $17.95
***RETURN OF THE JEDI* SPECIAL EDITION**
ISBN: 1-56971-235-2 $9.95
MANGA EDITIONS
Translated into English
RETURN OF THE JEDI
VOLUME 1
ISBN: 1-56971-394-4 $9.95
VOLUME 2
ISBN: 1-56971-395-2 $9.95
VOLUME 3
ISBN: 1-56971-396-0 $9.95
VOLUME 4
ISBN: 1-56971-397-9 $9.95

CLASSIC SPIN-OFF ERA 5-25 YEARS AFTER STAR WARS: A NEW HOPE

MARA JADE
BY THE EMPEROR'S HAND
ISBN: 1-56971-401-0 $15.95
SHADOWS OF THE EMPIRE
EVOLUTION
ISBN: 1-56971-441-X $14.95
X-WING ROGUE SQUADRON
THE PHANTOM AFFAIR
ISBN: 1-56971-251-4 $12.95
BATTLEGROUND: TATOOINE
ISBN: 1-56971-276-X $12.95
THE WARRIOR PRINCESS
ISBN: 1-56971-330-8 $12.95
REQUIEM FOR A ROGUE
ISBN: 1-56971-331-6 $12.95
IN THE EMPIRE'S SERVICE
ISBN: 1-56971-383-9 $12.95
BLOOD AND HONOR
ISBN: 1-56971-387-1 $12.95
MASQUERADE
ISBN: 1-56971-487-8 $12.95
MANDATORY RETIREMENT
ISBN: 1-56971-492-4 $12.95
THE THRAWN TRILOGY
HEIR TO THE EMPIRE
ISBN: 1-56971-202-6 $19.95
DARK FORCE RISING
ISBN: 1-56971-269-7 $17.95
THE LAST COMMAND
ISBN: 1-56971-378-2 $17.95
DARK EMPIRE
DARK EMPIRE
ISBN: 1-56971-073-2 $17.95
DARK EMPIRE II
ISBN: 1-56971-119-4 $17.95
EMPIRE'S END
ISBN: 1-56971-306-5 $5.95
BOBA FETT
DEATH, LIES, & TREACHERY
ISBN: 1-56971-311-1 $12.95
CRIMSON EMPIRE
CRIMSON EMPIRE
ISBN: 1-56971-355-3 $17.95
COUNCIL OF BLOOD
ISBN: 1-56971-410-X $17.95
JEDI ACADEMY
LEVIATHAN
ISBN: 1-56971-456-8 $11.95

THE NEW JEDI ORDER ERA 25+ YEARS AFTER STAR WARS: A NEW HOPE

UNION
ISBN: 1-56971-464-9 $12.95
CHEWBACCA
ISBN: 1-56971-515-7 $12.95

INFINITIES — DOES NOT APPLY TO TIMELINE

***TALES VOLUME 1**
ISBN: 1-56971-619-6 $19.95
***TALES VOLUME 2**
ISBN: 1-56971-757-5 $19.95
***INFINITIES**
A NEW HOPE
ISBN: 1-56971-648-X $12.95
BATTLE OF THE BOUNTY HUNTERS POP-UP COMIC BOOK
ISBN: 1-56971-129-1 $17.95
DARK FORCES
Prose novellas, heavily illustrated
SOLDIER FOR THE EMPIRE
hardcover edition
ISBN: 1-56971-155-0 $24.95
paperback edition
ISBN: 1-56971-348-0 $14.95
REBEL AGENT
hardcover edition
ISBN: 1-56971-156-9 $24.95
paperback edition
ISBN: 1-56971-400-2 $14.95
JEDI KNIGHT
hardcover edition
ISBN: 1-56971-157-7 $24.95
paperback edition
ISBN: 1-56971-433-9 $14.95

** New •Prices and availability subject to change without notice.*

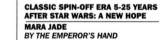

Available from your local comics shop or bookstore!

To find a comics shop in your area, call 1-888-266-4226
For more information or to order direct:
•On the web: www.darkhorse.com •E-mail: mailorder@darkhorse.com
•Phone: 1-800-862-0052 or (503) 652-9701 Mon.-Sat. 9 A.M. to 5 P.M. Pacific Time
*Prices and availability subject to change without notice

Dark Horse Comics: **Mike Richardson** *publisher* • **Neil Hankerson** *executive vice president* • **Tom Weddle** *vice president of finance* • **Randy Stradley** *vice president of publishing* • **Chris Warner** *senior editor* • **Sara Perrin** *vice president of marketing* • **Michael Martens** *vice president of business development* • **Anita Nelson** *vice president of sales & licensing* • **David Scroggy** *vice president of product development* • **Mark Cox** *art director* • **Dale LaFountain** *vice president of information technology* • **Kim Haines** *director of human resources* • **Darlene Vogel** *director of purchasing* • **Ken Lizzi** • *general counsel*

The Colours of Treasures and Trinkets

Les couleurs des trésors et des bibelots

Express Yourself in Colour • Exprimez-vous en couleurs

Pencil Patterns is an imprint of Telegraph Road Entertainment.
Création en couleur est une marque d'éditeur de Telegraph Road Entertainment.
© 2021 Telegraph Road Entertainment, Toronto, Ontario M1V 4Z7
ISBN 978-1-4876-0618-3

Senior Series Editor / Première directrice de publication
Georgia Green

Series and Cover Design / Conception de la série et de la couverture
Michael P. Brodey

For special bulk purchases, please contact:
Pour les achats en bloc spéciaux, veuillez vous adresser à :
sales@telegraph-rd.com

For other inquiries, please contact:
Pour toute autre demande, veuillez vous adresser à :
inquiries@telegraph-rd.com

With the participation of the Government of Canada
Avec la participation du gouvernement du Canada
Canadä

Printed in Canada • Imprimé au Canada

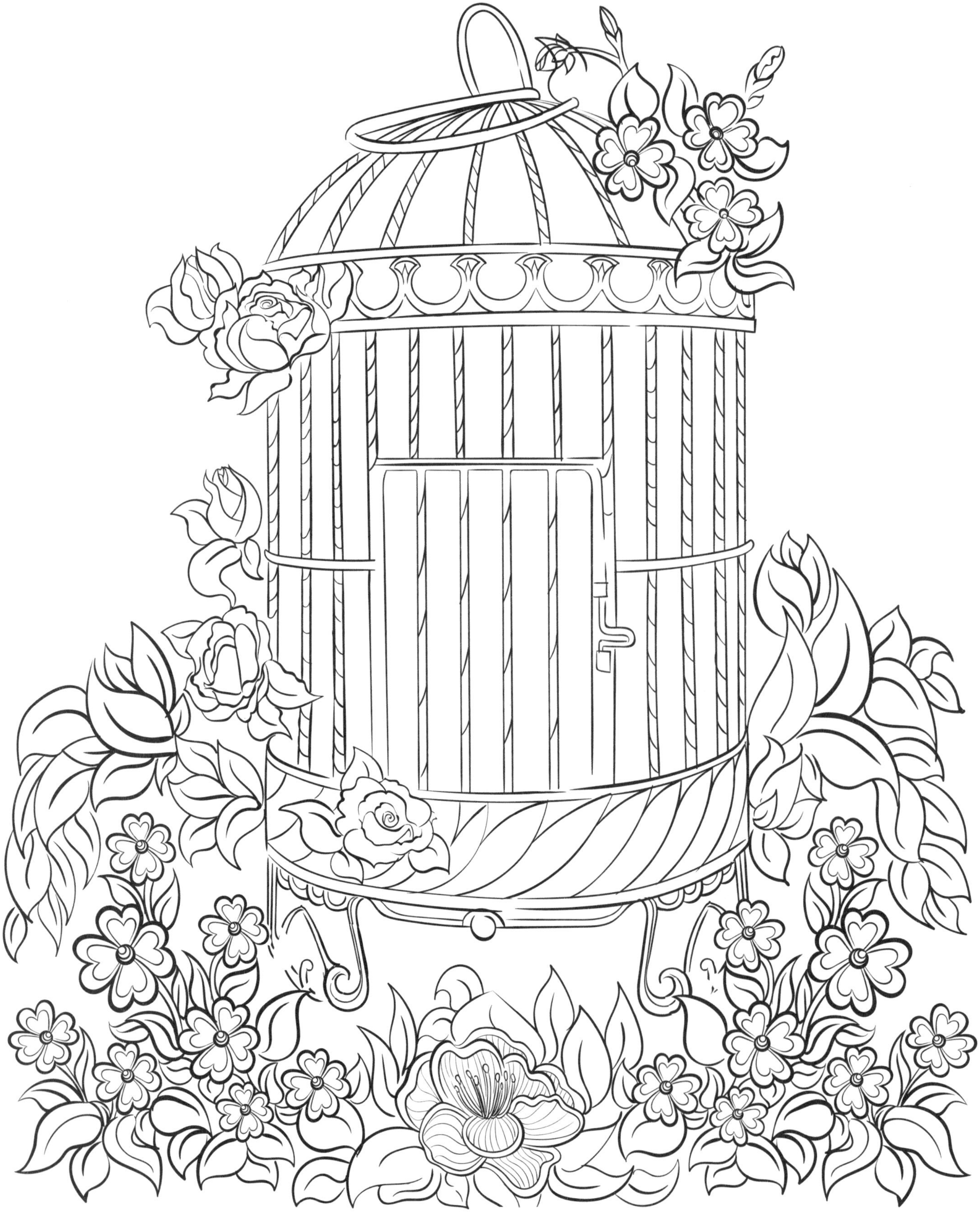

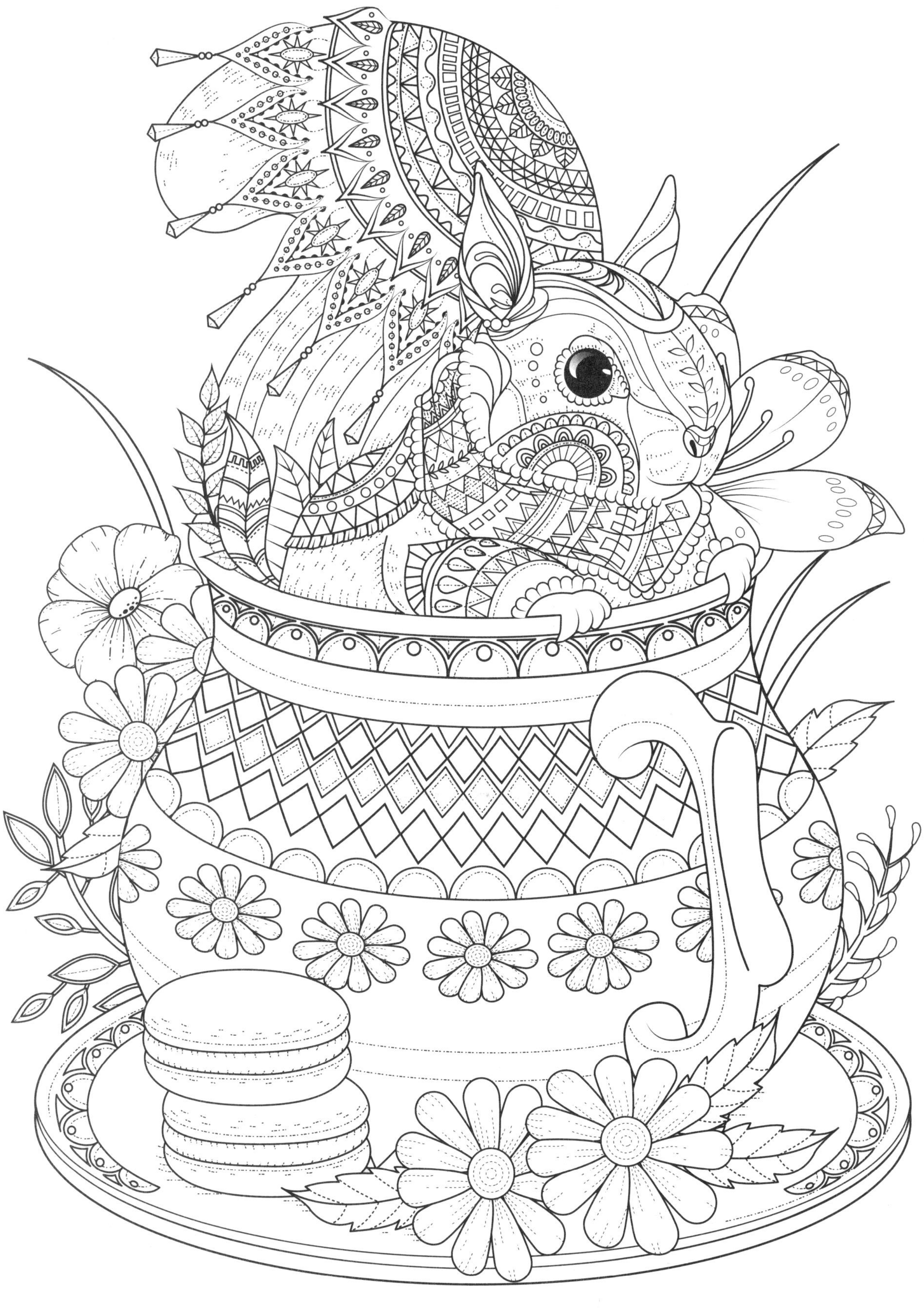

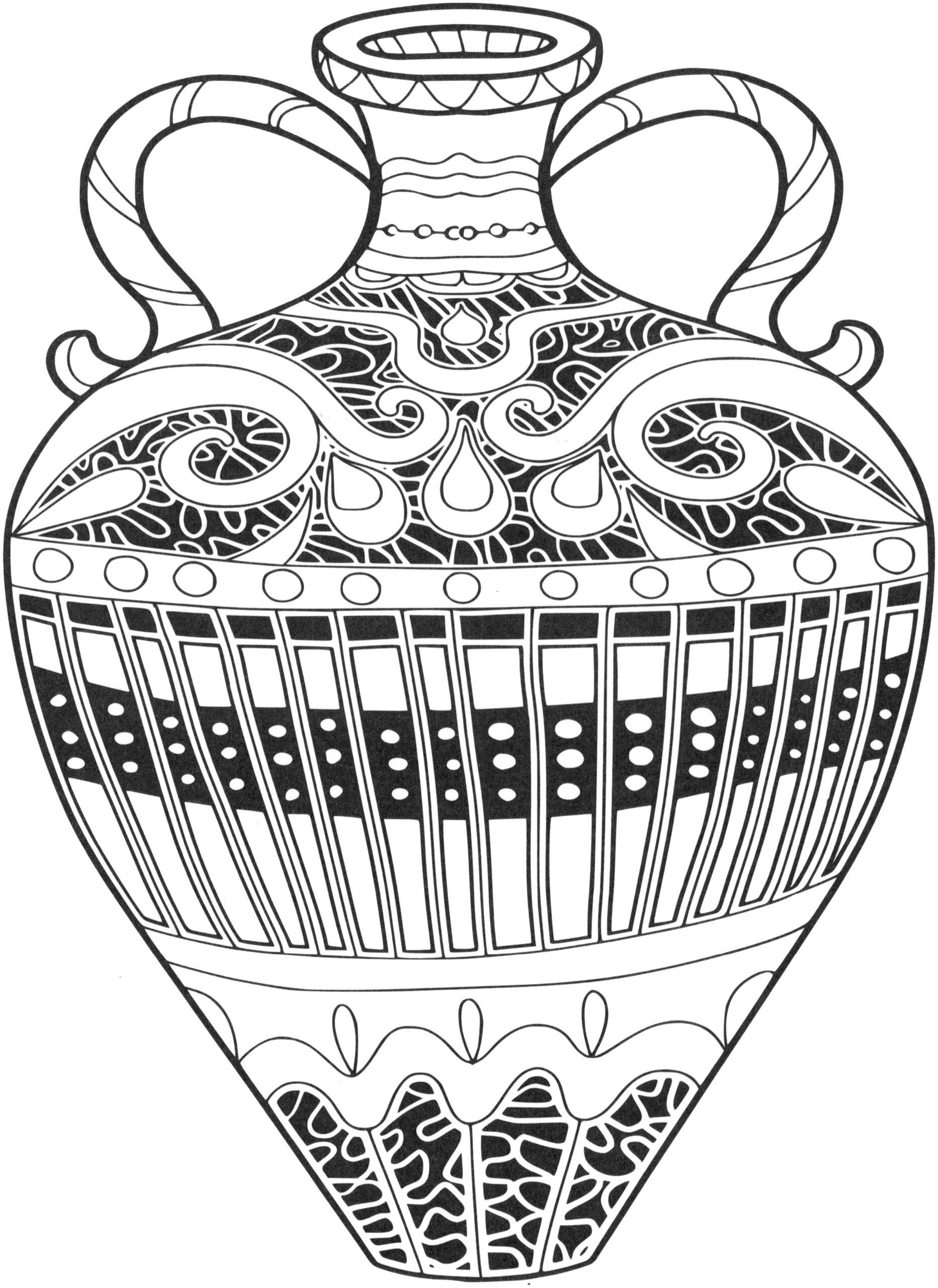

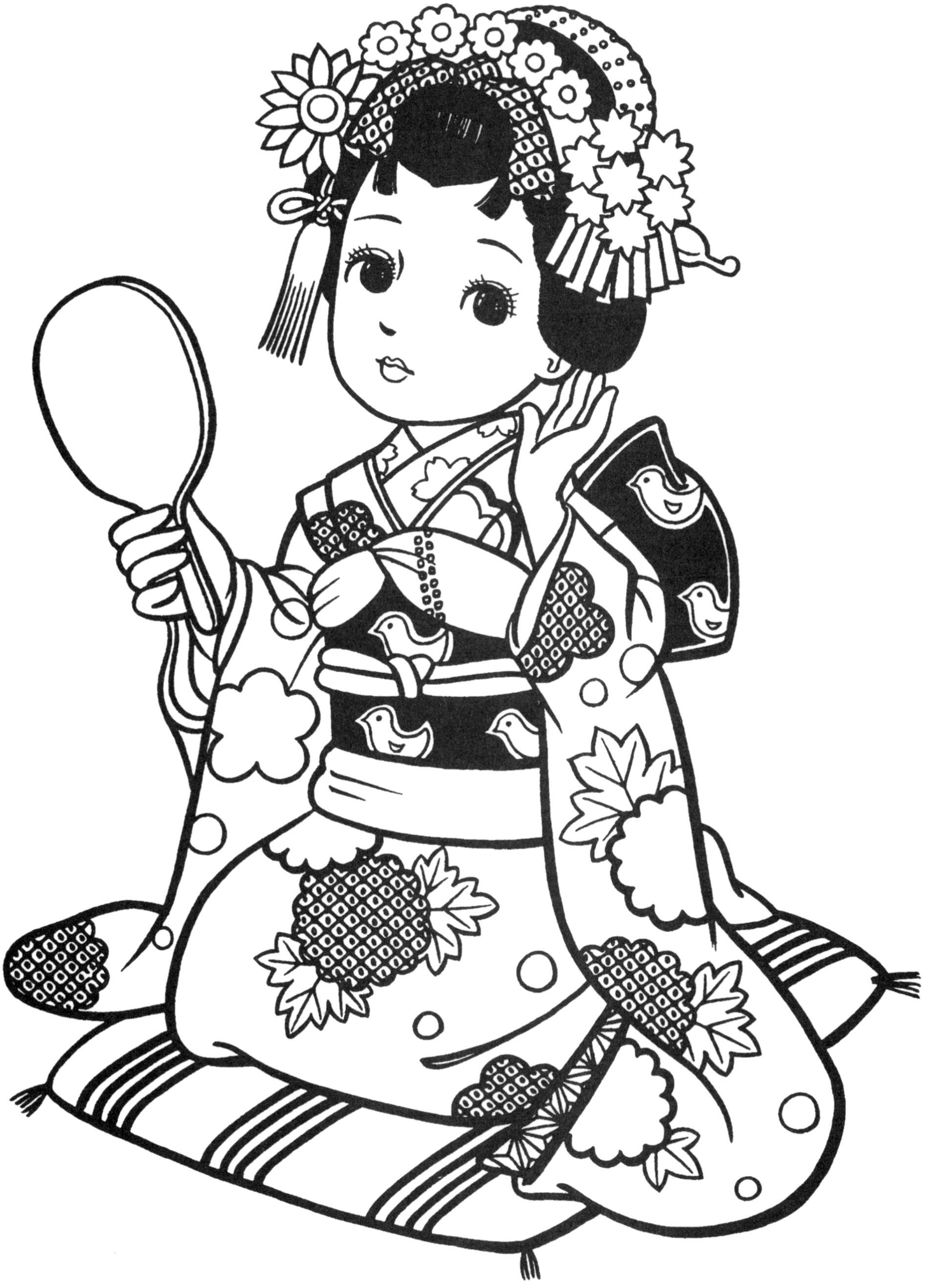

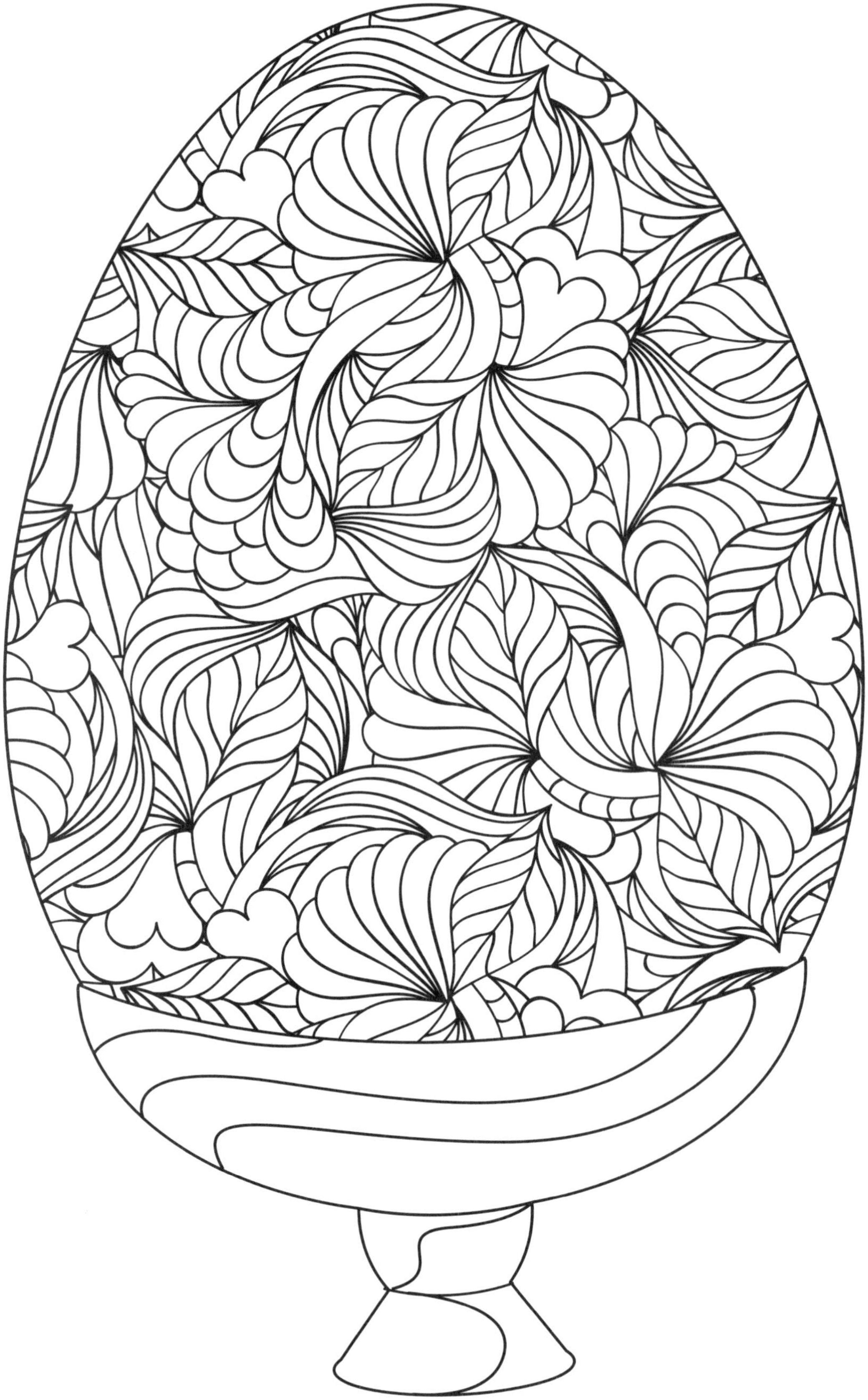

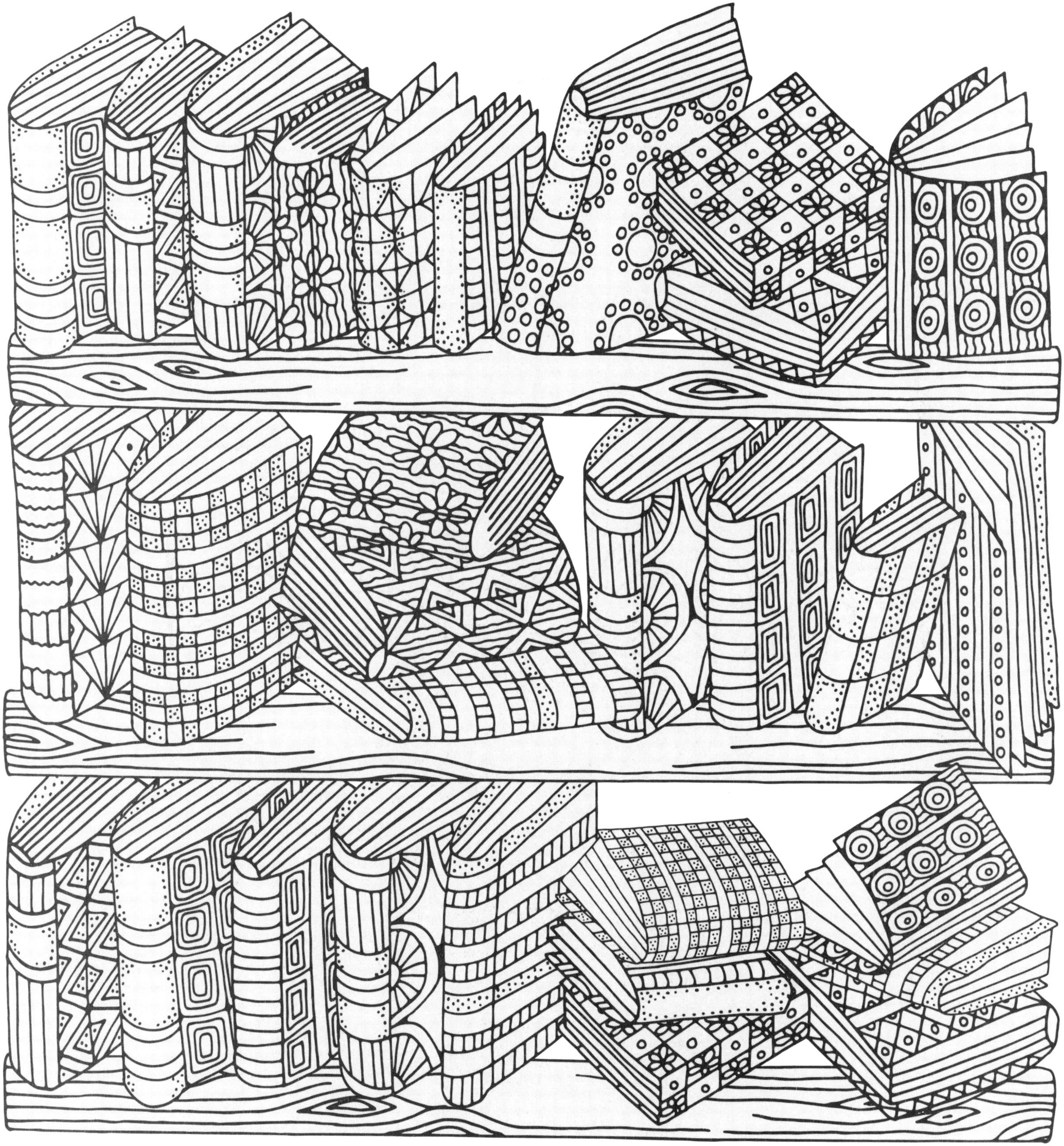

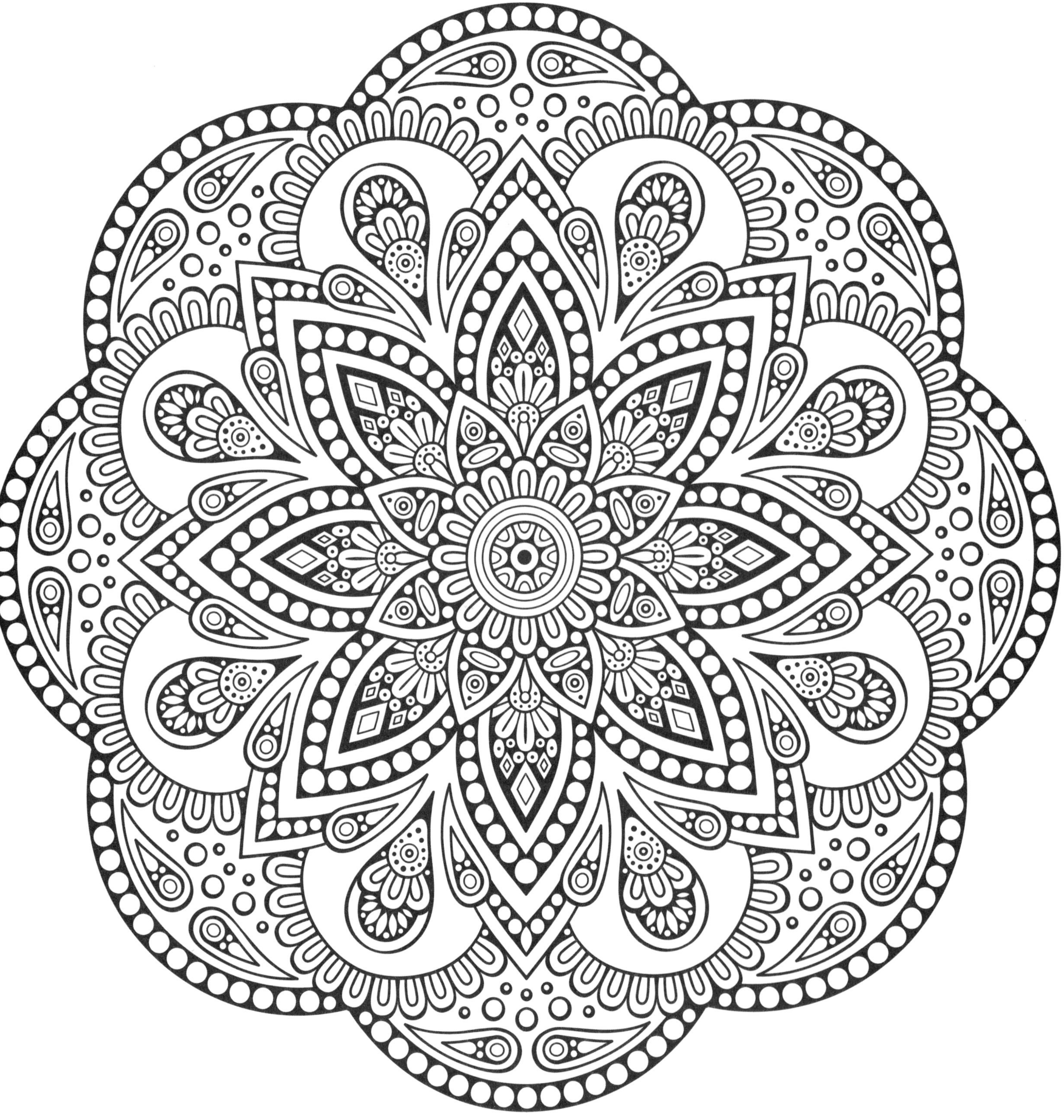

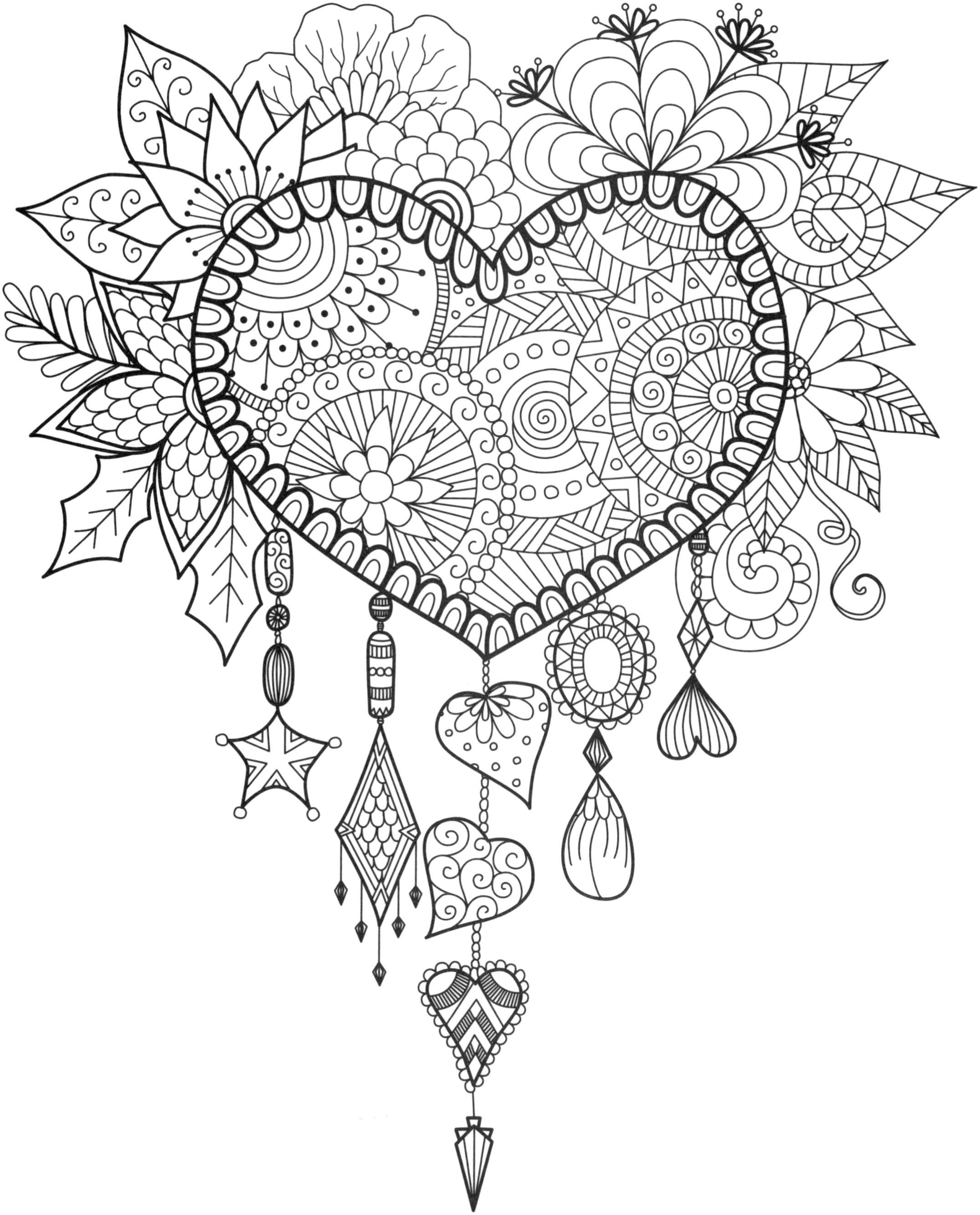

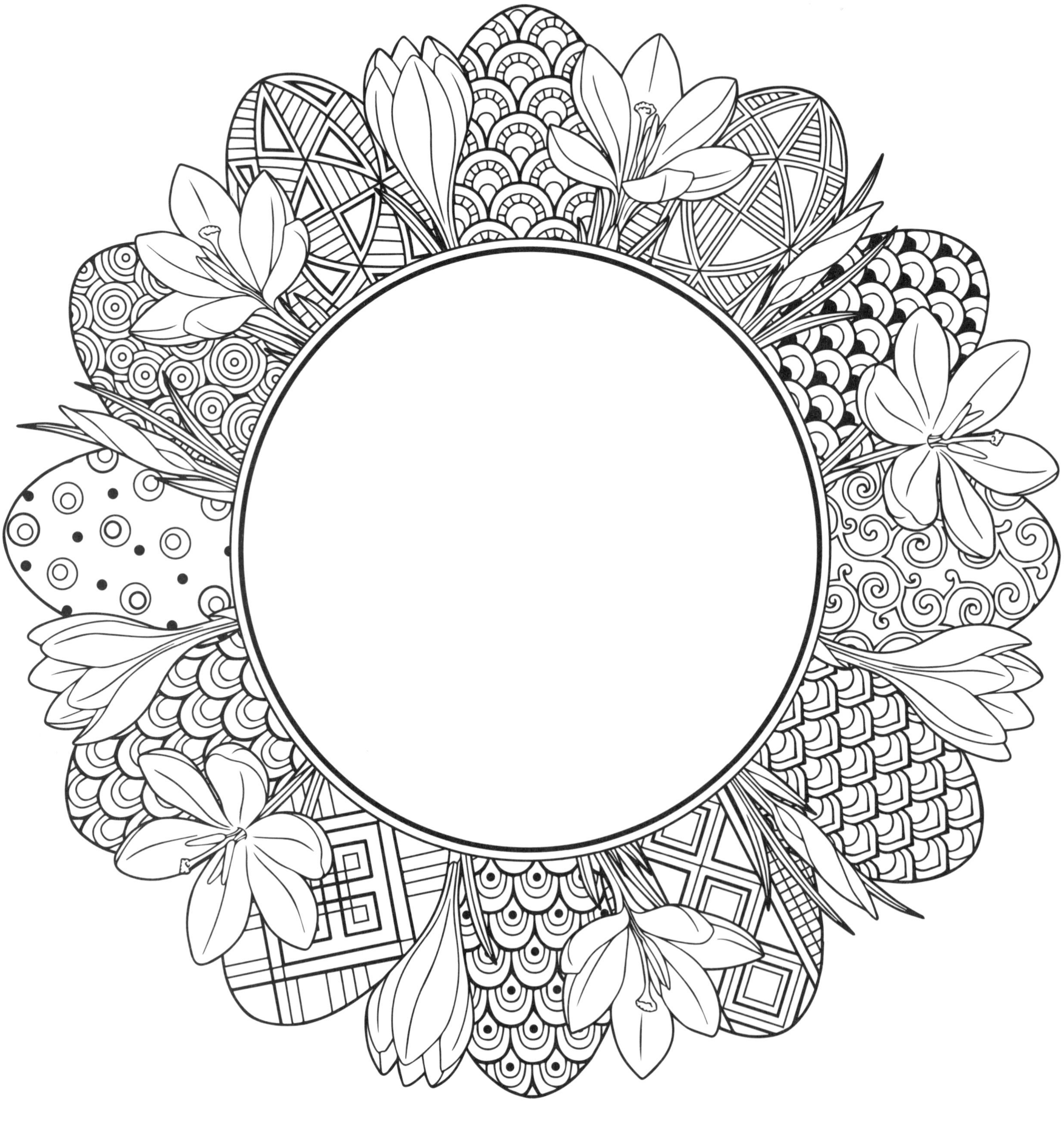

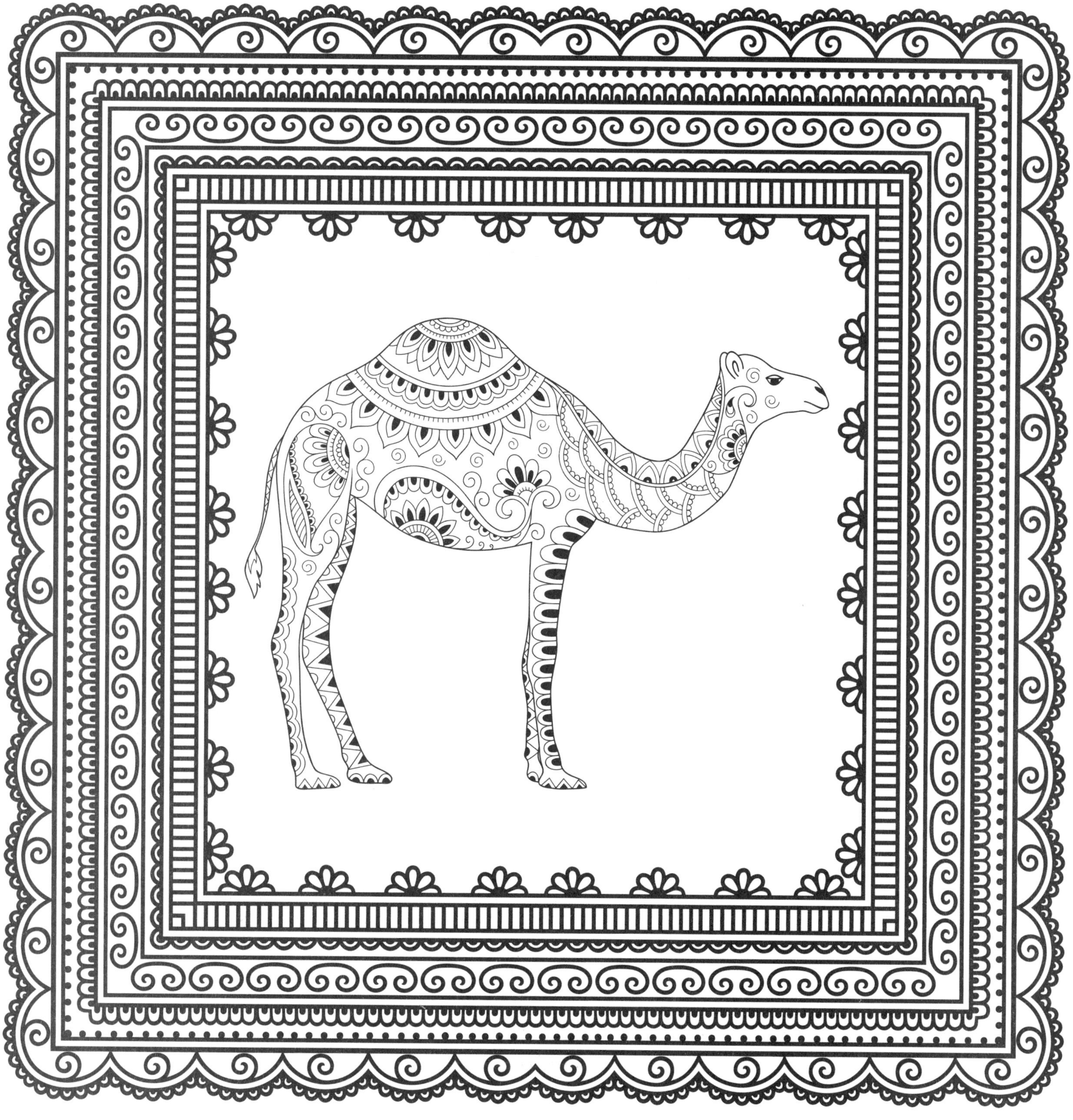

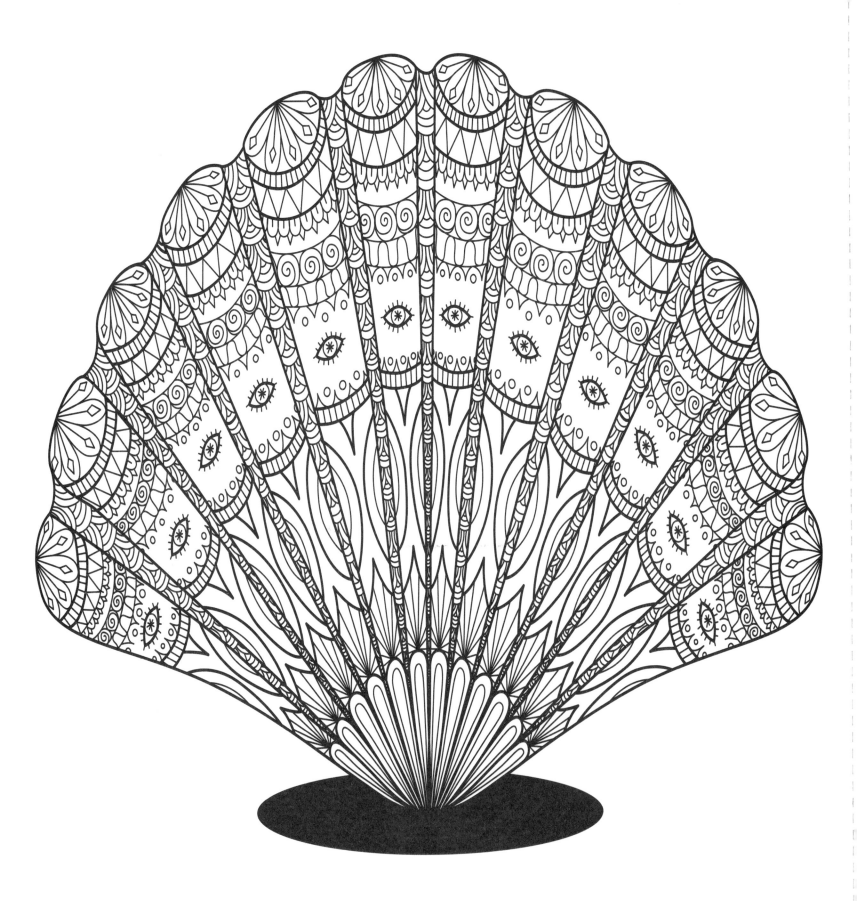

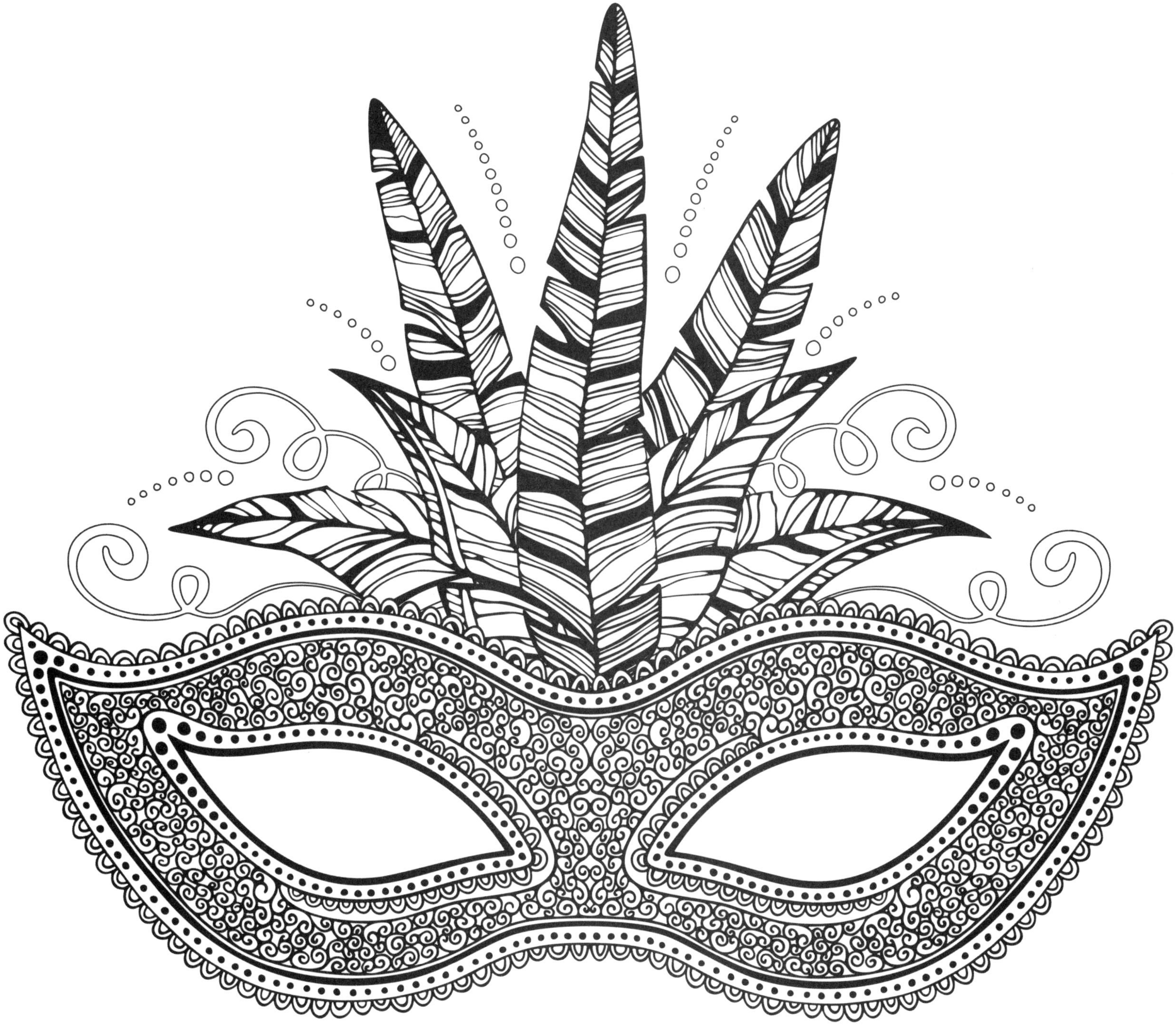

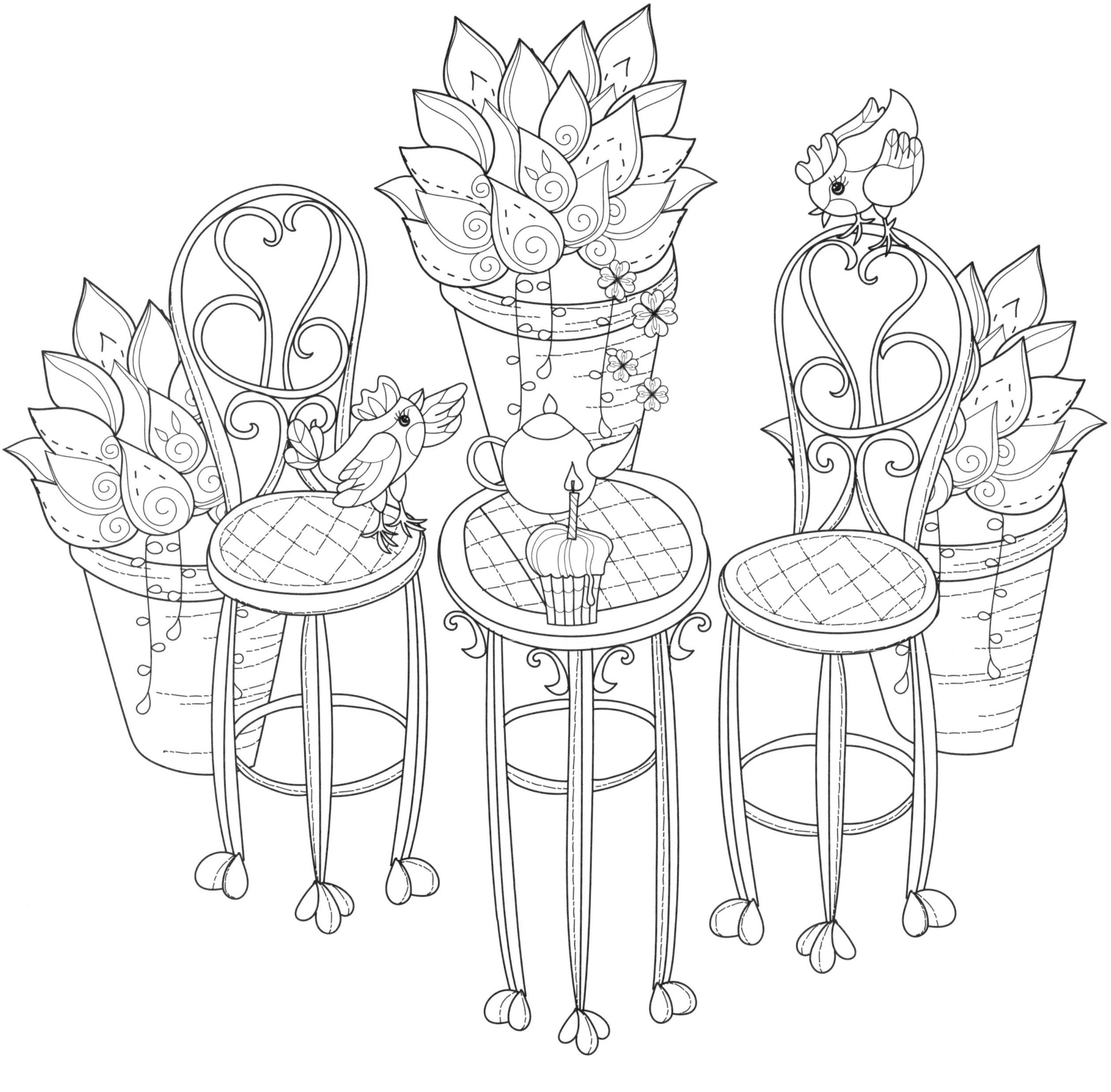

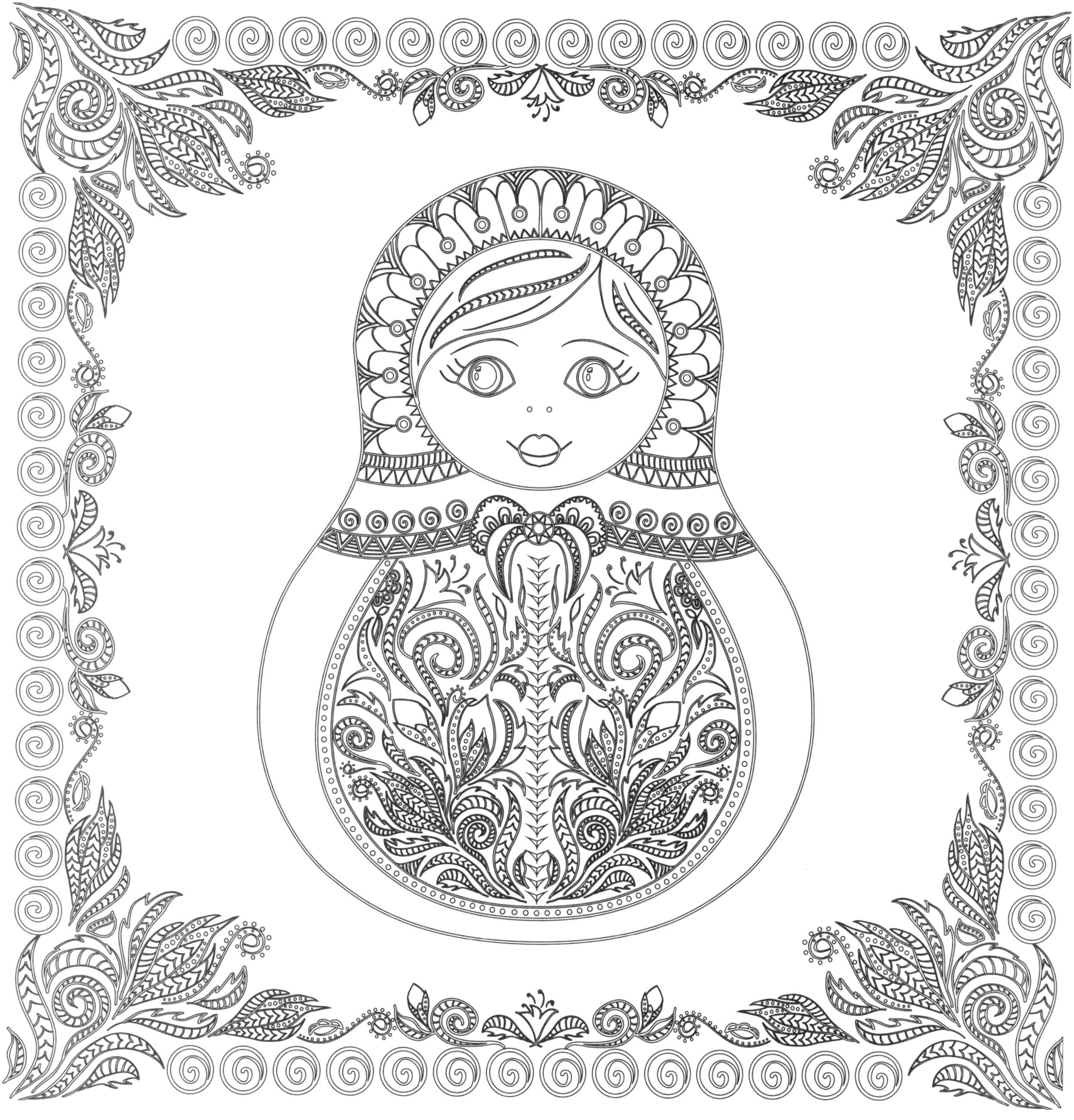

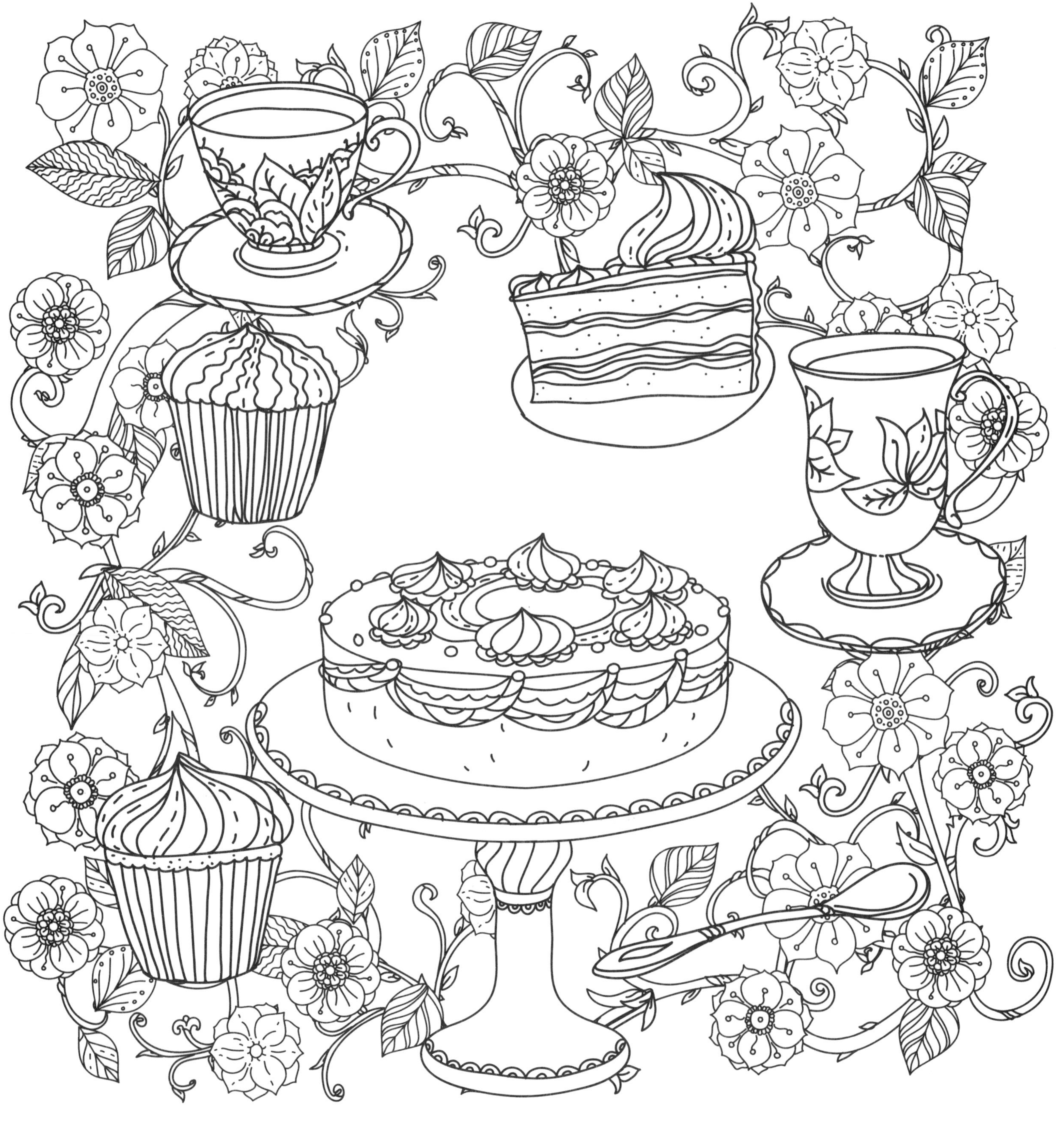

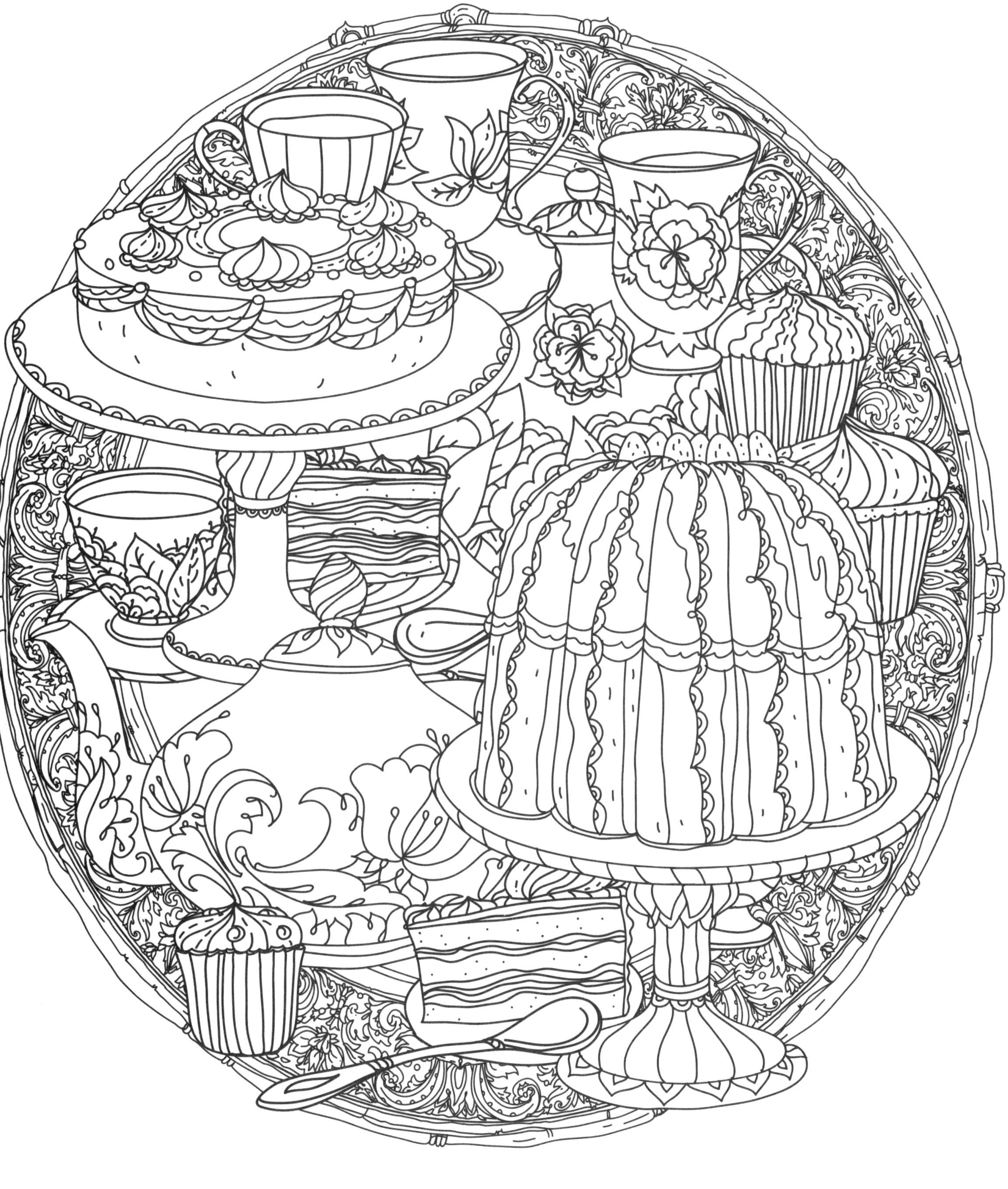

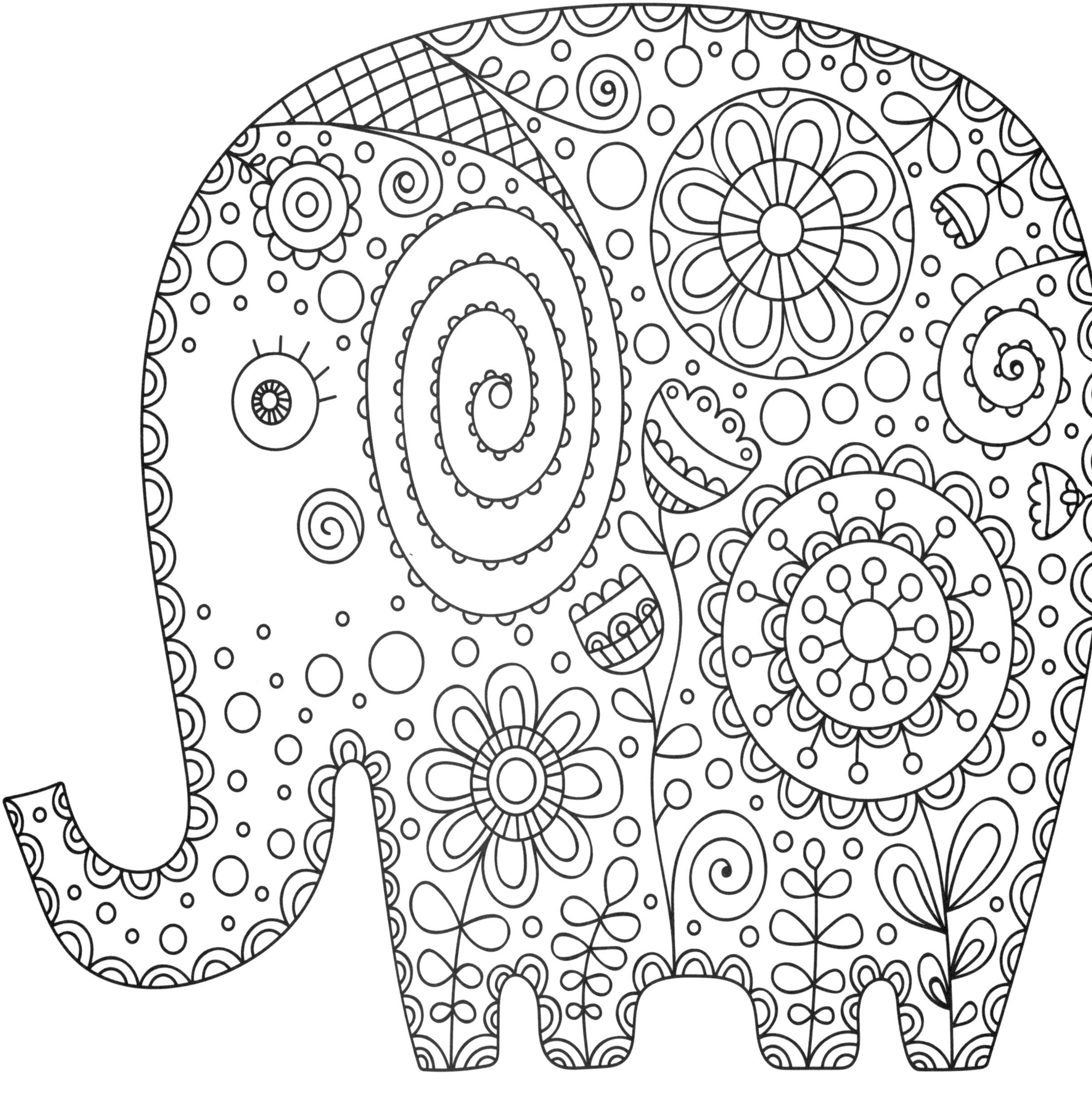

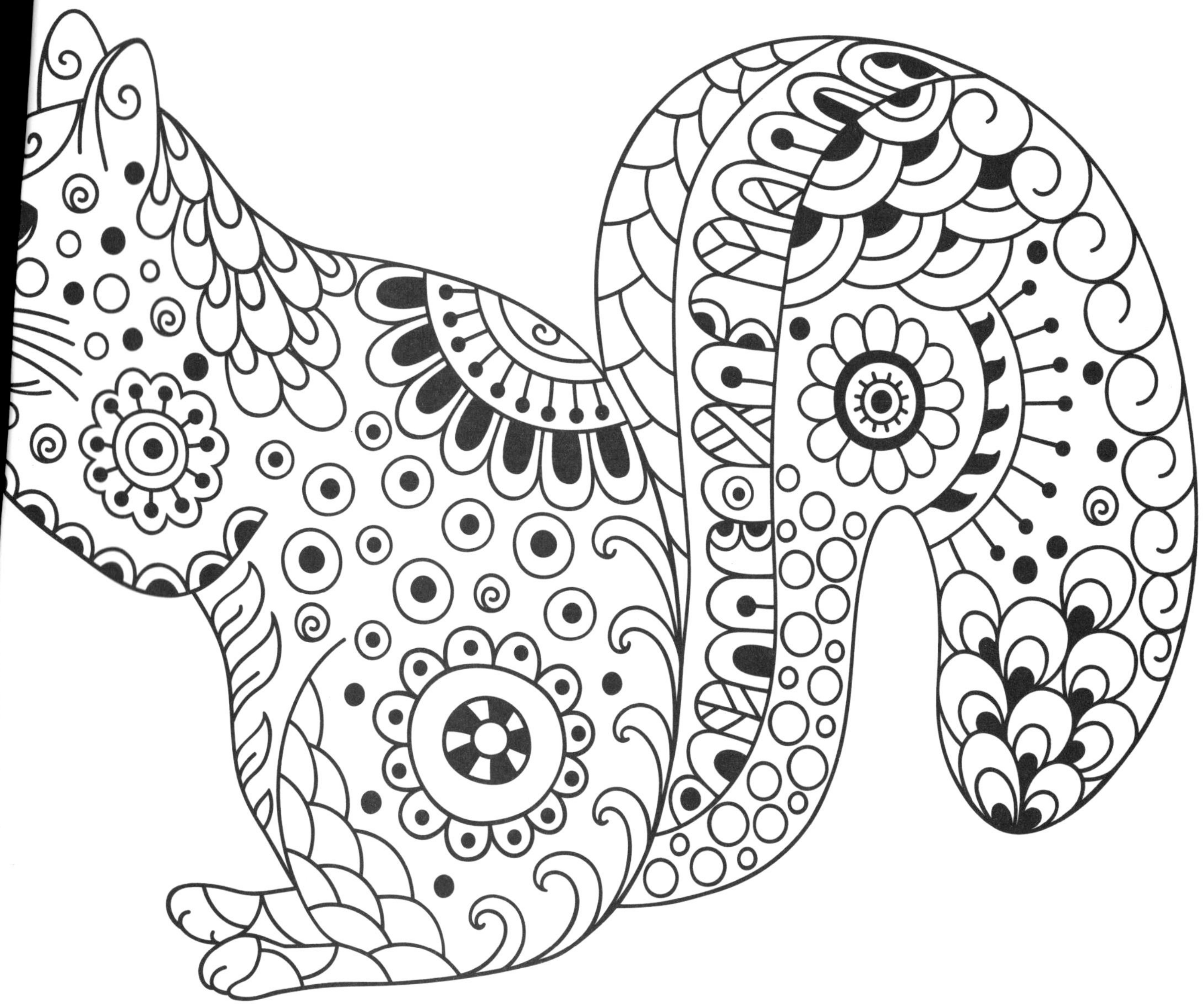

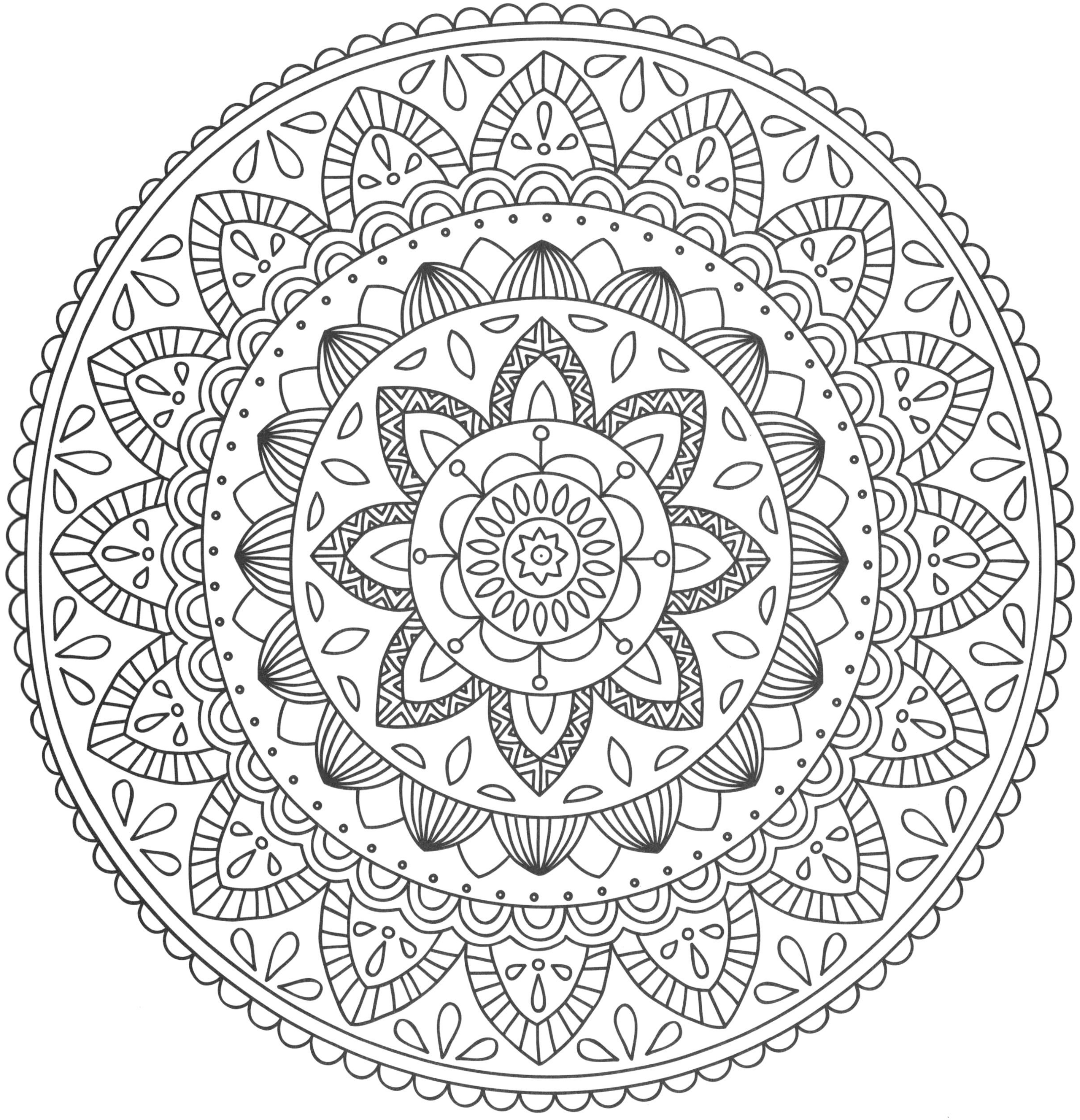

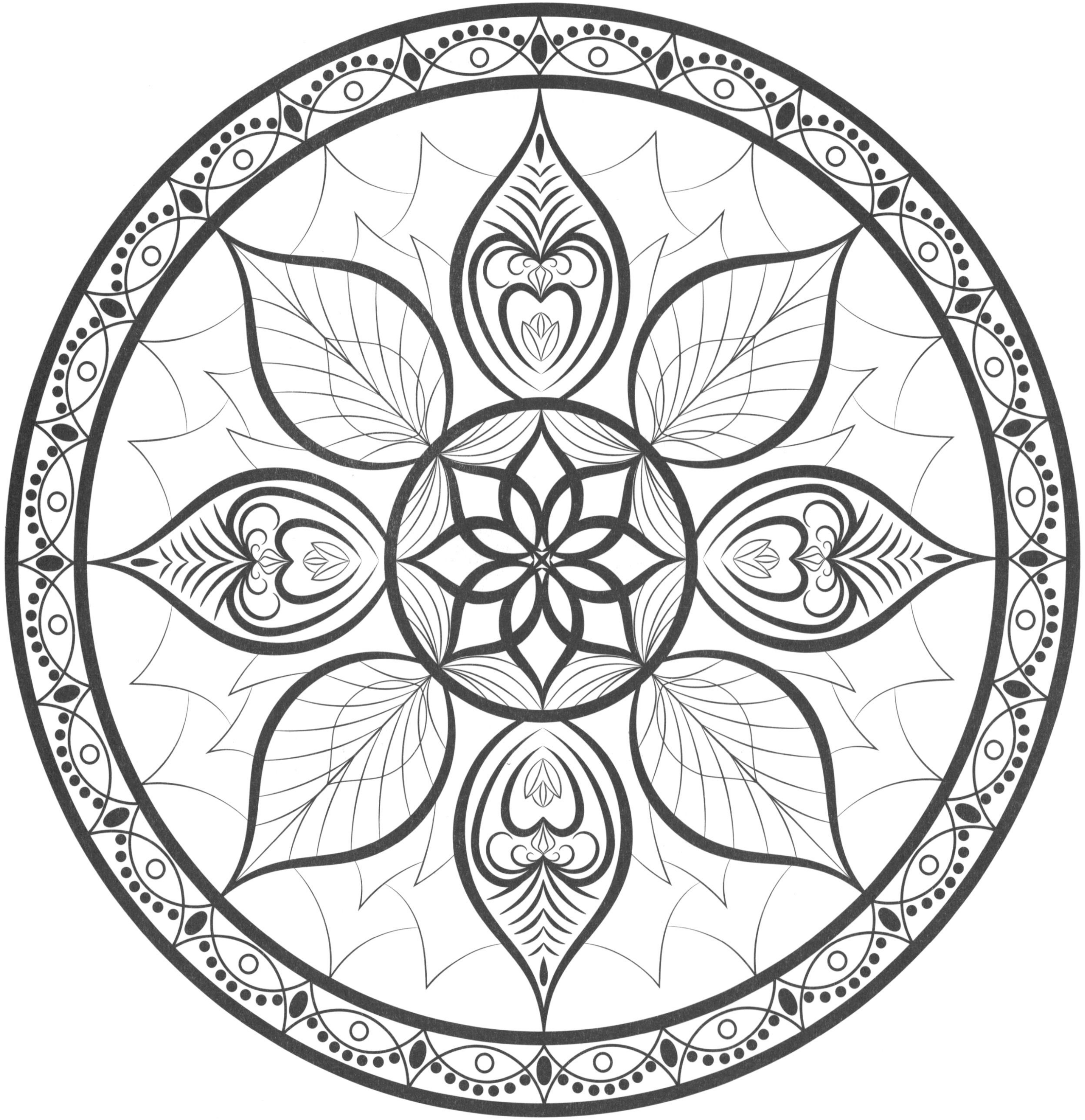

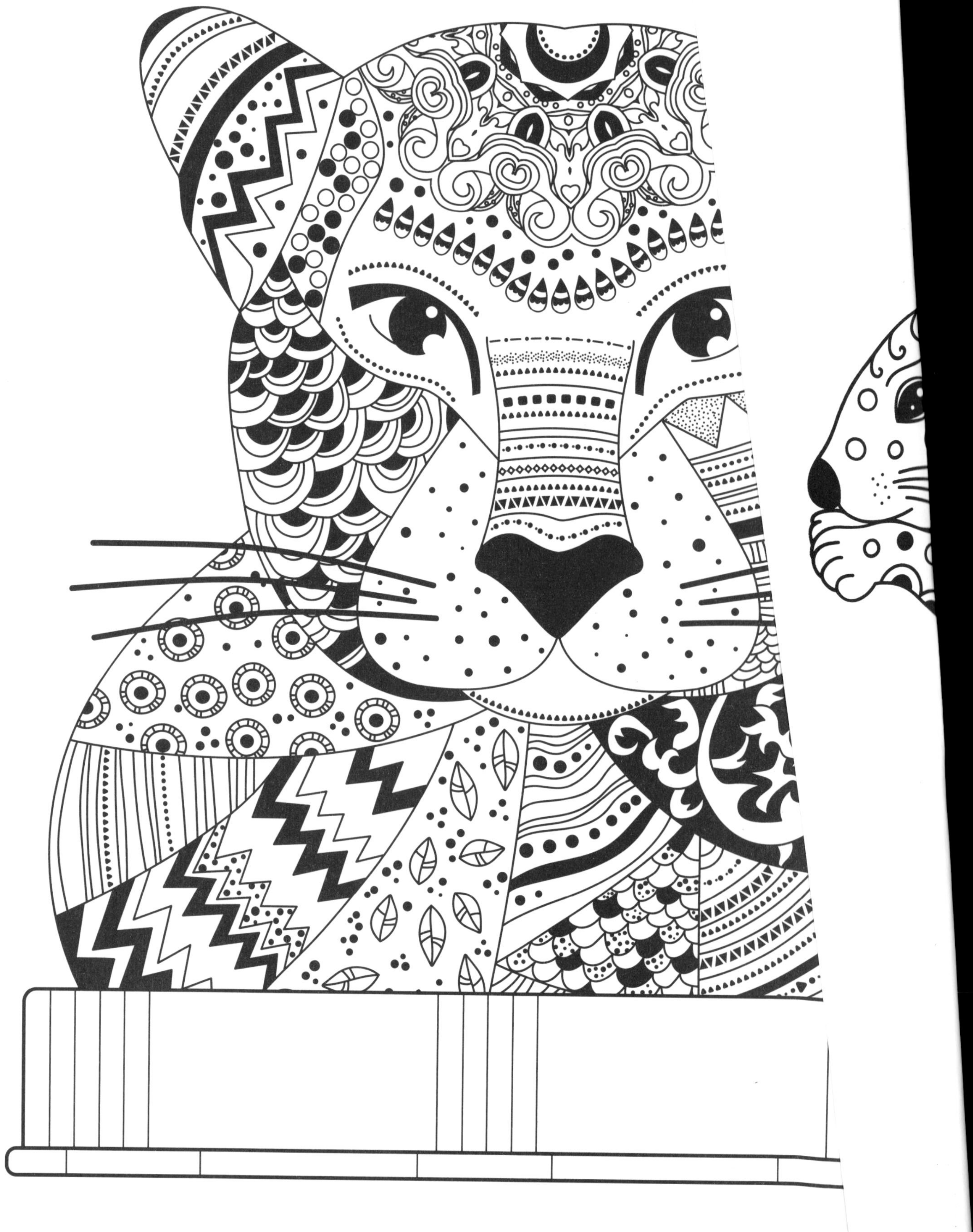

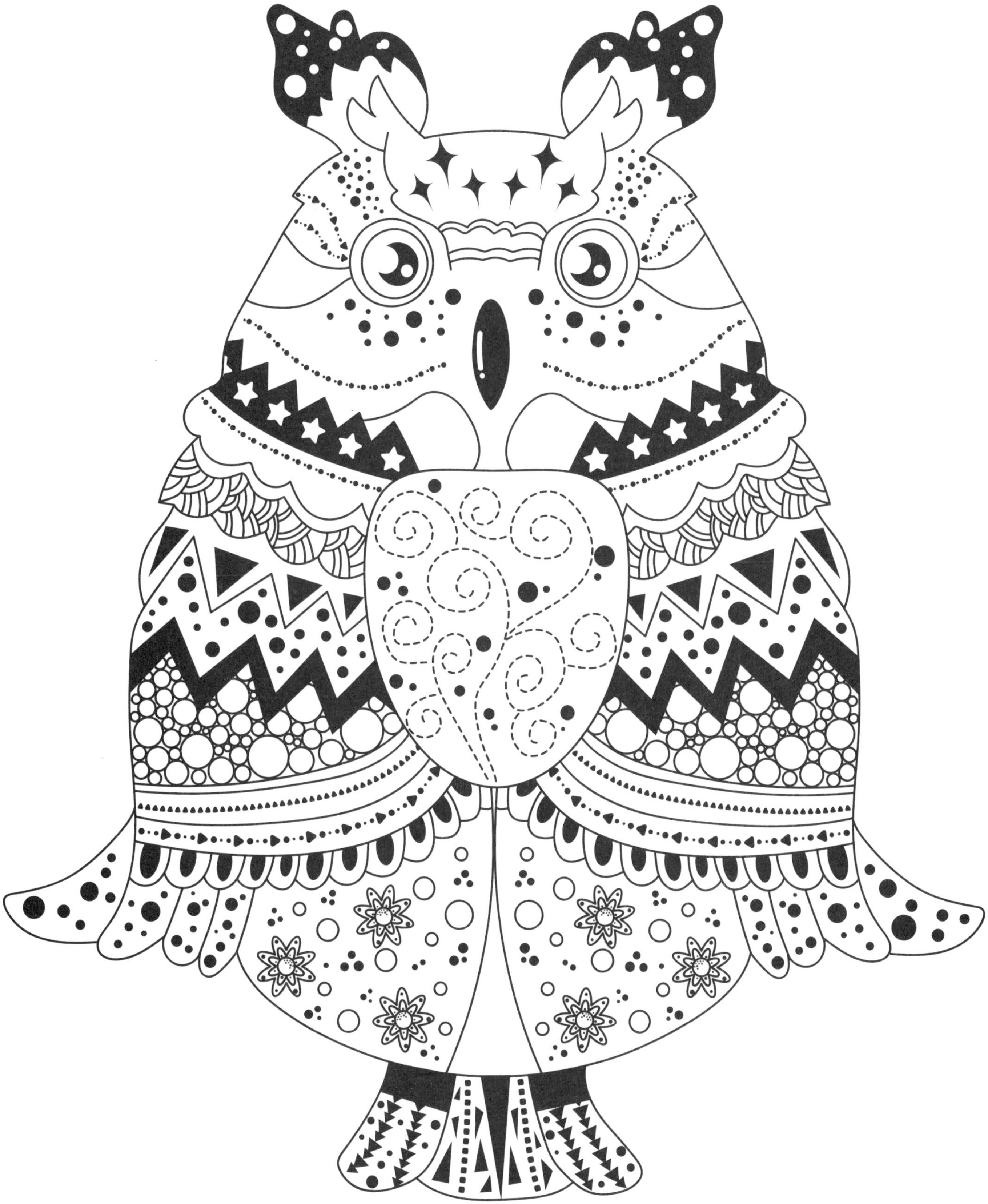

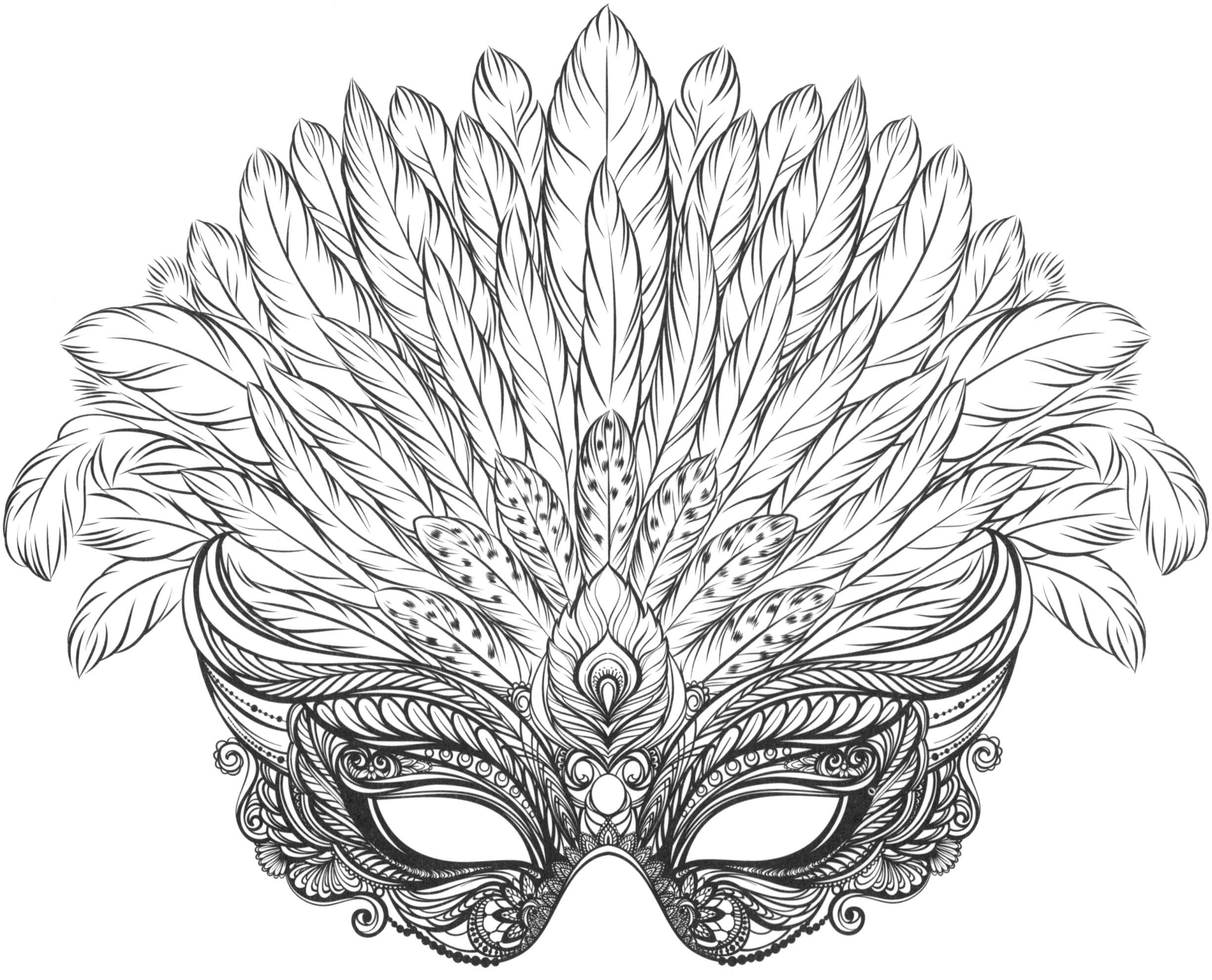

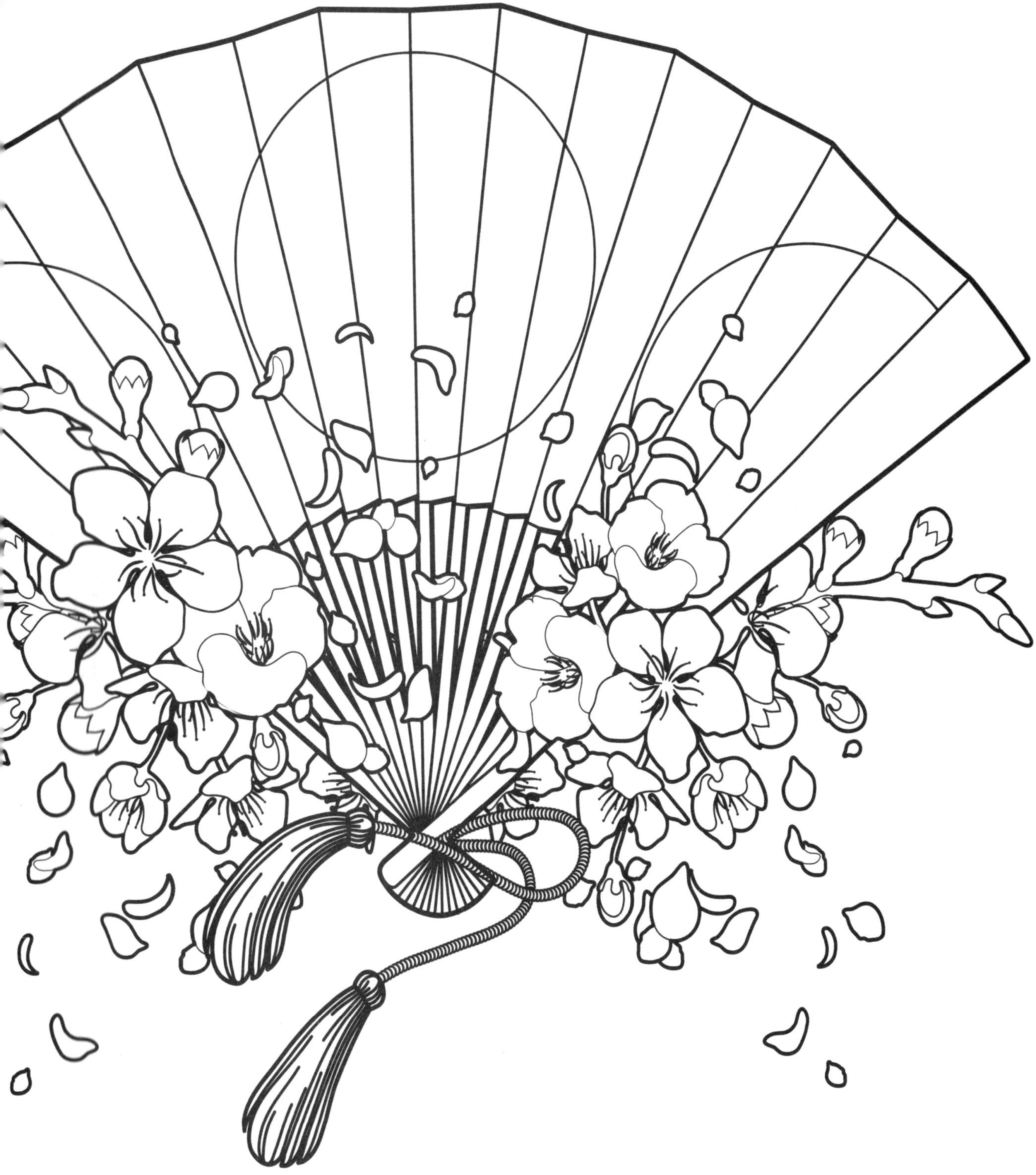

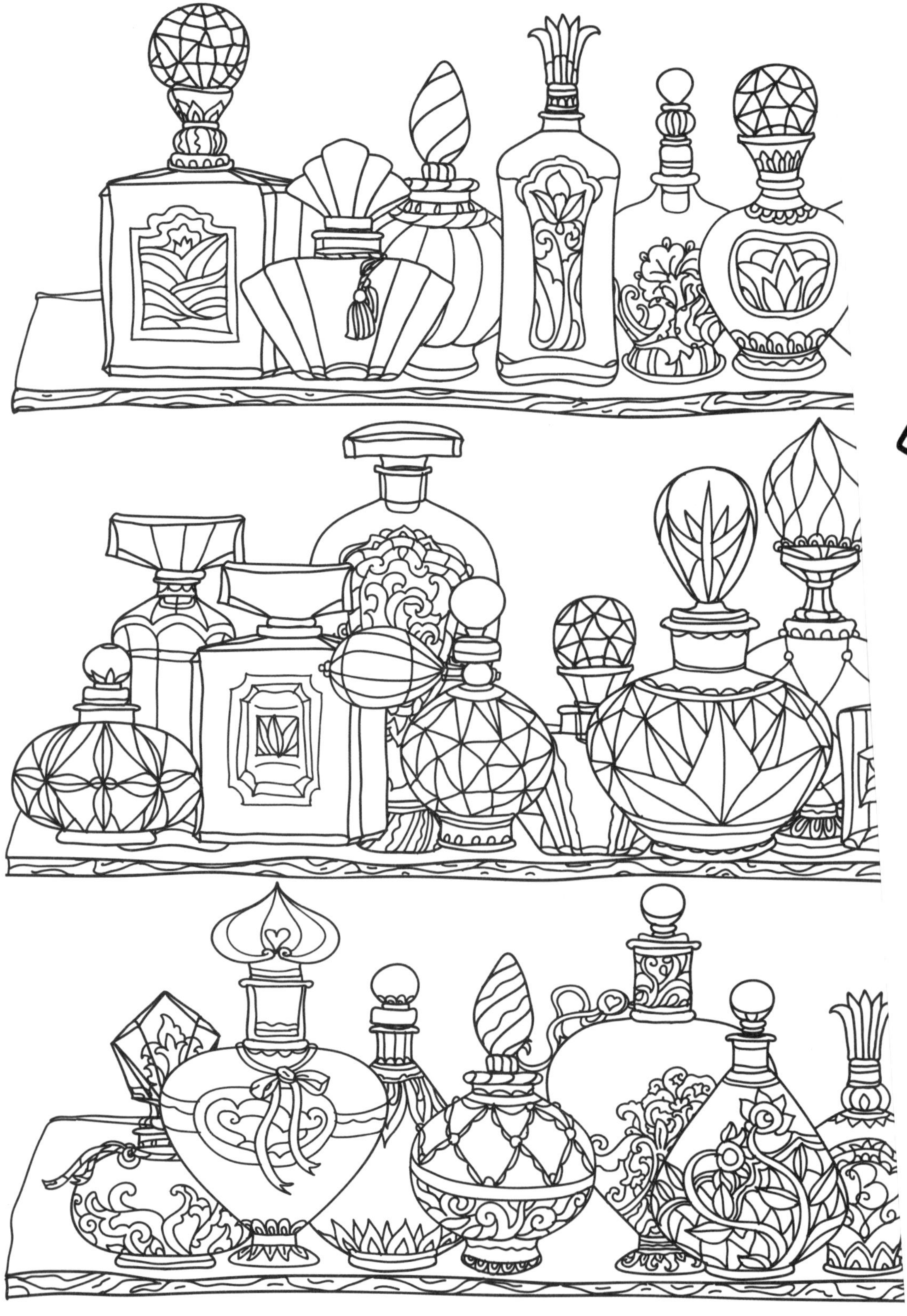
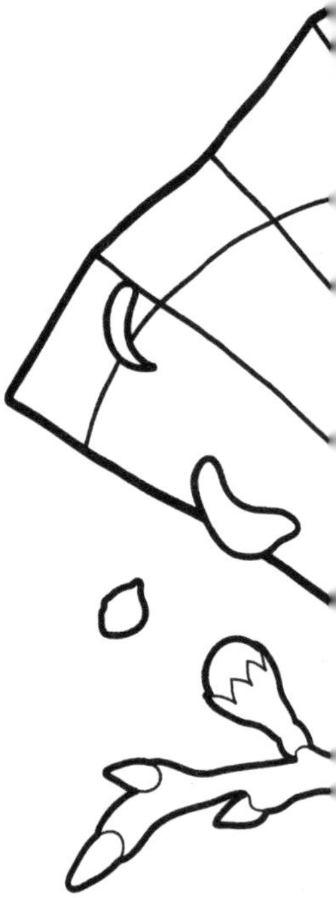

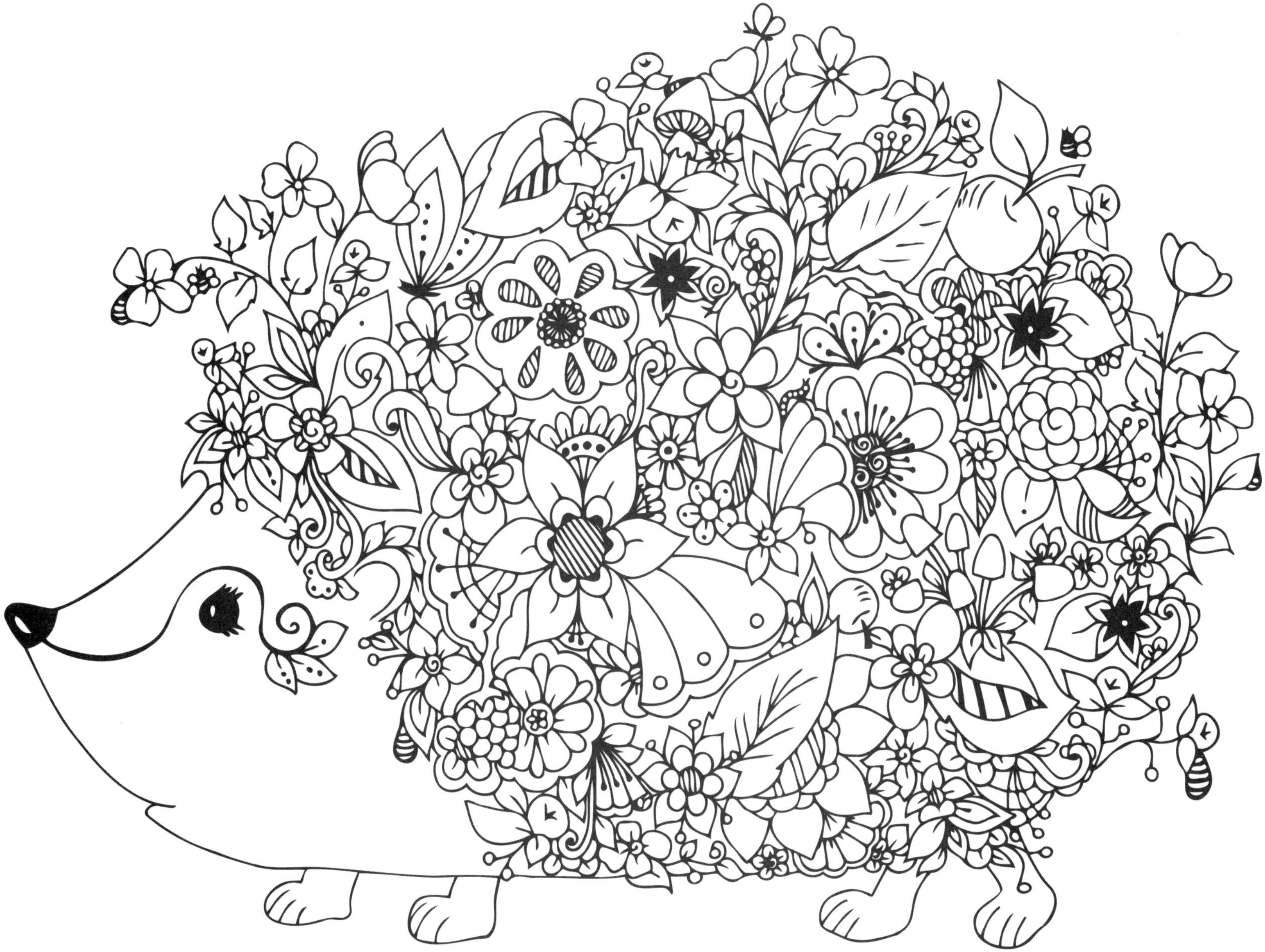

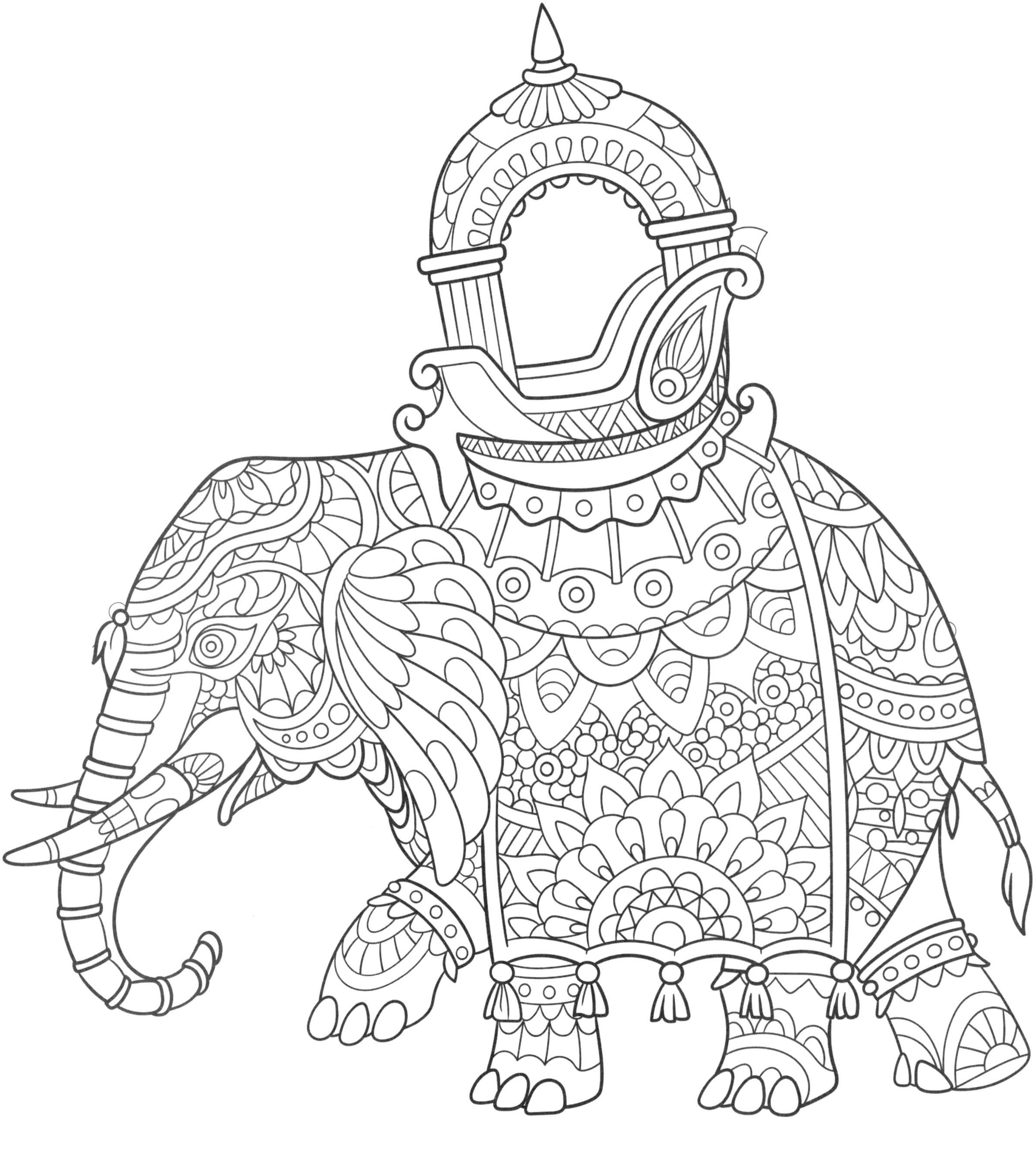

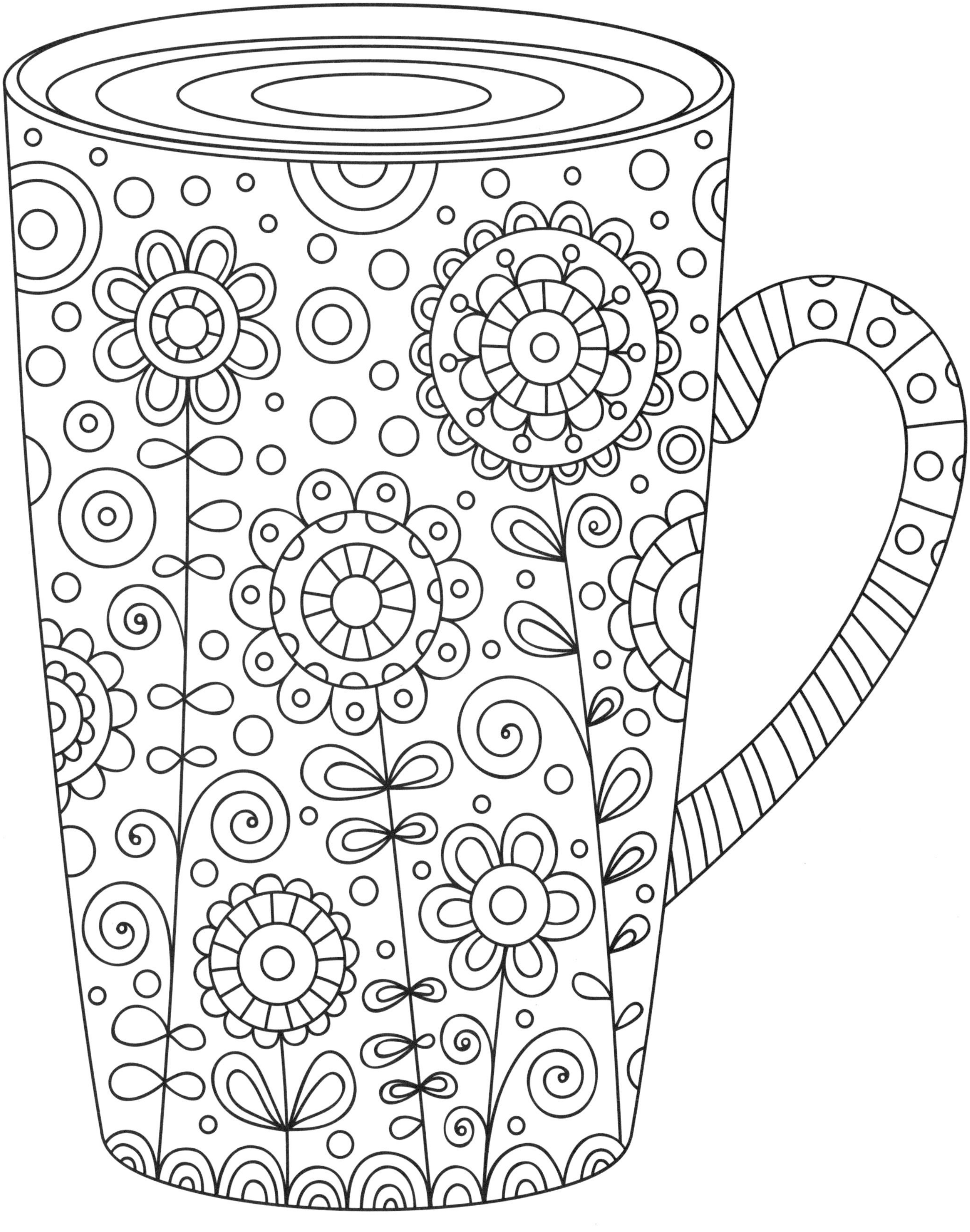

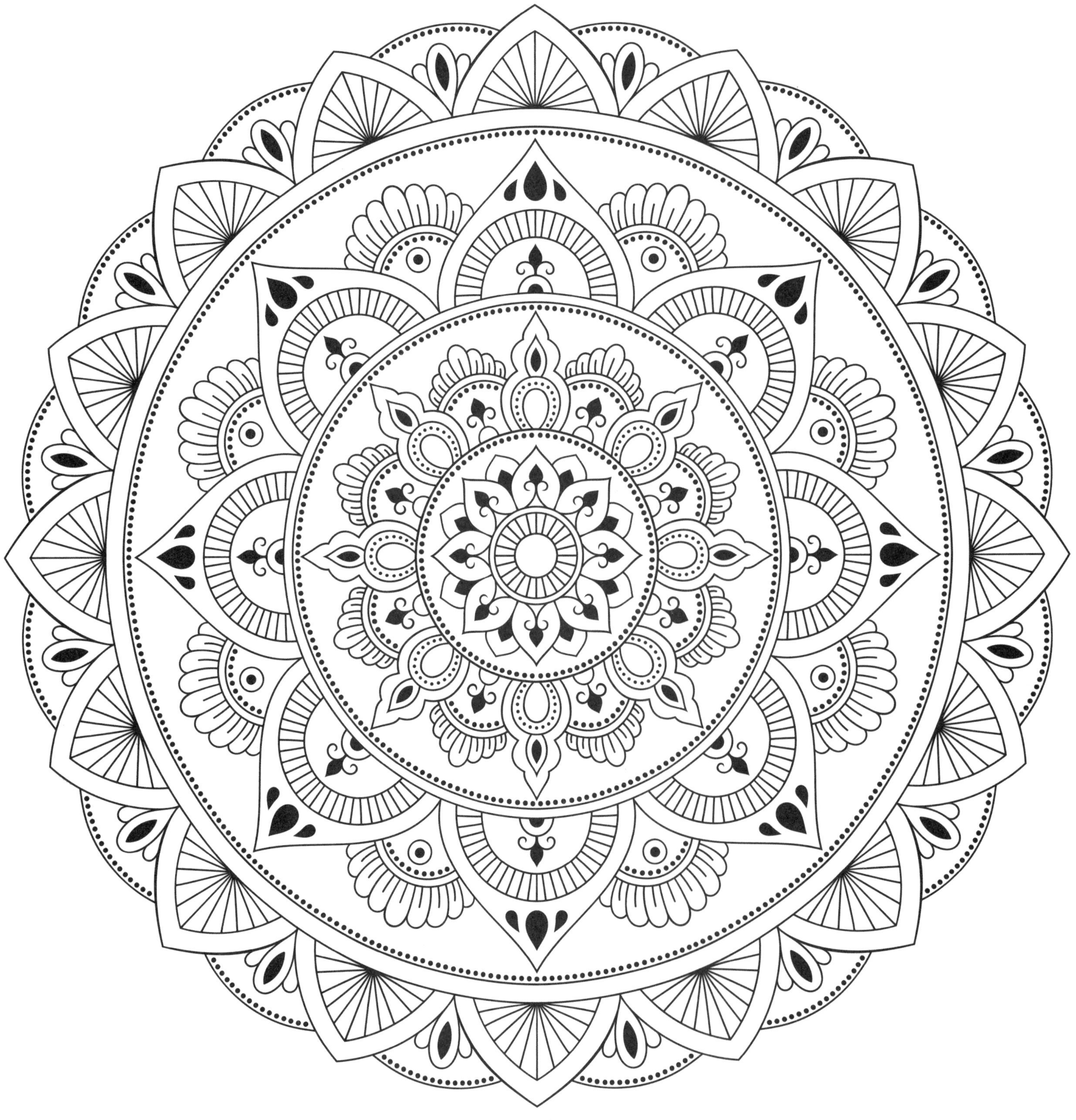

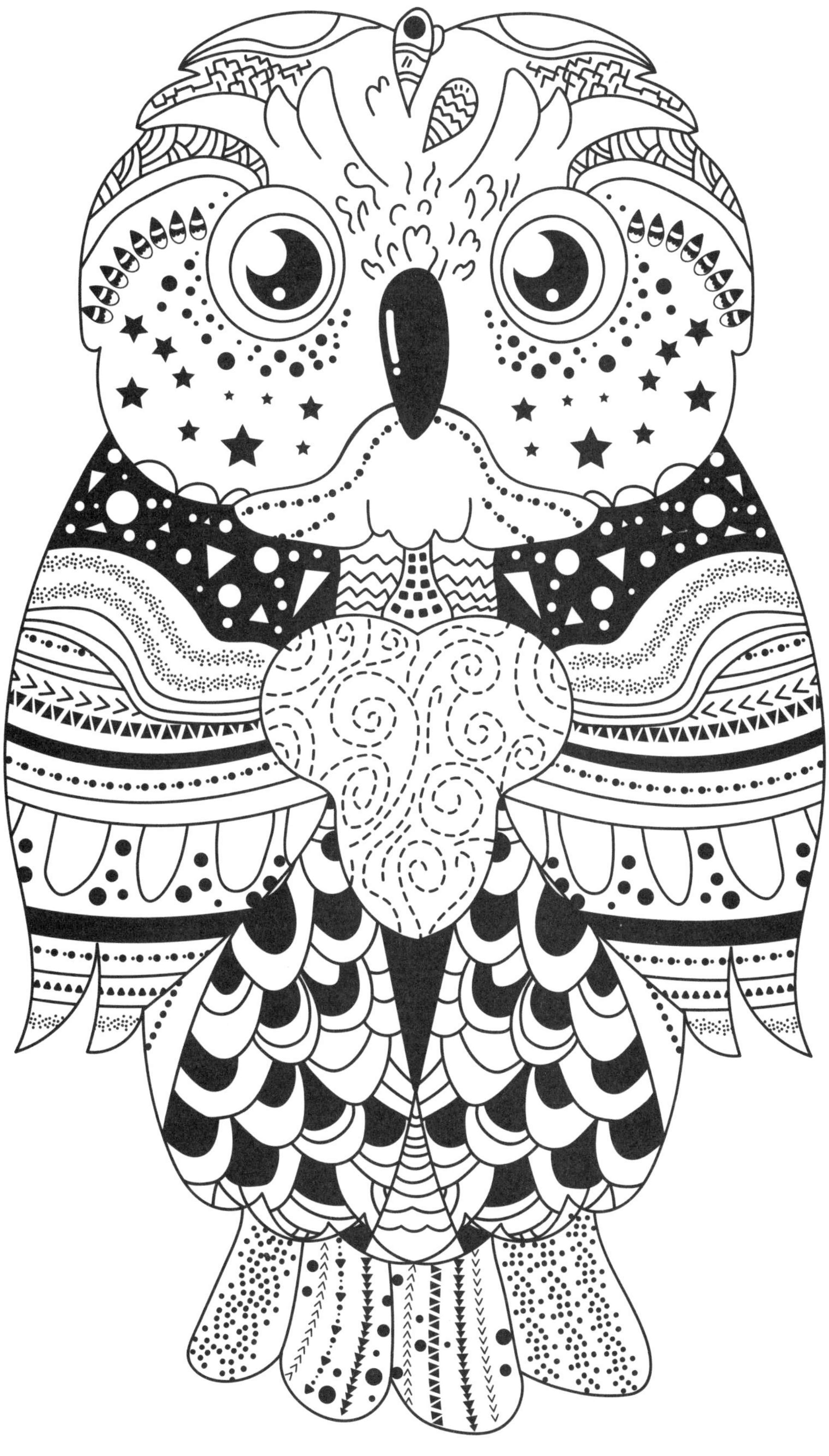

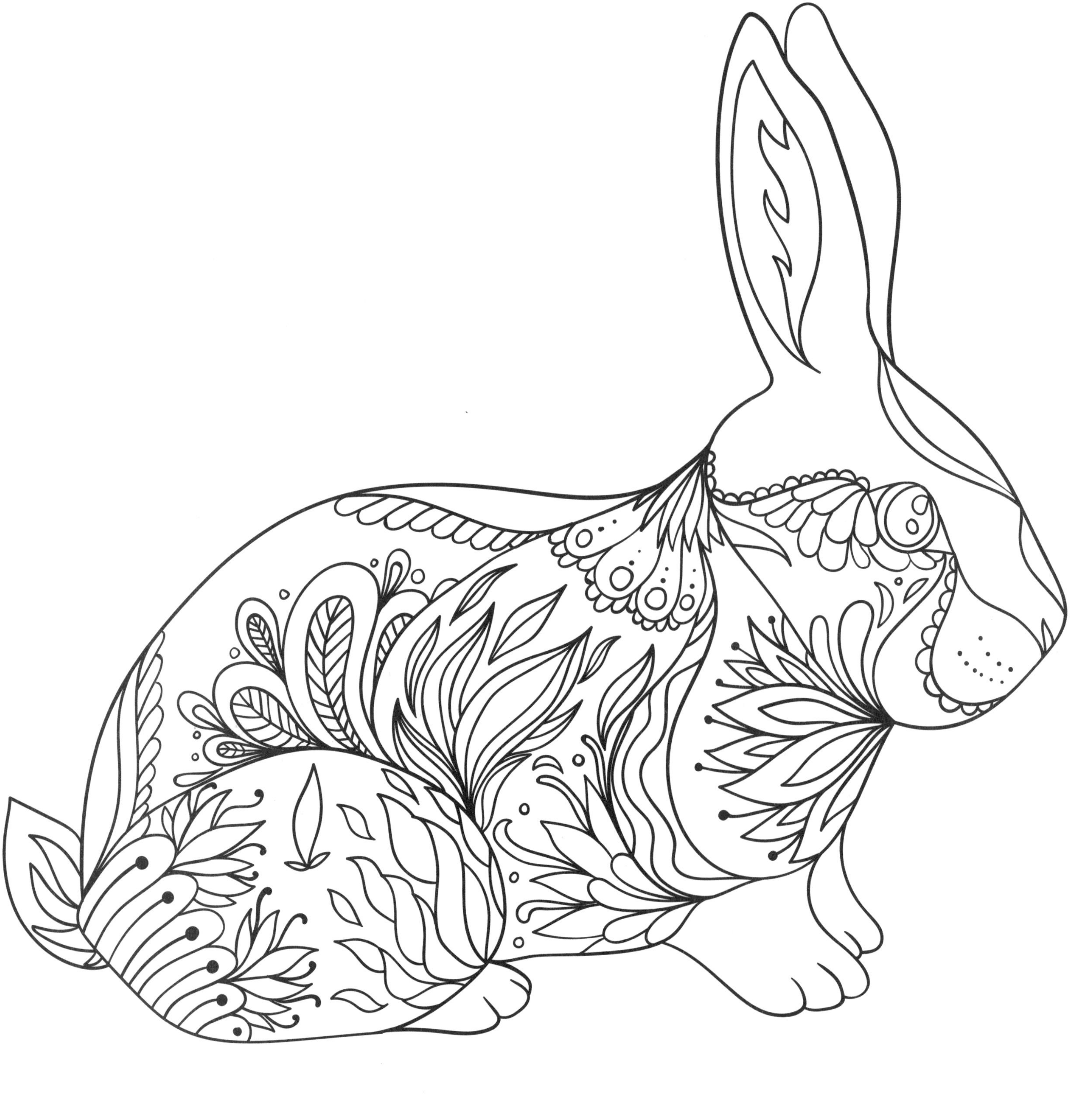

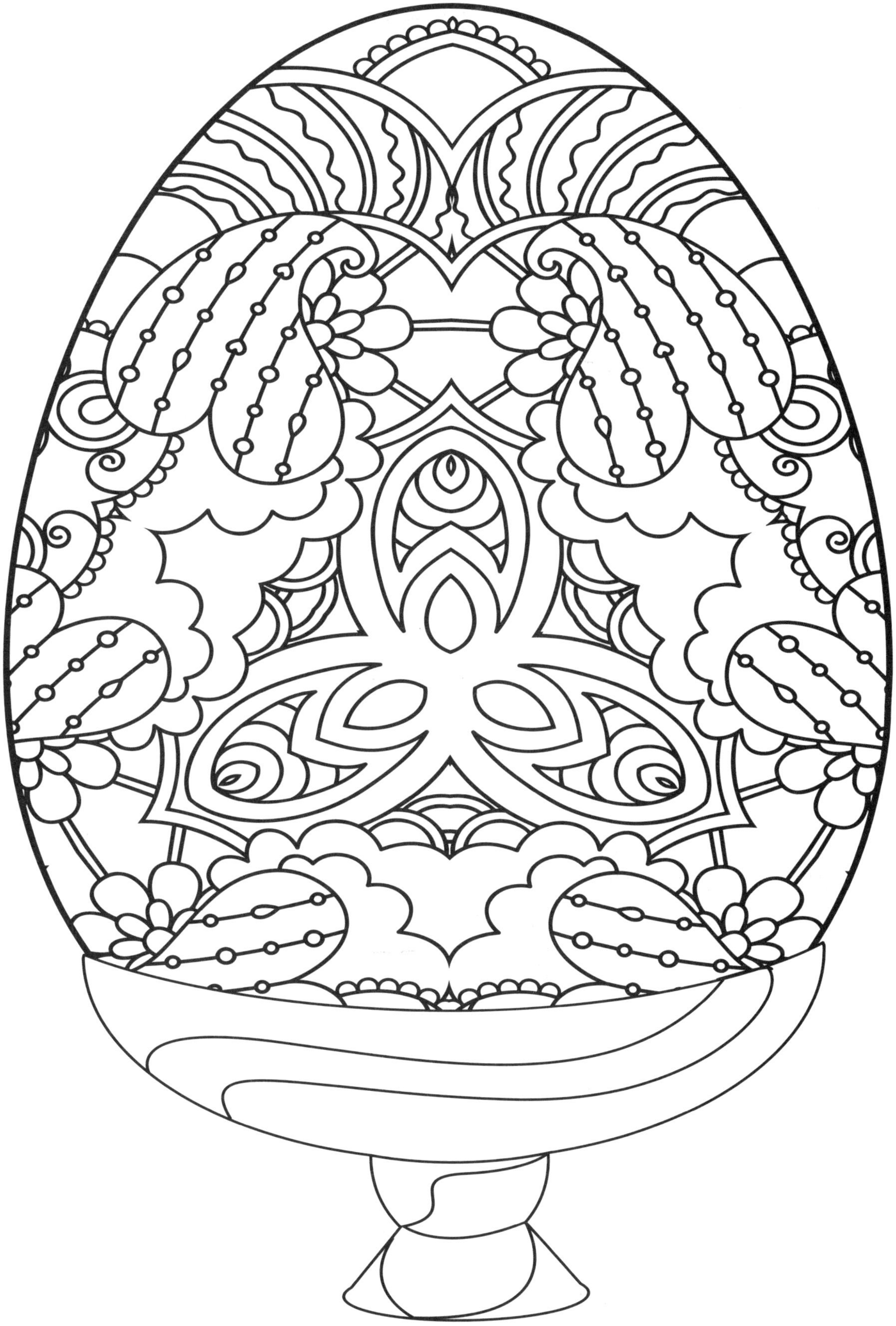

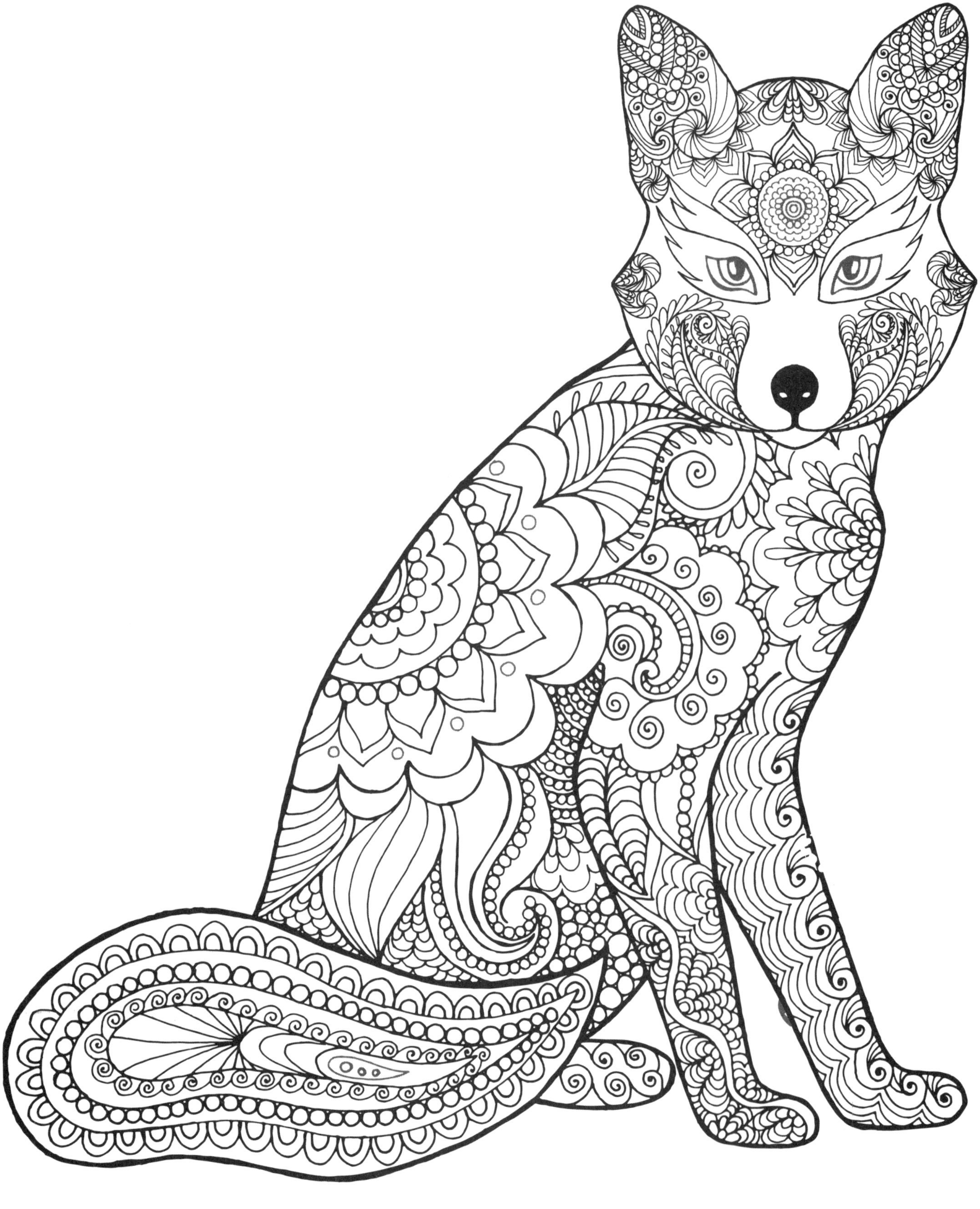

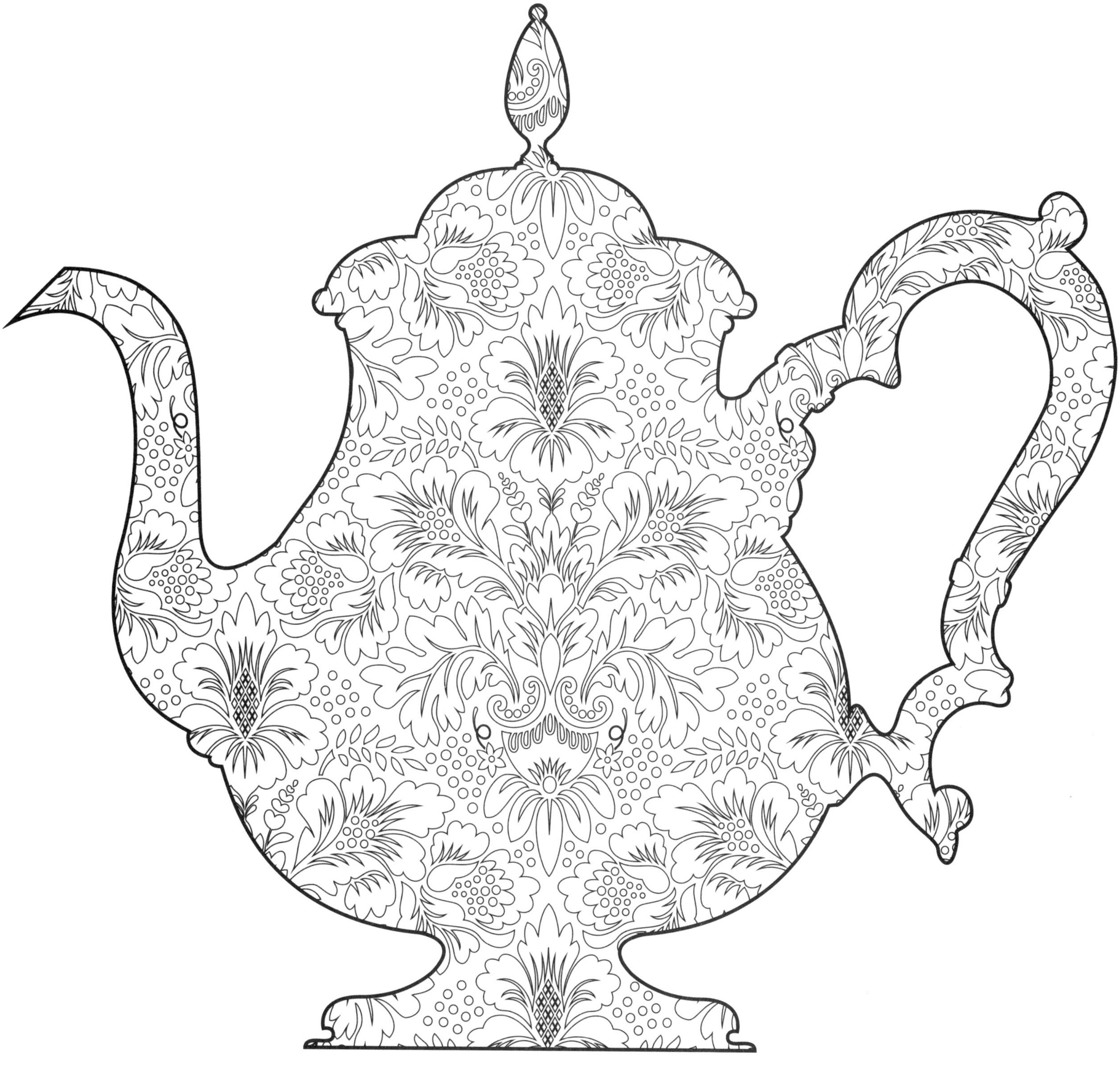

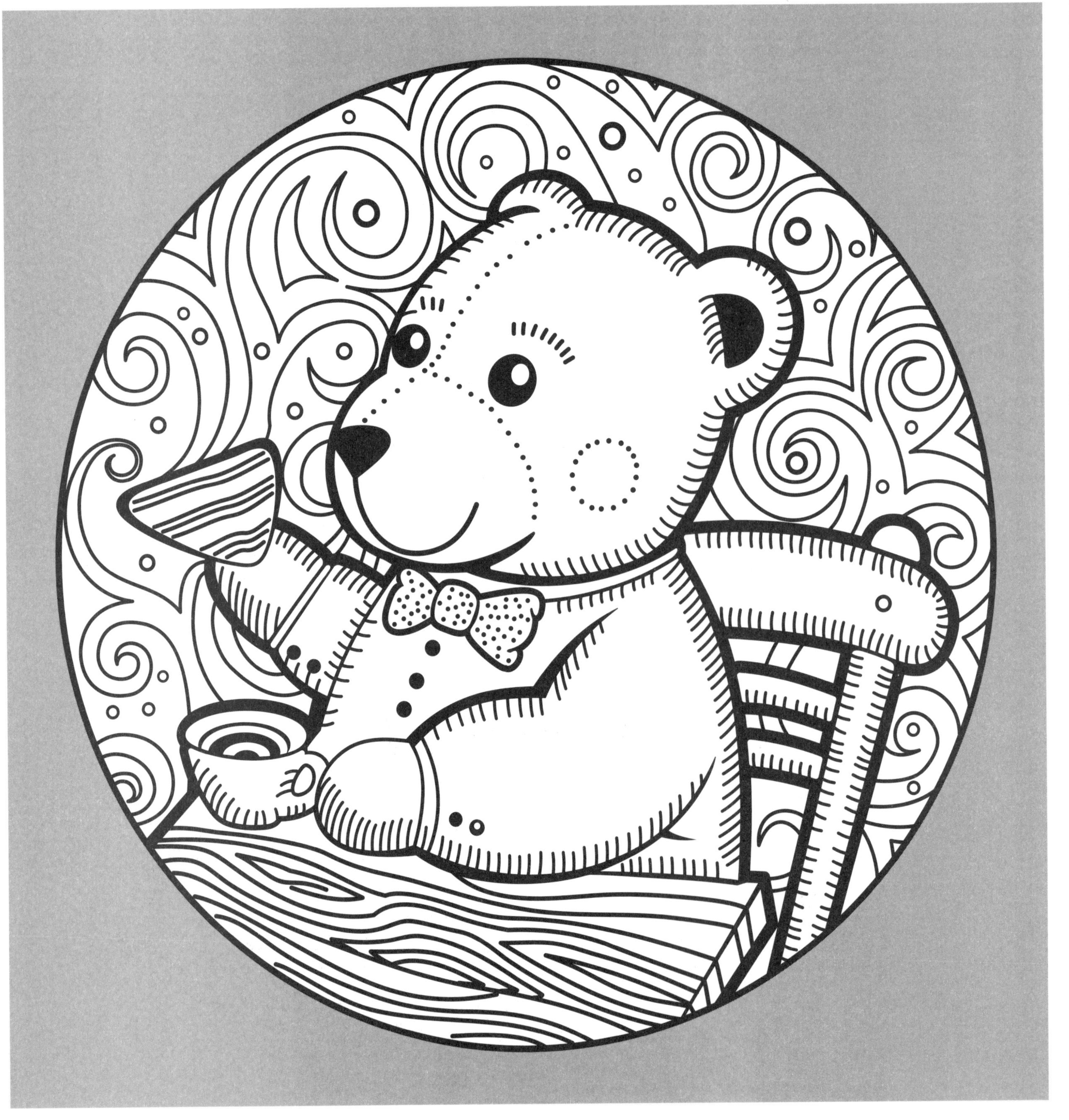

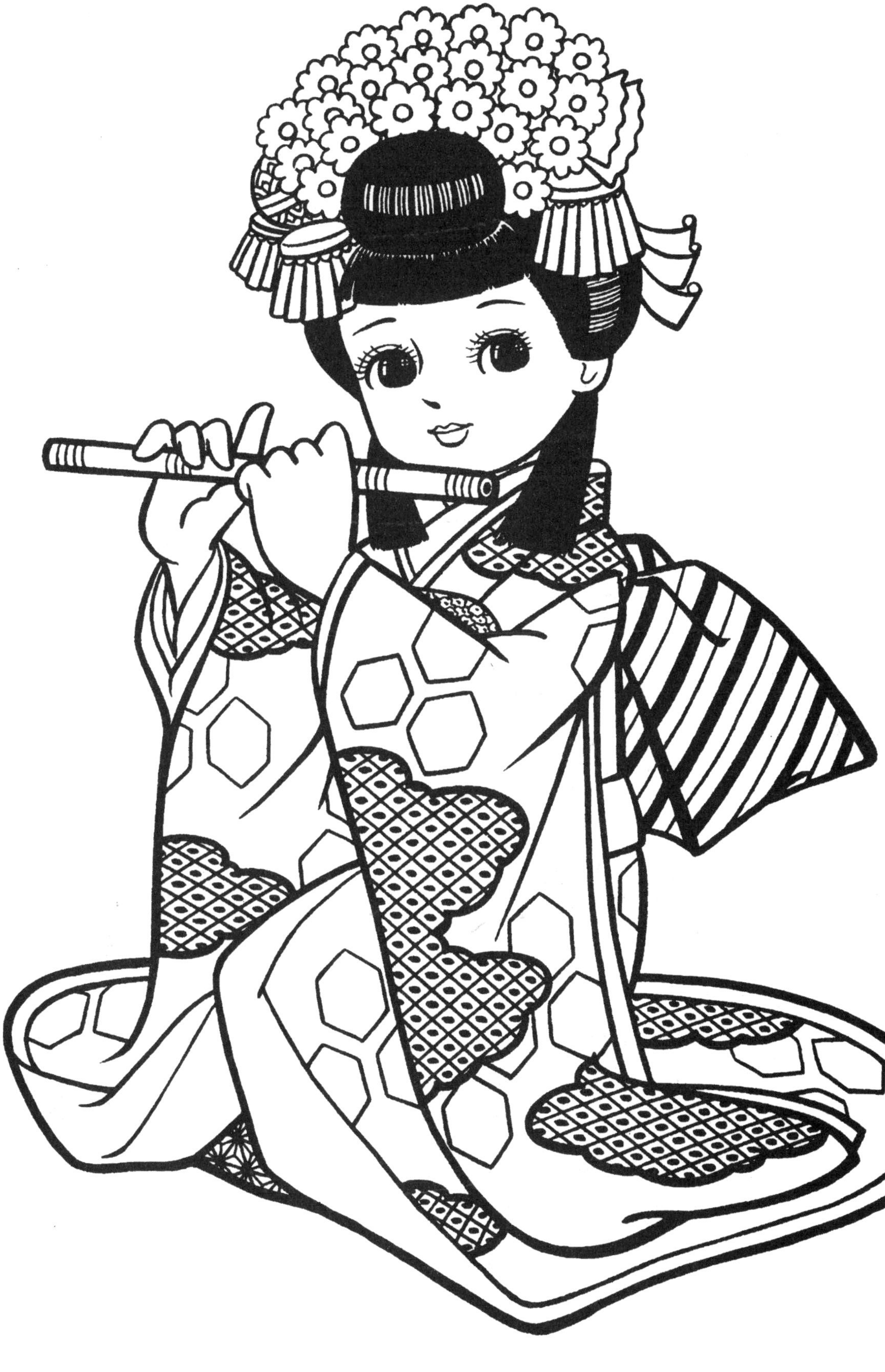

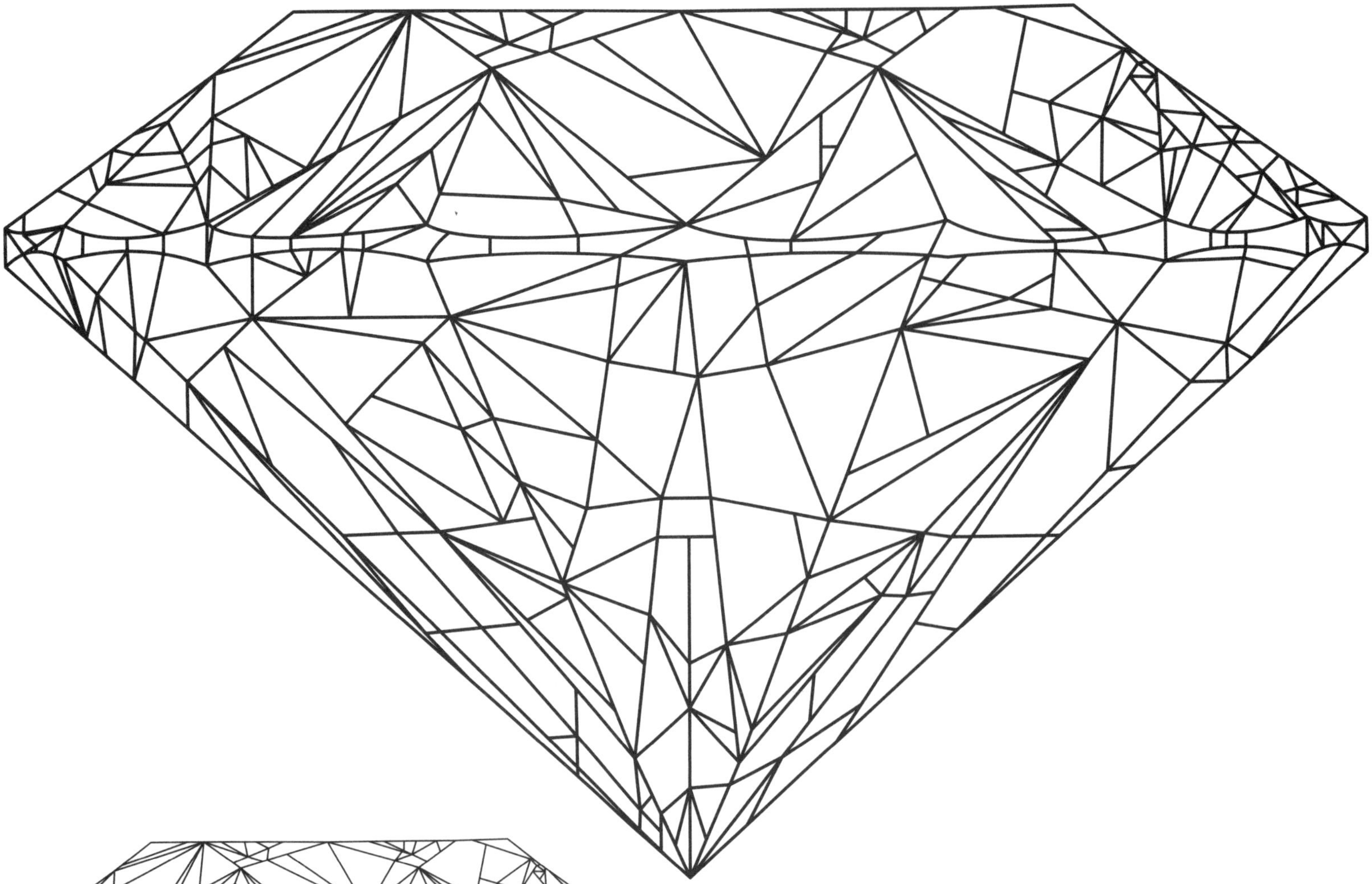

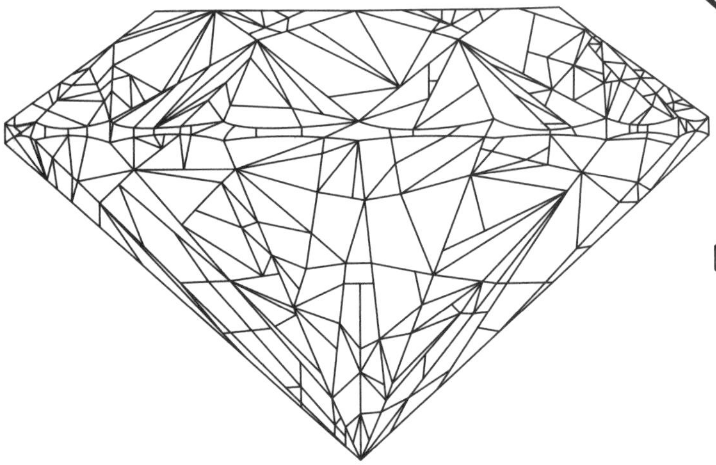

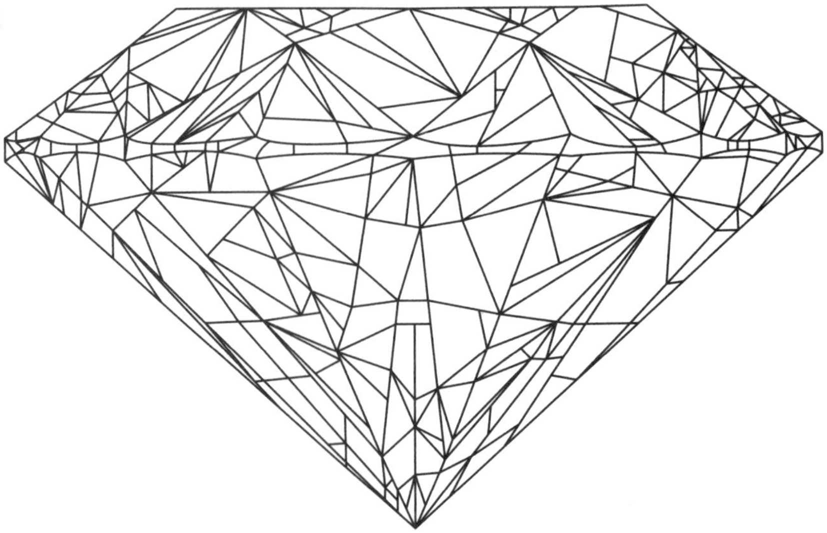

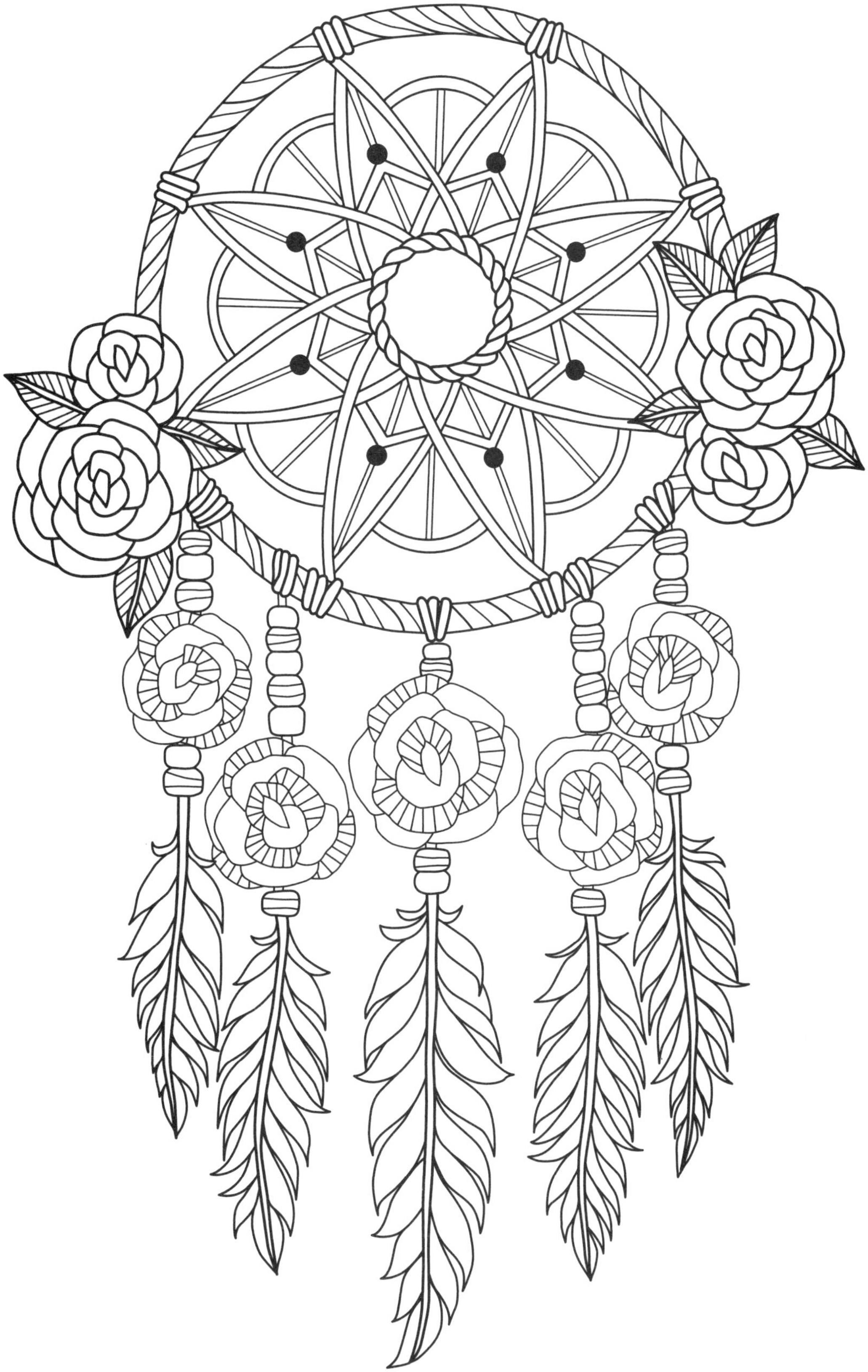

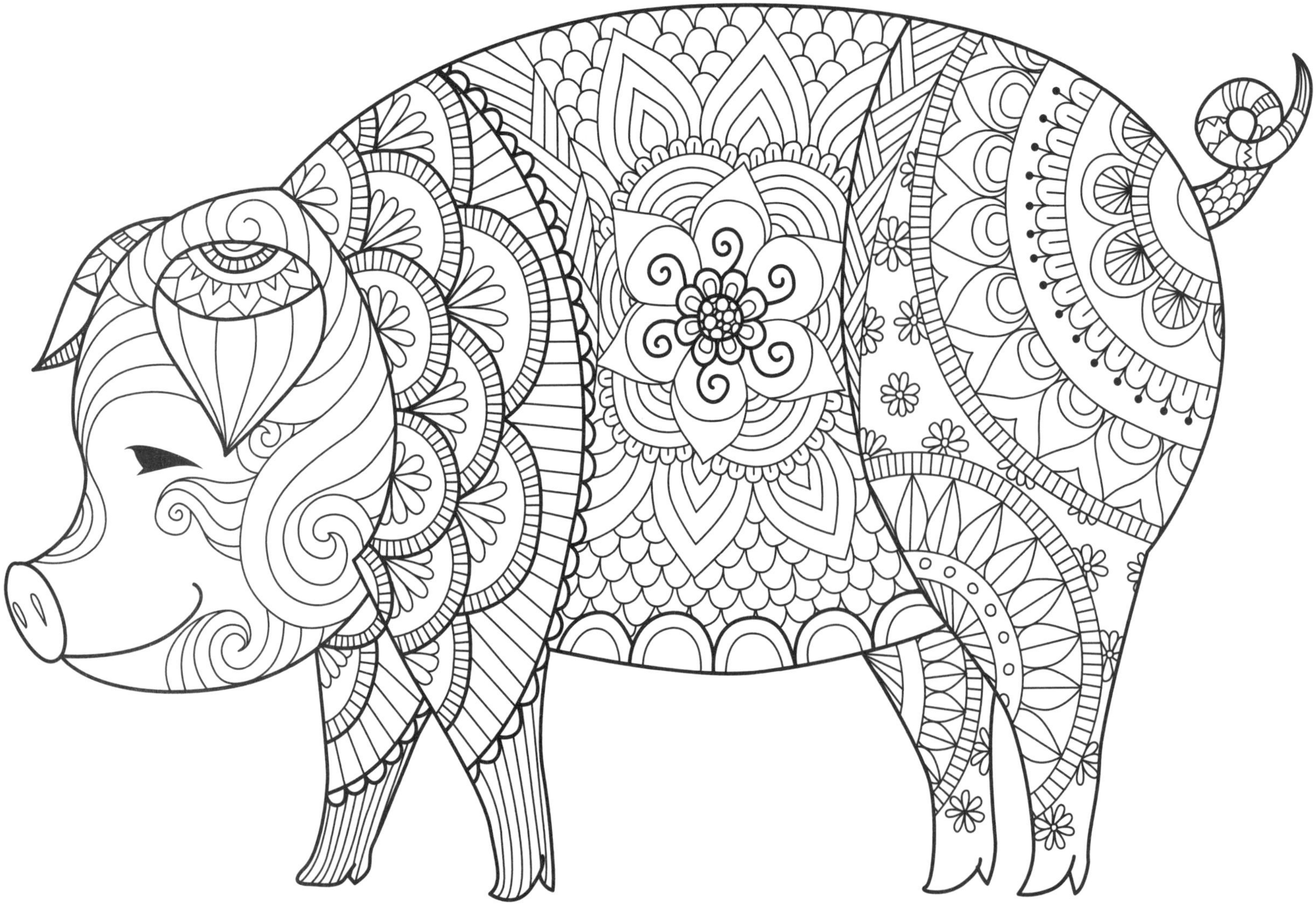

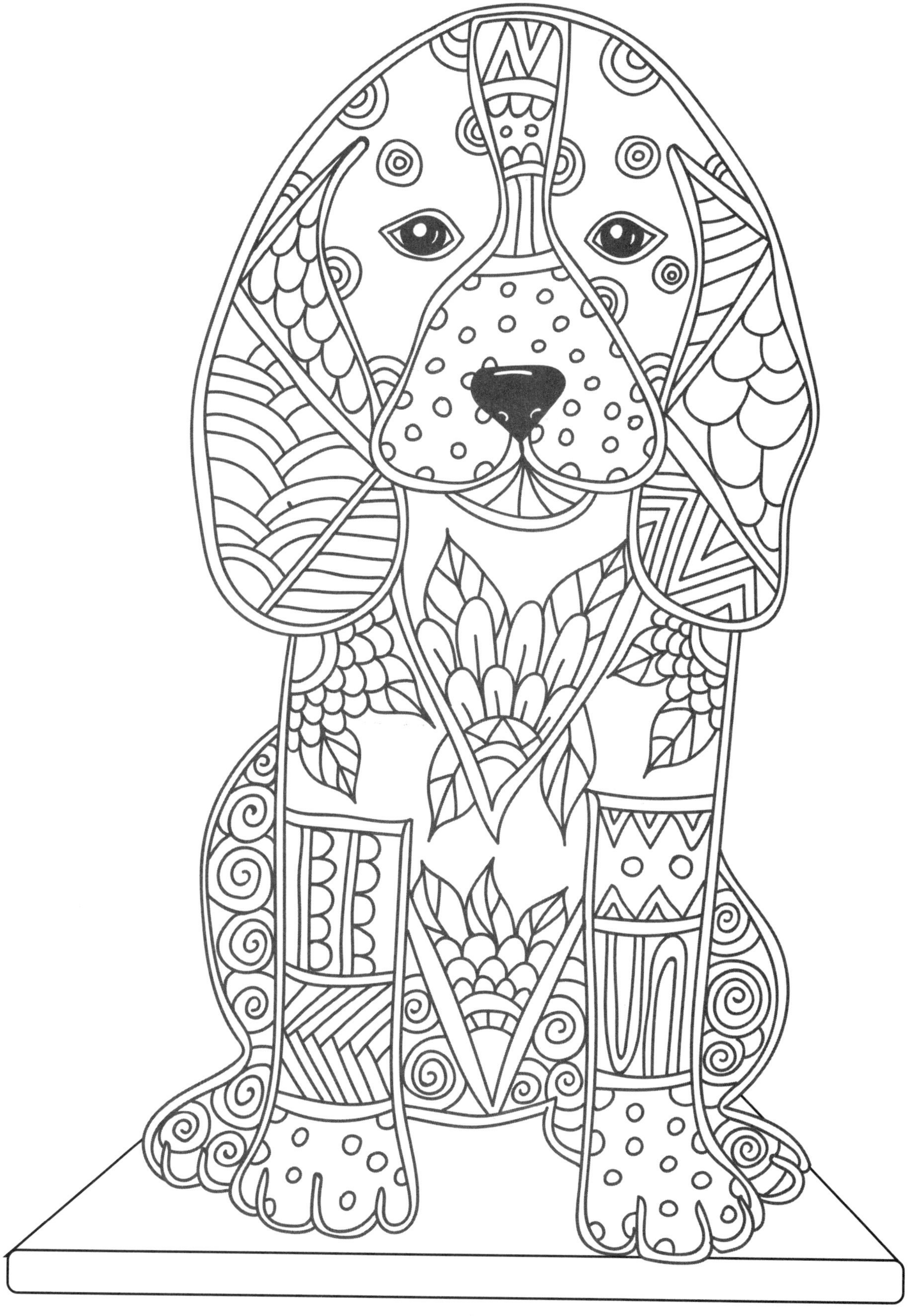

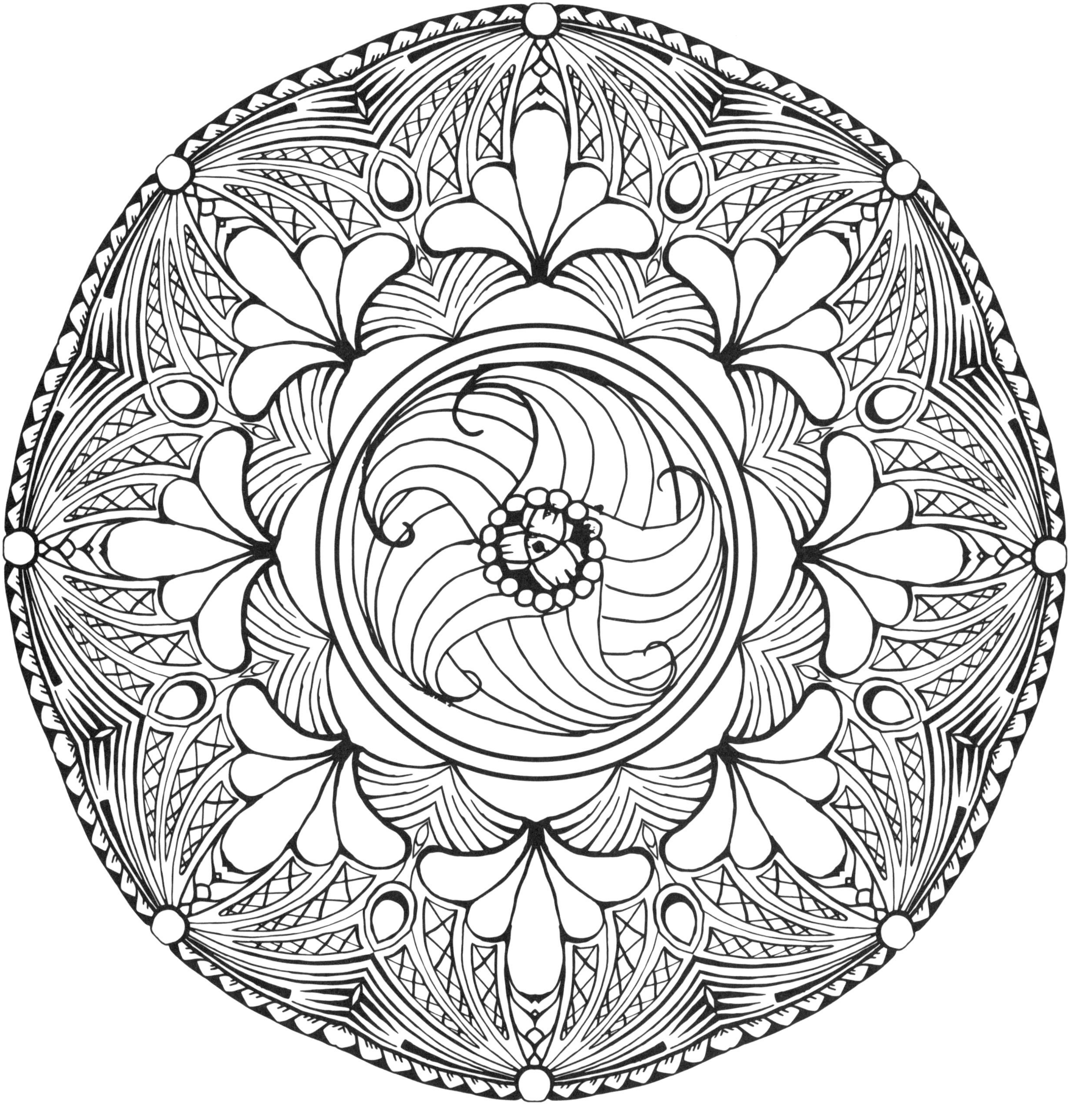

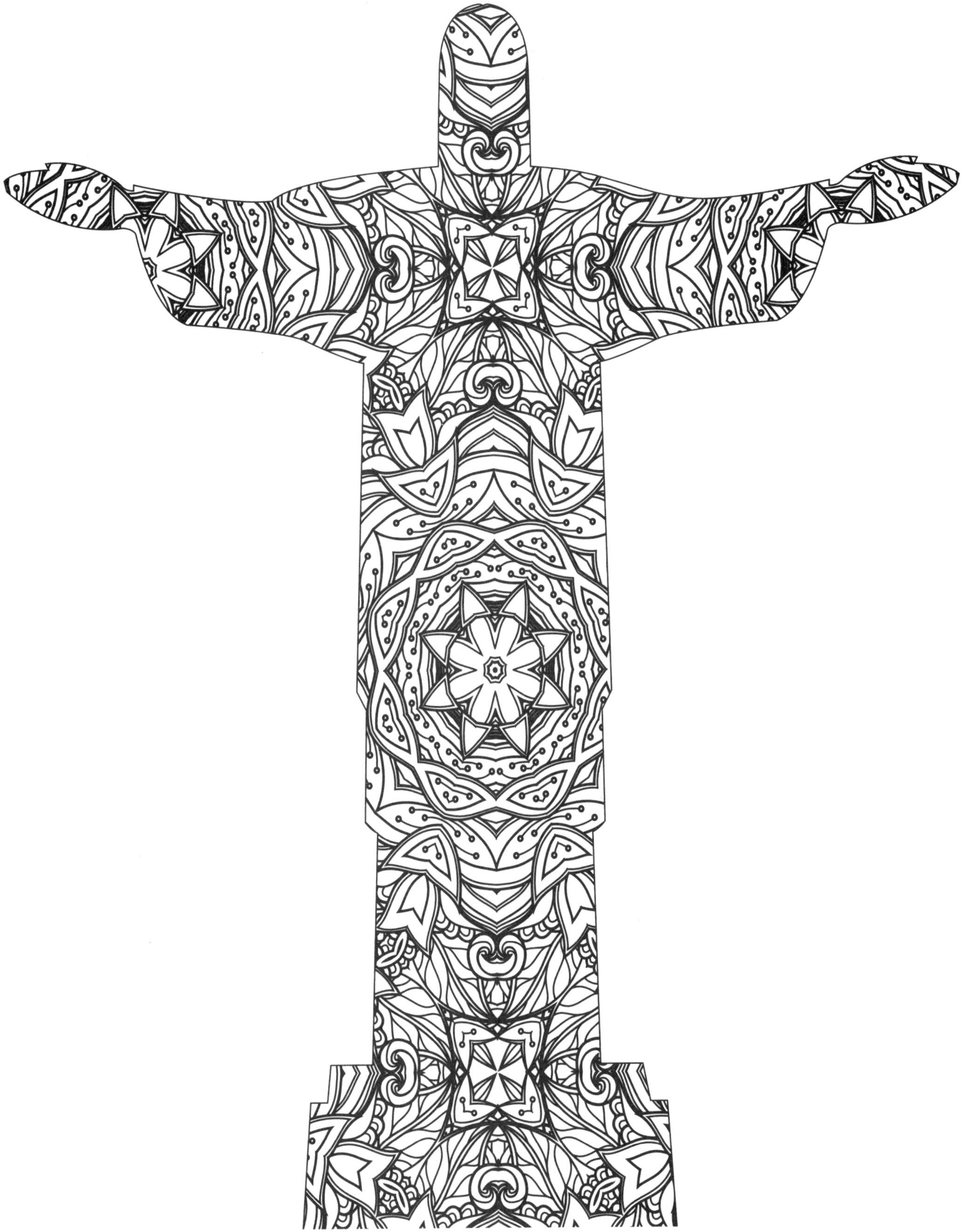

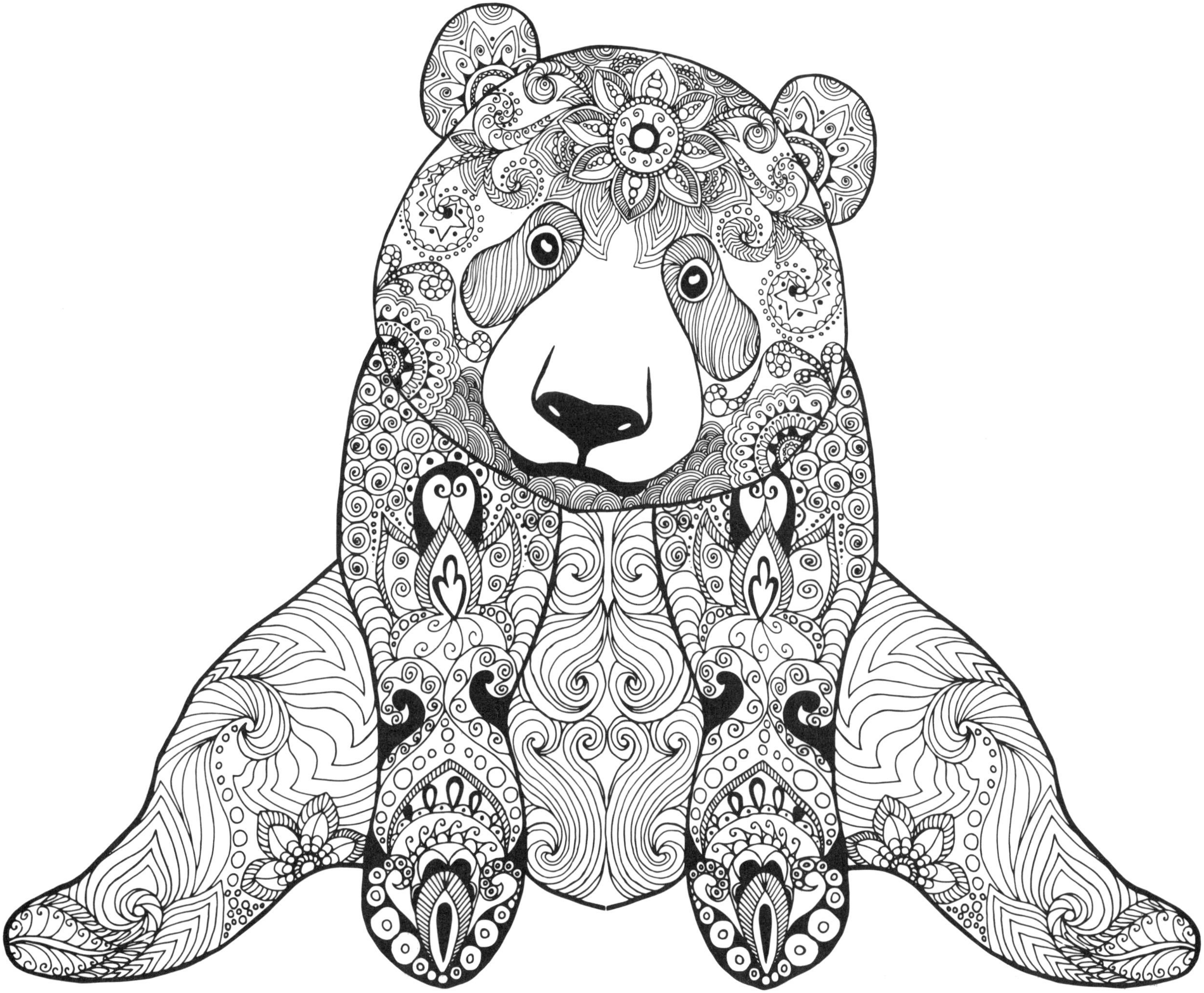

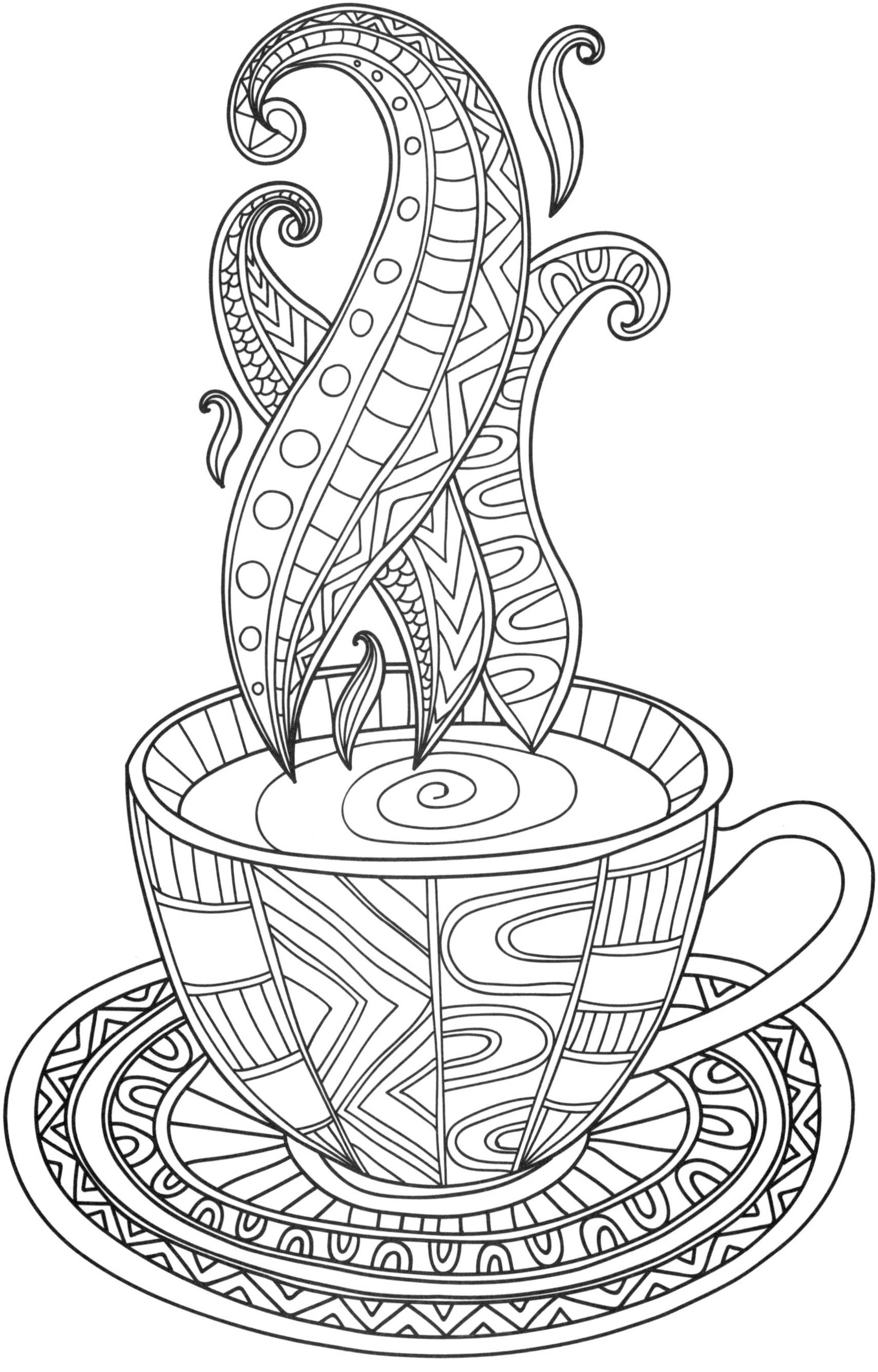

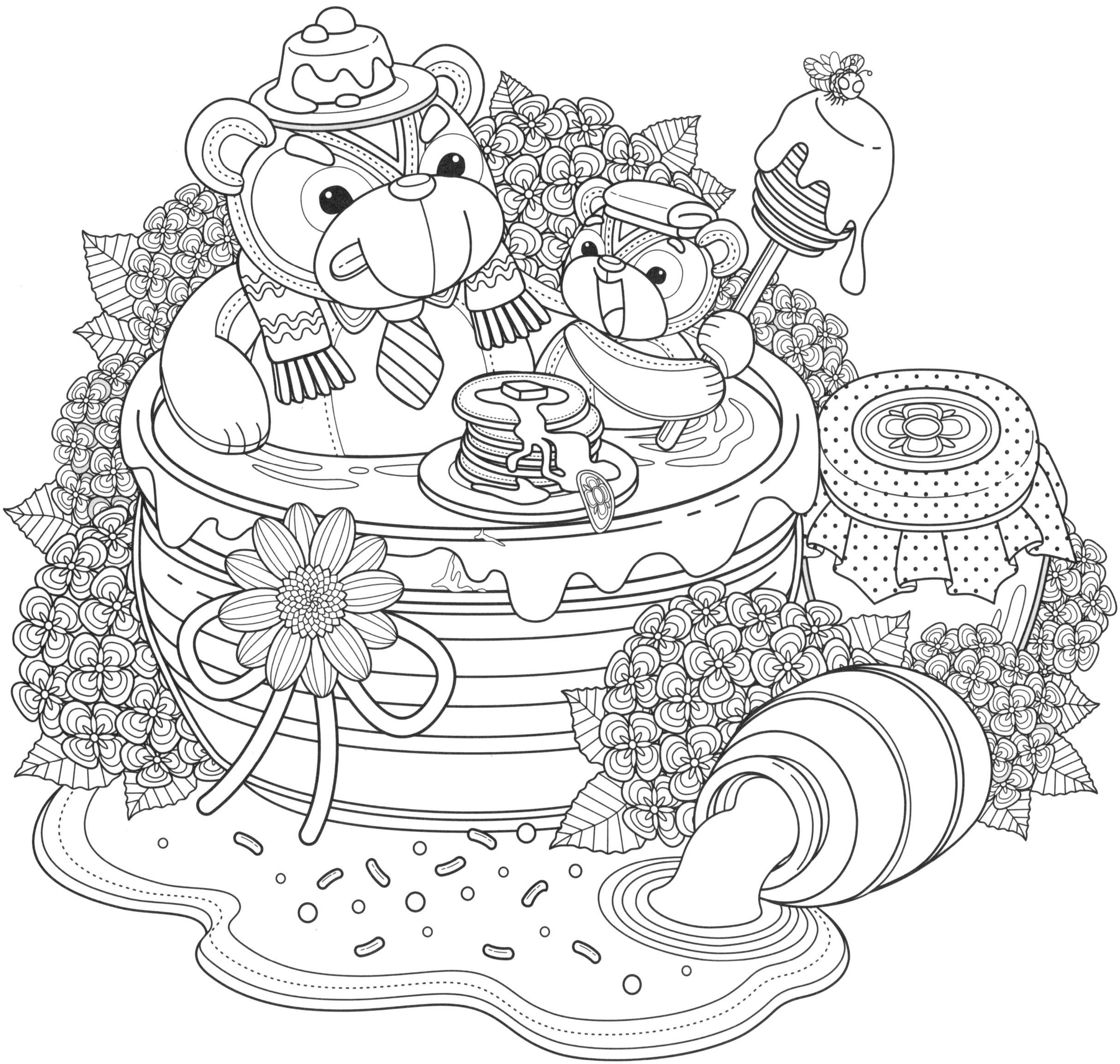

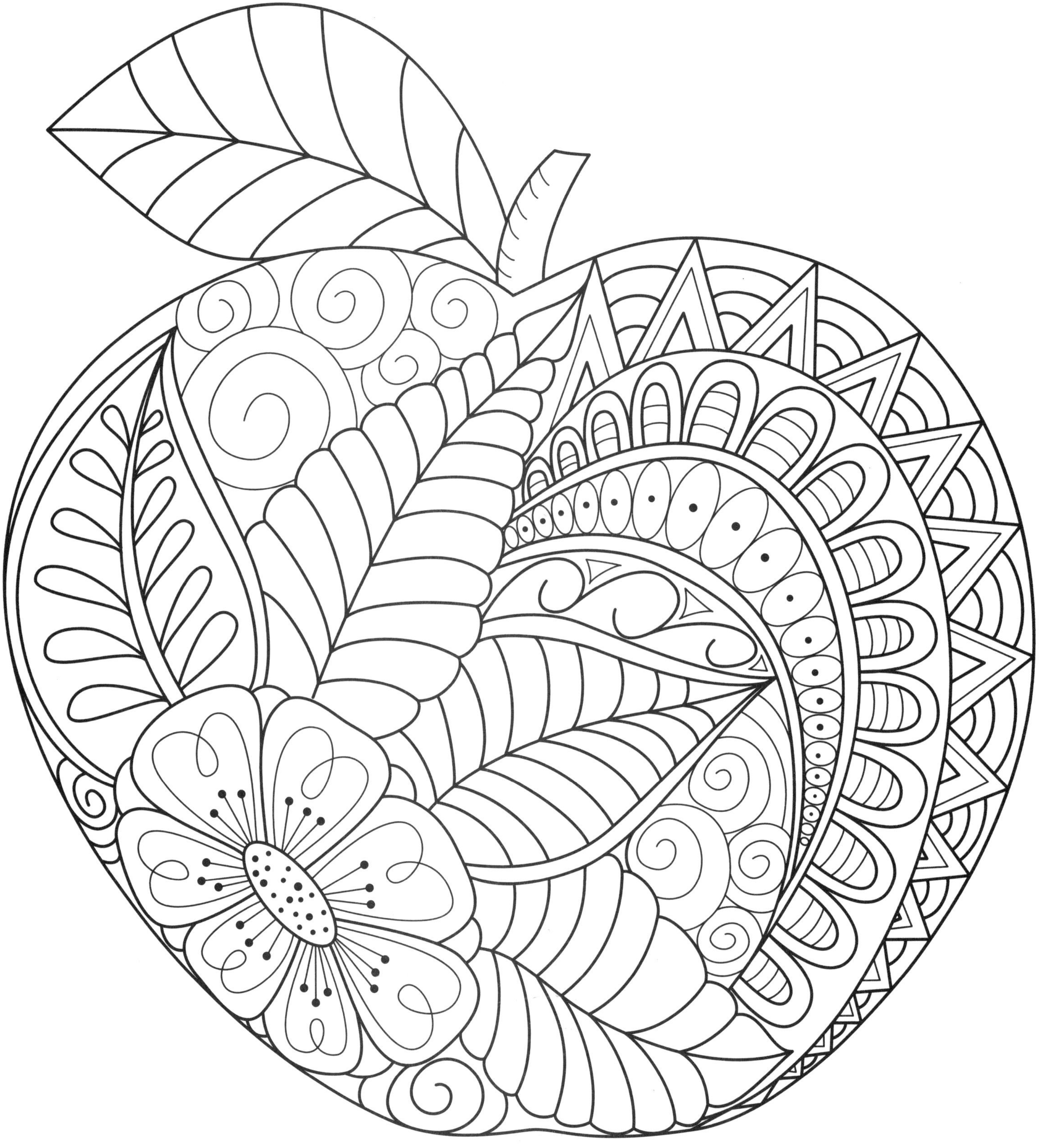

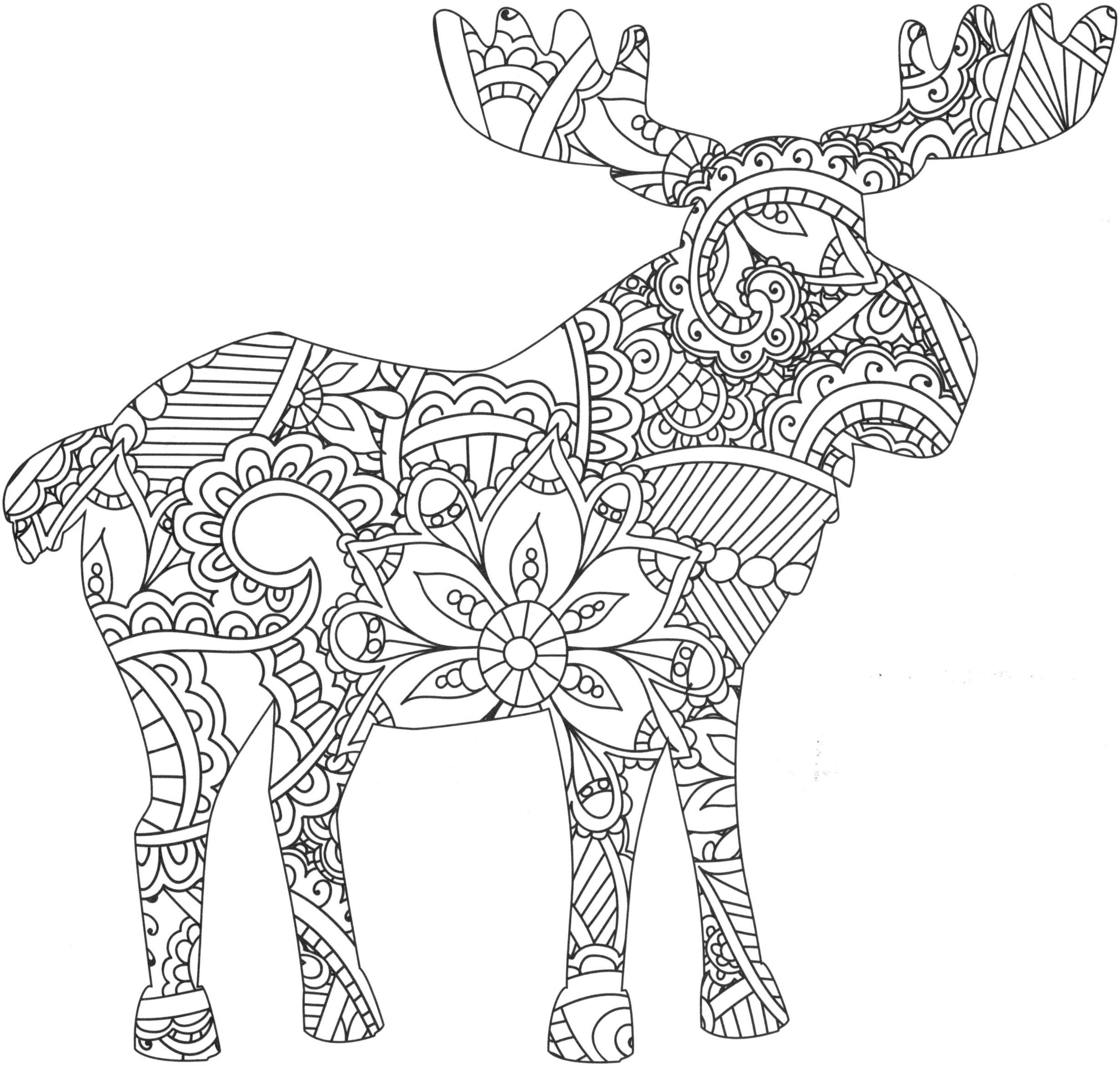

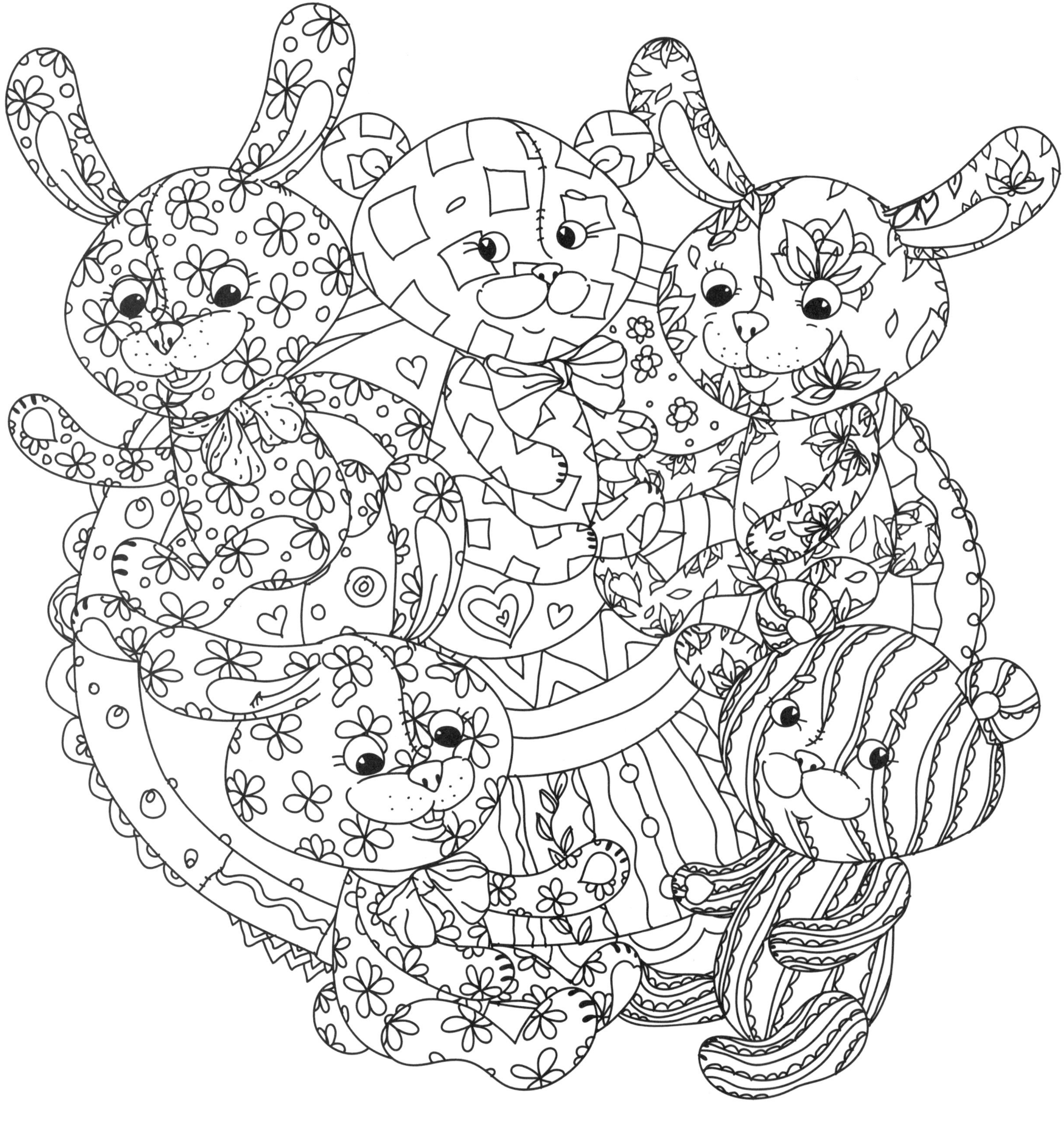

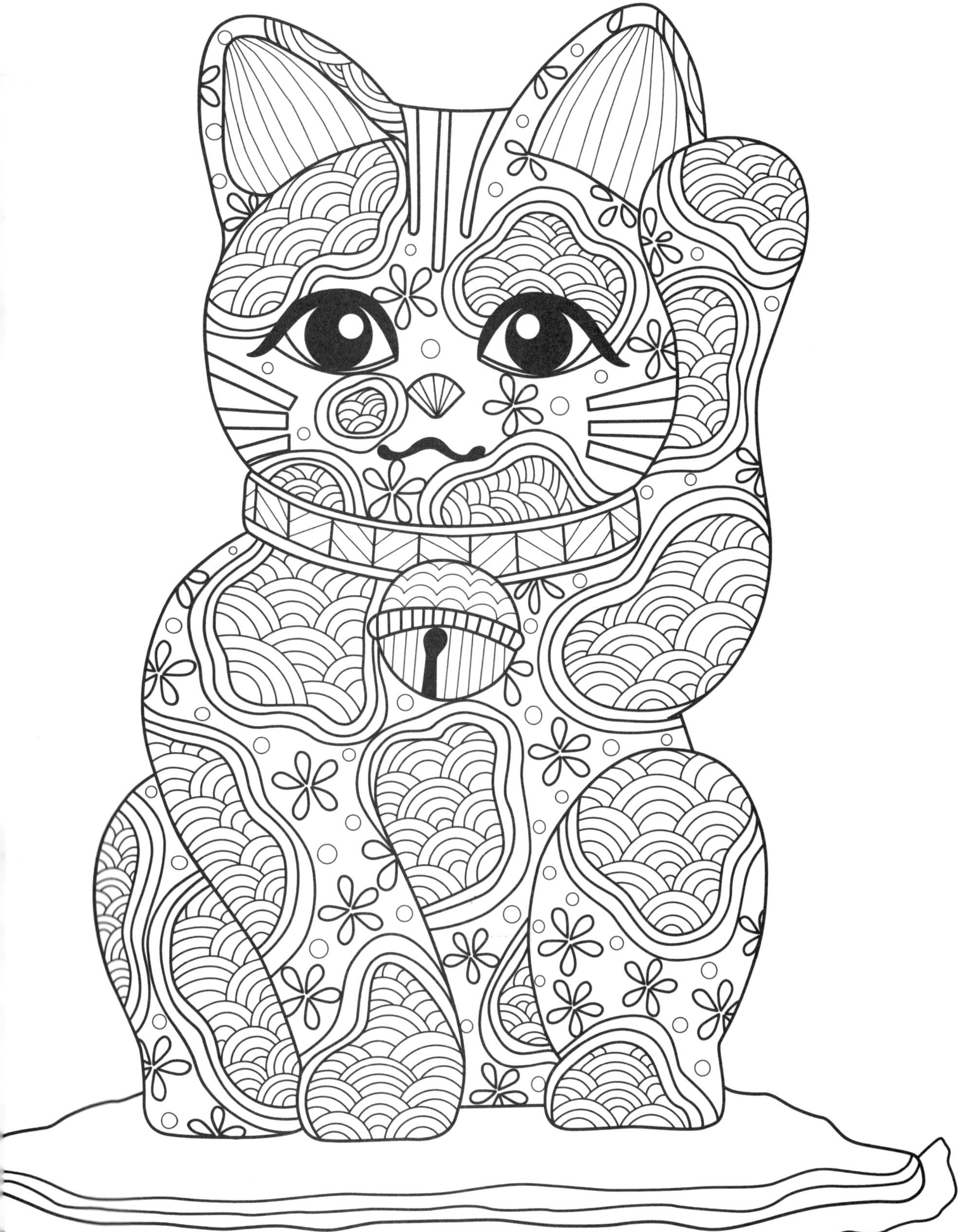

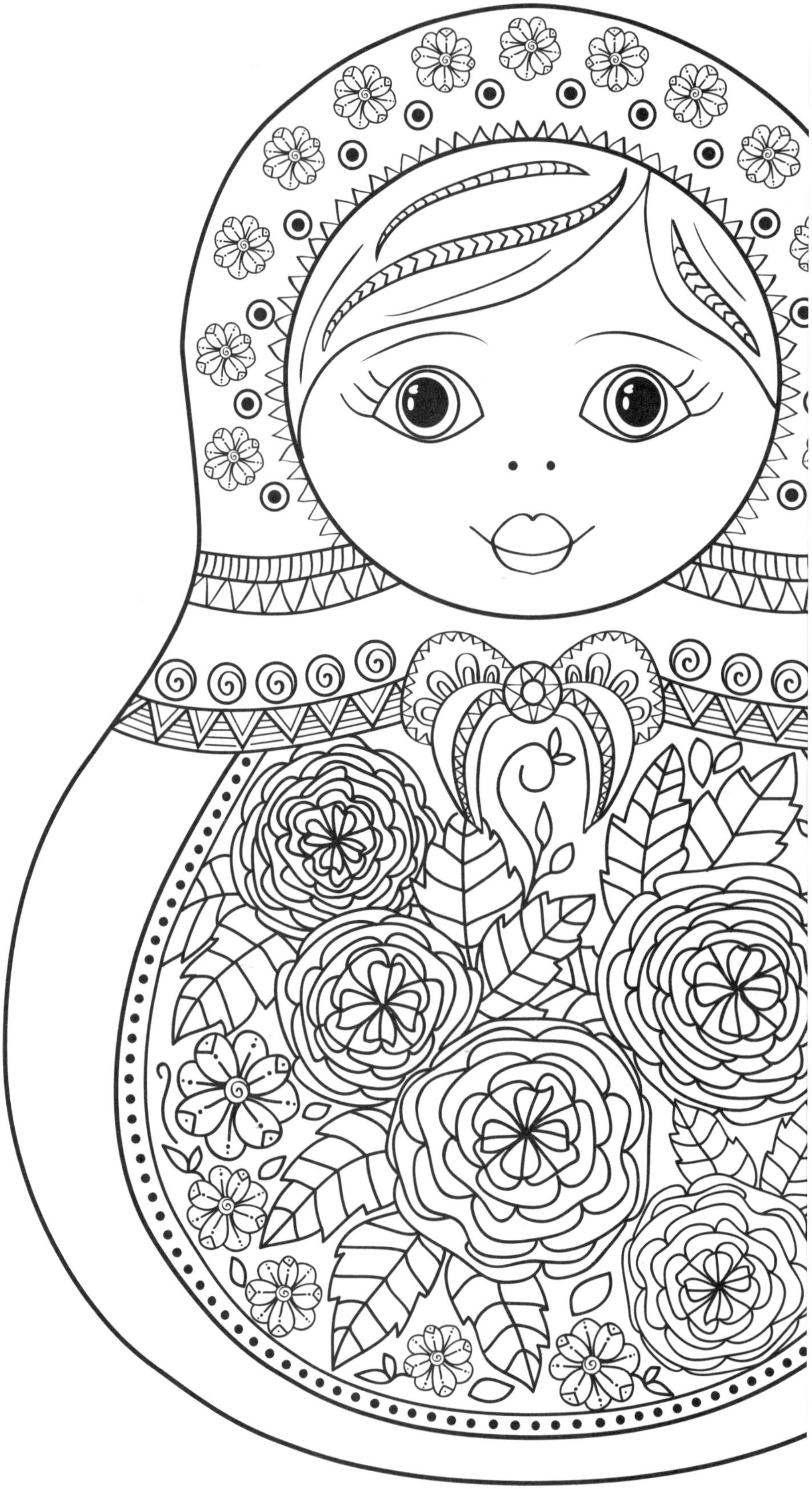